Informatik-Fachberichte

Herausgegeben von W. Brauer
im Auftrag der Gesellschaft für Informatik

1

Programmiersprachen

4. Fachtagung der GI
Erlangen, 8.–10. März 1976

Herausgegeben von
H.-J. Schneider und M. Nagl

Springer-Verlag
Berlin Heidelberg New York 1976

Herausgeber
Prof. Dr. Hans-Jürgen Schneider
Dr. Manfred Nagl
Universität Erlangen-Nürnberg
Institut für Mathematische Maschinen
und Datenverarbeitung (II)
Egerlandstr. 13
D–8520 Erlangen

AMS Subject Classifications (1970): 68-02, 68A05, 68A10, 68A30
CR Subjekt Classifications (1974): 1.3, 3.42, 3.8, 4.11, 4.12, 4.20, 4.21, 4.22,
4.32, 4.34, 5.22, 5.23, 5.24, 5.27, 8.2

ISBN-13:978-3-540-07619-3   e-ISBN-13:978-3-642-66319-2
DOI: 10.1007/978-3-642-66319-2

Vorwort

Der vorliegende Band enthält die Vorträge, die anläßlich der 4. Fachtagung über Programmiersprachen der Gesellschaft für Informatik gehalten wurden. Die drei vorangegangenen Fachtagungen über dieses Gebiet fanden in München (1971), Saarbrücken (1972) und Kiel (1974) statt.

Die Aufforderung zur Vortragsanmeldung enthielt die folgenden Fachgebiete:

    Compiler und Interpreter
    Sprachen für Systemprogrammierung
    Dialogsprachen
    Programmiersprachen für besondere Anwendungen
    Prozeßrechnersprachen
    Erweiterbare Sprachen
    Nichtprozedurale Sprachen
    Programmiermethodik
    Semantik und Verifikation.

Sie fand ein erstaunlich starkes Echo. Der Programmausschuß bestand aus den Mitgliedern des Fachausschusses 2 der GI:

    Prof. Dr. K. Alber (Braunschweig)
    W. Frielinghaus (Konstanz)
    Prof. Dr. H. Langmaack (Kiel)
    Prof. Dr. M. Paul (München)
    Prof. Dr. B. Schlender (Kiel)
    Prof. Dr. G. Seegmüller (München).

Er war bemüht, diejenigen Vorträge auszuwählen, die am ehesten den gegenwärtigen Stand der Forschung und Entwicklung wiedergeben. Die bereits im Tagungsband einer früheren GI-Jahrestagung beklagten Verständigungsschwierigkeiten zwischen Forschern und Anwendern sind - wie das Verfahren der Vortragsauswahl zeigte - noch lange nicht überwunden. Im Vergleich zu den früheren Tagungsbänden stieg jedoch die Anzahl der Vorträge, die den Anwendungen zuzurechnen sind. Dennoch bleibt für weitere Fachtagungen in dieser Richtung noch viel zu tun.

Den Vortragenden sei an dieser Stelle für ihre Beiträge gedankt. Der Erfolg einer Tagung hängt in erster Linie von ihnen ab. Daneben gilt unser Dank den Sitzungsleitern und den Mitgliedern des Programmkomitees, sowie den Mitarbeitern des Lehrstuhls für Informatik II (Programmier- und Dialogsprachen, sowie ihre Compiler) der Friedrich-Alexander-Universität Erlangen-Nürnberg, die alle bei der Organisation der Tagung geholfen haben.

Zur Finanzierung dieser Tagung haben beigetragen:
Bundesministerium für Forschung und Technologie, Bonn
Siemens AG, Erlangen
IBM Deutschland GmbH, Böblingen
Computer Gesellschaft Konstanz
Diehl Datensysteme GmbH, Nürnberg
Digital Equipment GmbH, München
Honeywell Bull GmbH, Köln
Stadt- und Kreissparkasse Erlangen
Control Data GmbH, Frankfurt
Softlab, München
Universität Erlangen-Nürnberg

Schließlich gebührt ein besonderer Dank dem Springer-Verlag, der die Veröffentlichung des Tagungsbandes in so kurzer Frist ermöglichte, daß er vor Beginn der Tagung den Teilnehmern bereitgestellt werden konnte.

Erlangen, im Januar 1976   Hans-Jürgen Schneider
                                            Manfred Nagl

INHALT / CONTENTS

GRUNDLEGENDE KONZEPTE/FOUNDATIONAL CONCEPTS

PROGRAMMIERSPRACHEN FÜR SPEZIELLE ANWENDUNGEN/PROGRAMMING
LANGUAGES FOR SPECIAL APPLICATIONS

FORMALE SPRACHEN UND SYNTAXANALYSE/FORMAL LANGUAGES AND SYNTAX
ANALYSIS

HAUPTVORTRÄGE/INVITED LECTURES

THE SEMANTICAL DEFINITION OF PROGRAMMING LANGUAGES IN TERMS OF THEIR DATA SPACES

Armin Cremers and Thomas N. Hibbard
University of Southern California, Los Angeles, California 90007

INTRODUCTION

In this paper we extend the notion of data type with a control structure to define "data spaces" that are useful in describing semantical aspects of programming languages as well as properties of software systems. The latter, in fact, are included in the former, since a programming language usually serves as a vehicle for expressing something that a computer system does.

Typically, the designer of a programming language begins with an excellent idea of <u>what</u> he wants to express before he decides <u>how</u> it should be expressed. That is, he has in mind some "virtual machine." The problem we address is: what is the general nature of this virtual machine?

We take the point of view that first there is some stepwise processor which transforms values on some given domain. Second, this domain is not just an a-morphous collection of states, but there are some functions reflecting the structure of the state space of the virtual machine and describing the "meaning" of the state transitions of the processor.

With just these "minimal" assumptions about virtual machines, it is possible to identify a variety of notions important to the designer, implementor, and user of a programming language. Among these notions are program, implementation, virtual processor, macro, subroutine, and concurrency.

The theory presented here could probably be called a "constructive approach" to the semantics of programming languages (in the notation of [3]). An important difference in our objective is to disentangle the syntax entirely from the semantics in order to be able to speak of the semantics before the syntax exists.

The fundamental model for our approach, viz. the concept of a data space, is defined in Section 1, where we also introduce the formal notion of a program. In Sections 2 respectively 3, we express the semantics of a few small procedure-oriented respectively function-oriented programming languages in terms of their data spaces. In particular, the notion of a virtual data space is developed and illustrated by means of another programming language example.

1. THE DATA SPACE MODEL

In accordance with the Introduction, a data space can be viewed as a "data type," i.e., essentially a set X together with a collection $\mathcal{J}$ of functions defined on X, combined with a "processor" p which is simply defined to be a relation on X.

As a first transparent example, consider the data space $\mathcal{D} = (X, \mathcal{J}, p)$, where $X = N \times S$, N the natural numbers and S the data space of natural number stacks. Suppose $\mathcal{J}$ has two functions, $i : X \to N$ and $s : X \to S$. Then the "procedure"

<pre>   while s not null and i ≠ 0 do
    begin i: = top(s); s: = pop(s) end</pre>

can be modelled as an execution sequence $p(x), p^2(x), p^3(x), \ldots$ of the processor p defined as the following function on X:

<pre>   p(x) = if s(x) = null or i(x) = 0
           then undefined
           else y such that i(y) = top(s(x)) and s(y) = pop(s(x)).</pre>

From a more general point of view, X represents "memory states," $\mathcal{J}$ consists of "memory descriptors" which allow us to extract data structures from memory states, and p serves as "sequence control" realizing the control structures desired for the data type $(X, \mathcal{J})$. Thus without the function set $\mathcal{J}$, the pair (X, p) can be viewed as a "mathematical machine" in the usual sense, whereas the full model of a data space comprises the functions used in determining the meaning of the state transitions of the mathematical machine.

Clearly there is to be expected a strong connection between p and $\mathcal{J}$, such as that p changes only a few of the functions in $\mathcal{J}$, and that the action of p depend on only a few of them. E.g., if some functions of $\mathcal{J}$ have numerical values then we expect p to do some arithmetic. For a formal study of the relationship between a "procedure" p and its "environment" as described by $\mathcal{J}$, the reader is referred to [2].

About $\mathcal{J}$ itself we can make some general statements:

In order for $\mathcal{J}$ to serve as a <u>concise</u> and <u>comprehensive</u> description of "memory," we incorporate two restrictions about $\mathcal{J}$ into our model of a data space: <u>orthogonality</u> and <u>completeness</u>.

The idea of the functions in $\mathcal{J}$ being orthogonal expresses the lack of dependence of the f in $\mathcal{J}$ on each other. This property can be formally defined as follows:

<u>Definition</u>: Two functions f and g (on X) are <u>orthogonal</u>, if for all x, y in X there exists z in X such that $f(z) = f(x)$ and $g(z) = g(y)$.

Orthogonal functions are protected against each other in an ideal way: they have no common information. We regard them as opening compartments of the memory states S, and these compartments must be disjoint. (Note that the functions i and s of the previous example are orthogonal.)

We shall wish to speak of the data spaces of programming languages, which allow arbitrarily many variables. Thus, we have to generalize the definition of orthogonality to function sets of infinite cardinality:

<u>Definition</u>: $\mathcal{J}$ is <u>orthogonal</u> for X if for every function $\eta : \mathcal{J} \to X$ there exists y in X such that for all f in $\mathcal{J}$ we have $f(y) = f(\eta(f))$.

Completeness of $\mathcal{J}$ as a set of descriptors of "memory" states can be formally defined in a straightforward way:

<u>Definition</u>: $\mathcal{J}$ is <u>complete</u> for X if for all x, y in X, $f(x) = f(y)$ for all f in $\mathcal{J}$ implies x = y.

$\mathcal{J}$ in the previous example is also complete.

For the sequel we assume that we always deal with function sets which are non-trivial in the sense that they contain at least one nonconstant function.

It is interesting to note that an orthogonal and complete set of functions $\mathcal{J}$ provides us with a <u>minimal</u> description of the "memory" of a data space in the following sense:

<u>Minimality Theorem</u>: Let $\mathcal{J}$ be orthogonal and complete for X. If we delete any nonconstant function in $\mathcal{J}$, then the function set is no longer complete for X.

<u>Remark</u>: It is somewhat surprising that $\mathcal{J}$ can be complete and not have a minimal complete subset. This is the case for the following rational encoding of bit strings: let X be the set of all sequences of bits and let $f_i = \sum_{j=0}^{i} x_j 2^{-j}$ where x_j is the $(j+1)^{st}$ bit from the right. Note that, in accordance with the theorem above, $\mathcal{J}=\{f_i \mid \text{all } i\}$ is not orthogonal.

We are now ready to give the formal definition of our data space model:

<u>Definition</u>: A data space $\mathcal{D}$ is a triple $(X, \mathcal{J}, p)$ where X is a set, the set of <u>states</u>, p is a relation on $X \times X$, called the <u>processor</u>, and $\mathcal{J}$ is an orthogonal and complete set of functions on X. If the processor p is a partial function then $\mathcal{D}$ is said to be <u>deterministic</u>.

Our main interest here is in deterministic data spaces. The more general definition models certain properties of concurrent processes. In the sequel a data space will be assumed deterministic unless specified otherwise.

We now turn to a brief discussion of the notion of a program in a data space.

Some fundamental properties of what are intuitively called "programs" are the following: (1) Programs are invariant. (2) A program drives some processor, i.e., the processor always consults the program to determine what its next step is.

The first property says that if a state x has a program "written" in it in some sense, then p(x) will have the same program written in it. Formally, this means simply that there is a subset X' of X (namely all the x having that program in them) such that if x is in X' then p(x) is in X'.

On the other hand, the fact that a program drives some processor suggests that it must be possible to "reach in" and change the program at the point where the processor is looking at it, to make the processor give a different result in the data, represented by the function g in the definition which these considerations now lead to:

<u>Definition</u>: A <u>program</u> of a data space $\mathcal{D} = (X, \mathcal{J}, p)$ is a subset X' of X such that $p(X') \subseteq X'$ and such that there is some function g on X with the following properties: (i) $\{g\}$ is a complete set for X'. (ii) For all x in X' there exists y in X such that $g(y) = g(x)$ and $g(p(y)) \neq g(p(x))$.

Note that this definition is not to imply that all properties of a program are fixed. However, for example, even when a program is "relocated" there is an invariant function which tells us what the program is and that the program counter is pointing to that program.

A program in the usual sense of a set of instructions in memory which does not modify itself nor transfer control out of itself, gives rise to a program in the sense of the definition. X' is the set of all states having those instructions in the required place in memory and having the program counter somewhere in the set. The function g can be the program counter and the rest of memory. Given a state x in X' the state y required by the definition is obtained by putting an appropriate jump instruction at location g(x).

For a different kind of example consider the set of all Turing machines. This set can be viewed as a data space, a state of which is a set of quintuples ("transitions"), a tape, a location on the tape, and a machine state variable. It is easy to show that the set of all states having a common set of quintuples is a program for this data space.

Definition: If X' is a program of the data space $\mathcal{D} = (X, \mathcal{J}, p)$ and if $\mathcal{J}'$ is complete and orthogonal with respect to X' then we define the data space $\mathcal{D}/X' = (X', \mathcal{J}', p')$ where p' is just p restricted to X'.

This definition reflects the fact that while what is called the program is data from the CPU's point of view, it is itself a machine from the programmer's point of view.

It may happen that $\mathcal{D}/Y$ also has a program Z. If so, then Z is also a program of $\mathcal{D}$, and in fact $(\mathcal{D}/Y)/Z = \mathcal{D}/Z$.

2. PROCEDURE-ORIENTED LANGUAGES

Programming languages can be compared and classified with respect to the methods and concepts that went into their design and implementation. One important clue to the understanding of a language is its sequence control. Relative to this criterion, it is customary to speak of procedure-oriented languages and function-oriented languages. Procedure-oriented languages such as ALGOL 60 usually have a wide set of control structures, whereas the sequence control in function-oriented languages such as LISP is kept very simple.

The purpose of the present section is to apply the data space model to the semantical definition of procedure-oriented languages. To illustrate this approach, we select two small high-level languages. The first language was used in [5] to specify the primitive-recursive functions, the second language is a version of the small ALGOL-like language which served as an example in [3].

2.1 Primitive-Recursive Function Language

In [5], computational models are discussed which are similar to digital computers and their languages. One way to distinguish certain classes of recursive functions is to vary the instruction set of a computational model.

Consider the language with the following grammar G

$$P ::= P; S \mid S$$
$$S ::= I^+ \mid I^0 \mid RPT\ (I)\ (P)$$
$$I ::= X_n \text{ for } n \in N \text{ (N the natural numbers).}$$

The grammar allows lists of statements to be formed in which each statement is of one of the three kinds given. The statements concern actions on variables X_n.

We now specify the semantics of this language with a data space $\mathcal{D} = (X, \mathcal{J}, p)$. The function set $\mathcal{J}$ and the processor p will be given explicitly, and X is the obvious set of states for which $\mathcal{J}$ is orthogonal and complete.

Let $\mathcal{J} = \{L\} \cup \{v_I \mid I = X_n \text{ for some } n\}$, where, for each x in X, $v_I(x)$ is in N, and $L(x)$ is a list, each element of which is one of the following:

$$I^+ \text{ for some I,}$$
$$I^0 \text{ for some I,}$$
$$RPT(I)L' \text{ for some I and some list } L'.$$

The processor p is defined as follows:

```
if L(x) is empty then p(x) is undefined
else case first (L(x)) of
I⁺:        begin
           v_I(p(x)) = v_I(x)+1
           L(p(x)) = rest(L(x))
           v_I'(p(x)) = v_I'(x) for I' ≠ I
           end
I⁰:        begin
           v_I(p(x)) = 0
           L(p(x)) = rest(L(x))
           v_I'(p(x)) = v_I'(x) for I' ≠ I
           end
RPT(I)L':  begin
           L(p(x)) = [L']^{v_I(x)}  concatenated with rest (L(x))
           v_I(p(x)) = v_I(x) for all I
           end
    end {case}
```

(Our "case" statement is essentially that of PASCAL, and our functions "first" and "rest" correspond to "car" and "cdr" for lists in LISP 1.5.)

The data space $\mathcal{D}$ defined above "computes" [5] all and only primitive-recursive functions. (Formal notions of computability in data spaces, as suggested by e.g. Scott's theory [8], will be explored in a subsequent paper.)

Note that $\mathcal{D}$ gives a "syntax-free" definition of the semantics of this language. We submit that $\mathcal{D}$, or its equivalent, would be the first thing that someone would want to know about this language. Only then would he want to know the relation between the set of strings (syntax) and the data space. In fact, the grammar could just as well define S as, say, $S ::= I^+ \mid I^0 \mid (P, I)$ and be related to $\mathcal{D}$ in the obvious way.

It might seem that since $\mathcal{D}$ keeps "erasing" its instructions it cannot be said to have a program as defined in Section 1. On the contrary, every state x of $\mathcal{D}$ belongs to a program. For X' (of the definition) we take the set of all states y such that $L(y)$ is either a suffix of $L(x)$, or a suffix of $L(x)$ with an initial $RTP(I)\ L'$ replaced by $(L^1)^k$ for some k.

2.2 ALGOL-Like Sample Language

We now consider a small procedure-oriented language which contains only assignment statements, compound statements, conditional statements, and repetitive statements (<u>while</u> loops). The language is a slight modification of the one used in [3]. For a BNF definition of the language the reader is referred to [3]. For our purpose the following grammatical specification is sufficient:

$$P:: = P;S \,|\, S$$
$$S :: = I^e \,|\, b \to (P), (P) \,|\, b*(P)$$
$$I:: = X_n \text{ for } n \in N.$$

For this language, Hoare and Lauer have given several semantical definitions each illustrating a different approach to the semantics of programming languages. The theory that comes closest to ours has been called the "interpretive approach" [4]. The interpretive approach basically consists in constructing a mathematical machine (X, p) and describing the stepwise execution of a program by means of the state transition function p. It seems that the main novel attribute of our data space approach consists in combining the concept of a mathematical machine (X, p) with that of a data type $(X, \mathcal{J})$ in order to be able to study the properties of the semantical descriptors of machine states explicitly and to apply these properties (i. e. orthogonality, completeness, etc.) to a further understanding of the principles of programming languages.

According to our approach, the semantics of the sample language is given by a data space $\mathcal{B} = (X, \mathcal{J}, p)$ for which X and $\mathcal{J}$ are very similar to the sets used for the primitive-recursive function language. Again, we have $\mathcal{J} = \{L\} \cup \{v_I \,|\, I = X_n \text{ for some } n\}$. Since we are mainly concerned with the procedural aspects of the language, we simply assume that for every expression e an "expression evaluator" val_e is defined. In the following, we give a complete specification of the processor p:

```
        if L(x) is empty then p(x) is undefined
        else case first (L(x)) of
        Iᵉ:             begin
                        v_I(p(x)) = val_e(x)
                        L(p(x)) = rest(L(x))
                        v_I'(p(x)) = v_I'(x) for I' ≠ I
                        end
        b→ L', L'':     begin
                        if val_b(x) then L(p(x)) = L' concatenated with rest (L(x))
                                    else L(p(x)) = L'' concatenated with rest (L(x))
                        v_I(p(x)) = v_I(x) for all I
                        end
        b * L':         begin
                        if val_b(x) then L(p(x)) = L' concatenated with L(x)
                                    else L(p(x)) = rest (L(x))
                        v_I(p(x)) = v_I(x) for all I
                        end
        end {case}
```

The language studied in [4] contains concurrent statements of the form $S_1 \underline{\text{ or }} S_2$. Their semantics can be easily expressed in terms of <u>nondeterministic</u> data spaces in which the processor is a relation $p \subseteq X \times X$ instead of a function. For a study of nondeterministic data spaces and their applications in software design, operating systems in particular, the reader is referred to [1].

3. FUNCTION-ORIENTED LANGUAGES

We first define a grammar for an alternative language for expressing primitive-recursive functions. The syntax-free semantics of this language is then given by a data space $(X, \mathcal{J}, p)$ the states of which are pairs (E, m) where E is an "expression tree" and m is a node in E. Intuitively, to evaluate a functional expression, the processor p moves through the tree E making local transformations in it.

More formally, the language that specifies primitive-recursive functions has the following grammar:

$$\langle \text{function} \rangle ::= S \mid Z \mid PR(\langle \text{function} \rangle, \langle \text{function} \rangle) \mid$$
$$C(\langle \text{function} \rangle, \langle \text{function list} \rangle)$$
$$\langle \text{function list} \rangle ::= \text{null} \mid \langle \text{function} \rangle \langle \text{function list} \rangle$$
$$\langle \text{expression} \rangle ::= \langle \text{function} \rangle (\langle \text{argument list} \rangle)$$
$$\langle \text{argument list} \rangle ::= \text{null} \mid \langle \text{natural number} \rangle \langle \text{argument list} \rangle$$

S denotes the <u>successor function</u> "$S(x, L) = x+1 = x'$," Z denotes the <u>zero function</u> "$Z(L) = 0$," $PR(g, h)$ means the <u>primitive recursion schema</u>, and C denotes <u>composition</u> [5]. All functions are defined on all argument lists which are long enough, e.g. $S(x_1, x_2, x_3) = x_1 + 1$.

A data space for defining the semantics of this language is $\mathcal{J} = (X, \{I\}, p)$, where I is the identity function and X and p will now be defined.

<u>Notation:</u> We represent a tree

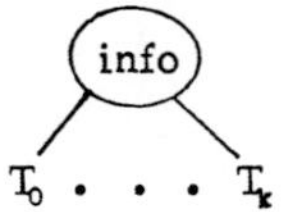

by $(\text{info}; T_0, \ldots, T_k)$ where info denotes the contents of the root node and the T_i are subtrees.

To specify p, we first define two auxiliary notions, function trees and expression trees.

<u>Definition:</u> A <u>function tree</u> is either S, or Z, or

$$(PR; g, h)$$

where g and h are function trees, or

$$(C; g_1, \ldots, g_k)$$

where the g_i are function trees.

An <u>expression tree</u> is either a natural number or

$$(T; a_1, \ldots, a_\ell)$$

where T is a function tree and the a_i are expression trees. (Note that T is the <u>contents</u> of the root node of the expression tree.)

The elements of X are now defined to be ordered pairs (E, m), where E is an expression tree and m is a node of E.

To define p we distinguish several cases:

1. If the contents of m is a natural number, then $p(E, m) = (E, m')$ where m' is the

father of m, except that if m has no father then $p(E, m)$ is undefined.

2. Suppose the subtree at m is $(T; a_1, \ldots, a_\ell)$.

(a) If not all the a_i are numbers, then let i be the first index for which a_i is not a number and let n be the corresponding node. Then $p(E, m) = (E, n)$.

(b) Suppose all the a_i are numbers. If $T = S$ (respectively Z), then the subtree at m is replaced by $a_1 + 1$ (respectively 0), giving a new expression tree E', and $p(E, m) = (E', m)$. If T is the function tree (PR; g, h), we have to consider two subcases: if $a_1 = 0$, the subtree at m is replaced by $(g; a_2, \ldots, a_\ell)$, giving a new tree E'. If $a_1 \neq 0$, then the subtree at m is replaced by

$$(h; (T; a_1 - 1, a_2, \ldots, a_\ell), a_1 - 1, a_2, \ldots, a_\ell)$$

giving a new tree E'. In either case, $p(E, m) = (E', m)$. If T is the function tree $(C, g_1, \ldots, g_k)$ then the subtree at m is replaced by

$$(g_1; (g_2; a_1, \ldots, a_\ell), \ldots, (g_k; a_1, \ldots, a_\ell))$$

giving a new tree E', and $p(E, m) = (E', m)$.

The definition of the data space $\mathcal{D}$ is now complete. It is intuitively clear that the functions "computable" in $\mathcal{D}$ are exactly the primitive-recursive functions.

Observe that the processor p of $\mathcal{D}$ can be easily modified to take advantage of concurrency.

It should be relatively straightforward from the data space given above to specify the semantics of other (perhaps more practical) function-oriented languages such as LISP-like languages, whose control structure consists of a simple sequencing of calls on functions which are defined as list structures (binary trees).

4. IMPLEMENTATION

In order to implement a "higher level" data space $\mathcal{D}_q = (Y, \mathcal{G}, q)$ in a "lower level" data space $\mathcal{D}_p = (X, \mathcal{F}, p)$ we need: For each $y \in Y$ at least one (possibly more) states in X which represents y, and, if $x \in X$ represents $y \in Y$ then p operating one or more times should take x to a state which represents $q(y)$.

The following definition makes these notions precise:

<u>Definition:</u> Let $\mathcal{D}_p = (X, \mathcal{F}, p)$ and $\mathcal{D}_q = (Y, \mathcal{G}, q)$ be data spaces. A partial function α from X onto Y is said to be an <u>implementation</u> of $\mathcal{D}_q$ in $\mathcal{D}_p$ if for every x in the domain of α there exists $k > 0$ such that $\alpha(p^k(x)) = q(\alpha(x))$ and such that $p^j(x)$ is not in the domain of α for $0 < j < k$. $\mathcal{D}_q$ is said to be a <u>virtual data space</u> of $\mathcal{D}_p$ if there exists an implementation of $\mathcal{D}_q$ in $\mathcal{D}_p$.

In practice we would expect simple links between $\mathcal{F}$ and $\mathcal{G}$, such as that a certain set of bits of $\mathcal{F}$ specify a certain integer of $\mathcal{G}$. But at the present level of generality the most we can say is that for a state x in the domain of α, the values of $f(x)$ for all f in $\mathcal{F}$, together with α, uniquely determine any g in $\mathcal{G}$ for the state represented by x.

In software development, an implementation of $\mathcal{D}_q$ in $\mathcal{D}_p$ corresponds to a step from higher "level of abstraction" to a lower "level of abstraction." Yet, upon a closer look, one such step actually consists of a composition of two "atomic" implementations. When embedding a "virtual" data space $\mathcal{D}_q$ in some "real" data space $\mathcal{D}_p$, we usually first go to a data space $\mathcal{D}_{p'}$ which might be called a "macro" data space, which offers us a number of different representation algorithms, i.e., a single state transition of p, say $p(a_1) = a_2$, may correspond to more than one state transition of p', say $p'(b_1) = b_2$ and $p'(b_3) = b_4$. We call it a "design decision" to select one among these representation choices. This is done in the second atomic step, namely in the implementation of $\mathcal{D}_{p'}$ in $\mathcal{D}_p$ which also has the effect to realize the selected state transitions of p' as state transition sequences of the "real" processor p.

A different and somewhat informal approach to the implementation of software modules, inspired by [6], has been given in [7]. The idea of our approach is made precise in the following definition. An example follows the definition.

<u>Definition</u>: A <u>macro processor</u> of $\mathcal{D}_p = (X, \mathcal{J}, p)$ is a partial function $p': X' \to X'$, where X' is a subset of X such that for all x in X' there exists $k > 0$ such that $p^k(x)$ is in X', and $p'(x) = p^k(x)$ for the least $k > 0$ such that $p^k(x)$ is in X'.

A virtual data space is essentially a data space mapped in a one-to-one way to a macro data space. This reflects the way in which virtual data spaces are implemented in practice. The mapping to the macro data space consists in deciding how to represent the data. The remaining task is then to do the required transformations with p, and that amounts to specifying the details of the macros.

To illustrate the notion of a macro processor consider a "classical" computer whose program has some locations dedicated to complex numbers, and at various points performs <u>complex arithmetic</u> on them. (For a formal data space definition of a classical computer architecture see [1].) The processor p here includes the program, the program being "factored out" of the data space as described in Section 1. We suppose that p does the complex arithmetic in a series of real arithmetic operations and performs no other operation on the complex data, so that we can always tell when p is about to begin a complex operation. X' is then the set of states which are not intermediate states in a complex operation.

We now relate the notion of a virtual data space to that of a program.

<u>Theorem</u>: If $\mathcal{D}_q$ is a virtual data space of $\mathcal{D}_p$ and if Y' is a program of $\mathcal{D}_q$, then

$$X' = \{p^k(x) \mid x \in \alpha^{-1}(Y'),\ k \geq 0\}$$

is a program of $\mathcal{D}_p$.

The key point in the proof is the following. Let g_q be the function which plays the role of g (of the definition of program) for Y'. The required function g_p for X' is the following. For $x \in X'$ let k be the first integer such that $p^k(x) \in \alpha^{-1}(Y')$. Then $g_p(x) = g_q(\alpha(p^k(x)))$.

The concepts developed in this section can be applied to make the notion of a <u>subroutine</u> precise. Use of a subroutine generates a virtual data space. The macro domain X' is the set of states external to the subroutine. The virtual data space lacks both the subroutine and all its local variables, and may otherwise be identical to the main data space. (But note that ALGOL own variables must be found in the virtual data space.)

Each programming language assumes some data space $\mathcal{B}_q$ which is virtual with respect to some data space $\mathcal{B}_p$. It is the mission of the compiler to create a state x such that when p starts at x there is a macro domain X' and a mapping α such that the associated virtual data space is $\mathcal{B}_q$ and $\alpha(x)$ is the start state of $\mathcal{B}_q$ requested by the programmer.

We conclude this section with a discussion of a small implementation example. The main point of the example is that, in practical program design, the data types of a given level of abstraction have to be implemented as part of the "context" in which they are used, i.e. as part of the data space in which they arise. In other words, the implementation of data types cannot be expected to meet any given efficiency requirements if it is done independently from the implementation of the control structures.

Suppose that a data space $\mathcal{B}_q = (Y, \mathcal{B}, q)$ has multibranching trees as one of its data types (i.e., some of the functions in $\mathcal{B}$ have multibranching trees as their values). Such a data space arises whenever we have a programming problem which is "naturally" expressed in terms of multibranching trees. Here, since our main interest is the problem and not the data space itself (as it would be if we were building a compiler for the data space), we are not likely to take the trouble to make a complete formal specification of the data space. We will only specify enough of its properties to formulate a "higher-level" algorithm which solves the given programming problem. For example, we might say that SUB(i, T) is the ith subtree of T and write (as part of the higher-level algorithm)

$$\underline{for}\ i = 1\ \underline{to}\ n\ \underline{do}\ S(SUB(i, T)).$$

The collection of all such statements specified will have some underlying formal data space. In fact there probably will be a great many, all of them having properties which do not seem useful for the problem at hand (for otherwise we would have specified them).

Now to implement the higher-level algorithm in a completely specified data space requires that we choose one of the possible underlying data spaces. This choice will usually not be made directly, for we will probably proceed by obtaining the properties which interest us in, say, FORTRAN, and thereby introduce some additional properties. It could be that when we see these additional properties we will not like some of them.

For example, suppose we represent multibranching trees as binary trees with the functions firstson and brother; so that a statement U : = SUB(i, T), as part of the statement S(SUB(i, T)), could be executed by

$$U := \text{firstson}(T); \; \underline{\text{for}} \; j = 1 \; \underline{\text{to}} \; i\text{-}1 \; \underline{\text{do}} \; U := \text{brother}(U) \; .$$

The inefficiency of substituting this for $U := \text{SUB}(i, T)$ in the $\underline{\text{for}}$ statement is obvious. Yet, that is exactly what might happen if we regarded the multibranching tree data type as the important property, and implemented it without regard for its "context."

We might guess at the outset that implementation will force us to choose a data space in which $\underline{\text{firstson}}$ and $\underline{\text{brother}}$ are primitive. Then we would write, instead of the $\underline{\text{for}}$-statement,

$$U := \underline{\text{firstson}}(T); \; S(U); \; \underline{\text{for}} \; i=1 \; \underline{\text{to}} \; n\text{-}1 \; \underline{\text{do}} \; \underline{\text{begin}} \; U := \underline{\text{brother}}(U); \; S(U) \; \underline{\text{end}}$$

Someone implementing this without regard to the context might feel that the statement $U := \underline{\text{brother}}(U)$ would have to produce a new copy of U. Whether it does or not is going to be a property of the higher-level data space, and one which is of interest with respect to storage efficiency.

<u>REFERENCES</u>

1. Cremers, A. and T.N. Hibbard, "Formal Modeling of Virtual Machines," submitted for publication, 1975.

2. Cremers, A. and T.N. Hibbard, "On the Relationship between a Procedure and Its Data," in preparation, 1975.

3. Hoare, C.A.R. and P.E. Lauer, "Consistent and Complementary Formal Theories of the Semantics of Programming Languages," <u>Acta Informatica</u> 3, 135-153, 1974.

4. Lauer, P.E., "Consistent Formal Theories of the Semantics of Programming Languages," IBM Laboratory, Vienna, Technical Report, TR.25.121, 1971.

5. Minsky, M.L., <u>Computation: Finite and Infinite Machines</u>, Prentice-Hall, 1967.

6. Parnas, D.L., "A Technique for Software Module Specification with Examples," <u>Communications of the ACM</u> 15, 330-336, 1972.

7. Robinson, L., K.N. Levitt, P.G. Neumann, A.R. Saxena, "On Attaining Reliable Software for a Secure Operating System," <u>Proceedings International Conference on Reliable Software</u>, Los Angeles, 1975.

8. Scott, D., "Data Types as Lattices," Lecture Notes, Advanced Course in Programming Languages, Amsterdam, 1972.

ANWENDUNG DER AXIOMATISCHEN DEFINITIONSMETHODE
AUF HÖHERE PROGRAMMIERSPRACHEN

Wolfgang Polak
Fakultät für Informatik, Universität Karlsruhe

0. Einleitung

Ziel der folgenden Überlegungen ist es, Probleme aufzuzeigen, die bei der Anwendung der axiomatischen Definitionsmethode [1,2] auf andere höhere Programmiersprachen als PASCAL entstehen. Ausgehend von der PASCAL-Definition werden zwei Gruppen von Problemen betrachtet. Einmal erfordert der Übergang von anweisungs- zu ausdrucksorientierten Sprachen eine detailliertere Beschreibung gewisser Sprachelemente. Zum anderen entstehen Probleme durch komplexere Variablenkonzepte als das von PASCAL (etwa das Referenzkonzept von ALGOL68).

In Ergänzung zu [1,2] sei auf folgende Punkte hingewiesen. Formeln der Art $\{P\}$ S $\{Q\}$ heissen dynamische Assertionen (dA), sie beschreiben die Wirkung der Ausführung des Programmstückes S (dynamisch). Statische Assertionen (sA) beschreiben statische Eigenschaften von Objekten (etwa $\text{Typ}(x)=\text{INT}$ o.ä.). Ist D eine Menge von Vereinbarungen, so bezeichne H(D) eine sA, die die Eigenschaften der vereinbarten Objekte beschreibt.

Die Prädikate P, Q sind Formeln einer "Logik der Datenobjekte" (LD). Wir nennen eine Abbildung der Datenobjekte auf Werte einen Speicherzustand. Jede Formel P der LD beschreibt eine Menge von Speicherzuständen.

Eine Substitution der Form $P*\langle x/y\rangle$ beschreibt die Ersetzung aller freien x in P durch y. $P*\langle x_1/y_1,x_2/y_2,.....\rangle$ bedeutet die simultane Ersetzung der x_i durch die y_i.

1. Probleme des Referenzkonzeptes

1.1 Mehrfache Zugriffswege

Das folgende Beispiel illustriert das Problem der mehrfachen Zugriffswege.

```
BEGIN REF INT xx; INT y, z;
y:=3; xx:=y; y:=5; z:=xx END
```

Wendet man auf dieses Programm die Axiomatik aus [1] unreflektiert an, so könnte man etwa deduzieren:

```
{3=3} y:=3 {cont(y)=3}
{cont(y)=3} xx:=y {cont(cont(xx))=3}
{cont(cont(xx))=3} y:=5 {cont(cont(xx))=3}
{cont(cont(xx))=3} z:=xx {cont(z)=3}
```

also

```
{true} BEGIN......END {cont(z)=3}
```

Darin verbergen sich zwei Fehler. Einmal ist das Vorgehen logisch nicht korrekt, es werden in der Deduktion Substitutionen von Termen und nicht nur von freien Variablen vorgenommen. Zum anderen möchte man für obiges Programm nicht

    {true} BEGIN.....END {cont(z)=3}
sondern

    {true} BEGIN.....END {cont(z)=5}
ableiten. Das Problem dabei ist, dass in

    {cont(cont(xx))=3} y:=5 {cont(cont(xx))=3}
cont(y) und cont(cont(xx)) das gleiche Objekt bezeichnen. An dieser Stelle müsste die Zuweisung daher durch das Axiom

    {5=5} y:=5 {cont(cont(xx))=5}
beschrieben werden. Die Deduktion ist falsch, da zu einem Objekt mehrere Zugriffswege existieren. Derartige mehrfache Zugriffswege treten in folgenden Fällen auf:
a) bei Feldern (A[i]=A[j], falls i=j),
b) bei Prozeduraufrufen (p(x,x)),
c) bei Gleichheitsvereinbarungen und
d) bei Namensnamen.
[2] bietet eine Lösung für den Fall a) und verbietet verbal mehrfache Zugriffswege im Fall b).

1.2 Theoretische Überlegungen

In PASCAL bezeichnet eine Variable (VAR x :INT) ein Objekt, welches durch eine Zuweisung (x:=y) verändert werden kann. Dies wird in der Axiomatik durch eine Substitution <x/y> ausgedrückt.

In einer Sprache mit Referenzkonzept können nur Bezugsobjekte verändert werden (Bezugsobjekte sind Variable). Eine Zuweisung x:=3 bewirkt eine Veränderung des Bezugsobjektes von x. Bezeichne Cx das Bezugsobjekt von x (cont(x)=Cx), so entspricht x:=3 einer Substitution <Cx/3>. Wir notieren eine solche Veränderung eines Objektes als Pseudozuweisung Cx<-3.

Damit ergibt sich folgende Situation: Bezeichner des Programmes treten als Variablensymbole der LD auf, sie bezeichnen ein Objekt. Ist dieses Objekt ein Name, so führen wir ein neues Variablensymbol ein, welches stets das Bezugsobjekt dieses Namens bezeichnet (in der Regel gibt es keinen Bezeichner des Programmes, der dies leistet). Die Beziehung (cont(x)=Cx) dieser beiden Variablensymbole zueinander gilt, solange x existiert, sie kann daher als sA formuliert werden.

Wir sind jetzt in der Lage, durch Substitution von Variablensymbolen durch Terme (<Cx/y>), die Zuweisung logisch korrekt zu beschreiben. Es verbleibt das Problem der mehrfachen Zugriffswege, was in obiger Terminologie so formuliert werden kann: zu jedem Bezugsobjekt, darf es in der LD nur ein Variablensymbol geben, welches dieses Objekt bezeichnet.

1.3 Beseitigung mehrfacher Zugriffswege

Mathematisch ist die Lösung des Problems trivial. Mehrere Bezeichner bezeichnen das gleiche Objekt, sie bilden eine Äquivalenzklasse. Verwenden wir in der LD statt Bezeichner Äquivalenzklassen von Bezeichnern, so wäre das Problem gelöst. Leider lassen sich solche Äquivalenzklassen nicht statisch bestimmen, jede Zuweisung an einen Namensnamen ändert die Klasseneinteilung.

Zur Lösung verhilft folgender Sachverhalt: zu jedem Bezugsobjekt lässt sich statisch ein Variablensymbol eindeutig bestimmen, welches stets dieses Objekt bezeichnet. Zeichnen wir dieses eindeutig bestimmte Variablensymbol als Repräsentanten einer Klasse aus, so kann jede Veränderung dieses Objekts durch eine Substitution dieses Repräsentanten durch den neuen Wert beschrieben werden.

Sei V ein Prädikatensymbol, welches den eindeutigen Repräsentanten einer Klasse auszeichnet, so erzeugt eine Vereinbarung INT x die sA s {Typ(x)=REF INT, Typ(Cx)=INT, cont(x)=Cx, V(Cx)}. Eine Gleichheitsvereinbarung REF INT x=y erzeugt die sA {Typ(x)=REF INT}. Ein entsprechendes Cx existiert nicht, vielmehr lässt sich aus cont(y)=Cy und x=y folgern cont(x)=Cy.

Betrachten wir die korrekte Deduktion des Programmes aus 1.1. Für die Vereinbarungen gilt folgende sA:

    Typ(xx)=REF REF INT & Typ(Cxx)=REF INT & cont(xx)=Cxx &
    V(Cxx) & Typ(y)=Typ(z)=REF INT & Typ(Cy)=Typ(Cz)=INT &
    cont(y)=Cy & cont(z)=Cz & V(Cy) & V(Cz)

womit wir ableiten können:

    {true} y:=3 {true}
    {true} xx:=y {Cxx=y}
    {Cxx=y} y:=5 {Cxx=y & Cy=5}
    {Cxx=y & Cy=5} z:=xx {Cxx=y & Cy=5 & Cz=5}

also

    {true} BEGIN.....END {Cz=5}.

1.4 Attribute von Objekten

Datenobjekte besitzen gewisse Eigenschaften, sie sind von einem bestimmten Typ und haben eine bestimmte Lebensdauer. Bei komplexeren Variablenkonzepten sind auch Attribute wie Bezugseigenschaft, Umbenennbarkeit, Variableneigenschaft denkbar [3,7].

Auch die oben eingeführten Bezeichner Cx werden verwendet, um Eigenschaften der Bezugsobjekte, Attribute der Namen, zu beschreiben.

Je nach Anforderungen der Sprache kann ein Attribut statisch oder dynamisch beschrieben werden. Dies bedeutet, dass entsprechende Aussagen in den sA oder in den Formeln der LD, damit in den dA, enthalten sind. Das Attribut Typ ist in PASCAL statisch [2], während in Euler Typen dynamisch behandelt werden müssen. Wir können dabei analog verfahren wie in 1.3. Ist x Bezeichner eines Namens, so enthält eine sA die Aussagen:

    cont(x)=Cx & Typ(x)=Tx.

Eine Zuweisung an x wird nun durch eine Substitution
   <Cx/Wert-rechte-Seite,Tx/Typ-rechte-Seite>
beschrieben.

Das Lebensdauerattribut wird in einigen Sprachen benötigt, um Vorbedingungen für die Zuweisung zu formulieren (Lebensdauer der rechten Seite darf nicht kleiner sein als die der linken). Schwierigkeiten bei der Beschreibung von Attributen treten bei Prozeduren auf. Betrachten wir obige Lebensdauerregel. Bei der Vereinbarung einer Prozedur erfolgt eine Deduktion, die die Bedeutung dieser Prozedur für jeden Aufruf festlegt. Zum Zeitpunkt der Deklaration ist lediglich bekannt, dass die Lebensdauer der globalen Objekte grösser als die der lokalen Objekte ist. Damit ist die Menge der beschreibbaren Prozeduren sehr stark eingeschränkt, nicht einmal die Bedeutung von
PROC p = (REF REF INT x, REF REF INT y) :. x:=y
ist erklärbar. Dies ist ein Hinweis auf das (hier nicht behandelte) Problem einer adäquaten Beschreibung von Prozeduren.

2. Anweisungs- und ausdrucksorientierte Sprachen

2.1 Anforderungen durch Programmstrukturen

In anweisungsorientierten Sprachen (statement languages) gibt es kleinste semantische Einheiten (Zuweisung, Prozeduraufruf), die wie in PASCAL durch Axiome beschreibbar sind. Dies setzt voraus, dass bei ihrer Abarbeitung keine Nebeneffekte auftreten. Nebeneffekt heisst in diesem Zusammenhang, dass bei der Beschaffung der linken oder rechten Seite oder eines aktuellen Parameters Datenobjekte verändert werden. Bei ausdrucksorientierten Sprachen (expression languages) sind Operanden selbst wieder Programmabschnitte, die Datenobjekte manipulieren. Nebeneffekte in obigem Sinn sind also von der Sprache intendiert, es ist daher notwendig, sie zu beschreiben, um der Sprache gerecht zu werden. Hieraus ergeben sich zwei Forderungen:
a) Gewisse syntaktische Strukturen liefern als Ergebnis ein Objekt. Für diese Objekte müssen Bezeichnungen geschaffen werden.
b) Operationen ebenso wie die Zuweisung sind nicht mehr durch Axiome beschreibbar. Vielmehr setzt sich ihre Bedeutung aus der der Operanden und der Verknüpfung zusammen, sie sind daher durch eine Ableitungsregel zu beschreiben.

2.2 Kollateralität

Operanden werden entweder in einer bestimmten Reihenfolge oder kollateral beschafft. Im ersten Fall treten keine Schwierigkeiten auf, im zweiten Fall ist, bevor eine Regel entwickelt werden kann, zu klären:
a) unter welchen Bedingungen zwei Klauseln kollateral erarbeitet werden können und

b) wie Vor- und Nachbedingung für kollaterale Klauseln bestimmt
   werden.

Man kann zwei kollateral ausgeführte Programmstücke als parallele
Prozesse auffassen, die nicht miteinander synchronisiert werden. Zur
axiomatischen Beschreibung paralleler Prozesse existieren Vorschläge
von Hoare [4] und Gries [5]. Für die folgende Diskussion sei
angenommen, dass eine Methode existiert, {P} (A,B) {Q} abzuleiten,
wobei (A,B) die kollaterale Abarbeitung von A und B andeutet.

2.3 Artanpassung

Bei der Beschreibung der Operationen in Abhängigkeit von den
Operanden, ist es möglich, die Wirkung der implizierten
Anpassoperationen zu erfassen. Diese Wirkung ist nicht immer trivial,
da etwa "Deprozedurieren" beliebige Nebeneffekte erzeugen kann.

Nehmen wir an, dass das Attribut Typ statisch behandelt wird, so
sind drei Beschreibungsformen denkbar.

a) Alle Anpassoperationen werden durch eine Vorbehandlung des
   Programmes explizit eingefügt, eine Deduktion erfolgt über ein
   modifiziertes Programm.

b) Zu jedem Zwischenergebnis sind die apriori und aposteriori Typen
   [6] bekannt. Während der Deduktion werden die notwendigen
   Anpassoperationen auf Grund dieser Informationen (sA) impliziert.

c) Die Bestimmung der korrekten Anpassoperationen und der apriori und
   aposteriori Typen sowie die Operator.identifikation erfolgen während
   der Deduktion. Dies ist sicher möglich, wenn man jedem
   Zwischenergebnis als Attribut eine syntaktische Position [6]
   zuordnet.

Der Fall b soll hier näher untersucht werden. Zu einer syntaktischen
Struktur S, die ein Objekt als Ergebnis liefert, seien $\underline{S}$ und S´ zwei
Variablensymbole der LD. Beide bezeichnen das Ergebnis von S, $\underline{S}$ ist
vom apriori Typ, S´ ist vom aposteriori Typ [6]. Sind diese Typen
statisch bekannt, so auch die Anpassequenz, die $\underline{S}$ in S´ überführt. Die
Notation S´<-Anpop($\underline{S}$) soll andeuten, dass eine Folge von
Anpassoperationen (Anpop) auf $\underline{S}$ angewendet wird.

2.4 Regeln für Operationen

Zur Ableitung dieser Regeln wird die Ausführung der Operationen in
kleinere Aktionen aufgegliedert, deren Bedeutung sich dann in
einfacher Weise beschreiben lässt. Eine Formel AoB wird in folgenden
Schritten erarbeitet:

(i)   (A,B) - die Operanden werden kollateral beschafft, dabei erhält
      man die Ergebnisse A´ und B´.

(ii) Ausführung der Operation, dies entspricht einer Pseudozuweisung
      an den entsprechenden Bezeichner, $\underline{AoB}$<-A´oB´

(iii) Artanpassung von apriori zu aposteriori Art, dies entspricht
      einer Pseudozuweisung (AoB)´<-Anpop($\underline{AoB}$), wobei Anpop eine von
      AoB abhängige Folge von Anpassoperationen ist.

Das Beschaffen der Operanden (i) wird gemäss 2.2 beschrieben. Die
Pseudozuweisung (ii) entspricht einer Substitution
$\{P*\langle AoB/A´oB´\rangle\}$ AoB<-A´oB´ $\{P\}$.
Die Aktionen (i)-(iii) werden sequentiell ausgeführt, damit erhält man
unmittelbar die Regel:

$$\frac{\{P\}\ (A,B)\ \{Q*\langle AoB/A´oB´\rangle\},\{Q\}\ (AoB)´\text{<-Anpop}(AoB)\ \{R\}}{\{P\}\ AoB\ \{R\}}$$

Das Zeichen "o" geht dabei textuell in die Vorbedingung ein, die
eigentliche Operation wird damit wie in [2] durch die Axiomatisierung
der Datentypen beschrieben.
Etwas anders sieht die Regel für die Zuweisung aus, da ":=" nicht in
den Prädikaten auftreten soll, sondern durch eine Substitution zu
beschreiben ist. Durch eine Aufgliederung wie oben erhält man die
Regel:

$$\frac{\text{cont}(A´)=Y}{\{P\}(A,B)\{Q*\langle A:=B/A´,Y/B´\rangle\},\{Q\}(A:=B)´\text{<-Anpop}(A:=B)\{R\}}$$
$$\{P\}\ A:=B\ \{R\}$$

Es wird AoB als frei von Nebeneffekten bezeichnet, wenn für alle P die
Beziehung $\{P\}(A,B)\{P\}$ gilt und keine Anpassoperationen zu implizieren
sind (also stets S=S´). Man sieht unmittelbar, dass obige Beschreibung
mit [1,2] konsistent ist; falls alle Operationen frei von
Nebeneffekten sind, sind die Regeln äquivalent mit dem
Zuweisungsaxiom.

2.5 Implikationen

Eine adäquate Beschreibung von expression languages erfordert einige
weitere Änderungen. Werden Nebeneffekte bei der Zuweisung beschrieben,
so ist es sinnvoll sie auch bei Ausdrücken zu erfassen, die in anderer
syntaktischer Position stehen. Beispiele dafür sind initialisierende
Vereinbarungen und boolsche Ausdrücke in IF und WHILE Konstruktionen.
Da auch komplexe Sprachkonstruktionen Objekte als Ergebnis liefern
können (IF oder CASE), muss bei deren Beschreibung die Pseudozuweisung
dieses Ergebnisses an das entsprechende Variablensymbol berücksichtigt
werden.
   Die Beschreibung von initialisierenden Vereinbarungen kann in
Analogie zum Vorgehen des Übersetzerbauers geschehen. Man trennt
Vereinbarungen von Initialisierungen. Die Vereinbarungen werden wie in
[2] behandelt. Die Deduktion über den Block beginnt mit der Behandlung
der Initialisierungen.
   Die Beschreibung der Nebeneffekte der boolschen Formel einer WHILE
Schleife kann etwa durch folgende Regel erfolgen:

$$\frac{\{P\}\ B\ \{Q\},\{Q\ \&\ B'\}\ S\ \{P\}}{\{P\}\ \text{WHILE}\ B\ \text{DO}\ S\ \text{DONE}\ \{Q\ \&\ \text{notB}'\}}$$

Ist B frei von Nebeneffekten, so gilt {P} B {P}; die Regel ist identisch mit der aus [2].

Der Wert einer IF Klausel wird durch Zuweisungen der Ergebnisse der Teilformeln an die gesamte Struktur beschrieben. Dies führt etwa zu der Regel:

$$\{P\}\ B\ \{Q\},\{Q\ \&\ B'\}\ A1\ \{R*<\underline{IF...FI}/A1'>\}$$
$$\{Q\ \&\ \text{notB}'\}\ A2\ \{R*<\underline{IF...FI}/A2'>\}$$
$$\{R\}\ (IF...FI)'<\text{-Anpop}(\underline{IF...FI})\ \{T\}$$
$$\overline{\{P\}\ IF\ B\ THEN\ A1\ ELSE\ A2\ FI\ \{T\}}$$

3. Literatur

[1] Hoare, C. A. R., "An axiomatic basis for computer programming", CACM 12/576-581 (1969)

[2] Hoare, C. A. R., Wirth, N., " Axiomatic definition of the programming language PASCAL", Acta Informatica 2/335-355 (1973)

[3] Goos, G., "Some thoughts on variables", Bericht Nr. 19/74, Fakultät für Informatik, Universität Karlsruhe (1974)

[4] Hoare, C. A. R., "Towards a theory of parallel programming", International Seminar on Operating System Techniques, Belfast, Northern Ireland (1971)

[5] Gries, D., "An exercise in proving properties of parallel programs", International Summerschool, Marktoberndorf 1975

[6] van Wijngaarden, Mailloux, Peck, Koster, "Report on the algorithmic language Algol68" Numerische Mathematik, 14/79-218 (1969)

[7] Goos, G., "Die Programmiersprache BALG", Bericht Nr. 6/75, Fakultät für Informatik, Universität Karlsruhe (1975)

SYSTEMATISCHE ANALYSE SEMANTISCHER ABHAENGIGKEITEN

Uwe Kastens
Fakultaet fuer Informatik der Universitaet Karlsruhe

1. Ueberblick

Die statische Semantik einer Programmiersprache kann beschrieben werden, indem man den Sprachkomponenten Attribute zuordnet und Abhaengigkeiten zwischen den Attributen angibt. In diesem Bericht wird beschrieben, wie solche Zusammenhaenge systematisch untersucht werden koennen. Es wird ein Verfahren angegeben, mit dem aus der syntaktischen und semantischen Definition einer Sprache eine Vorschrift ermittelt wird, nach der die semantischen Eigenschaften und Zusammenhaenge jedes Satzes der Sprache ermittelt werden koennen. Der Algorithmus kann zusammen mit einem Algorithmus zur Generierung eines Zerteilers den Kern eines Uebersetzer-erzeugenden Systems bilden. Mit solch einem System koennen die Uebersetzer-Prozeduren, die die semantische Analyse durchfuehren, automatisch aus der Sprachdefinition generiert werden. Die Komplexitaet der ausdrueckbaren semantischen Zusammenhaenge wird durch das Verfahren nicht beschraenkt.

Dieses Verfahren unterscheidet sich von den bisher bekannten dadurch, dass zur Analyse der semantischen Zusammenhaenge eine andere Methode angewandt wird als zur Ermittlung der syntaktischen Struktur. Solch ein Vorgehen erscheint uns zweckmaessig, da die Algorithmen zur syntaktischen und semantischen Analyse unterschiedliche Anforderungen hinsichtlich des zu betrachtenden Kontextes stellen. Systematische Verfahren zur syntaktischen Analyse sind im allgemeinen so konzipiert, dass die Struktur eines Satzes der Sprache in einem einzigen Durchgang unter Betrachtung eines moeglichst geringen Kontextes ermittelt werden kann (z.B. LR- oder LL-Verfahren). Die Analyse der Semantik vieler Programmiersprachen erfordert jedoch die Betrachtung eines groesseren Kontextes und in den meisten Faellen mehrere Durchgaenge durch den syntaktisch analysierten Satz der Sprache. Sie kann deshalb - zumindest nicht vollstaendig - in das Verfahren zur syntaktischen Analyse integriert werden.

Unser Verfahren basiert auf dem Ansatz von Knuth in [Kn68]. Dort werden semantische Eigenschaften von Sprachkomponenten durch Zuordnen von Attributen beschrieben und die Abhaengigkeiten zwischen den Attribut-Werten durch Graphen dargestellt. Knuth zeigt, wie aus der Untersuchung dieser Graphen festgestellt werden kann, ob die semantischen Definitionen der Sprache so beschaffen sind, dass zu jedem Satz der Sprache alle Attribut-Werte ermittelt werden koennen. Eine Sprache mit dieser Eigenschaft nennt er dann "semantisch wohldefiniert". Diese Untersuchungen wurden in modifizierter Form in unser Verfahren aufgenommen.

Wir gehen davon aus, dass die abstrakte syntaktische Struktur eines Satzes zu einer gegebenen Grammatik durch einen Ableitungs-Baum (AB) beschrieben wird. Jeder Knoten in einem AB repraesentiert ein Symbol des Vokabulars der Grammatik. Alle Knoten, die das gleiche Symbol repraesentieren, nennen wir der gleichen "Knoten-Klasse" zugehoerig. Alle Knoten, die zusammen mit ihren direkten Nachfolge-Knoten eine Anwendung der gleichen Ableitungsregel repraesentieren, nennen wir vom gleichen "Knoten-Typ".

Die semantischen Eigenschaften von Sprachkomponenten werden durch Attribut-Werte beschrieben, die den Knoten des AB zugeordnet sind. Allen Knoten einer Klasse werden die gleichen Attribute zugeordnet. Sie koennen abhaengig vom Kontext, in dem der jeweilige Knoten steht, verschiedene Werte annehmen. Den so erweiterten AB nennen wir einen "attributierten Ableitungs-Baum (AAB)".

Zu jeder syntaktischen Regel der Grammatik werden Vorschriften angegeben, nach denen die Berechnung der Werte bestimmter Attribute von Nichtterminalen erfolgt, die in dieser Regel auftreten. In den Berechnungsvorschriften koennen die Werte anderer Attribute verwendet werden.

Um die Werte aller Attribute in einem AAB zu berechnen, muss man im allgemeinen den AAB oder einige seiner Unterbaeume mehrfach in unterschiedlicher Richtung durchlaufen. Unser Verfahren ordnet jedem Knoten-Typ p (d.h. jeder Regel p) eine Sequenz von "Besuchen" zu, die beschreibt, in welcher Reihenfolge beim Durchlauf durch den AAB von einem Knoten des Typs p zu den Knoten in seiner direkten Nachbarschaft uebergangen werden muss. (Dabei koennen Knoten mehrfach besucht werden.) Ausserdem wird ermittelt, welche Attribut-Werte zwischen zwei solchen Besuchen berechnet werden koennen.

Diese Besuchssequenzen legen eindeutig fest, wie jeder zulaessige AAB zu einer bestimmten Sprache durchlaufen werden kann, damit die Werte aller Attribute berechnet werden koennen. Aus den Besuchssequenzen koennen fuer einen Uebersetzer die Programmstrukturen (z.B. rekursive Prozeduren oder Koroutinen) konstruiert werden, mit denen der AAB durchlaufen und die Attribute berechnet werden.

In Abschnitt 12 wird die Anwendung des Verfahrens am Beispiel einer einfachen Programmiersprache demonstriert.

[Kn68]   Knuth, D.E., Semantics of Context-Free Languages, Mathematical Systems Theory, vol. 2, pp. 127-145, 1968

2. Notation

Die hier angegebenen Schreibweisen und Abkuerzungen werden in den folgenden Abschnitten nur mit der hier festgelegten Bedeutung verwendet. (Indizes werden in eckigen Klammern notiert; z.B. X[i], b[i,l].)

G=(V,T,P,S)	(kontext-freie) Grammatik
V	Vokabular
T∈V	Terminal-Symbole
P	Menge der syntaktischen Regeln
S∈V\T	Zielsymbol
U,W,X,Y,Z ∈ V\T	beliebige Nichtterminale
u,v,w,x,y ∈ V*	beliebige Zeichenfolgen
p,q,r,s,t ∈ P	syntaktische Regeln
p:Y→X[1]....X[n]	Notation einer Regel p. Dabei werden Terminal-Symbole auf der rechten Seite nicht angegeben, da sie in diesem Zusammenhang keine Bedeutung haben.
M,N	Mengen von Attributen
A(X)	Menge der Attribute von X
A[der](X)	Menge der abgeleiteten (derived) Attribute von X
A[in](X)	Menge der erworbenen (inherited) Attribute von X
a∈A(X)	Attribut
a=g[p](a[1],...,a[n])	semantische Vorschrift zur Berechnung des Wertes von a, die der Regel p zugeordnet ist
C[p]	Graph zur Beschreibung der durch alle g[p] gegebenen Abhaengigkeiten
D[p]	durch Huellenbildung aus C[p] gewonnener Graph
E[p]	durch Huellenbildung aus D[p] gewonnener Graph (Falls die Zuordnung zu einer Regel p nicht wesentlich ist, wird auch C,D,E geschrieben.)
k=(a[1],a[2])	Kante in einem Graphen von a[1] nach a[2]
w[p](a)=(up,down)	Wertepaar, das dem Attribut a in einem E[p] zugeordnet ist.
<	lineare Ordnungsrelation ueber den Wertepaaren (up, down)
b[i,l]	l-ter Besuch eines Knotens X[i]
F[p]	Besuchs-Sequenz (Folge von Attributen und Besuchen)

3. Voraussetzungen zur Sprachdefinition

Fuer unser Verfahren wird vorausgesetzt, dass die Grammatik G kontext-frei ist und keine unnoetigen Regeln enthaelt. Fuer jedes Y∈V\T gilt also: Es gibt eine Zeichenfolge uYv, die aus S ableitbar

ist, und jedes w in einer Regel p:Y→w gilt: w ist zu einer terminalen
Zeichenfolge ableitbar.

Die semantischen Eigenschaften und Zusammenhaenge der Sprache
werden durch Attribute formuliert. Jedem Nichtterminal X ist eine
Menge von Attributen A(X) zugeordnet. Ein Attribut kann unterschiedliche Werte annehmen, abhaengig vom Kontext, in dem das Nichtterminal
steht und von den Attribut-Werten anderer Nichtterminale in diesem
Kontext. Die Vorschriften (semantische Regeln), nach denen die Werte
der Attribute zu ermitteln sind, werden den syntaktischen Regeln
zugeordnet. Wir nennen a∈A(X) ein abgeleitetes (derived) Attribut von
X, wenn es zu einer Regel p:X→v eine Berechnungsvorschrift fuer a
gibt. a∈A(X) heisst erworbenes (inherited) Attribut von x, wenn es zu
einer Regel p:Y→uXv eine Berechnungsvorschrift fuer a gibt.

In den weiteren Untersuchungen wird vorausgesetzt, dass fuer die
Attribute und Berechnungsvorschriften folgende Aussagen gelten:

a)   Kein Attribut kann zugleich abgeleitet und erworben sein, d.h.
      fuer jedes X∈V\T muss gelten
      A[der](X) v A[in](X) = A(X) und
      A[der](X) ∧ A[in](X) = ∅.
b)   Fuer jedes abgeleitete (bzw.erworbene) Attribut von X muss es zu
      jeder Regel p:X→v (bzw. p:Y→uXv) eine Berechnungsvorschrift
      geben.
c)   Fuer das Zielsymbol S gilt A[in](S) = ∅.

Fuer die Untersuchungen in den Abschnitten 7 bis 10 wird ausserdem
die "semantische Wohldefiniertheit" der Sprache vorausgesetzt. In
Abschnitt 6 wird diese Eigenschaft definiert und ein Verfahren zu
ihrer Pruefung angegeben.

4. Strategie des Baum-Durchlaufes

Es ist das Ziel unseres Verfahrens, aus den semantischen Abhaengigkeiten Vorschriften zu ermitteln, die angeben, wie jeder AB zu
durchlaufen ist, damit alle Attribut-Werte aller Knoten bestimmt
werden koennen. Nimmt man an, dass der AB vollstaendig aufgebaut ist,
bevor die Attribut-Werte berechnet werden, so kann man zu jeder Regel
p:Y→X[1]...X[n] eine "Besuchssequenz" angeben, die die Wege durch
jeden Knoten der Klasse Y und des Typs p und die bei jedem Besuch des
Knotens berechenbaren Attribute bestimmt. Haengt die Berechnung von
Attribut-Werten ab, deren Berechnungsvorschriften nicht p zugeordnet
sind (a∈A[in](Y)vA[der](X[i])), so wird der entsprechende, benachbarte
Knoten besucht (X[i] oder der Vorgaenger von Y).

Unser Verfahren erlaubt es darueber hinaus, die Besuchssequenzen so
zu bestimmen, dass schon beim Aufbau des AB Attribute berechnet werden

koennen. in diesem Fall bestimmt die Ordnung, in der der Baum
aufgebaut wird, die Reihenfolge der Besuche im ersten Durchlauf.
Derartige Annahmen wirken sich nur auf den in Abschnitt 8 (Bewertung
der Abhaengigkeits-Graphen) beschriebenen Teil unseres Verfahrens aus.
Wir nehmen dort an, dass der AB von den Endknoten zur Wurzel hin
aufgebaut wird (bottom-up) und dass dabei schon Attribut-Werte
bestimmt werden, soweit es die Abhaengigkeiten zulassen. In Abschnitt
11 wird angegeben, wie das Verfahren zu modifizieren ist, falls eine
andere Durchlaufstrategie vorgegeben wird (z.B. top-down-Aufbau des
AAB, oder Ermittlung der Attribut-Werte nach dem vollstaendigen Aufbau
des AA).

5. Beschreibung semantischer Abhaengigkeiten durch Graphen

Zu jeder Regel $p:Y \to X[1]...X[n]$ sind durch die Berechnungsvorschriften fuer die Attribut-Werte Abhaengigkeiten zwischen den
Attributen von $Y, X[1],...,X[n]$ definiert.

Es wird nun zu jeder Regel p ein gerichteter Graph $C[p]$ konstruiert, der diese Abhaengigkeiten beschreibt.

Die Knoten von $C[p]$ sind alle Attribute $a \in A(Y) \vee A(X[1]) \vee...\vee A(X[n])$. In $C[p]$ fuehrt genau dann eine Kante $k=(a[i],a)$ von $a[i]$ nach
a, wenn es zu p eine Berechnungsvorschrift fuer a gibt, in der der
Wert von a von dem Wert von $a[i]$ abhaengt: $a=g[p](a[1],...,a[i],...a[m])$.

Wegen der Voraussetzung b in Abschnitt 3 hat jeder Graph C die
Eigenschaften

a)   Nur fuer $a \in A[der](Y) \vee A[in](X[1]) \vee...\vee A[in](X[n])$ gibt es zu
     der Regel p Berechnungsvorschriften $g[p]$. In $C[p]$ muenden deshalb
     nur in diese Knoten Kanten.
b)   Ist in einer Berechnungsvorschrift $a=g[p]$ $g[p]$ eine konstante
     Funktion (d.h. der Wert von a wird unabhaengig von anderen
     Attribut-Werten berechnet), so muenden in $C[p]$ keine Kanten in a.

In den folgenden Abschnitten werden wir die Graphen C so vervollstaendigen, dass sie auch alle Abhaengigkeiten zwischen Attributen
beschreiben, die durch jede moegliche Zusammensetzung solcher Graphen
zu einem AAB verursacht werden koennen. Dieser Vorgang ist als
Huellenbildung ueber den Graphen bezueglich der Kontext-Abhaengigkei-
ten zu verstehen.

6. Semantische Wohldefiniertheit

Wir wollen nach [Kn68] eine Grammatik "semantisch wohldefiniert"
nennen, wenn zu ihr kein AAB konstruiert werden kann, in dem einige
Attribute zyklisch voneinander abhaengen, und ihre Werte deshalb nicht
berechnet werden koennen.

Diese Eigenschaft der Grammatik kann mit Hilfe der Graphen C
ueberprueft werden. Dazu vervollstaendigen wir jeden Graphen $C[p]$ zu
einer Regel $p:Y \rightarrow X[1] \ldots X[n]$, so dass er auch alle Abhaengigkeiten
zwischen den Attributen von $Y, X[1], \ldots, X[n]$ beschreibt, die durch
jede moegliche Ableitung der $X[i]$ gegeben sind (Regeln $q:X[i] \rightarrow u$).

Zu jedem Graphen $C[p]$ wird ein Graph $D[p]$ konstruiert. Die
Knotenmengen von $C[p]$ und $D[p]$ sind gleich. $D[p]$ enthaelt eine Kante
$k=(a[1],a[2])$ von $a[1]$ nach $a[2]$ genau dann, wenn k in $C[p]$ enthalten
ist oder wenn gilt $a[1] \in A(X[i])$ und $a[2] \in A[der](X[i])$, $1 \leq i \leq n$ und
es gibt einen Graphen $D[q]$ zu einer Regel $q:X[i] \rightarrow u$, in dem ein Weg
von $a[1]$ nach $a[2]$ fuehrt. Die in $D[p]$ aber nicht in $C[p]$ enthaltenen
Kanten nennen wir "durch die Regeln q in $D[p]$ induziert".

Sind alle Graphen $D[p]$ zyklenfrei, so kann man keinen AAB konstruieren, der einen Zyklus enthaelt - die Grammatik ist semantisch
wohldefiniert.

Enthaelt ein Graph $D[p]$ zu einer Regel $p:Y \rightarrow X[1] \ldots X[n]$ einen
Zyklus, so sind folgende Faelle zu unterscheiden:

a)   Auf dem Zyklus liegen mindestens zwei Kanten, die durch verschiedene Regeln $q:X[i] \rightarrow u$ und $r:X[i] \rightarrow v$ in $D[p]$ induziert sind.
In diesem Fall fuehrt weder die Ableitungssequenz
$Y \Rightarrow X[1] \ldots X[i] \ldots X[n] \Rightarrow X[1] \ldots u \ldots X[n]$ noch
$Y \Rightarrow X[1] \ldots X[i] \ldots X[n] \Rightarrow X[1] \ldots v \ldots X[n]$
zu einem Zyklus im AAB. Falls keine weiteren Zyklen auftreten,
ist die Grammatik semantisch wohldefiniert. Der Zyklus in $D[p]$
kann durch eine Transformation der Grammatik beseitigt werden:
Man ersetzt die Regel p durch zwei Regeln $p[1]:Y \rightarrow X[1] \ldots u \ldots X[n]$
und $p[2]:Y \rightarrow X[1] \ldots v \ldots X[n]$.

b)   In allen anderen Faellen laesst sich ein AAB konstruieren, der
einen Zyklus enthaelt. Die Grammatik ist dann nicht semantisch
wohldefiniert.

Alle weiteren Untersuchungen setzen voraus, dass alle Graphen $D[p]$
zyklenfrei sind.

7. Erweiterung der Abhaengigkeits-Graphen

Die in Abschnitt 6 konstruierten Graphen D werden durch weitere Huellenbildung zu Graphen E vervollstaendigt.

Die Knotenmengen jedes D[p] und E[p] sind gleich. Ein Graph E[p] zu einer Regel p:Y→X[1]...X[n] enthaelt genau dann eine Kante k=(a[1],a[2]), wenn eine der folgenden Bedingungen erfuellt ist:

a)   k ist in D[p] enthalten.

b)   a[1]∈A(Y) und a[2]∈A[in](Y) und es gibt einen Graphen E[q] zu einer Regel q:Z→uYv, in dem ein Weg von a[1] nach a[2] fuehrt. Diese Kanten beschreiben die Abhaengigkeiten zwischen Attributen von Y, die durch jede moegliche Einbettung von Y in einen Kontext verursacht werden.

c)   a[1]∈A(Y) und a[2]∈A[der](Y) und es gibt einen Graphen D[r] zu einer Regel r:Y→w, der eine Kante von a[1] nach a[2] enthaelt.

d)   a[1]∈A(X[i]) und a[2]∈A[in](X[i]) und es gibt einen Graphen E[s] zu einer Regel s:U→xX[i]y, der eine Kante von a[1] nach a[2] enthaelt.

Die in c und d eingefuegten Kanten beschreiben Abhaengigkeiten zwischen Attributen, die bestehen, falls Y bzw. X[i] in einem anderen als durch die Regel p gegebenen Kontext stehen. (Diese Kanten gewaehrleisten, dass die Bewertung der Graphen und die Ermittlung der Besuchssequenzen zunaechst fuer jeden Graphen E[p] unabhaengig durchgefuehrt werden kann.)

Wir nennen die in E[p] aber nicht in D[p] enthaltenen Kanten "durch die Regeln q in E[p] induziert".

Es ist moeglich, dass die so konstruierten Graphen E Zyklen enthalten. In diesem Fall kann man jedoch die Grammatik so transformieren, dass ein solcher Graph durch mehrere zyklenfreie Graphen ersetzt wird. Da alle Graphen D zyklenfrei sind, muss ein Zyklus in einem Graphen E[p] mindestens zwei Kanten enthalten, die durch verschiedene Regeln q in E[p] induziert sind. Setzt man nun die Regel q in p ein und/oder fuehrt neue Nichtterminale fuer ein X[i] mit entsprechenden neuen Regeln ein, so enthalten die Graphen E den urspruenglichen Zyklus nicht mehr.

Bei den folgenden Untersuchungen setzen wir voraus, dass alle Graphen E zyklenfrei sind.

8. Bewertung der Abhaengigkeits-Graphen

In diesem Abschnitt werden den Attributen a in den Graphen E[p]
Wertepaare (up,down)=w[p](a) zugeordnet. Sei p:Y->X[1]...X[n], dann
bedeutet w[p](a)=(m,n):
a kann berechnet werden, bevor von Y aus zum m+1-ten mal der Vorgaen-
ger-Knoten besucht wird und bevor zwischen zwei Besuchen des Vorgaenger-Knotens (bzw. vor dem 1. Besuch falls m=0) zum n+1-ten mal ein
Knoten X[i] besucht wird.

Zwei Wertepaare w(a[1])=(m[1],n[1]) und w(a[2])=(m[2],n[2]) sind
gleich, wenn sie komponentenweise gleich sind.

Es wird eine Relation < wie folgt definiert:
w(a[1])=(m[1],n[1])<w(a[2])=(m[2],n[2])
genau dann,wenn
m[1]<m[2] oder (m[1]=m[2] und n[1]<n[2]).

Die Bewertung der Attribute erfolgt so, dass a[1] vor a[2]
berechnet werden kann, wenn w(a[1])<w(a[2]), und a[1] und a[2] beim
gleichen Besuch berechnet werden koennen, wenn gilt w(a[1])=w(a[2]).

Zunaechst wird in einem Graphen E[p] zu einer Regel p:Y->X[1]...
X[n] denjenigen Attributen, deren Wert beim ersten Besuch des Knotens
Y berechnet werden kann, das Wertepaar (0,0) zugeordnet.

Dies sind alle Attribute a∈A[der](Y)vA[in](X[i]), 1≤i≤n, zu denen
es eine konstante Berechnungsvorschrift a=g[p] gibt.

Aufgrund der gewaehlten Strategie fuer den Durchlauf durch den AAB
kann in E[p] auch allen Attributen von X[i], die ohne einen Besuch des
Vorgaenger-Knotens berechnet werden koennen, das Wertepaar (0,0)
zugeordnet werden. Dies sind die Attribute a∈A[der](X[i]), in die in
E[p] keine Kanten muenden.

Wir nehmen zunaechst an, dass alle Attribute a∈A[in](Y), in die
keine Kanten muenden, nach dem ersten Besuch des Vorgaenger-Knotens
berechnet sind, und ordnen ihnen das Wertepaar (1,0) zu. Nach der
Bewertung aller Graphen wird diese Annahme in Abschnitt 10 ueberprueft
und - falls erforderlich - korrigiert.

Alle uebrigen Attribute in E[p] werden nun sukzessive wie folgt
bewertet. Sei a ein noch nicht bewertetes Attribut in E[p], k[j]
=(a[j],a) alle Kanten, die in a muenden und alle a[j] seien bewertet.
Dann kann a ein Wertepaar zugeordnet werden. Es sind dabei folgende
Faelle zu unterscheiden:

a)   Falls gilt a∈A[der](Y) v A[in](X[i]), 1≤i≤n (es gibt dann eine
     Berechnungsvorschrift a=g[p](....)), dann ist w(a)=max(w(a[j])).
     Die Maximum-Bildung erfolgt gemaess der Relation <.

b)   Falls $a \in A[der](X[i])$, $1 < i \leq n$, so sind alle Kanten $k[j]$ durch Regeln $q:X[i] \rightarrow v$ induziert und es ist ein Besuch des Knotens $X[i]$ erforderlich, um die zu q angegebene Berechnungsvorschrift fuer a auszuwerten. Sei $(m,n')=max((up(a[j],down(a[j]+1)))$, und sei n der kleinste Wert fuer den gilt $n \geq n'$, und fuer kein $a' \in A[der](X[1])$ gilt $(w(a)=(m,n)$ und $i \neq 1)$, dann ist $w(a)=(m,n)$. Hierdurch wird sichergestellt, dass die Besuche verschiedener Knoten $X[i]$ und $X[1]$ zu verschiedenen down-Werten der dabei berechneten Attribute fuehren, und dass bei einem Besuch eines Knotens $X[i]$ moeglicherweise mehrere Attribute aus $A[der](X[i])$ berechnet werden koennen. (Um die Zahl der Besuche einzelner Knoten $X[i]$ klein zu halten, ist es zweckmaessig, ein Attribut nach dieser Regel erst dann zu bewerten, wenn moeglichst viele Attribute $a \in A[im](X[i])$ bewertet sind.)

c)   Falls gilt $a \in A[in](Y)$, so ist zur Berechnung von a ein Besuch des Vorgaenger-Knotens erforderlich. Es ist dann $w(a)=(m,\emptyset)$, wobei m der kleinste Wert ist, fuer den gilt:

$w(a[j]) \leq (m,\emptyset)$, falls $a[j] \in A[in](Y)$, und

$w(a[j]) < (m,\emptyset)$ andernfalls.

9. Aufstellung der Besuchs-Sequenzen

Sind in einem Graphen $E[p]$ zu einer Regel $p:Y \rightarrow X[1]...X[n]$ alle Attribute bewertet, so kann festgestellt werden, in welcher Reihenfolge die Knoten in der Umgebung eines Knotens des Typs p besucht werden muessen, und welche Attribute zwischen je zwei solchen Besuchen berechnet werden koennen.

Wir stellen zu $E[p]$ eine Besuchs-Sequenz $F[p]$ auf, die eine lineare Folge von Attributen $a \in A[der](Y)$ v $A[in](X[i])$, $1 < i \leq n$ (nur fuer diese gibt es Berechnungs-Vorschriften zu p) und Besuchen $b[i,1]$ ist. Dabei bezeichnet $b[i,1]$ den 1-ten Besuch des Knotens $X[i]$, falls $1 < i \leq n$, bzw. des Vorgaenger-Knotens von Y, falls $i=\emptyset$.

$F[p]$ hat die folgenden Eigenschaften:

a)   Alle Attribute $a \in A[der](Y)$ v $A[in](X[i])$, $1 < i \leq n$ treten genau einmal in $F[p]$ auf.

b)   Fuer je zwei Attribute $a[1]$, $a[2]$ gilt: $a[1]$ steht in $F[p]$ vor $a[2]$, falls $w(a[1]) < w(a[2])$ (Die Anordnung von Attributen mit $w(a[1])=w(a[2])$ ist bedeutungslos.)

c)   Zwischen je zwei Attributen $a[1]$ und $a[2]$ mit $w(a[1]) < w(a[2])$ steht ein Besuch $b[i,1]$. Es gilt $i=\emptyset$, falls es ein Attribut $a[k]$ in $F[p]$ vor $b[i,1]$ gibt mit $a[k] \in A[in](Y)$ und $w(a[k])=w(a[1])$. Anderenfalls gibt es in $F[p]$ vor $b[i,1]$ mindestens ein $a[k] \in A[der](X[i])$ mit $w(a[k])=w(a[1])$. Mit 1 werden alle Besuche des gleichen Knotens (bei 1 beginnend) in der Reihenfolge ihres Auftretens in $F[p]$ durchnumeriert.

d)   Gilt fuer das erste Attribut a in F[p] w(a)=(1,∅), so geht ihm ein Besuch b[∅,1] voraus.

e)   Auf jedes Attribut a∈A[in](X[i]) muss in F[p] ein Besuch b[i,1] folgen.

Die F[p] stellen Vorschriften dar zur Auswertung der Attribute von Knoten des Typs p.

10. Anpassung der Bewertung von Graphen

Sind alle Graphen E[p] bewertet, so muss ueberprueft werden, ob die Annahme aus Abschnitt 8 gilt, dass alle Attribute a∈A[in](Y), in die in E[p] keine Kanten muenden, beim ersten Besuch des Vorgaenger-Knotens berechnet werden koennen. Trifft dies fuer ein oder mehrere Nichtterminale nicht zu, so sind die Bewertungen der Graphen in geeigneter Weise anzupassen, oder die Grammatik ist zu transformieren.

Sei M die Menge der Attribute a∈A[in](Y), in die in den Graphen E[p] zu Regeln p:Y→u keine Kanten muenden. Zu jeder Regel q:Z→vYw wird nun eine Menge N[q] gebildet mit
N[q] = [a | a∈M und a steht in F[p] nach dem ersten Besuch von Y]
Es sind dann folgende Faelle zu unterscheiden:

a)   N[q]=∅ fuer alle q.
     Dann gilt die obige Annahme und E[p] und F[p] bleiben unveraendert.

b)   Alle N[q] sind gleich und nicht leer.
     In diesem Fall muessen die Graphen neu bewertet werden. Dabei erhalten die Attribute a∈M\N das Wertepaar (1,∅) und a∈N das Wertepaar (2,∅). Die Bewertung der uebrigen Attribute und die Bestimmung der Besuchs-Sequenz erfolgt wie in den Abschnitten 8 und 9 beschrieben.

c)   Es gibt mehrere paarweise verschiedene N[q1],...,N[qm]. In diesem Fall ist die folgende Transformation der Grammatik erforderlich:
     Zu jedem N[qj]≠∅ wird die Regel qj:Z[j]→vYw ersetzt durch qj´:Z[j]→vY[j]w, wobei Y[j] ein neues Nichtterminal der Grammatik ist. Zu jeder Regel p:Y→u wird eine neue Regel pj:Y[j]→u eingefuehrt.
     Die Graphen E[qj] und die Besuchs-Sequenzen F[qj] sind gleich E[q] bzw. F[q]. Die E[pj] und F[pj] werden wie im Fall b neu bestimmt.

11. Modifikationen des Algorithmus

In Abschnitt 4 wurden Annahmen zur Strategie gemacht, die beim Aufbau und Durchlaufen des AAB anzuwenden ist. Wie zeigen hier, wie der Algorithmus modifiziert werden muss, falls stattdessen die folgenden Annahmen gelten:

a) Der AAB wird von der Wurzel zu den Endknoten hin aufgebaut. Dabei werden die Knoten zu einer Regel $p:Y \rightarrow X[1]...X[n]$ in der Reihenfolge $Y,T(X[1]),...,T(X[n])$ generiert; $T(X[i])$ bezeichnet den Teilbaum, dessen Wurzel $X[i]$ ist. Damit ist die Reihenfolge der ersten Besuche jedes Knoten festgelegt. Sollen beim ersten Besuch eines Knotens der Klasse p alle Berechnungsvorschriften $g[p]$ ausgewertet werden, die keinen erneuten Besuch des Vorgaenger-Knotens erfordern, so ist nur der Abschntt 8 so zu veraendern, dass die Anfangsbewertung der Attribute $a \in A[der](X[i])$, in die keine Kanten muenden nicht $(0,0)$ sondern $(0,i)$ ist.

b) Die Auswertung der Berechnungsvorschriften beginnt erst, wenn der AB vollstaendig aufgebaut ist. Der Durchlauf durch den AB beginnt bei seiner Wurzel.
In diesem Fall kann auch die Reihenfolge der ersten Besuche der Knoten $X[i]$ (zu einem Knoten-Typ $p:Y \rightarrow X[1]...X[n]$) aus den semantischen Abhaengigkeiten bestimmt werden. Dies wird durch folgende Aenderungen der Regeln zur Bewertung der Graphen (Abschnitt 8) beruecksichtigt:

Die Attribute $a \in A[der](X[i])$, in die keine Kanten muenden, werden zunaechst nicht bewertet. Stattdessen wird ein Fall d) wie folgt ergaenzt:

> d) Ist schon ein Attribut $a[1] \in A[der](X[i])$ bewertet, so wird allen $a \in A[der](X[i])$, in die keine Kanten muenden, das Wertepaar $w(a[1])$ zugeordnet; andernfalls das Wertepaar (u,d), wobei gilt $(u,d-1)=max(w[p](a[1]))$ und $a[1]$ sind alle schon bewerteten Attribute in $E[p]$. (Um die Anzahl der Besuche von $X[i]$ gering zu halten, sollte diese Regel moeglichst spaet angewandt werden.)

12. Beispiel

In diesem Abschnitt wird die Anwendung des Verfahrens anhand einer einfachen Programmiersprache demonstriert. Die statische Semantik wurde hier auf die Identifikation vereinbarter Bezeichner und auf eine einfache Bestimmung und Anpassung von Arten beschraenkt. Die Attribute haben folgende Bedeutung:

ACCESS   Menge der jeweils gueltigen Bezeichner
DECL   Vereinbartes Objekt
PRIMODE.   Art vor der Artanpassung
POSTMODE   Art nach der Artanpassung

Zu jeder syntaktischen Regel der Grammatik sind die Berechnungs-vorschriften fuer die semantischen Attribute, die C-, D- und E-Graphen und die ermittelte Besuchs-Sequenz angegeben. Es wird die folgende Notation verwendet:
- Nichtterminale werden in <,> eingeschlossen, z.B. <EXPRESSION> .
- Attribute werden durch Nichtterminal.Attribut angegeben (bzw. Nichtterminal.Attribut-ganze Zahl, falls das Nichtterminal mehrfach in der Regel auftritt). z.B. <EXPRESSION>.ACCESS bzw. <EXPRESSION>-1.ACCESS

Die C-,D- und E-Graphen sind jeweils fuer eine Regel zu einem Graphen zusammen gefasst und werden durch die Kennzeichnung der Kanten unterschieden:
  --->   Kanten im C-,D- und E-Graph
  - ->   Kanten im D- und E-Graph
  ...>   Kanten im E-Graph

Zu jedem Knoten ist die Bewertung (up,down) des Attributes angegeben.

Regel 1:
<PROGRAM>   : <EXPRESSION>,
    <EXPRESSION>.ACCESS : EMPTY,
    <EXPRESSION>.POSTMODE   : <EXPRESSION>.PRIMODE.

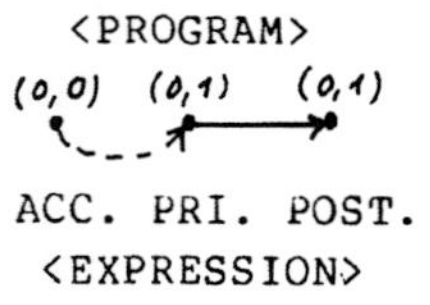

$$\langle \text{PROGRAM} \rangle$$
$$(0,0) \quad (0,1) \quad (0,1)$$

ACC. PRI. POST.
<EXPRESSION>

F[1]=<EXPRESSION>.ACCESS,B[1,1],<EXPRESSION>.POSTMODE,B[1.2]

Regel 2:.
<EXPRESSION> :. BEGIN <DECLARATION> ; <EXPRESSION> END,
    <DECLARATION>.ACCESS : <EXPRESSION>-1.ACCESS,
    <EXPRESSION>-2.ACCESS :
       INCLUDE(<DECLARATION>.DECL,<EXPRESSION>-1.ACCESS),
    <EXPRESSION>-1.PRIMODE : <EXPRESSION>-2.PRIMODE,
    <EXPRESSION>-2.POSTMODE : <EXPRESSION>-1.POSTMODE.

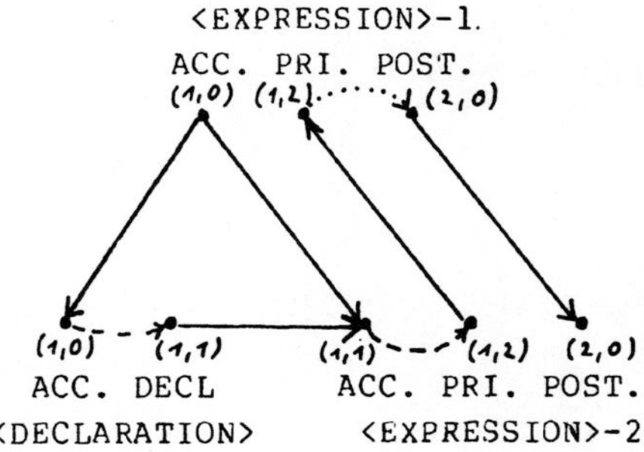

F[2]=B[0,1],<DECLARATION>.ACCESS,B[1,1],<EXPRESSION>-2.ACCESS,
    B[2,1],<EXPRESSION>-1.PRIMODE,B[0,2],<EXPRESSION>-2.POSTMODE

Regel 3:
<EXPRESSION> :. IDENTIFIER := <EXPRESSION>,
    <EXPRESSION>-2.ACCESS : <EXPRESSION>-1..ACCESS,
    <EXPRESSION>-2.POSTMODE :
       COERCE(<EXPRESSION>-2.PRIMODE,<EXPRESSION>-1.PRIMODE),
    <EXPRESSION>-1.PRIMODE :
       IDENTIFY(IDENTIFIER,<EXPRESSION>-1..ACCESS).

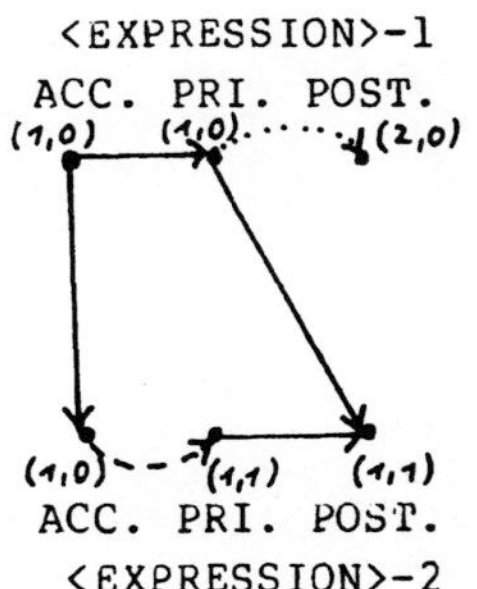

F[3]=B[0,1],<EXPRESSION>-2.ACCESS,<EXPRESSION>-1..PRIMODE,B[1,1],
    <EXPRESSION>-2.POSTMODE,B[0,2],B[1,2]

Regel 4:
<EXPRESSION> : IDENTIFIER,
    <EXPRESSION>.PRIMODE :   IDENTIFY(IDENTIFIER,<EXPRESSION>.ACCESS).

<EXPRESSION>
ACC. PRI.POST.

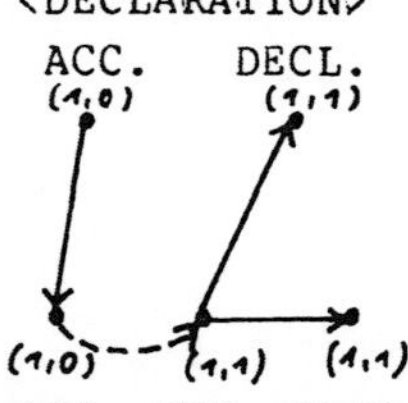

F[4]=B[0,1],<EXPRESSION>.PRIMODE,B[0,2]

Regel 5:
<EXPRESSION> : CONSTANT,
    <EXPRESSION>.PRIMODE. :   MODE(CONSTANT)

<EXPRESSION>
ACC. PRI.POST.

F[5]=<EXPRESSION>.PRIMODE,B[0,1],B[0,2]

Regel 6:.
<DECLARATION> : NEW IDENTIFIER = <EXPRESSION>,
    <DECLARATION>.DECL :   DECLARE(IDENTIFIER,<EXPRESSION>.PRIMODE),
    <EXPRESSION>.POSTMODE :   <EXPRESSION>.PRIMODE,
    <EXPRESSION>.ACCESS :   <DECLARATION>.ACCESS

<DECLARATION>
ACC.   DECL.

ACC. PRI. POST.
<EXPRESSION>

F[6]=B[0,1],<EXPRESSION>.ACCESS,B[1,1],<DECLARATION>.DECL,
    <EXPRESSION>.POSTMODE,B[1,2]

EIN ALGEBRAISCHER ANSATZ FÜR KOMPILERKORREKTHEITSBEWEISE

Hartmut Schmeck
Institut für Informatik und Praktische Mathematik
Christian-Albrechts-Universität Kiel

1. Einleitung

In dieser Arbeit soll ein algebraisches Verfahren vorgestellt
werden, mit dem das Problem, die Korrektheit von Kompilern einfacher
Programmiersprachen zu beweisen, behandelt werden kann. Es lehnt sich
an eine Arbeit von Morris [6] an, die auf Ergebnissen von Burstall und
Landin [2], [3], [5] aufbaut. In [7] ist dieses gegenüber [6] weiter-
entwickelte Verfahren ausführlich dargestellt.

Die Frage nach der Korrektheit eines Kompilers läßt sich reduzieren
auf die Frage nach der Kommutativität des Diagramms

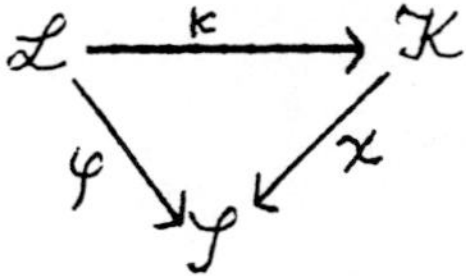

wobei $\mathcal{L}$ und $\mathcal{K}$ die Ausgangs- und Zielsprache sind und $\mathcal{S}$ den "Bedeutungsraum" darstellt. κ bezeichnet die vom Kompilerprogramm berechnete
Kompilierungsfunktion, φ und χ ordnen jedem Programm seine Bedeutung
zu. Die Abbildung χ kann aufgespalten werden in zwei Abbildungen ψ
und δ , so daß sich ein leicht modifiziertes Diagramm ergibt

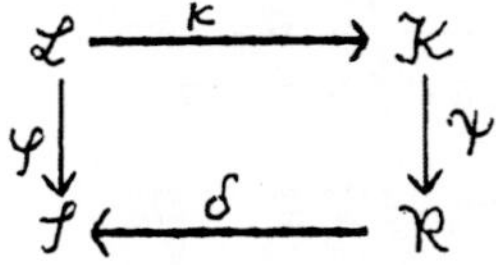

ψ entspricht der Ausführung eines Programms auf einer "Maschine" und
ordnet jedem Programm die von ihm berechnete Relation zwischen Anfangs-
zustand der Maschine bei der Startanweisung und dem Endzustand nach
der letzten Anweisung des Programms zu. δ "dekodiert" die so gewonnene
Darstellung der Bedeutung eines Programms in einem Bedeutungsraum $\mathcal{R}$
in die Darstellung der Bedeutung in $\mathcal{S}$.

2. Algebraische Beschreibung von Programmiersprachen

Programmiersprachen als durch Grammatiken erzeugte Teilmengen eines
freien Monoids tragen von sich aus keinerlei algebraische Struktur.
Gewisse Teile der üblichen Programmiersprachen lassen sich jedoch in
natürlicher Weise als (universelle) Algebren auffassen. Ein naheliegen-
des Beispiel ist die Sprache der arithmetischen Ausdrücke (im folgenden
durch "AA" abgekürzt). Worte dieser Sprache können mit Hilfe der arithmetischen Operatoren zu neuen Worten zusammengesetzt werden :

$$w_1 = a+b \; , \; w_2 = c*d \in AA \implies w_1/w_2 = (a+b)/(c*d) \in AA$$

d.h. auf AA können auf natürliche Weise Verknüpfungen definiert werden.
Treten dabei typisierte Variablen auf, so ist die Verknüpfung der
Ausdrücke erst durch Angabe des Typs der Argumente und des Ergebnisses
vollständig definiert.

Die folgenden Definitionen ermöglichen eine algebraische Formalisierung dieser Überlegungen.

2.1 Definition: Ein Operatorsystem ist ein Tripel $(\Omega, \propto, T)$, für das
gilt :

   (i) Ω ist eine Menge von Operatoren.

   (ii) $\propto: \Omega \longrightarrow \mathbb{N}_o$ gibt die Stelligkeit der Operatoren an.

   (iii) T ist eine nichtleere Typmenge.

   (iv) Für jedes $\omega \in \Omega$ legt die partielle Typfunktion $\tau_\omega : T^{\propto(\omega)} \xrightarrow{\sim} T$
   den Typ der Argumente und des Ergebnisses fest.

2.2 Definition: Eine Interpretation eines Operatorsystems $(\Omega, \propto, T)$
ist ein Paar (I, M), für das gilt :

   (i) $M = \{M_t\}_{t \in T}$ ist eine Familie nichtleerer Mengen.

   (ii) I ordnet jedem Operator $\omega \in \Omega$ mit $\propto(\omega) = k$ für alle
   $(t_1, \ldots, t_k) \in \text{Def}(\tau_\omega)$ eine Operation

$$\omega_I : M_{t_1} \times \cdots \times M_{t_k} \longrightarrow M_{\tau_\omega(t_1, \ldots, t_k)} \qquad zu.$$

2.3 Definition: Eine Ω-Algebra ist ein Quintupel $(A, \{A_t\}_{t \in T}, \Omega, \propto, T)$,
für das gilt :

   (i) $(\Omega, \propto, T)$ ist ein Operatorsystem.

   (ii) $(A, \{A_t\}_{t \in T})$ ist eine Interpretation von $(\Omega, \propto, T)$.

Die Mengen A_t heißen Trägermengen. Wird aus dem Zusammenhang klar, in
welcher Algebra wir uns befinden, so wird der Index der interpretierten
Operatoren fortgelassen. Ist $|T| = 1$, so heißt die Ω-Algebra homogen,
sonst heterogen. Für $(A, \{A_t\}_{t \in T}, \Omega, \propto, T)$ schreiben wir abkürzend
$A = (\{A_t\}_{t \in T}, \Omega)$.

Die so definierte Ω-Algebra ist bis auf die Typfunktion mit der

von Birkhoff und Lipson [1] definierten Algebra identisch. In [6] sind
nur homogene Ω-Algebren erlaubt.

2.4 Definition: Sei $X = \{X_t\}_{t \in T}$ eine Familie beliebiger Mengen,
(Ω, α, T) ein Operatorsystem. Die <u>Wortalgebra über X</u> ist die
Ω-Algebra $W_\Omega(X) := (\{W_t\}_{t \in T}, \Omega)$, definiert durch

   (i) $\forall t \in T \quad X_t \subseteq W_t$

  (ii) $\forall \omega \in \Omega$ mit $\alpha(\omega)=k \; \forall (t_1, \ldots, t_k) \in \text{Def}(\tau_\omega)$

$$\forall (u_1, \ldots, u_k) \in W_{t_1} \times \cdots \times W_{t_k}$$

$$\omega(u_1, \ldots, u_k) := \omega u_1 \cdots u_k \in W_{\tau_\omega(t_1, \ldots, t_k)}$$

(iii) Für alle $t \in T$ enthält W_t keine anderen als durch (i) und (ii)
      erzeugten Elemente.

Die Anwendung der Definitionen sei an zwei einfachen Beispielen
demonstriert :

(1) <u>Anweisungsfolgen (AF)</u>

Sei A eine Menge von "Anweisungen", ";" eine zweistellige Operation
auf A, die Konkatenation. Dann ist die Sprache der Anweisungsfolgen
die homogene $\{;\}$-Algebra $AF = W_{\{;\}}(A)$.

Sollen Vereinbarungen hinzugenommen werden, so darf in keinem
"Programm" eine Anweisung vor einer Vereinbarung stehen. Dies kann
durch die Typfunktion bewirkt werden :

Sei $T = \{a,v,z\}$, $F_a := A$, F_v die Menge der Vereinbarungen und $F_z := \emptyset$,
ferner $\quad \tau_; : (v,v) \longmapsto v \qquad , : (a,a) \longmapsto a$

$\qquad\qquad\qquad : (v,a) \longmapsto z \qquad , : (z,a) \longmapsto z$

Dann erfüllt $W_{\{;\}}(\{F_a, F_v, F_z\})$ die gestellte Forderung.

(2) <u>Arithmetische Ausdrücke (AA)</u>

Sei X eine Menge von Variablen, $\Omega = \{+,-,*,/\}$ die Menge der arithmetischen Operatoren. Dann ist die Sprache der arithmetischen Ausdrücke
die Algebra $AA = W_\Omega(X)$.

Sind die Variablen typisiert, z.B. $X = \{X_{\text{INTEGER}}, X_{\text{REAL}}\}$, so wird AA
zu einer heterogenen Algebra. Hier zeigt sich wieder der Vorteil der
von uns eingeführten Typfunktion. τ_+ könnte etwa definiert werden als

$\qquad \tau_+ : (\text{INTEGER, INTEGER}) \longmapsto \text{INTEGER}$

$\qquad\qquad : (\text{INTEGER, REAL}) \longmapsto \text{REAL}$

$\qquad\qquad : (\text{REAL, INTEGER}) \longmapsto \text{REAL}$

$\qquad\qquad : (\text{REAL, REAL}) \longmapsto \text{REAL}$

Ein Operator reicht also zur Beschreibung vier verschiedener Operationen aus.

Das von Morris in [6] entwickelte Verfahren erweist sich durch die

Beschränkung auf homogene Algebren als unbrauchbar zur Behandlung beider Beispiele.

Ω-Algebren, die Programmiersprachen darstellen, seien in Zukunft auch <u>Sprachalgebren</u> genannt.

3. Algebraische Beschreibung von Übersetzern

Entsprechend dem vorigen Abschnitt können die im eingangs erwähnten Kompilerdiagramm auftauchenden Programmiersprachen durch Ω-Algebren dargestellt werden. Daraus ergibt sich die sinnvolle Forderung, daß die Abbildungen des Diagramms strukturerhaltend sein sollen.

<u>3.1 Definition</u>: Seien $A = (\{A_t\}_{t \in T}, \Omega)$ und $B = (\{B_t\}_{t \in T}, \Omega)$ Ω-Algebren. Sei $\varphi = \{\varphi_t\}_{t \in T}$ eine Familie von Abbildungen $\varphi_t : A_t \longrightarrow B_t$. φ heißt <u>Morphismus</u> von A nach B $: \Longleftrightarrow$

$$\forall \omega \in \Omega \text{ mit } \alpha(\omega) = k \quad \forall (t_1, \ldots, t_k) \in \text{Def}(\tau_\omega)$$

$$\omega_B \circ (\varphi_{t_1} \times \cdots \times \varphi_{t_k}) = \varphi_{\tau_\omega(t_1, \ldots, t_k)} \circ \omega_A \quad .$$

Für die Anwendungen wird vor allem der folgende Fortsetzungssatz benötigt :

<u>3.2 Satz</u>: Sei $X = \{X_t\}_{t \in T}$ eine Familie beliebiger Mengen, $B = (\{B_t\}_{t \in T}, \Omega)$ eine Ω-Algebra. Sei $\bar{\varphi} = \{\bar{\varphi}_t\}_{t \in T}$ eine Familie von Abbildungen $\bar{\varphi}_t : X_t \longrightarrow B_t$. Dann gibt es genau einen Morphismus $\varphi = \{\varphi_t\}_{t \in T}$ von $W_\Omega(X)$ nach B mit $\varphi|_X = \bar{\varphi}$.

$$
\begin{array}{ccc}
X & \xrightarrow{\quad \bar{\varphi} \quad} & B \\
{\scriptstyle 1_X}\downarrow & \nearrow{\scriptstyle \varphi} & \\
W_\Omega(X) & &
\end{array}
$$

Beweis: [1]

Läßt sich die Ausgangsprogrammiersprache durch eine Wortalgebra darstellen, so ist der Kompiler also bereits durch Angabe seiner Wirkung auf dem Erzeugendensystem vollständig definiert.

<u>3.3 Definition</u>: Sei $A = (\{A_t\}_{t \in T}, \Omega)$ eine Ω-Algebra, $X = \{X_t\}_{t \in T}$ eine Familie von Mengen mit $X_t \subseteq A_t$ für alle $t \in T$. Sei $\bar{\varphi} = \{\bar{\varphi}_t\}_{t \in T}$ die Familie von Abbildungen $\bar{\varphi}_t : X_t \longrightarrow A_t$ mit $\bar{\varphi}_t(x) = x$ für alle $t \in T$ und $x \in X$. A wird <u>erzeugt</u> von X $: \Longleftrightarrow$ A ist das Bild von $W_\Omega(X)$ unter der Fortsetzung von $\bar{\varphi}$ zu einem Morphismus.

Um ausdrücken zu können, daß ein Kompiler Programmiersprachen stets in gleichwertige oder niedrigere Sprachen übersetzt, wird ein weiterer Begriff eingeführt :

Programme zerfallen normalerweise in eine Reihe von Anweisungen. Versieht man jede dieser Anweisungen mit einer Marke, so ist die

Reihenfolge der Abarbeitung dadurch gegeben, daß hinter jeder Anweisung
die Marke der Anweisung steht, die anschließend ausgeführt werden soll.
In [4] definiert Hotz zum Beispiel einige einfache Sprachen auf diese
Art.

Faßt man die Anweisungen als Relationen zwischen den Marken auf, so
ist ein Programm gegeben durch die Menge M der Marken und eine Menge
von Relationen auf M. Die transitive Hülle der Vereinigung all dieser
Relationen ergibt dann die Menge der möglichen Anweisungsfolgen. Die
sich anbietende Formalisierung dieser Überlegungen ergibt

3.4 Definition: Ein markiertes Programm (oder Relationsalgebra) ist ein
Paar $\underline{P} = (M, \Gamma)$, wobei M die nichtleere Markenmenge (oder Trägermenge),
Γ die Operatorenmenge von $\underline{P}$ ist und alle $\gamma \in \Gamma$ als nichtleere
Relationen $\gamma_{\underline{P}}$ auf M interpretiert werden.

3.5 Definition: Sei $\underline{P} = (M, \Gamma)$ ein markiertes Programm, $S, T \subseteq M$.
(a) $\sum \underline{P} := \bigcup_{\gamma \in \Gamma} \gamma_{\underline{P}}$ heißt Summe über $\underline{P}$.
(b) $\underline{P}$ heißt eindeutig (oder determiniert) $: \Longleftrightarrow$ $\underline{P}$ ist eine partielle
   Funktion.
(c) $er(\underline{P}) := \bigcup_{n=0}^{\infty} (\sum \underline{P})^n$ heißt Erreichbarkeitsrelation von $\underline{P}$.
(d) $er(\underline{P})\big|_S^T$, die Einschränkung der Erreichbarkeitsrelation im
   Argumentbereich auf S und im Bildbereich auf T heißt die durch $\underline{P}$
   berechnete Relation von S nach T.
(e) $er(\underline{P})\big| S := er(\underline{P})\big|_S^S$ ist die von $\underline{P}$ berechnete Relation auf S.

Ist S die Menge der Anfangs- und T die Menge der Endmarken eines
markierten Programmes $\underline{P}$, so gibt $er(\underline{P})\big|_S^T$ die in $\underline{P}$ möglichen Anweisungs-
folgen an. Falls $\underline{P}$ eindeutig und es nicht möglich ist, von einer End-
marke ins Programm zurückzuspringen ($\sum\underline{P}\big|_T = \emptyset$), so berechnet $\underline{P}$ eine
partielle Funktion [7].

Der Begriff "Kompiler" kann nun festgelegt werden :

3.6 Definition: Seien A und B Sprachalgebren mit identischen Operatorsystemen. Die Elemente der Trägermengen von B seien markierte Programme. Morphismen $\kappa : A \longrightarrow B$ heißen dann Kompiler.

Bei dieser Definition bleiben zwei Gesichtspunkte unberücksichtigt :

(1) In der Praxis ist ein Kompiler stets ein Programm, dessen Input-
   Output-Funktion unserem Morphismus entsprechen soll. Es müßte also
   auch gezeigt werden, daß das Programm die gewünschte Kompilierungsfunktion berechnet.

(2) Der Kompiler ist nur auf korrekt gebildeten Programmen der Sprachalgebra A definiert, kann also keine syntaktische Analyse durchführen.

Da markierte Programme Elemente der Trägermengen von Sprachalgebren sein sollen, muß die Wirkung von Operatoren auf ihnen interpretiert werden. Für eine genaue Durchführung sei auf [7] verwiesen. Hier genüge die Erläuterung der Verknüpfung markierter Programme im Rahmen des folgenden Beispiels :

Die Sprache der arithmetischen Ausdrücke ist in Abschnitt 2 als $AA = W_\Omega(X)$ eingeführt worden. Ein Kompiler κ sei auf den Erzeugenden definiert durch

$$\forall \, x \in X \qquad \kappa : x \longmapsto \quad START \quad LOAD \; x \quad HALT$$

$\kappa(u), \kappa(v)$ mit $u, v \in AA$ seien gegeben. $\kappa(u)$ habe $n+2$ Marken, $\kappa(v)$ habe $m+2$ Marken, d.h. sie können dargestellt werden als

$$START \;\longmapsto\; (\kappa(u)) \longrightarrow HALT$$
$$1\ldots\ldots n$$

$$START \;\longmapsto\; (\kappa(v)) \longrightarrow HALT$$
$$1\ldots\ldots m$$

Dann sei $(+(u,v)) = +(\ (u),\ (v))$ dargestellt als

$$START \;\longmapsto\; (\kappa(u)) \longrightarrow n+1 \longmapsto (\kappa(v)) \longrightarrow n+m+2 \;\xrightarrow{ADD}\; HALT$$
$$1\ldots\ldots n \qquad n+2\ldots\ldots n+m+1$$

d.h. $\kappa(u)$ und $\kappa(v)$ werden "aneinandergereiht", die Marken von $\kappa(v)$ werden umbenannt und ein zu "+" gehöriges markiertes Programm wird "angehängt".

Für die restlichen Operatoren erfolgt die Verknüpfung analog.

4. Algebraische Beschreibung der Semantik

Wie schon vorher erwähnt soll die Bedeutung eines Programms stets durch die von ihm berechnete Relation oder partielle Funktion gegeben sein.

4.1 Definition: Die <u>Semantik</u> einer Sprachalgebra $A = (\{A_t\}_{t \in T}, \Omega)$ ist ein Paar (SA, φ), wobei SA eine Ω-Algebra von Relationen ist, die <u>semantische Algebra</u>, und φ ein Morphismus von A nach SA, der <u>semantische Morphismus</u>.

Ein einfaches Beispiel ermöglicht die Sprache der Anweisungsfolgen $AF = W_{\{;\}}(A)$:

Jedem $x \in A$ sei durch $\tilde{\varphi} : A \longrightarrow \mathcal{P}(Z \times Z)$ eine Relation auf einer Menge Z zugeordnet. Sei $SAF := (S, \{;\})$ die von $\tilde{\varphi}(A)$ bezüglich der Komposition von Relationen erzeugte $\{;\}$-Algebra. Dann existiert nach Satz 3.2 die Fortsetzung von $\tilde{\varphi}$ zu einem Morphismus $\varphi : W_{\{;\}}(A) \longrightarrow SAF$. Die Semantik von AF ist also das Paar (SAF, φ).

Den markierten Programmen kann relativ einfach ihre Bedeutung zugeordnet werden. Wie in der Einleitung bereits erwähnt, werden die Programme an einer gewissen "Maschine" $\underline{M}$ gerechnet. Die Bedeutung eines Programmes $\underline{P}$ kann also durch die Relation zwischen Anfangs- und Endzustand von $\underline{M}$ nach Ausführung von $\underline{P}$ angegeben werden. Diese Ausführung von $\underline{P}$ auf $\underline{M}$ ist nur dann möglich, wenn jeder Anweisung von $\underline{P}$ eine nichtleere Relation auf den Zuständen von $\underline{M}$ entspricht, d.h. die Maschine $\underline{M}$ kann ebenfalls durch eine Relationsalgebra und die Ausführung von $\underline{P}$ auf $\underline{M}$ als Produkt $\underline{P} \boxtimes \underline{M}$ von Relationsalgebren im Sinne der folgenden Definition dargestellt werden.

4.2 Definition: Das <u>Produkt</u> von Relationsalgebren $\underline{P} = (P, \Gamma_1)$ und $\underline{Q} = (Q, \Gamma_2)$ ist definiert durch

$$\underline{P} \boxtimes \underline{Q} := (P \times Q, \Gamma)$$

wobei $\Gamma = \Gamma_1 \cap \Gamma_2$ und für alle $\gamma \in \Gamma$ gilt $\gamma_{\underline{P} \boxtimes \underline{Q}} := \gamma_{\underline{P}} \times \gamma_{\underline{Q}}$.

Die Bedeutung eines markierten Programms $\underline{P}$ erhält man damit wie folgt :
  (1) Man bilde das Produkt von $\underline{P} = (P, \Gamma)$ mit der Maschine $\underline{M} = (M, \Gamma')$.
  (2) Man berechne $er(\underline{P} \boxtimes \underline{M})$.
  (3) Man schränke das Ergebnis auf die Menge A der Anfangs- und
      Endmarken von $\underline{P}$ ein, bilde also $er(\underline{P} \boxtimes \underline{M}) | A$.

Man kann zeigen [7], daß dadurch ein Morphismus auf eine Ω-Algebra von Relationen definiert wird.

    Als Beispiel sei eine vereinfachte Form einer Maschine angegeben, auf der kompilierte arithmetische Ausdrücke "berechnet" werden können :

    Sei $\underline{MAA} := (MA, \Gamma)$ definiert durch
$$MA := W^* x \ (X \longrightarrow W) \quad , \qquad \Gamma := \{ \text{LOAD } x \mid x \in X \} \cup \{ \text{ADD} \}$$
Dabei sei X die Variablenmenge, $W = (W, \Omega)$ eine Ω-Algebra als Wertebereich für die Variablen, W^* das freie Monoid über W und $(X \longrightarrow W)$ die Menge aller Abbildungen von X in W.

    Die Elemente von Γ seien interpretiert als partielle Funktionen :
Für $x \in X$, $w_1, w_2 \in W$, $w \in W^*$, $i : X \longrightarrow W$ sei

        LOAD x : $(w, i) \longmapsto (i(x)w, i)$
        ADD   : $(w_2 w_1 w, i) \longmapsto (+_W(w_1, w_2), i)$

Bei Ausführung des Programms

       START   LOAD x   1
           1   LOAD y   2
           2   ADD   HALT

würden unter Belegung der Variablen x und y mit Werten a bzw. b durch die Abbildung $i : X \longrightarrow W$ die folgenden Marken-Zustandspaare durchlaufen :

    $(START, (\varepsilon, i)) \longmapsto (1, (a, i)) \longmapsto (2, (ba, i)) \longmapsto (HALT, (+_W(a, b), i))$

Die im eingangs skizzierten Kompilerdiagramm auftauchende Dekodierungsfunktion ist im Allgemeinen einer Projektion auf die zweite Komponente der Marken-Zustandspaare vergleichbar.

5. Kompilerkorrektheit

Grundlage für das weitere Vorgehen ist der folgende rein algebraische Satz :

5.1 Satz: Seien L, K, S und R Ω-Algebren mit identischen Operatorsystemen. X und Y seien Erzeugendensysteme für L bzw. K. Sei $\tilde{\kappa}$: X $\longrightarrow$ Y surjektiv, seien φ: L $\longrightarrow$ S, ψ: K $\longrightarrow$ R, δ: R $\longrightarrow$ S Morphismen. Das Diagramm

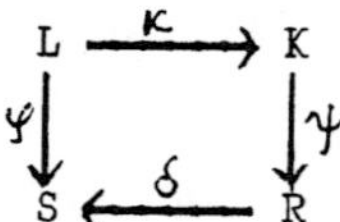

kommutiere. Existiert die Fortsetzung von $\tilde{\kappa}$ zu einem Morphismus κ, so ist das Diagramm

$$\begin{array}{ccc} L & \xrightarrow{\kappa} & K \\ \varphi \downarrow & & \downarrow \psi \\ S & \xleftarrow{\delta} & R \end{array}$$

kommutativ.

Beweis: [7]

Da ein Kompiler korrekt ist, wenn das Kompilerdiagramm kommutiert, ergibt sich folgendes "Verfahren" zum Nachweis der Kompilerkorrektheit:

(1) Man gebe einen semantischen Morphismus für die Ausgangssprachalgebra an.
(2) Man gebe eine Maschine (Relationsalgebra) $\underline{M}$ an, auf der die kompilierten Programme "rechnen" sollen.
(3) Man gebe die Dekodierungsfunktion an.
(4) Man zeige die Korrektheit des Kompilers auf dem Erzeugendensystem der Ausgangssprachalgebra.
(5) Man zeige, daß die Dekodierungsfunktion ein Morphismus ist.
(6) Man zeige, daß sich der auf den Erzeugenden gegebene Kompiler zu einem Morphismus fortsetzen läßt.

Die Bedeutung des Satzes 5.1 für Kompilerkorrektheitsbeweise liegt also darin, daß man sich darauf beschränken kann, die Kommutativität des Kompilerdiagramms für das Erzeugendensystem der Ausgangssprachalgebra zu zeigen. Wir nennen ihn deshalb den Kompilerkorrektheitssatz.
Eine wichtige Anwendung ergibt sich, wenn eine Programmiersprache Erzeugnis mehrerer verschiedener Sprachelemente ist (z.B. Vereinbarun-

gen, Wertzuweisungen, arithmetische Ausdrücke, <u>while</u>-Anweisungen), die
als Teilsprachen aufgefaßt werden können und für die jeweils ein
Kompiler gegeben ist. Werden die Teilkompiler in geeigneter Weise zu
einer Abbildung des Erzeugendensystems zusammengesetzt und kann die
Abbildung bezüglich der Verknüpfung der Sprachelemente zu einem
Morphismus fortgesetzt werden, so ergibt sich aus der Korrektheit der
Teilkompiler die Korrektheit des Kompilers für die vollständige
Sprache. In diesem Sinne gilt :

<u>5.2 Korollar</u>: Läßt sich ein auf den Erzeugenden gegebener Kompiler zu
    einem Morphismus fortsetzen, so ist er genau dann korrekt, wenn die
    auf den erzeugenden Sprachelementen definierten Teilkompiler korrekt
    sind.

6. Schlußbemerkungen

Die hier kurz dargestellte Theorie wird in [7] auf die folgenden
einfachen Sprachen angewendet :
- Anweisungsfolgen
- Vereinbarungsfolgen
- Arithmetische Ausdrücke
- Boolesche Ausdrücke
- Wertzuweisungen
- <u>while</u>-Anweisungen

Anschließend wird dann in mehreren Schritten eine Sprache aufgebaut,
die alle diese Sprachelemente enthält. Dabei geht entscheidend die
in [6] nicht vorhandene Möglichkeit ein, Sprachen durch heterogene
Algebren zu beschreiben. Vor allem die Einbeziehung von Vereinbarungen
und typisierten Variablen wäre sonst nicht möglich gewesen. Ferner
werden die für die einzelnen Sprachelemente definierten Kompiler zu
neuen Kompilern zusammengesetzt, deren Korrektheit mit Hilfe des
Kompilerkorrektheitssatzes gezeigt wird.

In [7] wird ferner der Versuch gemacht, über die algebraische, rein
theoretische Behandlung des Kompilerkorrektheitsproblems hinaus zu
einer praktischen Anwendung zu kommen. Vom Verfasser wurde dazu ein
Programmsystem entwickelt, das die Erzeugung allgemeiner Automaten mit
beliebig vielen Eingabe-, Keller- und Ausgabebändern erlaubt und
folgende Möglichkeiten bietet :

(1) Ausgehend von der algebraischen Beschreibung der Ausgangs- und
    Zielsprache und der auf den Erzeugenden gegebenen Kompilierungs-
    funktion kann ein Kompilerprogramm konstruiert werden, das die zum
    Morphismus fortgesetzte Kompilierungsfunktion realisiert. Ziel ist
    dabei die Erstellung eines Kompiler-Kompilers, der allein aus der

gegebenen algebraischen Beschreibung ein Kompilerprogramm erzeugt.
Die automatische Verknüpfung von Teilkompilern im Sinne des
Korollars 5.2 wird in [7] noch nicht erreicht, erscheint aber möglich.
(2) Die in dem Verfahren des Abschnitts 5 benötigte Maschine, auf der
die kompilierten Programme rechnen sollen, kann ebenfalls über einen
allgemeinen Automaten als Programm realisiert werden. Es akzeptiert
als Eingabe markierte Programme und gibt die von diesen Programmen
berechneten Relationen zwischen Anfangs- und Endwert der Variablen
aus.

In beiden Fällen wird jedoch die Umsetzung der algebraischen Beschrei-
bungen in die zur Erzeugung der entsprechenden Automaten nötige Form
noch per Hand durchgeführt. Diese Umsetzung verläuft in den ausgeführten Beispielen nahezu mechanisch. Wir hoffen daher, eine Klasse
von Sprachen und Semantiken, die sich durch algebraische Methoden
beschreiben lassen, so abgrenzen zu können, daß innerhalb dieser
Klasse die Umsetzung automatisch geschehen kann.

Soll der in der vorliegenden Arbeit dargestellte algebraische
Ansatz für Korrektheitsbeweise für Kompiler höherer Programmiersprachen
genutzt werden, so muß er allerdings erweitert werden, um die Beschreibung von Blockstrukturen, Prozeduren und ähnlichem zu ermöglichen.

<u>Literatur</u>:

[1]   Birkhoff, G., Lipson, J.D.: Heterogeneous Algebras.
        J. Comb. Theory 8, 115-133 (1970)

[2]   Burstall, R.M., Landin,P.J.: Programs and their Proofs: an
        Algebraic Approach. Mach. Int. 4, 17-43 (1969)

[3]   Burstall, R.M.: An Algebraic Description of Programs with
        Assertions, Verification, and Simulation.
        SIGPLAN Notices 7, 1, 7-14 (1972)

[4]   Hotz, G.: Grundlagen einer Theorie der Programmiersprachen.
        Berichte des Inst. f. Angew. Math. u. Inform.
        Universität des Saarlandes, Saarbrücken, (1970)

[5]   Landin, P.J.: A Program Machine Symmetric Automata Theory.
        Mach. Int. 5, 99-120 (1970)

[6]   Morris, F.L.: Correctness of Translations of Programming
        Languages. AIM 174, Stanford University, (1972)

[7]   Schmeck, H.: Korrektheit von Übersetzungen. Bericht Nr. 3/75
        des Inst. f. Inform. u. Prakt. Math., Universität Kiel, (1975)

EINE METHODE ZUR RECHNERGESTÜTZTEN VERIFIKATION VON WHILE-PROGRAMMEN

Alfred Lothar Luft

Institut für Mathematische Maschinen und Datenverarbeitung (Informatik)
der Universität Erlangen-Nürnberg

Zusammenfassung

Eine Methode zur Verifikation einfacher Programmiersprachen, deren
Kontrollstruktur außer der Sequenzierung nur bedingte Verzweigungen,
Exits und while-Schleifen zuläßt, wird skizziert und anhand eines Beispiels erläutert. Aufbauend auf einer operationellen Semantik von Programmiersprachen resultiert diese Methode aus einer mathematisch-logisch
exakten Präzisierung der Floyd/Hoare/Manna'schen Zusicherungsmethode
und unterscheidet sich von dieser insbesondere bezüglich dem Nachweis
der Programmterminierung.

1. Grundlegende Begriffe

Die Verifizierungsaufgabe für ein Programm beinhaltet die Untersuchung
folgender Teilaspekte:

    i)   Definiertheit der Programmoperationen (Nichtabblocken des Pro-
        gramms),

    ii)   Gültigkeit gewisser, vom Programmierer postulierter Eigenschaf-
        ten (Zusicherungen) an gewissen Programmpunkten und

    iii) Endlichkeit der Programmschleifendurchläufe.

Diese Verifizierungsaufgabe wird in zwei, durch den Bezug auf die gleichen Zusicherungen zusammenhängende, methodisch jedoch verschiedene Teil-
aufgaben zerlegt, nämlich in den Nachweis der partiellen Korrektheit
(i) und ii)) und den der Terminierung (iii)).

Die betrachteten Programmiersprachen enthalten außer dem üblichen Kommentar drei weitere Sprachelemente, die bei der Programmausführung über-
lesen werden, nämlich Zusicherungen, Hilfsvereinbarungen und Marken.
Zusicherungen müssen am Programmanfang, vor jedem Programmausgang und vor
jeder while-Anweisung stehen; zweckmäßig ist es auch Module mit Zusicherungen einzugrenzen. Die syntaktische Vorschrift, an gewissen Programmstellen Zusicherungen zu verlangen, orientiert sich an der Vorgehens-
weise bei der Programmverifikation, wo stets Programmvoraussetzung (An-
fangszusicherung), Programmzweck (Endzusicherungen) und Schleifenzu-
sicherungen benötigt werden; darüber hinaus bildet diese Vorschrift eine
Grundlage für das Begriffsnetz und die Begründung der hier gegebenen
Verifikationsmethode.
Bei der Programmverifikation nach der Zusicherungsmethode ist es in der
Regel notwendig, Objekte zur Verfügung zu haben, die bezüglich der Pro-
grammausführung durch den Computer keine Bedeutung besitzen. Derartige
Objekte und ihre Bedeutung (Funktionen, Relationen, Individuenvariable

und Individuenkonstante) sollen mittels <u>Hilfsvereinbarungen</u> in einem
Programm eingeführt werden. Solange davon ausgegangen wird, daß die
Grundlagen zum Beweis von Verifikationsbedingungen (z.B. Kalkül der
Zahlentheorie) nur informell vom Programmierer benutzt werden, genügt es,
die Bedeutung derartiger Objekte mittels informellem Kommentar anzugeben.
Um die Programmverifikation jedoch automatisch von einem Computer durchführen bzw. überprüfen zu können, ist es notwendig, die Bedeutung der
durch die Hilfsvereinbarungen eingeführten Objekte hinreichend streng
zu definieren.

<u>Marken</u> dienen im wesentlichen dazu, bei der Programmverifikation Bezüge
zu Zusicherungen und anderen Programmstellen einfach darstellen zu
können.

<u>Quasiinstruktionen</u> sind die kleinsten Elementarbausteine eines Programms.
Der Programmabschnitt "y $\Leftarrow$ SUB(y,1)<u>;</u> z $\Leftarrow$ ADD(z,x) <u>else</u> <u>C</u> Bereichsüberschreitung <u>$\supset$;</u> M 1.1.1<u>:</u> $\{\mathbf{T}\}$ <u>exit</u> " des späteren Beispielprogramms MULT
besteht z.B. aus den fortlaufend durchnummerierten Quasiinstruktionen
Q_i = y $\Leftarrow$ SUB(y,1), Q_{i+1} = <u>;</u> , Q_{i+2} = z $\Leftarrow$ ADD(z,x), Q_{i+3} = <u>else</u>, Q_{i+4} = <u>C</u>
Bereichsüberschreitung <u>$\supset$</u>, Q_{i+5} = <u>;</u> , Q_{i+6} = M1.1.1<u>:</u>, Q_{i+7} = $\{\mathbf{T}\}$ und
Q_{i+8} = <u>exit</u>.

Die zugrundegelegte operationelle <u>Semantik eines Programms</u> ist in [4]
formal definiert und durch die Begriffe "Interpretation" sowie "Belegung" mit der formalen Logik und durch "Konfiguration" und "Berechnung" mit der Berechenbarkeitstheorie verknüpft. Mittels eines Kalküls,
der im wesentlichen über diese Semantik in [4] begründet ist, werden
die Programmzusicherungen schrittweise entsprechend den jeweiligen
Quasiinstruktionen durch das Programm fortentwickelt. Eine quantorenlogische Aussage A heißt hierbei <u>Vorbedingung</u> einer Quasiinstruktion Q_i,
wenn jede "zulässige" Berechnung, die von einer beliebigen Zusicherung
direkt, d.h. ohne auf eine andere Zusicherung zu treffen, zum Programm-
punkt i führt, mit den am Punkt i erzielten Werten der Programmvariablen
die Aussage A erfüllen; außerdem muß hierbei garantiert sein, daß derartige Berechnungen nicht abblocken, bevor sie den Punkt i erreicht
haben. Ein Programm wird nun gerade dann als partiell korrekt bezeichnet,
wenn keine "zulässige" Berechnung abblockt und alle Zwischen- und End-
ergebnisse jeder "zulässigen" Berechnung die zugehörigen Zusicherungen
erfüllen ("zulässig" sind hierbei alle die Berechnungen, die an einer
beliebigen Zusicherung im Programm mit Werten beginnen, die diese Zusicherung erfüllen). Damit ergibt sich die in [4] bewiesene Tatsache,
daß ein Programm genau dann partiell korrekt ist, wenn alle seine Zusicherungen Vorbedingungen sind.

2. Methode zum Nachweis der partiellen Korrektheit

Die theoretische Absicherung der Methode zum Nachweis der partiellen
Korrektheit bildet die Tatsache, daß ein Programm genau dann partiell
korrekt ist, wenn alle seine Zusicherungen Vorbedingungen sind. Das
Kriterium dafür, ob Zusicherungen Vorbedingungen sind, kann schrittweise mithilfe des folgenden Kalküls konstruiert werden:

Kalkül zum Vorwärtsentwickeln von Vorbedingungen für Programme mit Ergibt-, if-then-else-, while-und exit-Anweisungen

Ist V Vorbedingung einer Quasiinstruktion Q_i, so gilt:

a) Jede quantorenlogische Aussage V', die aus V folgt, ist ebenfalls
   Vorbedingung von Q_i.

b) Falls Q_i eine Kommentaranweisung, jedoch keine Zusicherung, so ist
   V Vorbedingung von Q_{i+1}.

c) Falls Q_i eine Zusicherung, so ist diese Zusicherung Vorbedingung von
   Q_{i+1}.

d) Falls Q_i = $\underline{if}$ Φ $\underline{then}$ und der Wert von Φ für alle Werte der Programmvariablen, die V erfüllen, definiert (d.h. wahr oder falsch) ist,
   so ist $(V \wedge \Phi)$ Vorbedingung von Q_{i+1} und $(V \wedge \neg(\Phi))$ Vorbedingung von
   Q_{m+1} mit m = Index (korrespondierenden else).

e) Falls Q_i = $\underline{else}$ und f = Index (korr. $\underline{fi}$) oder wenn Q_i = $\underline{fi}$ und f =
   Index (korr. $\underline{else}$), so gilt:

e1) Wenn Q_{f-1} eine Exit-Anweisung[1], so ist V Vorbedingung von
    $Q_{\text{Index(korr. fi})+1}$.

e2) Wenn Q_{f-1} keine Exit-Anweisung und V' Vorbedingung von Q_f, so ist
    $(V \vee V')$ Vorbedingung von $Q_{\text{Index(korr. fi})+1}$.

f) Ist Q_i Anfang einer while-Anweisung und V' Vorbedingung von Q_e mit
   e = Index (korr. $\underline{elihw}$), so ist $(V \vee V')$ Vorbedingung von Q_{i+1}.

g) Falls Q_i = $\underline{while}$ Φ $\underline{do}$ und der Wert von Φ für alle Werte der Programmvariablen, die V erfüllen, definiert ist, so ist $(V \wedge \Phi)$ Vorbedingung von Q_{i+1} und $(V \wedge \neg(\Phi))$ Vorbedingung von $Q_{\text{Index(korr. elihw})+1}$.

h) Falls Q_i = $\underline{elihw}$ und V' Vorbedingung der ersten Quasiinstruktion Q_j
   der while- Anweisung ist, so ist $(V \vee V')$ Vorbedingung von Q_{j+1}.

i) Falls Q_i = xj $\Leftarrow$ TE und der Wert des Terms TE für alle Werte der Programmvariablen, die V erfüllen, definiert ist, so ist

i1) $\exists xo\ (V^{xj}_{xo} \wedge xj = TE^{xj}_{xo})$ Vorbedingung von Q_{i+1}, wobei xo eine
    Individuenvariable ist, die weder in V noch im Programm vorkommt.

   $(V^{xj}_{xo}$ bzw. TE$^{xj}_{xo}$ bezeichnet den Ausdruck, in den V bzw. TE durch die
   Substitution, die xj xo zuordnet, übergeht).

---

1) Neben dem Programmausgang am Ende der Programmzeichenkette sind Exit-
   Anweisungen nur in höchstens einem der beiden Zweige einer if-Anweisung
   erlaubt.

Spezialfälle:

i2) Falls xj weder in TE noch in V frei vorkommt, so ist $(V \wedge xj = TE)$ Vorbedingung von Q_{i+1}.

i3) Falls xj in TE vorkommt und V so äquivalent in ein V' umgeformt werden kann, daß xj in V' nur noch in Form des Terms TE vorkommt, so ist die Formel V", die man erhält, wenn in V' jeder Term TE durch xj ersetzt wird, Vorbedingung von Q_{i+1}.

Beispiel zum Nachweis der partiellen Korrektheit:

a) Angaben bezüglich den Fähigkeit des Programmausführers:

Er kenne
- die Funktionskonstanten HALB, DOP, SUB, ADD,
- die Relationskonstante GRGL
- die Individuenkonstanten 0, 1, IMAX
- die Individuenvariablen x, y, z.

Individuenbereich sei die Menge $\mathbb{D} = \{x \mid x \in \mathbb{N}_0 \wedge x \leq 2^{48}\}$.

Den Funktions-, Relations- und Ididuenkonstanten ordne der Programmausführer die durch die Bezeichnung nahegelegte mathematische Bedeutung mit der durch $\mathbb{D}$ implizierten Einschränkung zu:

$$J(HALB) = \left\langle \; x \; \longmapsto \begin{cases} \frac{x}{2} & \text{falls } x \text{ gerade oder } x = 0 \\ \frac{x-1}{2} & \text{sonst} \end{cases} \right\rangle \quad 1)$$

$$J(DOP) = \left\langle \; x \; \longmapsto \begin{cases} 2 \cdot x & \text{falls } x \leq 2^{47} \\ \Omega & \text{sonst} \end{cases} \right\rangle$$

$$J(ADD) = \left\langle \; (x,y) \longmapsto \begin{cases} x+y, & \text{falls } x+y \leq 2^{48} \\ \Omega & \text{sonst} \end{cases} \right\rangle$$

$$J(SUB) = \left\langle \; (x,y) \longmapsto \begin{cases} x-y & \text{falls } x \geq y \\ \Omega & \text{sonst} \end{cases} \right\rangle$$

$$J(ODD) = \left\langle \; x \; \longmapsto \begin{cases} \mathbf{T}, & \text{falls } x \text{ ungerade} \\ \perp, & \text{falls } x \text{ gerade} \end{cases} \right\rangle$$

$$J(GRGL) = \left\langle \; (x,y) \longmapsto \begin{cases} \mathbf{T}, & \text{falls } x \geq y \\ \perp, & \text{sonst} \end{cases} \right\rangle$$

$J(0)$ ist die Zahl 0, $J(1)$ die Zahl 1 und $J(IMAX)$ die Zahl 2^{48}.

("J" steht für "Interpretation von", "Ω" für "nicht definiert", "$\mathbf{T}$" für "wahr" und "$\perp$" für "falsch").

---

1) Mit $f = \langle x \longmapsto t(x) \rangle$ wird die Funktion f bezeichnet, die dem Argument x den Wert des Terms t(x) zuordnet.

b) <u>Aufgabenstellung:</u>

Für den Programmausführer von a) soll ein Programm für die Multi-
plikation zweier natürlicher Zahlen erstellt werden.

c) <u>Grundlage des Lösungsalgorithmus</u>

$$x \cdot y = \begin{cases} 2x \cdot \frac{y}{2} & \text{falls } y \text{ gerade.} \\ x \cdot (y-1) + x & \text{falls } y \text{ ungerade.} \end{cases}$$

d) <u>Programm</u>

MULT (x,y) A <u>:</u> { $xa = x \wedge ya = y$ }

       <u>C</u> Multiplikation zweier natürlicher Zahlen x,y durch
       einen Programmausführer vom Typ a) Ͻ ;

       <u>H</u> Der Wert von xa bzw. ya sei der Eingabewert von
       x bzw. y; die Interpretation der Funktionskonstan-
       ten FM sei die zahlentheoretische Multiplikation <u>H</u>;[1]

       $z \Leftarrow 0$<u>;</u>

M1 <u>:</u> { ADD(FM$(x,y),z$)) = FM(xa, ya) <u>}</u> <u>while</u> GRGL $(y, 1)$ <u>do</u>

   M 1.1 <u>:</u> <u>if</u> ODD(y)
      <u>then</u> <u>if</u> GRGL (SUB(IMAX, x), z)
         <u>then</u> $y \Leftarrow$ SUB$(y,1)$<u>;</u> $z \Leftarrow$ ADD(z,x)
         <u>else</u> <u>C</u> Bereichsüberschreitung Ͻ <u>;</u> M 1.1.1 <u>:</u> {T} <u>exit</u>
         <u>fi</u>

      <u>else</u> M 1.1.2 <u>:</u>
      <u>fi</u> <u>;</u>

   M 1:2 <u>:</u> { ADD(FM$(x,y),z$) = FM(xa, ya) $\wedge$ ⅂(ODD(y)))}<u>;</u>

      <u>if</u> GRGL(SUB(IMAX, x),x)
      <u>then</u> $y \Leftarrow$ HALB(y)<u>;</u> $x \Leftarrow$ DOP(x)
      <u>else</u> <u>C</u> Bereichsüberschreitung Ͻ <u>;</u> M 1.2.1 <u>:</u> {T} <u>exit</u>
      <u>fi</u>

   elihw
MULT(z)E <u>:</u> { z = FM(xa, ya)} <u>exit</u>

e) <u>Beweis der partiellen Korrektheit:</u>

Sei $Q_1 \ldots Q_n$ die Zerlegung des Programms MULT in Quasiinstruktionen;

$Z(M)$ bezeichne die auf die Marke M unmittelbar folgende Zusicherung

---

1) Von FM werden nur   axiomatisch gegebene Eigenschaften benutzt,
   ohne zu wissen, ob und wie die Funktionswerte berechnet werden können.

und $Q_{Z(M)}$ die auf die Marke M unmittelbar folgende Quasiinstruktion.
Wir wissen, daß das Programm MULT dann partiell korrekt ist, wenn
alle seine Zusicherungen Vorbedingungen sind.

α) Nachweis, daß Z(M1) Vorbedingung von $Q_{Z(M1)}$:
Alle zulässigen direkten Berechnungen, die zu $Q_{Z(M1)}$ führen, beginnen bei Z(MULT) oder Z(M1.2).

α1) Entwicklung von Z(MULT):
Vorbedingung von "M1:" ist nach Kalkülregel i2)
$(xa = x \wedge ya = y \wedge z = 0)$.

α2) Entwicklung von Z(M 1.2):
- "GRGL (SUB(IMAX,x),x)" kann nicht abblocken, da der Wert von x an
  dieser Stelle stets definiert ist (x kommt in Z(M 1.2) vor).
- Vorbedingung $V_{2)}$ von "y $\Leftarrow$ HALB(y)" ist nach Kalkülregel d) (Z(M1.2)
  $\wedge$ GRGL(SUB(IMAX,x),x)).
- "HALB(y)" kann nicht abblocken.
- Mit ⅂(ODD(y)) gilt DOP(HALB(y)) = y und mit GRGL(SUB(IMAX,x),x))
  kann "DOP(x)" nicht abblocken.
  Da $x \cdot y + z = xa \cdot ya$ äquivalent zu $2 x \cdot \frac{y}{2} + z = xa \cdot ya$, ist somit
  (ADD(FM(DOP(x), HALB(y)),z) = FM(xa,ya) $\wedge$ ⅂(ODD(y)) $\wedge$
  GRGL (SUB(IMAX,x),x)) äquivalent zu $V_{2)}$.

  Nach Kalkülregel a) ist damit auch (ADD(FM(DOP(x), HALB(y)),z) =
  FM(xa,ya) $\wedge$ GRGL(SUB(IMAX, x),x)) Vorbedingung von "y $\Leftarrow$ HALB(y)" und
  entsprechend Kalkülregel i3) liefert das Einsetzen von "y" für
  "HALB(y)" die Vorbedingung von "x $\Leftarrow$ DOP(x)" zu
  (ADD(FM(DOP(x),y),z) = FM(xa, ya) $\wedge$ GRGL(SUB(IMAX,x),x)).
- Daß "DOP(x)" nicht abblocken kann, wurde schon im vorigen Schritt
  mitbenutzt und gilt wegen GRGL(SUB(IMAX,x),x).
- Nach Kalkülregel i3) liefert das Einsetzen von "x" für "DOP(x)"
  nach dem Anwenden von Kalkülregel a) (ADD(FM(x,y),z) = FM(xa,ya))
  als Vorbedingung $V_{3)}$ des folgenden "<u>else</u>".
- Nach Kalkülregel e1) ist $V_{3)}$ Vorbedingung von "<u>elihw</u>".

Zusammenfassung der Ergebnisse von α1) und α2):
Nach Kalkülregel f) oder h) ist $(V_{3)} \vee (xa = x \wedge ya = y \wedge z = 0))$
Vorbedingung von $Q_{Z(M1)}$. Mit Kalkülregel a) bleibt zu zeigen, daß
Z(M1) aus dieser Vorbedingung folgt. Da $V_{3)}$ identisch mit Z(M1),
bleibt nur zu zeigen, daß Z(M1) aus $(xa = x \wedge ya = y \wedge z = 0)$ folgt.
Es gilt: ADD(FM(x,y),0) = FM(x,y). Passendes Einsetzen von z für 0,
sowie xa für x und ya für y liefert Z(M1).

β) Den Nachweis für Z(M1.2) und Z(MULT,E) führt man analog zu α).

3. Methode zum Nachweis der Terminierung einer while-Anweisung π

Die Methode ist in [4] begründet und besteht aus den folgenden Schritten:

i) Bestimme die Belegungen der Programmvariablen, die die Schleifenzusicherung von π erfüllen und für die

   α) die Testbedingung der while-Anweisung falsch ist ($\Gamma_{E1}(\pi)$),

   β) der while-Körper terminiert ($\Gamma_{E2}(\pi)$), bzw.

   γ) der while-Körper vollständig durchlaufen wird ($\Gamma_S(\pi)$).

ii) $f_{\pi k}$ sei die Bedeutung des while-Körpers von π. Bestimme die Funktion $f_{\pi k}|\Gamma_S(\pi)$, d. h. die Einschränkung von $f_{\pi k}$ auf $\Gamma_S(\pi)$ und setze

$$f_\Omega = \; < \Gamma \longmapsto \begin{cases} f_{\pi k}(\Gamma) & \text{falls } \Gamma \epsilon \Gamma_S(\pi) \\ \Omega & \text{sonst} \end{cases} > \; .$$

iii) Suche für ein beliebiges $\Gamma \epsilon \; \Gamma_S(\pi)$ eine natürliche Zahl n mit $f_\Omega^n(\Gamma) \epsilon \; \Gamma_{E1}(\pi) \cup \Gamma_{E2}(\pi) \cup \{\Omega\}$.

   Existiert für beliebiges $\Gamma \epsilon \; \Gamma_S(\pi)$ ein solches n, so terminiert π.

Beispiel: Es wird die Terminierung des Programms MULT bewiesen.

$\Gamma \epsilon \Gamma_J$ bezeichne eine beliebige Belegung der Programmvariablen über J, $\Gamma(x)$ den Wert der Programmvariablen x bei der Belegung Γ. Der Strukturgraph G_{MULT} des Programms MULT ist eine graphentheoretische Darstellung des zu diesem Programm gehörenden Programmschemas und gibt Aufschluß über alle Wege, auf denen Berechnungen das Programm durchlaufen können.

i) α) $\Gamma_{E1}(M1) = \{\Gamma \epsilon \Gamma_J \mid \Gamma(y) \cdot \Gamma(x) + \Gamma(z) = xa \cdot ya \; \wedge \; \Gamma(y) = 0\}$.

   β) Bestimmung von $\Gamma_{E2}(M1)$: Aus dem Strukturgraphen von MULT ergibt sich, daß $\Gamma \epsilon \; \Gamma_{E2}(M1)$ gdw. gilt:

   $(ODD(y)^{J,\Gamma} = T \; \wedge \; GRGL(Sub(IMAX,x),z)^{J,\Gamma} = \bot) \; \vee \; (ODD(y)^{J,\Gamma} = T \; \wedge$
   $GRGL(SUB(IMAX,x),z)^{J,\Gamma} = T \; \wedge \; GRGL(SUB(IMAX,x),x)^{J,\Gamma} = \bot) \; \vee \; (ODD(y)^{J,\Gamma}$
   $= \bot \; \wedge \; GRGL(SUB(IMAX,x),x)^{J,\Gamma} = \bot)$.

   Logisch äquivalente Umformung ergibt:
   $(ODD(y)^{J,\Gamma} = T \; \wedge \; GRGL(SUB(IMAX,x),z)^{J,\Gamma} = \bot) \; \vee \; GRGL(SUB(IMAX,x),$
   $x)^{J,\Gamma} = \bot$.

   Also gilt:

   $\Gamma_{E2}(M1) = \{\Gamma \epsilon \Gamma_J \mid \Gamma(x) \cdot \Gamma(y) + \Gamma(z) = xa \cdot ya \; \wedge \; \Gamma(y) \geq 1 \; \wedge \; ((\Gamma(y)$ ist ungerade $\wedge \; \Gamma(z) > 2^{48} - \Gamma(x)) \; \vee \; \Gamma(x) > 2^{48} - \Gamma(x))\}$.

   γ) Analog zu β) ergibt sich $\Gamma_S(M1)$ zu

   $\Gamma_S(M1) = \{\Gamma \epsilon \Gamma_J \mid \Gamma(x) \cdot \Gamma(y) + \Gamma(z) = xa \cdot ya \; \wedge \; \Gamma(y) \geq 1 \; \wedge \; \Gamma(x) \leq 2^{48} - \Gamma(x) \; \wedge$
   $(\Gamma(y)$ ist gerade $\vee \; \Gamma(z) \leq 2^{48} - \Gamma(x))\}$.

ii) Analog zu $\Gamma_{E2}(M1)$ läßt sich auch die Bedeutung des while-Körpers von M1 eingeschränkt auf $\Gamma_S(M1)$ mithilfe von G_{MULT} und $\Gamma_S(M1)$ weitgehend mechanisch gewinnen.

   Es ergibt sich:

$$f_\Omega = \; < \; \Gamma \longmapsto \begin{cases} < \begin{array}{l} x \longmapsto 2 \cdot \Gamma(x) \\ y \longmapsto (\Gamma(y)-1):2 \\ z \longmapsto \Gamma(z)+\Gamma(x) \end{array} > & \text{falls } \Gamma\epsilon\Gamma_S(M1) \wedge \Gamma(y) \text{ ungerade} \\[2em] < \begin{array}{l} x \longmapsto 2 \cdot \Gamma(x) \\ y \longmapsto \Gamma(y):2 \\ z \longmapsto \Gamma(z) \end{array} > & \text{falls } \Gamma\epsilon\Gamma_S(M1) \wedge \Gamma(y) \text{ gerade} \\[2em] \Omega & \text{falls } \Gamma\notin\Gamma_S(M1) \end{cases} >$$

iv) Abschätzung der maximalen Schleifendurchläufe von M1:

Sei $\Gamma\epsilon\Gamma_S(M1)$ beliebig. Es gilt ein $n(\Gamma)\epsilon N$ zu ermitteln mit $f_\Omega^n(\Gamma)\epsilon\{\Omega\} \cup \Gamma_{E1}(M1) \cup \Gamma_{E2}(M1)$.

α) 1. Abschätzung:

Sei $\Gamma(y) = y_w$. Bei jedem Schleifendurchlauf von M1 wird für $\Gamma(y)\geq2$ der Wert von y mindestens halbiert, für $\Gamma(y) = 1$ erhält y den Wert 0. Also gilt nach spätestens $n(y_w)\epsilon N$ Schritten mit $y_w:2^n\leq1$, daß $f_\Omega^{n+1}(\Gamma)(y)\epsilon\{0\}\cup\{\Omega\}$, also daß $f_\Omega^{n+1}\notin\Gamma_S(M1)$.
Man erhält: $y_w\leq2^n$, also $n\geq\lg_2(y_w)$.

β) 2. Abschätzung:

Sei $\Gamma(x) = x_w$. Bei jedem Schleifendurchlauf von M1 wird der Wert von x verdoppelt. Also gilt nach spätestens $n(x_w)\epsilon N$ Schritten mit $x_w\cdot2^n>2^{48}-x_w\cdot2^n$, daß $f_\Omega^n(\Gamma)\notin\Gamma_S(M1)$. Man erhält: $n>47-\lg_2(x_w)$.

Also gilt: M1 terminiert nach spätestens n' Schritten mit
$$n' = \text{Min } \{n\epsilon N \mid n>\lg_2(y_w) \vee n>47-\lg_2(x_w)\}.$$

4. Ansatzpunkte einer Rechnerunterstützung

Für experimentelle Untersuchungen ist die Implementierung eines Dialogsystems geplant. Dem Rechner sollen hierbei folgende Aufgaben übertragen werden:

i) Entwicklung von Vorbedingungen (bzw. Zusicherungen) nach dem angegebenen Kalkül unter Mithilfe des Programmierers.

ii) Kontrollaufgaben während der Programmverifikation (z.B. "Abhaken" derjenigen Zusicherungen, für die bewiesen wurde, daß sie Vorbedingungen sind),

iii) Ermittlung der Mengen Γ_S und Γ_{E2} sowie der Funktion, die der while-Körper realisiert, unter Mithilfe des Programmierers,

iv) Abschätzung der maximalen oder wahrscheinlichen Programmausführungsdauer.

Nachtrag: Die skizzierte Methode wurde inzwischen auf allgemeinere Schleifenstrukturen (die sog. RE_n-Strukturen) sowie auf hierarchisch verschachtelte (d.h. nicht rekursive) Unterprogramme ausgedehnt. Mit einer Erweiterung um Deklarationsvereinbarungen, rekursive Prozeduren und Parallelverarbeitung wurde begonnen.

5. Literaturangaben

[1] R.W. Floyd: "Assigning Meanings to Programs", *Proceedings of Symposia in Applied Mathematics*, Volume XIX, 19-32 (1967)

[2] C.A.R. Hoare: "An Axiomatic Basis for Computer Programming", CACM <u>12</u>,10, 576-583 (1969)

[3] D.C. Luckham/ D.M. Park/ M.S. Paterson: "On Formalized Computer Programs", J. Comput. System Sci. <u>4</u>, 22o - 249 (197o)

[4] A.L. Luft: "Grundlagen einer Methode für die rechnergestützte Verifikation von while-Programmen während der Programmerstellung" Arbeitsbericht des Instituts für Mathem. Maschinen und Datenverarbeitung Erlangen, Bd. 8, Nr. 7, August 1975

[5] Z. Manna: "Mathematical Theory of Computation" McGraw-Hill Book Company, New York 1974

EINE DIALOGSPRACHE FÜR DIE PROZESS-STEUERUNG

Peter Rütters

Brown, Boveri & Cie AG, Mannheim

Fachbereich Prozeß-Datenverarbeitung

1. Einführung

Der Einsatz der Datenverarbeitung in den verschiedensten Bereichen der Technik
hat gerade in den letzten Jahren rapide zugenommen. Die zu lösenden Aufgaben
werden in allen technischen Bereichen immer komplexer, so daß der Einsatz von
Datenverarbeitungsanlagen unumgänglich ist. Die Anforderungen an das technische
Personal nehmen demzufolge in allen Produktionsbereichen fortlaufend zu. Zur Be-
dienung der Produktionsanlagen werden qualifizierte Fachkräfte benötigt.

Mit dem im folgenden beschriebenen Programmsystem wird eine anwenderfreundliche Dialogsprache angeboten, die zum einen leicht verständlich und schnell erlernbar ist und zum anderen die durch den Prozeßrechnereinsatz bedingten erhöhten
Anforderungen an das Bedienungspersonal minimal hält.

Das Anwender-Programmsystem "Ablaufsteuerung DP 1000" ist in der prozeßorientierten höheren Programmierungssprache PAS 2, dem BBC-PEARL-Subset, abge-
faßt und dient zur Steuerung sequentieller Prozeßabläufe. Das Programmpaket wurde ausgehend von den Empfehlungen des NAMUR/VDI-Arbeitskreises 6 entwickelt
und mit führenden Anwendern in der chemischen Industrie abgestimmt.

2. Problemstellung und Randbedingungen

Bei der Realisierung der Ablaufsteuerung wurden die folgenden Randbedingungen
berücksichtigt:

- Verwendung der höheren Programmierungssprache PAS 2 (einfache Programmerstellung, übersichtlicher Programmaufbau und einfache Korrekturmöglichkeit)

- Modularer Aufbau des Programmsystems (einfache Ergänzung des Programm-
  pakets durch vom Anwender gewünschte Sonderroutinen)

- Generieren von Steuerungsprogrammen aus einem Vorrat von Steuerungsbefehlen
  (i)   on-line im Dialog-Betrieb
  (ii) durch Eingabe über Lochstreifen

- Kein erneutes Kompilieren oder Programm-Binden nach der Zusammenstellung
  einer Steuerkette (Folge von Steuerungsbefehlen)

- Quasi-paralleles Abarbeiten von k Steuerketten
- Starten eines Steuerungsprogramms im Dialog-Betrieb, durch Interrupt oder von einem Anwenderprogramm aus

- Bearbeitung weiterer PAS 2-Anwenderprogramme in Verbindung mit der Ablaufsteuerung

Wie die oben angeführten Randbedingungen zeigen, wurde bei der Erstellung des Programmsystems von der "On-line-Generierbarkeit und -Änderbarkeit" von Steuerungsprogrammen ausgegangen. Die On-line-Änderbarkeit ist insbesondere in den Anwendungsfällen von Vorteil, in denen eine bereits in Betrieb befindliche Anlage ergänzt werden soll. Zum Beispiel kann dann die Inbetriebnahme weiterer Anlagenteile vorgenommen werden, ohne daß die auf der Anlage bereits implementierten Prozesse unterbrochen werden müssen.

Die Befehle der Dialogsprache sind, je nach Funktion, in drei Befehlsgruppen unterteilt:

- Dialog-Befehle zum Generieren von Steuerungsprogrammen (bestimmt für den DV-Fachmann),
- Dialog-Befehle zum Bedienen der Ablaufsteuerung (bestimmt für das Bedienungspersonal) und die
- Befehlsliste der Steuerkettenbefehle.

3. Struktur des Programmsystems

Einen Überblick über die Einordnung der "Ablaufsteuerung DP 1000" in das Gesamtsoftwaresystem vermittelt das Blockdiagramm in Bild 1.

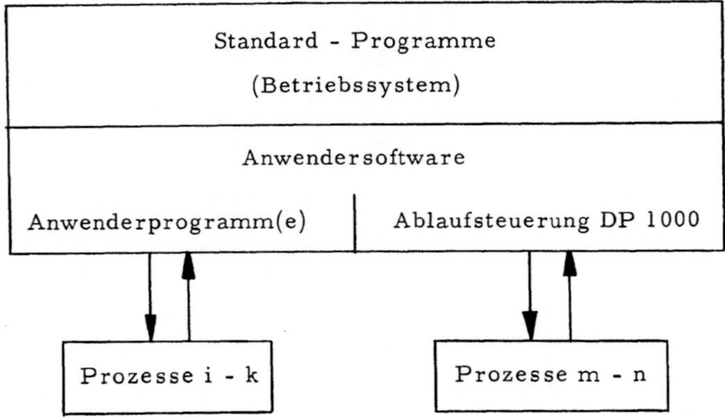

Bild 1 Blockdiagramm des Gesamtsystems

Die Anwendersoftware gliedert sich in zwei Blöcke, die einzeln anwenderspezifi-
schen Programme zur Kontrolle der Prozesse i bis k sowie die Ablaufsteuerung
zur Überwachung und Steuerung der Prozesse m bis n. Beide Programmblöcke werden durch die Standardroutinen der Systemsoftware unterstützt.

Der modulare Aufbau der Ablaufsteuerung ist im Blockdiagramm von Bild 2 wieder-
gegeben. Wie das Bild zeigt, handelt es sich um ein sogenanntes listeninterpretie-
rendes Programmsystem. Alle Programmblöcke (realisiert als Module, Tasks
oder Prozeduren) tauschen untereinander Informationen über Datenlisten oder Parametertabellen aus.

Datenlisten							
Prozeß-Ein-/Ausgabe	Dialog	Steuerketten-Abarbeitung	Meldungs-Protokollierung	Prozeßstellen-Überwachung	Meßwert-Protokollierung	Meßwert-Verarbeitung	... Erweiterungen ...

Bild 2 Blockdiagramm der Ablaufsteuerung

Zum Grundausbau des Programmsystems gehören neben den Parametertabellen,
die anlagenabhängig an den jeweiligen Hardware-Ausbau angepaßt werden können,
die folgenden Module:

"Prozeß-Ein-/Ausgabe"   Zyklische Ein-/Ausgabe von/zur Prozeß-
                               peripherie

"Dialog"   Generieren von Steuerungsprogrammen im
                               "On-line-Betrieb" sowie Bedienung der
                               Ablaufsteuerung

"Steuerketten-Abarbeitung"   Zyklisches quasi-paralleles Abarbeiten von
                               k Steuerketten

"Meldungs-Protokollierung"   Ausgabe von Meldungen und Anweisungen an
                               das Bedienungspersonal

Als Erweiterungen zu diesem Grundausbau sind unter anderem die folgenden Module vorgesehen:

"Prozeßstellen-Überwachung"   Zyklische Überwachung aller analogen und digitalen Prozeßstellen

"Meßwert-Protokollierung"   Protokollierung der Prozeßabläufe in Form von Meßwerttabellen

"Meßwert-Verarbeitung"   Auswertung und Protokollierung von Meß-ergebnissen gemäß vom Anwender zu definie-renden Algorithmen

"Notprogramm"   Anwenderspezifisches Programm zum rech-nergesteuerten Ergreifen von Notmaßnahmen, z. B. bei Grenzwertüberschreitungen

"Regelung"   DDC-Programmpaket mit Anschluß an die modulare Ablaufsteuerung

In den folgenden Abschnitten wird auf die Module des Grundausbaus näher eingegangen und dabei auf die wesentlichen Merkmale des Programmsystems hingewiesen.

4. Programmodule der Ablaufsteuerung

4.1 Prozeß-Ein-/Ausgabe

Der Modul "Prozeß-Ein-/Ausgabe" stellt die Verbindung zwischen dem Prozeß und der Ablaufsteuerung her. Er dient dem zyklischen Erfassen aller Prozeßvariablen und der Ausgabe von Steuerungsgrößen an den Prozeß.

Als mögliche Hardware-Konfiguration für ein Prozeßsteuerungssystem wird die folgende Ausbaustufe vorgeschlagen:

512   digitale Eingänge
      (einzeln oder jeweils 16 Eingänge zusammenhängend adressierbar)

256   digitale Ausgänge
      (einzeln oder jeweils 16 Ausgänge zusammenhängend adressierbar)

128   analoge Eingänge
 64   analoge Ausgänge
 32   Impulszähler (16 bit)

Jede andere Hardware-Ausbaustufe läßt sich programmtechnisch ohne weiteres realisieren. Eine zyklische Ein-/Ausgabe aller Prozeßvariablen in bedienbaren Zeitabständen - für analoge Größen sind drei unterschiedliche Zeitzyklen, für digitale Größen ein Zeitzyklus vorgesehen - bedeutet, daß zu jedem Zeitaugenblick eine Momentaufnahme des gesamten Prozesses im Speicher der Zentraleinheit vorliegt. Jeder Prozeßstelle ist also ein bestimmter Speicherplatz zugeordnet. Diese Programmorganisation ist unumgänglich, wenn eine quasi-parallele Abarbeitung von Steuerketten in einem festen Zeitraster eingehalten werden soll. Die direkte Ansprache von Prozeßstellen von der Ablaufsteuerung her hat beispielsweise im Falle einer integrierenden analogen Eingabe zur Folge, daß die Steuerketten-Abarbeitung für die Dauer der Eingabe unterbrochen und somit ein Einhalten eines vorgegebenen Zeitrasters gefährdet wird. Ein Zurückgreifen auf Speicherplätze hingegen garantiert kurze Befehlsausführungszeiten und ermöglicht eine zyklische Abarbeitung.

4.2 Der Dialog

Mit Hilfe des Moduls "Dialog" werden zum einen die Daten von Steuerketten für ein bestimmtes Steuerungsprogramm (Programm zur Steuerung eines Prozesses oder Teilprozesses) zusammengestellt. Zum anderen erfüllt der Dialog eine Vielzahl von Bedienungsfunktionen bei der späteren Anlagenbedienung. Die Dialogbefehle sind dementsprechend in Befehle zur Programmerstellung und Programmbedienungsbefehle unterteilt. Die erste Befehlsgruppe ist softwaremäßig verriegelt und kann somit nur einem bestimmten Personenkreis zugänglich gemacht werden. Eine Befehlsauswahl ist in Tabelle 1 zusammengestellt.

Wie der Auszug aus der Dialog-Befehlsliste zeigt, wurde eine benutzerfreundliche Programmbedienung angestrebt. Jeder Dialog-Befehl setzt sich aus einer Zeichenfolge von maximal 50 Zeichen zusammen. Das Leerzeichen dient hierbei als Trennungszeichen zwischen zwei Wörtern. Abgeschlossen wird ein Befehl entweder durch ein Semikolon oder aber bei Eingabe des 51. Zeichens.

Ein Befehlsinterpreter löst die Zeichenkette in vier einzelne Wörter auf. Der Dialog-Befehl wird ausgeführt, falls die entschlüsselte Zeichenkette dem Befehlsvorrat zugeordnet werden kann. Wird der Befehl hingegen nicht verstanden, z. B. wegen Verwendung eines nicht vereinbarten Schlüsselworts, eines unbekannten Namens oder eines unerlaubten Parameters, so wird als Ergebnis der erfolgten Plausibilitätskontrolle eine den Eingabefehler diagnostizierende Fehlermeldung ausgegeben.

Befehle zur Programmerstellung

KETTE XXXXXX INITIALISIEREN;

      (Steuerkette x initialisieren)

KETTE XXXXXX NACH YYYYYY;

      (Steuerkette x auf Steuerkette y kopieren)

PROTOKOLLIEREN;

      (die angewählte Steuerkette protokollieren)

STANDARDKETTE XXXXXX ANWAEHLEN;

      (Standard-Steuerkette x zur Korrektur
      anwählen)

SCHRITT ZZZ EINFUEGEN;

      (Steuerkettenschritte vor Schritt z einfügen)

NAME XXXXXX AEINGANG ZZZ;

      (Namensvereinbarung für Analogeingang z)

Bedienungsbefehle

KETTE XXXXXX ABFRAGEN;

      (den Zustand von Steuerkette x abfragen)

AEINGANG XXXXXX ABFRAGEN;

      (den Wert des Analogeingangs x anfordern)

DEINGANG XXXXXX UEBERBRUECKEN;

      (Digitaleingang x überbrücken; Kennzeich-
      nen eines defekten Eingangs)

ZEITZYKLEN ABLAUFSTEUERUNG AENDERN;

      (Zykluszeiten der Ablaufsteuerung ab-
      ändern)

INHALTSVERZEICHNIS;

      (Liste aller Steuerketten mit Steuerketten-
      parametern ausgeben)

ENDE;

      (den Dialog beenden)

Tabelle 1 Beispiele von Dialogbefehlen

    XXXXXX: Name, bestehend aus maximal 6 Zeichen
    ZZZ: positive ganze Zahl (max. 3 Ziffern)

Die Eingabe eines Dialog-Befehls wird vom Interpreterprogramm jeweils durch Ausgabe eines vereinbarten Steuerzeichens angefordert. Ein Sprung in eine untergeordnete Dialog-Ebene erfolgt immer bei Dialog-Befehlen, die die Eingabe neuer Steuerkettenbefehle oder die Modifikation von Steuerkettenbefehlen betreffen. Das Interpreterprogramm gibt ein zweites spezielles Steuerzeichen zur Befehlsanforderung aus und kehrt erst dann wieder in die übergeordnete Dialog-Ebene zurück, wenn anstelle eines neuen Befehls eine Endfile-Bedingung angetroffen wird.

Einige Beispiele aus der dritten Befehlsgruppe, den Steuerkettenbefehlen, sind in Tabelle 2 zusammengestellt. Charakteristisch für diesen Abschnitt des Dialogs ist ein mehrmaliger Frage-Antwort-Wechsel innerhalb einer abgeschlossenen Befehlseingabe.

---

1) Ausgabe eines Analogsignals:

Die analoge Ausgangsvariable x_1 soll den Wert 0,667 annehmen.

SETZEN, XX1;   ANALOGGROESSE

ZAHL? 0.667;

2) Abfragen eines digitalen Eingangssignals:

Die digitale Eingangsvariable x_2 wird auf den Wert "1" abgefragt. Ist die Bedingung $x_2 = 1$ erfüllt, so werden k Steuerkettenschritte übersprungen.

ABFRAGEN, XX2, K;   DIGITALGROESSE

ZAHL? 1;

3) Die Abarbeitung einer Steuerkette so lange unterbrechen, bis daß die Steuerkette x_3 beendet ist.

WARTEN, XX3;

4) Die Abarbeitung einer Steuerkette für k Sekunden unterbrechen.

PAUSE;

T/S? K;

Tabelle 2 Beispiele von Steuerkettenbefehlen

(_ _ _ _ _ _ _ Ausgaben des Interpreterprogramms)

Die Reihenfolge der verschiedenen Befehlsparameter kann aufgrund dieses Eingabe-
modus vom Anwender nicht verwechselt werden. Das Erlernen der unterschiedlichen
Steuerkettenbefehle wird dadurch auf die Kenntnis der Befehlsschlüsselwörter reduziert, also minimal gehalten. Nach jeder Eingabe eines Namens oder Parameters
erfolgt jeweils eine Parameterkontrolle. Falsche oder unerlaubte Eingaben werden
durch eine entsprechende Fehlermeldung diagnostiziert; für die als fehlerhaft er-
kannten Befehlsparameter wird die Eingabeanforderung erneuert.

Als ein weiterer Vorteil der Dialogsprache ist die hardwareunabhängige Ansprache
der Prozeßstellen bei der Steuerkettengenerierung oder bei Abfragen durch das
Bedienungspersonal hervorzuheben. Für alle Prozeßstellen kann ein Name, beste-
hend aus maximal 6 Zeichen, definiert werden. Diese Festlegung ist mit Hilfe
eines speziellen Dialog-Befehls einmal zu treffen und behält für alle weiteren Eingaben seine Gültigkeit. Eine Namensänderung ist über eine erneute Namensfestle-
gung einfach zu erreichen. Neben den Prozeßstellen sind Steuerketten, Standard-
Steuerketten, Relativzeitzähler, Vorrichtungen (z. B. Transportbänder, auf die
mehrere Teilanlagen Zugriff haben), Anwendertasks sowie Ergebnisvariable zur
Zwischenspeicherung ebenfalls mit frei wählbaren Namen adressierbar. Die mehrfache Verwendung des gleichen Namens für unterschiedliche Größen wird vom
Dialog-Programm überwacht und mit einer entsprechenden Fehlermeldung unterbun-
den.

4.3 Steuerketten-Abarbeitung

Wie bereits erwähnt wurde, werden die Daten aller Steuerketten in einem festen
Zeitraster abgearbeitet. Vorgesehen sind zwei unterschiedliche, bedienbare Zeitzyklen, die standardmäßig mit den Zykluszeiten $T_1 = 1$ s und $T_2 = 10$ s $(k \cdot T_1)$
initialisiert werden.

Um die Abarbeitung der Steuerketten zu beschleunigen, wurden zwei Tabellen (je
eine pro Zeitzyklus) angelegt, in die alle im Zustand "aktiv" (d. h. in Bearbeitung)
befindlichen Steuerketten eingetragen werden (siehe Bild 3). Hierdurch entfällt die
Abfrage sämtlicher Steuerketten auf Zustand und Zykluszeit vor jedem Steuerkettenschritt. Wie im Bild 3 dargestellt ist, wird beim Starten einer Steuerkette die
Steuerkettenkennung der vereinbarten Zykluszeit entsprechend in eine der Abarbei-
tungstabellen eingetragen; bei Beenden einer Steuerkette wird dementsprechend die
Kennung in diesen Tabellen wieder gelöscht. Ein quasi-paralleles Abarbeiten bedeutet für das vorgegebene Beispiel, daß pro Zyklus jeweils ein Steuerkettenschritt
(beim k-ten Zyklus z. B. die Schritte k_1, k_3 und k_i) der im Zustand "aktiv" befind-

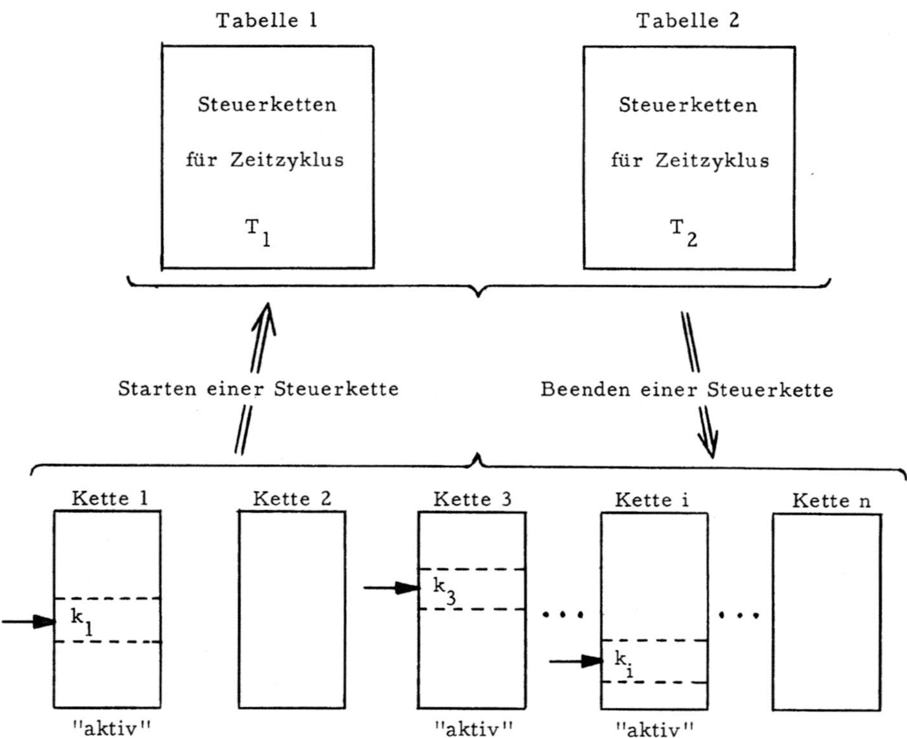

__Bild 3__ Verfahren der Steuerketten-Abarbeitung

lichen Steuerketten ausgeführt wird.

Nach den obigen Festlegungen wird pro Abarbeitungszyklus jeweils ein Steuerkettenschritt, also ein Steuerungsbefehl, ausgeführt. Bestimmte Anwendungen machen es
jedoch erforderlich, daß pro Zyklus mehrere Schritte oder Befehle einer Steuerkette abgearbeitet werden müssen, z. B. bei gleichzeitiger Abfrage von Ventilstel-
lungen. Darüber hinaus wird häufig eine Adressierung von Steuerkettenabschnitten
oder -phasen gewünscht. Diesen Anforderungen wird mit einem speziellen Steuer-
kettenbefehl Rechnung getragen. Durch Angabe des ersten Befehlsparameters kann
eine Phasennummer zur Identifizierung der Phase vergeben werden; mit dem zweiten Parameter wird die Schrittanzahl der Phase spezifiziert, die abweichend von
der quasi-parallelen Abarbeitung hintereinander auszuführen ist.

Reentrant-fähige Steuerungsprogramme, sogenannte Standard-Steuerketten, sind
für Anwendungsfälle vorgesehen, bei denen entweder gleiche Produkte auf unterschiedlichen Anlagen oder Produkte nach unterschiedlichen Rezepturvorschriften,

jedoch mit gleicher Befehlsfolge herzustellen sind. Bei Aufruf einer derartigen Standard-Steuerkette werden die formalen Befehlsparameter zunächst aktualisiert, sodann wird mit der Ausführung des modifizierten Steuerungsprogramms begonnen.

4.4 Meldungs-Protokollierung

Die Protokollierung von Meldungen wird aus denselben Gründen wie die direkte Ansprache von Prozeßstellen von der Steuerketten-Abarbeitung, bei der feste Zeitabstände einzuhalten sind, entkoppelt. Die Information über zu protokollierende Meldungen wird demzufolge zwischen beiden Modulen über eine Parameterliste ausgetauscht. Der Wörtervorrat, auf den bei der Zusammenstellung einer Meldung zurückgegriffen werden kann, ist vom Anwender im Dialog-Verkehr mit dem Rechner festzulegen.

5. Zusammenfassung

In den vorangegangenen Abschnitten wurde ein neues PEARL-Programmsystem zur Steuerung von diskontinuierlichen Prozeßabläufen vorgestellt. Hauptmerkmal dieses Systems ist eine anwenderfreundliche Dialogsprache, mit deren Hilfe zum einen on-line die gesamte Programmierung von Prozeßabläufen erfolgen kann, zum anderen das Gesamtsystem auf einfache Weise zu bedienen ist. Aufgrund der übersichtlichen Struktur und der Überschaubarkeit des Befehlsvorrats ist die Dialogsprache leicht erlernbar; sie setzt nicht die Kenntnis einer höheren Programmiersprache voraus. Der Befehlsvorrat wurde an die NAMUR-Empfehlungen angepaßt und kommt somit den Anforderungen des Anwenders sehr entgegen.

Der modulare Aufbau der Ablaufsteuerung und die Verwendung der prozeßorientierten höheren Programmierungssprache PAS 2 (also maschinenunabhängige Programmierung) sind Grundlage für ein flexibles Programmsystem. Zum einen lassen sich Ergänzungen zu diesem System ohne großen Aufwand einfügen; zum anderen ist das Programmpaket mit anderen PEARL-Anwenderprogrammen verträglich. Die Ablaufsteuerung kann ohne weiteres zu anderen Anwenderprogrammen gebunden und gemäß einer vorgegebenen Prioritätenverteilung zusammen mit diesen Programmen zur Ausführung gelangen.

6. Literatur

[1] Merkmale der Grundsoftware zur Steuerung von Chargenprozessen. Hrsg. von NAMUR/VDI-Ausschuß, Regelung und Steuerung in der chemischen Verfahrenstechnik, Arbeitskreis 6: Automatisierung diskontinuierlicher Prozesse.

[2] PAS 2, BBC-PEARL-Subset, Sprachbeschreibung. Hrsg. von BBC Brown, Boveri & Cie AG, Mannheim. Druckschriften-Bestell-Nr. D EG 40424D.

[3] G. Müller: PAS 2, (BBC-PEARL-Subset), eine höhere, prozedurorientierte Programmiersprache für Prozeßrechensysteme. Rundfunktechn. Mitteilungen, Jahrg. 19 (1975), H. 1, S. 31 - 36.

ZUR PROGRAMMIERUNG VON ECHTZEITRECHNERSYSTEMEN MIT RÄUMLICH VERTEILTEN
PROZESSORSTATIONEN

Hartwig Steusloff
Institut für Informationsverarbeitung in Technik und Biologie der
Fraunhofer-Gesellschaft, Karlsruhe

1. Konzept und Struktur der Gerätetechnik

Ein Echtzeitrechnersystem (ERS) zur Automatisierung eines in Echtzeit ablau-
fenden technischen Prozesses muß grundsätzlich zwei Anforderungen genügen: Es
muß die Echtzeitbedingungen des technischen Prozesses einhalten und die geforderte Automatisierungsleistung an räumlich verteilten Komponenten des technischen Prozesses erbringen können.

Die herkömmliche zentrale Struktur von ERS und ihre Programmierung mittels
Assembler hat verschiedene Nachteile. Folgende Problemkreise haben heute besonderes Gewicht:

. Die geforderte hohe Zuverlässigkeit des Automatisierungssystems ist durch
  den Einsatz von back-up-Systemen allein aus Kostengründen nicht mehr zu erreichen. Das Automatisierungssystem muß vielmehr in sich eine hohe Grund-
  Zuverlässigkeit mit der Eigenschaft eines in kleinen Stufen erfolgenden Lei-
  stungsabfalls bei Störungen vereinigen.

· Eine zentrale Rechnerstruktur kann bei großen technischen Prozessen zu Lei-
  stungsengpässen führen, deren Beseitigung - falls überhaupt möglich - sehr
  kostenintensiv ist. Dieses Problem ist durch den Einsatz von heute preis-
  wert erstellbarer paralleler Verarbeitungskapazität (Mikroprozessorsysteme)
  lösbar.

· Die Nutzung der Leistungsfähigkeit neuer Rechnergenerationen bedingt bei
  zentraler Rechnerstruktur einen völligen Austausch der vorhandenen Installa-
  tion. Eine aufgabenspezifische, gleitende Modernisierung des ERS ohne er-
  hebliche Betriebsunterbrechungen ist schon aus wirtschaftlichen Gründen zu
  fordern.

· Bei großen technischen Prozessen betragen heute die Verkabelungskosten zu
  einem zentralen ERS bis zum Dreifachen der für das Rechnersystem (ohne Da-
  tenperipherie und Externspeicher) einzusetzenden Kosten.

· Die zunehmend dominierenden Kosten für die Programmerstellung, die Dokumen-
  tation, die Programmpflege und -weiterentwicklung sind nur durch den Einsatz
  eines anwendungsbezogenen Programmierungshilfsmittels beherrschbar.

· Flexibilität, Inbetriebnahme und Überwachung sind bei zentraler Struktur des
  ERS und der hohen Komplexität moderner technischer Systeme erschwert.

Diese Situation führt auf ein ERS mit räumlich verteilten Prozessorstationen, dessen gerätetechnische Struktur in Bild 1 dargestellt ist /1/.

Die wesentlichen Eigenschaften dieses ERS sind:

• Prozessorstationen mit Rechnerkern, Arbeitsspeicher und Prozeß-Ein/Ausgabe erbringen die in ihrer räumlichen Umgebung geforderte Automatisierungsleistung. Die Prozessorstationen enthalten Mikroprozessoren und sind u. a. durch geringe Leistungsaufnahme für einen robusten Vor-Ort-Einsatz im Gußkastengehäuse geeignet.

• Die Prozessorstationen arbeiten möglichst autonom. Erforderliche Kommunikation zwischen verschiedenen Prozessorstationen wird über ein Sammelleitungssystem hergestellt, das alle Prozessorstationen miteinander verbindet. Aus Sicherheitsgründen ist für die Steuerung des Sammelleitungssystems ein dezentrales Konzept vorgesehen /2/, das auf einer automatischen Verlagerung der Steuerungsfunktion auf die einzelne Prozessorstationen nach vorgegebener Reihenfolge beruht.

• Bei Störungen eines Prozessors schaltet die Stationssteuerung das Ein/Ausgabewerk der Staion direkt auf die Sammelleitung.

• Besonders wichtige Meß- und Stellgrößen des technischen Systems können an die Ein/Ausgabe-Werke mehrerer Prozessorstationen angeschlossen sein.

• Die gerätetechnische Ausstattung der Prozessorstationen ist den lokalen Automatisierungsforderungen angepaßt und kann - auch hinsichtlich der Prozessortypen - unterschiedlich sein.

• Aus Sicherheitsgründen erhalten die normalen Prozessorstationen keine fest angeschlossene Standardperipherie; für Wartungs- und Inbetriebnahmefunktionen sind Stecker zum Anschluß von transportabler Standardperipherie vorgesehen. Lediglich einige ausgezeichnete Stationen verfügen über Massenspeicher und weitere Standardperipherie für die Aufgaben der Programmerstellung und der Kommunikation zwischen Mensch, technischem System und Rechnersystem.

Von besonderer Bedeutung für die Programmierung ist die Adressierungsmethode innerhalb des ERS. Es ist ein das gesamte ERS überdeckender "globaler" Adressraum vorgesehen. Eine "globale Adresse" kann, wie in Bild 2 dargestellt, auf zweierlei Weise in lokalen Adressen umgesetzt werden, wobei die 2. Methode den Vorteil einer lückenlosen Ausnutzbarkeit des Adressraumes mit dem Aufwand einer Adreßrechnung für jede globale Adresse erkauft.

2. Anforderungen an das Programmierungshilfsmittel

Ein effizienter Einsatz der dargestellten gerätetechnischen Lösung für ein ERS mit räumlich verteilten Prozessorstationen ist nur über ein Programmierungshilfsmittel möglich, das es dem Programmierer gestattet, die lokale Automatisierungsaufgabe geschlossen und weitgehend ohne Rücksicht auf die gerätetechnische Struktur des gesamten Rechnersystems zu formulieren. Diese Forderung gilt insbesondere auch für den Zugriff zu globalen Daten, d. h. Daten, die in verschiedenen Stationen des ERS vorliegen. Weiterhin müssen die gerätetechnisch bereitgestellten Möglichkeiten zur Sicherung der Verfügbarkeit der Automatisierungsleistung durch den Programmierer einfach nutzbar sein.

Bei der grundsätzlichen Auswahl eines Programmierungshilfsmittels für das ERS mit räumlich verteilten Prozessorstationen führt eine Wertanalyse auf die Verwendung einer höheren Programmiersprache. Bild 3 zeigt die Bewertung einer Hierarchie von Programmierungshilfsmitteln anhand von sechs Bewertungskriterien. Die Überlegenheit der höheren Sprache ist evident. Das niedrige Gewicht des Kriteriums "Programmeffizienz" resultiert aus den weiter sinkenden Kosten für Speicherplatz und der zunehmend kleiner werdenden Differenz der Laufzeit von assemblierten bzw. kompilierten Programmen.

Diese höhere Sprache muß besondere Anforderungen erfüllen, die in der folgenden Tabelle zusammengestellt sind.

<u>Auf Sprachebene</u> müssen formulierbar sein:

<u>Echtzeitbetrieb und räumliche Verteilung des Rechnersystems:</u>

1. Die Zeit- und Synchronisationsbedingungen ("Tasking")
2. Die Betriebsmittelverwaltung und Dateiverwaltung
3. Die Prozeß-Ein-/Ausgabe
4. Die Bearbeitung von Prozessinformationen beliebigen Wertebereiches ("Bit-Handling")
5. Die Beschreibung von Prozessortypen, -orten und -kennungen oder -adressbereichen
6. Die Zuordnung von Programmen und Prozessorstationen
7. Die Zuordnung von E/A-Geräten und Daten aus dem technischen System zu Variablen im Problemprogramm
8. Die Programmkommunikation und
9. Der Datenverkehr über die Sammelleitung

<u>Vorkehrungen zur Ausfallsicherung</u>

10. Zuordnung von Programm und Prozessorstation abhängig vom Betriebszustand des Rechnersystems
11. Beschreibung der Gewinnung von Ersatzwerten für Prozessdaten, abhängig vom Betriebszustand der E/A-Werke, der Meßfühler und Stellglieder sowie des Rechnersystems.

Allgemeine Anforderungen

12. Algorithmischer Sprachteil universell einsetzbar

13. Aussicht auf internationale Standardisierung

Nach diesen Kriterien ist z. Z. die Sprache PEARL am besten für die Programmie-
rung des ERS mit räumlich verteilten Prozessorstationen geeignet /3/, /4/. Das
Beispiel auf Bild 4 zeigt charakteristische Eigenschaften von PEARL gegenüber
Prozeß-FORTRAN. Im Beispiel ist die Aufgabe gestellt, Teile eines Eingangs-
Bitmusters logisch zu verknüpfen (UND-Funktion) und als Bitmuster rechtsbündig
auszugeben. Wesentlich ist die Vermischung der Prozeß-Ein-/Ausgabe, CALL DINP
(IN) bzw. CALL DOAP (IOUT), mit der eigentlichen Datenumformung im FORTRAN-
Beispiel, wobei die in den Steuerlisten IN und IOUT enthaltenen Parameter und
Daten vom Programmierer formal an festgelegten Stellen einzusetzen sind. Bei
PEARL ist die Beschreibung der Prozeß-Ein-/Ausgabe im SYSTEM-Teil durch direkt
die Gerätetechnik bezeichnende Sprachelemente möglich und zudem vom algorith-
mischen Teil des Programmes, dem PROBLEM-Teil, formal getrennt. Änderungen der
Prozeß-Ein-/Ausgabe sind somit bei PEARL leicht und fehlerarm durchführbar.
Weiterhin verwendet PEARL einfache, der Fachsprache entnommene Sprachelemente
(TAKE, SEND), die gute Eigendokumentationseigenschaften besitzen; gleiches
gilt für den zyklischen Start des Programms (EVERY --- ACTIVATE).

Anforderungen 6 bis 11 (teilweise auch 5) sind jedoch auch bei PEARL nicht erfüllt. Daher sind Erweiterungen der Sprache PEARL erforderlich, die im folgenden vorgestellt werden. Wesentlich ist dabei,

• ein erweitertes PEARL möglichst frei von Eingriffen in das bisher definierte
  PEARL zu halten,
• das Konzept von PEARL, funktionell abteilbare Programmeinheiten auch formal
  zu trennen (SYSTEM-Teil/PROBLEM-Teil), auszunutzen.

Die vorgeschlagenen Erweiterungen sind als vorläufiger Sprachvorschlag zu verstehen. Im Rahmen eines vom BMFT geförderten Forschungsvorhabens wird ein de-
finierter Sprachvorschlag erarbeitet.

3. Erweiterungen der Sprache PEARL

Eine neu hinzukommende Programmsektion dient zur Beschreibung der Prozessorstationen. Diese Einheit ist im Sinne von PEARL ein eigener Modul mit aus-
schließlich globalen Referenzen. Bild 5 zeigt diese Stationsbeschreibung zwischen den Schlüsselwörtern STATION und STAEND. Die Stationsbeschreibung wird
anhand der gerätetechnischen Konfiguration des ERS erstellt, einmal in eine
Tabelle umgewandelt und später nur geändert, wenn gerätetechnische Änderungen
im ERS vorgenommen wurden. Änderungen solcher Art bedingen lediglich eine neue
Codegenerierung der betroffenen Programme, sofern die im SYSTEM- und PROBLEM-

Teil beschriebene bzw. bearbeitete Prozeßinformation unverändert bleibt. Dies
wird insbesondere auch dadurch erreicht, daß - im Gegensatz zum bisher definierten PEARL - die selten veränderten Adressen der Prozeß-Ein-/Ausgabegeräte
im STATION-Teil mit Namen verknüpft sind und daher im SYSTEM-Teil nur über
diese Namen angesprochen werden. Dies dient der Portabilität von PEARL-Programm-
men.
Weiter enthält der STATION-Teil Angaben über die Eigenschaften des vorhandenen
lokalen Betriebssystems (OS), so daß schon zur Übersetzungszeit der Compiler
prüfen kann, ob die im Programm aufgerufenen Betriebssystemdienste im Betriebssystem der betreffenden Prozessorstation vorhanden sind.

Eine weitere, neu hinzukommende Programmeinheit für jeden PEARL-Modul ist der
Ladeteil, auf Bild 5 zwischen den Schlüsselworten LOAD und LODEND. Der Ladeteil gibt an, in welcher Prozessorstation, abhängig vom Systemstatus, der Modul auszuführen ist. Hier steht dem Programmierer das Werkzeug zur geplanten
Rekonfiguration des Automatisierungssystems bei Störungen des Rechnersystems
zur Verfügung. Bild 5 zeigt, daß im NORMAL-Zustand des Rechnersystems, identisch mit dem Urstart, der Modul in eine oder auch mehrere (AND) Prozessorstationen unter Angabe einer Ladepriorität PRIO geladen wird. Abhängig vom
Systemstatus, gekennzeichnet durch einen Statuscode, startet der Lader den
in einer Ausweichstation bereits residenten Modul (Attribut RES) oder verlagert den Modul in die angegebenen Ausweichstationen. Die Ladepriorität PRIO
("pgz" bedeutet "positive ganze Zahl") dient zur Lösung von Konfliktfällen,
die auftreten können, wenn mehrere Module in dieselbe Station ausweichen.

Bild 6 zeigt unterhalb des Doppelstriches Ladeanweisungen für die Module MOD1
und MOD2, die normalerweise in den Stationen STA1 bzw. STA2 ablaufen sollen;
im Falle einer Prozessorstörung von STA1 (STA1PR) soll MOD1 in STA3 ablaufen,
falls STA3 ebenfalls gestört ist (STA3PR), wird MOD1 nach STA2 verlagert.

Jedes lokale Betriebssystem enthält dazu eine Modulverlagerungstabelle (V-
Tabelle), in die der zentrale Lader beim System-Urstart die in Bild 6 dargestellte Eintragung macht. Weiterhin ist jedes lokale Betriebssystem ständig
über den gesamten Systemstatus informiert und untersucht bei Eintreffen neuer
Statusmeldungen seine V-Tabelle auf erforderliche Reaktionen. Diese bestehen
im selbständigen Start residenter Ersatzmodule (Station 3) oder in einem Aufruf des zentralen Laders, der die angeforderten Module lädt (Station 2), wobei
unter Berücksichtigung der Ladepriorität ein Überladen anderer Module möglich
ist (MOD1 überlädt MOD2 in Station 2). Nach Beseitigung der Störungen stellt
der zentrale Lader den Normalzustand wieder her.
Der LOAD-Teil enthält Anweisungen, die auf die Steuersprachen der einzelnen
Betriebssysteme zurückzuführen sind und prinzipiell mit diesen Steuersprachen
formulierbar wären. Der Grund für die Einführung des LOAD-Teiles auf Sprach-

ebene ist neben der z. Z. noch fehlenden Standardisierung von Betriebssystem-
Steuersprachen vor allem die Notwendigkeit, die zum Sicherheitskonzept des ERS
gehörenden Maßnahmen programmtechnisch geschlossen formulieren zu können und
nicht den wichtigen Teil der Rekonfiguration mit nicht standardisierten Hilfs-
mitteln nachtragen zu müssen.

Der SYSTEM-Teil von PEARL ist im bisher vorliegenden Sprachvorschlag ein rei-
ner Adressenvermittler. Reaktionen auf Störungen der Ein-/Ausgabegeräte und
eine evtl. Ersatzwertbeschaffung sind im PROBLEM-Teil vorzusehen.

Im Rahmen der gerätetechnischen Sicherheitsmaßnahmen des ERS mit räumlich
verteilten Prozessorstationen ist eine große Vielfalt von Möglichkeiten der
Ersatzwertbeschaffung und -ausgabe für gestörte Prozeß-Ein-/Ausgaben vorge-
sehen, die für den Programmierer leicht anwendbar sein sollten. Der PROBLEM-
Teil sollte jedoch mit diesen Aufgaben aus Gründen der Übersichtlichkeit nicht
mehr belastet sein; es liegt nahe, eine konsequente Trennung von Daten-Ein-/
Ausgabe und Datenverarbeitung durchzuführen. Dem trägt der Vorschlag für eine
Erweiterung des PEARL-SYSTEM-Teils auf Bild 7 Rechnung. Wesentlich ist das
Vorhandensein von Fortsetzungszeilen für die Gewinnung oder Ausgabe einer Pro-
zeßinformation, die Möglichkeit, Korrekturangaben zu formulieren (CORR) sowie
einen errechneten Ersatzwert (REP) auszugeben, falls alle vorgesehenen Prozeß-
Ein-/Ausgabegeräte gestört sind.

Der PEARL-SYSTEM-Teil in dieser Fassung ist zu einem eigenständigen Ein-/Aus-
gabeprogramm geworden. Es ist nun leicht möglich, über weitere Schlüsselwörter
Standardoperationen wie Mittelwertbildung, Glättung oder Redundanzreduzierung
im SYSTEM-Teil anzusprechen und den Problemteil dadurch zu entlasten und übersichtlicher zu machen.

Das System zum Übersetzen, Bereitstellen und Laden der Programme zeigt Bild 8.
Der Übersetzer erzeugt eine maschinenunabhängige Zwischensprache MUZ, die über
verschiedene Codegeneratoren - entsprechend dem LOAD-Teil eines jeden Moduls -
in Maschinencode für die angegebenen Prozessorstationen umgesetzt wird. Ein
Binder erzeugt ladefähige, relativ adressierte Phasen, die vom dynamischen
Lader in Abhängigkeit von den LOAD-Angaben, dem Status des Rechnersystems und
evtl. Operatoranweisungen in die Prozessorstationen geladen und den dortigen
lokalen Betriebssystemen übergeben werden. Es wird hier deutlich, daß Änderungen der Gerätetechnik, die in die STATION-Tabelle eingetragen werden (z. B.
Adressenänderungen) bei unveränderten Verarbeitungsalgorithmen allein durch
eine neue Codegenerierung schon berücksichtigt sind. Damit ist die zu Beginn
genannte Forderung nach einfacher Nutzbarkeit neuer Gerätegenerationen erfüllt.

4. Struktur des Betriebssystems

Eine der charakteristischen Eigenschaften von PEARL ist die Formulierung der
Aufrufe von Betriebssystemfunktionen auf der Ebene der Programmiersprache,
also ohne Benutzung einer besonderen Betriebssystem-Steuersprache. Dies bedingt das Vorhandensein der von der Programmiersprache her geforderten Funktionen,ohne jedoch ihre Realisierung festzulegen /5/. Für die Realisierung
der Betriebssystemfunktionen, insbesondere im Hinblick auf mikroprogrammier-
bare Mikroprozessoren, sind drei abgestufte Wege denkbar:

a) Zusammenfassung _aller_ von der Programmiersprache geforderten Betriebssystemfunktionen in einem residenten Betriebssystem.

b) Residentes Betriebssystem enthält von allen Programmen häufig angesprochene
   Funktionen. Spezielle, von wenigen Programmen geforderte Funktionen werden
   als Standardprozeduren in die Programme eingebunden.

c) Zusätzlich zum Fall b) existieren für häufig benutzte, zeitkritische Betriebssystemfunktionen Mikroprogramme, die durch einen speziellen Befehl
   anzusprechen sind.

Der Umfang einer Realisierung des Betriebssystems nach a) wird in der Regel
den Einsatz auf den Mikroprozessorstationen des hier behandelten ERS verbie-
ten. Die Realisierung nach b), ggf. unterstützt durch mikroprogrammierte Funktionen, gestattet eine flexible und optimierbare Auslegung des Betriebssystems
für die einzelnen Prozessorstationen unter Berücksichtigung der jeweiligen Automatisierungsaufgabe.

Das Betriebssystem für das hier vorgestellte ERS gliedert sich in drei Teile,
die lokalen Betriebssysteme, das zentrale Betriebssystem und das Warten-Betriebssystem (Bild 9). Die lokalen Betriebssysteme enthalten alle Funktionen für den
Ablauf der Prozeßprogramme sowie für die Kommunikation über das Sammelleitungssystem. Sie sind in der Lage, bei Ausfall der Verbindung zur Sammelleitung die
betroffene Station im Inselbetrieb weiterzuführen, ggf. mit verringerter Lei-
stung.

Die problemangepaßte Generierung eines residenten lokalen Betriebssystems ein-
schließlich evtl. vorteilhafter Mikroprogramme kann mit Hilfe der nach dem
Schlüsselwort OS im STATION-Teil gemachten Angaben (siehe Bild 5) erfolgen.
Verwendet der Programmierer Sprachelemente, die weitere, in den für den Ablauf
eines Programms vorgesehenen Prozessorstationen (LOAD-Teil) nicht residente
Betriebssystemfunktionen ansprechen, so werden diese Funktionen durch vom
Binder eingebundene Standardprozeduren realisiert.

Das zentrale Betriebssystem enthält neben den Funktionen für die Prozeßführung
(lokales Betriebssystem) Funktionen für die Programmerstellung, den Systemstart

(Urstart) und einige zentrale Hilfsfunktionen. Es ist in einer der größeren
Stationen des ERS vorhanden, die auch über Massenspeicher und weitere Standardperipherie verfügt. Die zentralen Hilfsfunktionen, z. B. der dynamische Lader,
sind so ausgelegt, daß bei Ausfall der "zentralen" Prozessorstation die Lei-
stung des gesamten ERS zwar zurückgeht aber nicht völlig zusammenbricht.

Das Warten-Betriebssystem dient über ein besonderes Bildschirmsystem der Kommunikation zwischen Mensch, Rechnersystem und technischem Prozeß.

Das im Rahmen des erwähnten Forschungsvorhabens zu realisierende System besteht
aus zwei Prozessorstationen für die reine Prozeßführung; hier werden Mikroprozessoren - z. B. vom Typ INTEL 3000 - eingesetzt. Die "zentrale" Prozessorstation wird durch einen Rechner DP 1000 realisiert, während die Warten-Prozessor-
station ein Ein-/Ausgabe-Farbbildschirmsystem mit dem Rechner Siemens 310 sein
wird.

Für das zentrale Betriebssystem wird ein Standard-Echtzeitbetriebssystem zum
Einsatz kommen, erweitert um die erwähnten Hilfsfunktionen. Das lokale Betriebssystem werden wir, unter Anlehnung an vorhandene Konzepte und laufende Arbeiten
zur aufgabenadaptiven Betriebssystemgenerierung, selbst realisieren.

Literatur:

/1/ Syrbe, M.: Höhere Zuverlässigkeit von Prozeßrechnersystemen und niedrigere
    Peripheriekosten durch verteilte Mikroprozessoren. Regelungstechnik 1974,
    Heft 9, S. 264 - 268.

/2/ Heger, D.: Konstruktion von Prozeßrechnersystemen mit verteilten Mikropro-
    zessoren. IITB-Mitteilungen 1974, S. 2 - 8.

/3/ Eichenauer, B. et al.: PEARL, eine prozeß- und experimentorientierte Pro-
    grammiersprache. Angewandte Informatik 1973, Heft 9, S. 363 - 372.

/4/ BBC-PEARL-Subset Prozeß-Automatisierungs-Sprache, Sprachbeschreibung. BBC,
    Mannheim, D GEG 31003 D.

/5/ Bösmann, H., Tarabout, A.: Der Kern eines allgemeinen PEARL-Betriebssystems.
    Fachtagung Prozeßrechner 1974. Lecture Notes in Computer Science Band 12,
    S. 528 - 543, Springer-Verlag

Dieser Beitrag enthält Ergebnisse aus einem Forschungs- und Entwicklungsvorha-
ben "Echtzeitrechnersystem mit verteilten Mikroprozessoren" (GMD-081 5604 75)
des BMFT.

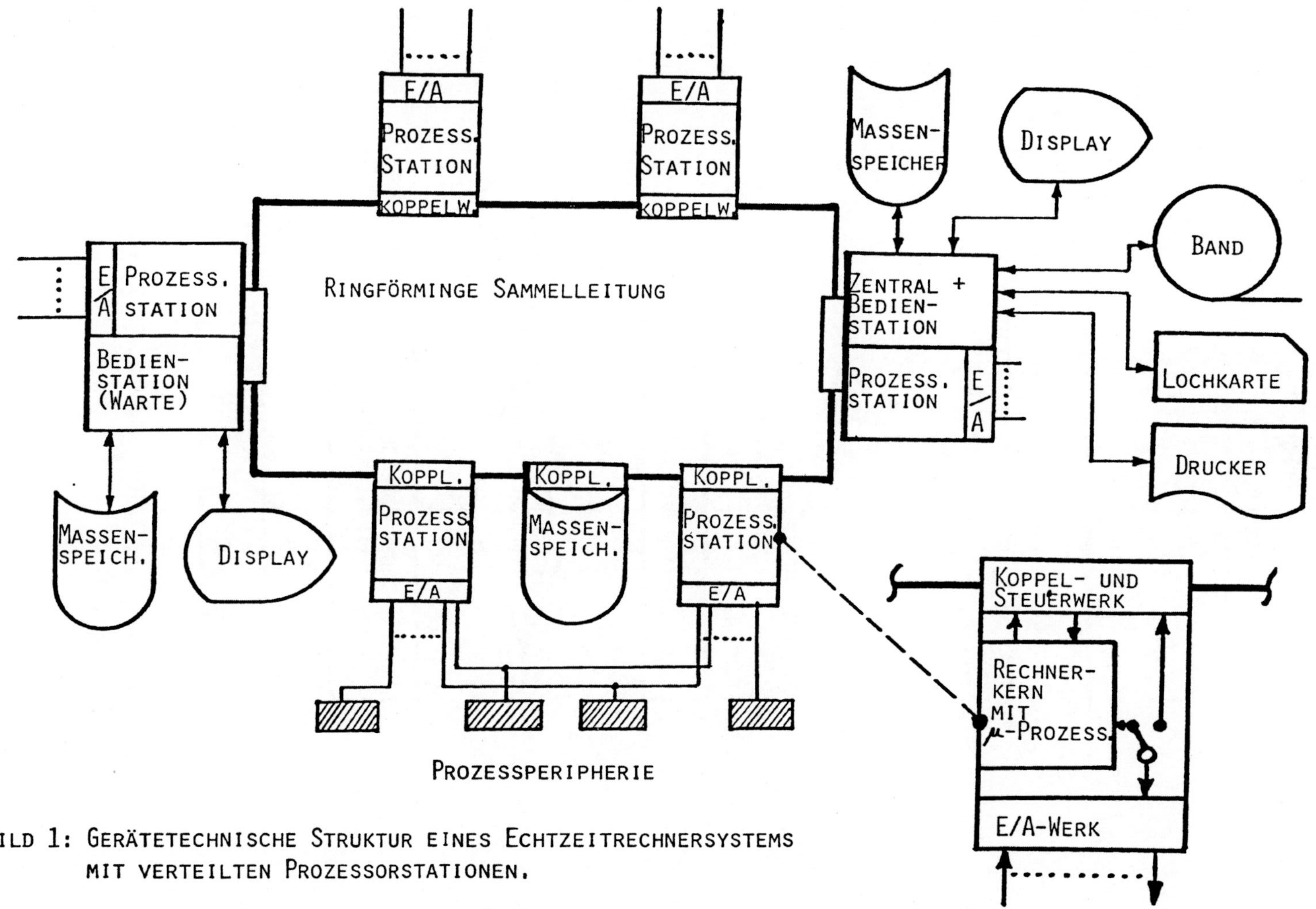

BILD 1: GERÄTETECHNISCHE STRUKTUR EINES ECHTZEITRECHNERSYSTEMS MIT VERTEILTEN PROZESSORSTATIONEN.

GLOBALE ADRESSIERUNG IM RÄUMLICH
VERTEILTEN RECHNERSYSTEM

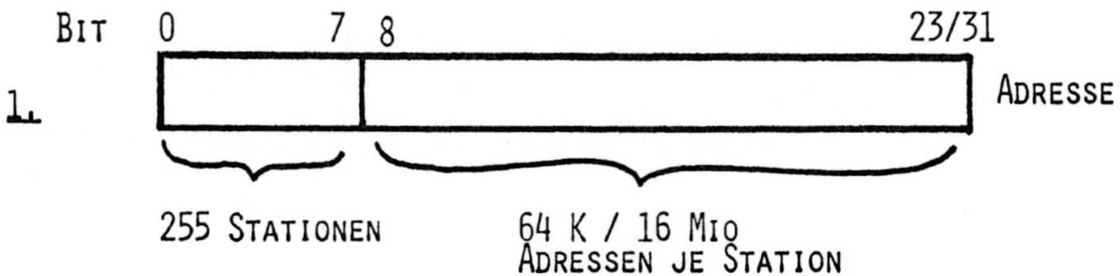

1.

2.   OBERE ⎫ GLOBALE ADRESSGRENZE JE STATION
      UNTERE ⎭ ZUGETEILT UND GESPEICHERT
      ADRESSRECHNUNG:

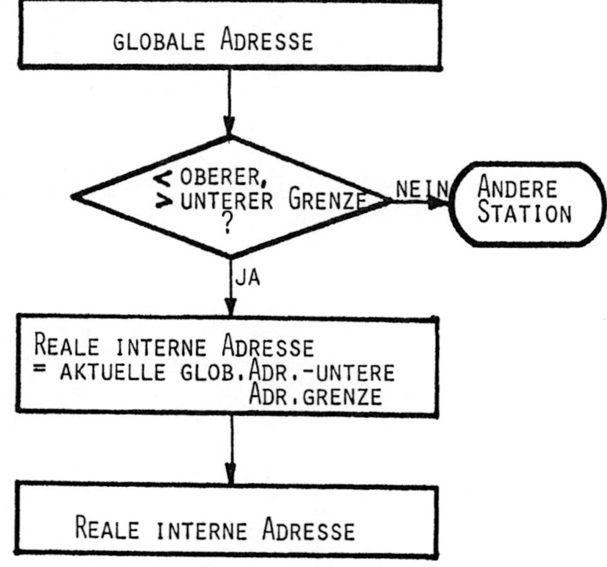

BILD 2: GLOBALE ADRESSIERUNG IM RÄUMLICH VERTEILTEN
RECHNERSYSTEM.

		Wert	1	2	3	4	5	6	Bewertungskriterium
			6	5	4	3	2	1	Gewichtsfaktor
Echtzeitprogrammier-sprachen	PEARL	70	++	+	0	++	++	+	
	RT-FORTRAN	53	0	+	0	+	+	+	
Deskriptive, problem-orientierte Sprachen	ANAGOL	64	+	++	−	++	++	0	
	PROSPRO	64	+	++	−	++	++	0	
Operative Spezialspr.	APT	53	0	+	(−)/0	+	+	+	
Allgem. algorithmische operative Sprachen	FORTRAN	53	0	+	0	+	+	+	
	PL/1	53	0	+	0	+	+	+	
	COBOL	57	0	+	+	+	++	−	
	ALGOL	56	0	+	+	+	+	0	
Höhere Sprachen									
Maschinenorientierte Sprachen	ASSEMBLER	26	−	−	−	0	−	(+)/+	
Maschinensprachen	MASCH.CODE	13	−	−	−	−	−	++	

Bewertungskriterien:

1. Open ended design
2. Wenig Kenntnisse über Rechner-gerätetechnik und rechnerinterne Abläufe nötig.
3. Portabilität
4. Wirtschaftliche Programmerstel-lung (Fehlerarme Programmierung, wenig Testaufwand).
5. Gute Eigendokumentation
6. Effizienz der ablauffähigen Programme

Bewertung: Punktzahl

++	Gut erfüllt	4
+	Erfüllt	3
0	Indifferent	2
−	Schlecht erfüllt	1
−−	Nicht erfüllt	0

Bild 3: Wertanalytischer Vergleich verschiedener Programmierungs-hilfsmittel

Prozess-FORTRAN (IBM 1800, MPX)

HAUPTPROGRAMM

```
        ⋮
   CALL REPET (INOUT,15,3)
        ⋮
UNTERPROGRAMM INOUT:
   SUBROUTINE INOUT
   DIMENSION IN (12), IOUT (12)
C      EIN-AUSGABE ADRESSEN
       IN(11) = 67
       IOUT (11) = 126
        ⋮
   CALL DINP (IN)
        ⋮
   I1 = ISRL (IN(12),4)
   I2 = ISRL (IN(12),8)
   IOUT(12) = IAND (I1,I2)
   IOUT(12) = IAND (IOUT(12), IMASK)
   CALL DAOP (IOUT)
        ⋮
```

EINGANGSMUSTER   IN (12)

| 0110 | 1011 | 1110 | 0010 |

SIG2   SIG1

AUSGANGSMUSTER   IOUT (12)

| 0 | | 0 | 1010 |

OUTBIT

PEARL (PAS2 VON BBC)

```
MODULE;
SYSTEM;
DEVADDR DI1005   =   1024;
SIG1    BIT(4):  -> DI1005*8
SIG2    BIT(4):  -> DI1005*4
DEVADDR DO1006   =   2048
OUTBIT  BIT(4): <- DO1006*12
SYSEND;


PROBLEM
MAIN: TASK MAIN;
        ⋮
EVERY 3 SEC ACTIVATE INOUT;
        ⋮
INOUT: TASK

DCL(SIG1, SIG2) DEVICE;
DCL I1 BIT(4), I2 (BIT(4), IOUT BIT(4);
TAKE SIG1 INTO I1;
TAKE SIG2 INTO I2;
IOUT = I1 & I2;
SEND: OUTBIT FROM IOUT
PROBEND;
MODEND;
```

BILD 4: VERGLEICH VON PROZESS-FORTRAN UND PEARL ANHAND EINES BEISPIELS

```
STATION;

NAME = STATIONSNAME;

KEY  = UNTERE GLOBALE ADRESSGRENZE, OBERE GLOBALE ADRESSGRENZE;

TYPE = STATIONSTYPE;

STATEADR = GLOBALE ADRESSE DER STATIONSSTATUSINFORMATION;

STATEID  = BEZEICHNER FÜR STATUSCODES

DEVICEn  = NAME,

             DEVADR: (GLOBALE BEFEHLS-, DATEN-, STATUS-, INTERRUPT-
                      ADRESSEN),

             DRIVER: (EXTERN-REFERENZEN DES GERÄTETREIBERPROGRAMMS),

             CHANID: KANALBEZEICHNER,

             BITID:  BITBEZEICHNER,

             MODE:   MODE-BEZEICHNER;

OSRES    = ANGABE DER RESIDENTEN BETRIEBSSYSTEMFUNKTIONEN;

OSPROC   = ANGABE DER ÜBER EINGEBUNDENE PROZEDUREN ANSPRECHBAREN
           BETRIEBSSYSTEMFUNKTIONEN;

OSMICRO  = ANGABE DER ALS MIKROPROGRAMM RESIDENTEN BETRIEBS-
           SYSTEMFUNKTIONEN;

STAEND;

MODULE LIB NAME;

LOAD;

NORMAL TO STATIONSNAME PRIO PGZ
       AND STATIONSNAME PRIO PGZ    ;

STATE    = STATUSBEZEICHNER
             TO STATIONSNAME PRIO PGZ   RES ;

/* STATE-ANWEISUNGEN SIND BELIEBIG OFT ZUGELASSEN */

LODEND;
```

BILD 5: STATIONSBESCHREIBUNG UND LADEANWEISUNGEN

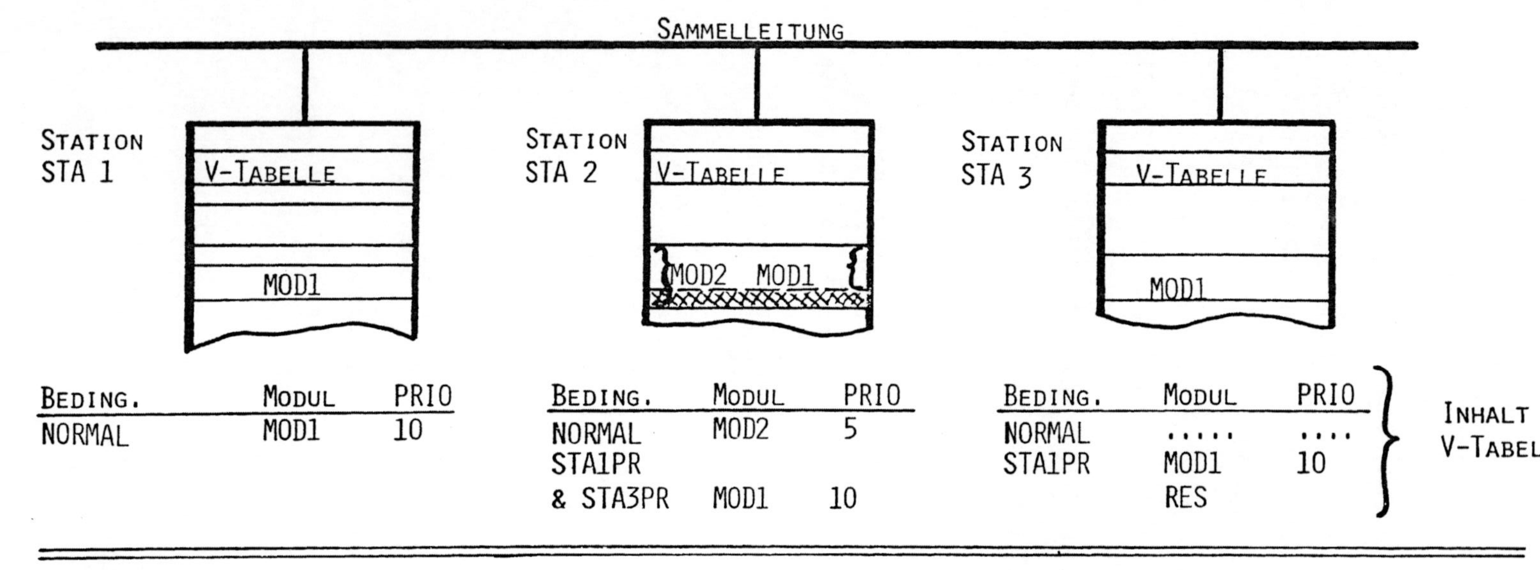

BILD 6: AUSFÜHRUNG VON LADEANWEISUNGEN

SYSTEM:

NAME FÜR

PROZESSVARIABLE
$: \left\{ \begin{array}{c} \rightarrow \\ \leftrightarrow \\ \leftarrow \end{array} \right\}$
GERÄTENAME, KANAL- ODER BITBEZEICHNER,

MODE = BEZEICHNER, STATE = NAME FÜR

STATUSINFORM.,

/* 1. ALTERNATIVE */

$\left\{ \begin{array}{c} \rightarrow \\ \leftrightarrow \\ \leftarrow \end{array} \right\}$
GERÄTENAME, KANAL- ODER BITBEZEICHNER,

MODE = BEZEICHNER, STATE = NAME FÜR

STATUSINFORM.,

$\left[\text{CORR} = \left\{ \text{AUSDRUCK/PROC:NAME} \right\}, \right]$

/* WEITERE ALTERNATIVEN, FALLS GERÄTETECHNISCH

SINNVOLL */

$\text{REP} = \left\{ \text{WERT/PROC:NAME/TASK:NAME} \right\},$

$\left[\text{SPEC} = \text{GLAET (PARAMETER),} \right.$

$\vdots$

$\left. \text{REDØ (PARAMETER)} \right];$

SYSEND;

BILD 7: SYSTEMTEIL

PROGRAMMÜBERSETZUNG,
PROGRAMMBEREITSTELLUNG

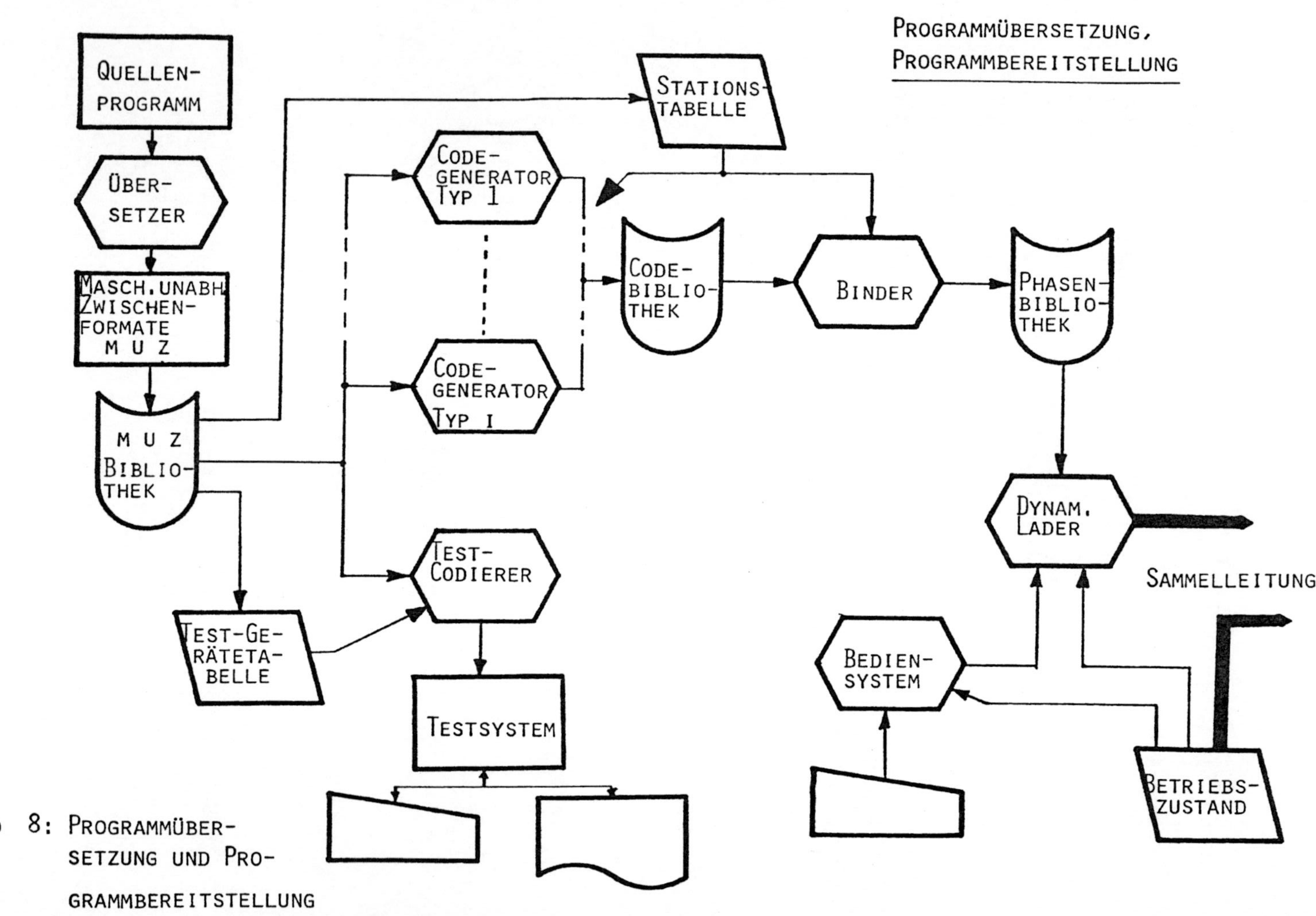

BILD 8: PROGRAMMÜBER-SETZUNG UND PRO-GRAMMBEREITSTELLUNG

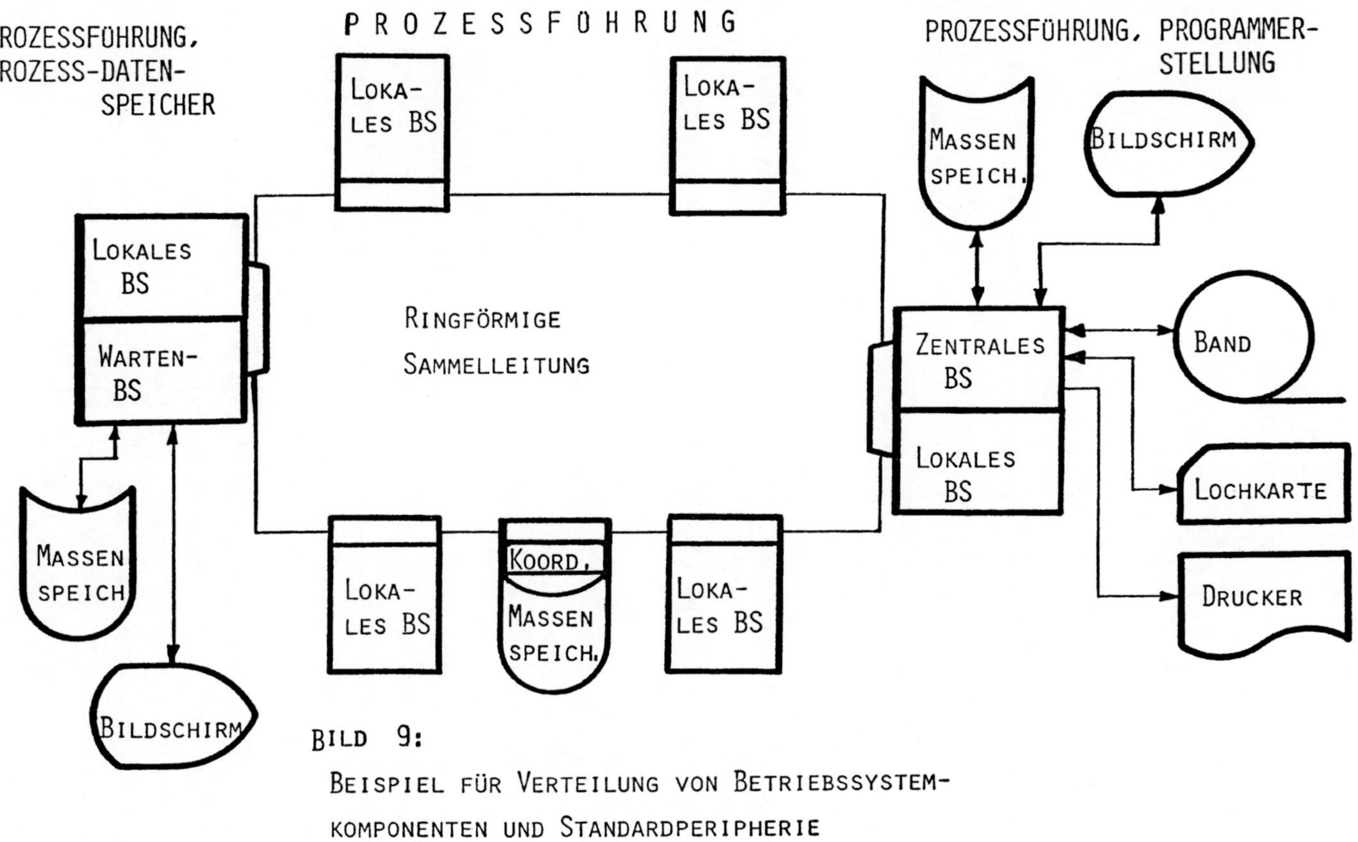

BILD 9:

BEISPIEL FÜR VERTEILUNG VON BETRIEBSSYSTEM-KOMPONENTEN UND STANDARDPERIPHERIE

PROGRAMMING-IN-THE-LARGE

VERSUS

PROGRAMMING-IN-THE-SMALL

F. L. DEREMER

H. H. KRON

Abstract

We distinguish the activity of writing large programs from that of
writing small ones. By large programs we mean systems consisting of
many small programs ("modules") written by different people, possibly
in different languages.

We need languages for programming-in-the-small, i.e. languages not un-
like the common programming languages, for writing modules. We also
need a "module interconnection language" for knitting those modules
together, and for providing an overview that formally records the in-
tent of the programmers and that can be checked for consistency.

1. Introduction

Programming a large system in any typical programming language available today is an exercise in obscuration. We work hard at discovering
the inherent structure in a problem and then structuring our solution
in a compatible way. Research into "structured programming" (Dijkstra
1972) tells us that this approach will lead to readable, provable, and
modifiable solutions. However, current languages discourage the accu-
rate recording of the overall solution structure; they force us to
write programs in which we are so preoccupied with the trees that we
lose sight of the forest, as do the readers of our programs!

Let us refer to typical languages as "languages for programming-in-the-
small" (LPSs). Let us use the term "module" to refer to a segment of
LPS code defining one or more named "resources". Each resource is a
variable, constant, procedure, data structure, class, or whatever is
definable in the LPS. Preferably a module is one to a few pages long
and is easily comprehensible by a single person who understands the in-

---

Work reported herein was supported in part by the National Science
Foundation via grant number GJ 36339.

tended environment and function of the module.

We argue that structuring a large collection of modules to form a "system" is an essentially distinct and different intellectual activity from that of constructing the individual modules. Correspondingly, we believe that essentially distinct and different languages should be used for the two activities, rather than that existing constructs for programming-in-the-small should be overextended. We refer to a language for describing system structure as a "module interconnection language" (MIL); it is one necessity for supporting programming-in-the-large.

System design. Modularization helps in finding reliable solutions to complex problems by applying the traditional method of "divide and conquer". Programming-in-the-large should be recognized as a separate activity that relies, as heavily as does programming-in-the-small, on a language providing abstraction, structure, and style. An MIL must encourage the structuring of one level at a time, since we humans do not usually deal effectively with several levels simultaneously. Given a job, a programmer should be able to switch to the role of chief programmer (Mills 1970) for his subtask, assigning subproblems to his assistant programmers via an MIL program, just as he was given his job assignment.

That current languages fail to support the global task of composing large systems was well argued by Wulf and Shaw in their paper "Global variables considered harmful" (Wulf 1973). Improvements have been suggested (Clark 1971, White 1972, George 1973, Ichbiah 1974); we believe that some of the mechanisms proposed were appropriate, but that they were inappropriately placed in the LPS.

Programming. The results of the system design phase must be communicated to and among the members of the programming team. Such communication concerns, among other things, the position of each module in the system hierarchy, the resources each module must provide, and the access rights with which each module is endowed. It is unreasonable to expect that this information can be reliably transmitted via anything but a formal language, or enforced by anything less than a rigorous compiling system.

The MIL must include facilities for specifying and enforcing "module disconnectivity" via information hiding (Parnas 1971), establishing layers of virtual machines (Dijkstra 1972), closing off subsystems, etc. The lack of such facilities invites undisciplined or even unsocial programming, as shown by one of Weinberg's case studies (Weinberg 1971, pp. 71-75).

<u>Compiling</u>. Presumably, an MIL does not provide any ways of specifying
the type of a resource or of defining language extensions. Rather, it is
used to specify <u>paths</u> for transmitting relevant information from one
module to another during compilation. Such paths may be defined for any
named entity that has its defining and applied occurences distributed
over different LPS modules. It is assumed that the total LPS + MIL
compiling system will do as much bookkeeping as necessary to perform
all static type checking as soon as the relevant information is available. This will require a nontrivial file system so that the compiler
may keep summaries of each module and its external connections for use
in subsequent compilations and recompilations. A modification of
Liskov's "description units" (Liskov 1974) seems to be well-suited
for such bookkeeping.

<u>Linking</u>. One may regard an MIL as being a higher-level language for
specifying how a "linker" is to prepare for loading a program comprising
separately compiled segments (Presser 1972). Roughly, the linker must
resolve static references to external names, i.e. names external to each
separately compiled module. A distinction, however, is that we do not
expect the linkage to happen after compilation but rather as part of it.

Where an MIL is not available, module interconnectivity information is
usually buried partly in the modules, partly in the linkage-editor instructions, and partly in the informal documentation of the project.
Each of these areas is ill-suited to express interconnectivity, and the
smearing of the information over disjoint media is highly unreliable.

<u>Testing and proving</u>. A substantial amount of testing is done by indepen-
dently exercising each module. However, there is a gap between testing
individual modules and testing the system as a whole. Performing only
these two kinds of tests involves too big a jump in levels of abstraction
and results in a gap of confidence. MILs that are designed around a
hierarchical subsystem concept support a more flexible and gradual
bottom-up development. Working with small modules, we may also find it
less prohibitive to prove their correctness ("proving-in-the-small").
Then, we may be able to prove on the MIL level that the correct modules
work together correctly ("proving-in-the-large").

<u>Maintenance and modification</u>. Each connection and dependency between
modules is durably documented in the MIL program. No link between modules
can be left out of the documentation and be forgotten -- the compiling
system will complain. Thus, system modifications are more likely to be
successful. Furthermore, the MIL makes it easy to replace modules and/or

subsystems; and the compiler can support modifications by providing
graphs of system structure, access rights, and dependencies. Finally,
the modified system structure can be automatically checked for consistency.

2. The Semantics of MIL 75

We now present a particular language, MIL 75, for describing inter-
connections among modules. The universe of discourse of MIL 75 consists
of names: the names of resources originating in the modules, the names
of the modules themselves, and the names of subsystems or systems
containing these modules. An MIL 75 program addresses the question of
who knows whom within a collection of modules; it defines the scopes of
definition of names across module and subsystem boundaries.

We define the language by starting with a simple algebraic structure
(a tree) and refining it stepwise. Simultaneously, the language concepts
are motivated and illustrated by the stepwise development of the subsystem "Thrm_prover" of a theorem-proving program written by Professor
Sharon Sickel at the University of California, Santa Cruz.

2.1 System hierarchy

We concentrate on the overall system structure first. MIL 75 imposes a
tree structure on the system under construction. This "system tree" expresses nothing but the hierarchical relation between systems and subsystems; for now, we do not contemplate modules or resources at all.
This will happen later, possibly forcing us to refine the system tree
during the development of an actual project. Figure 1 shows the tree of
the system Thrm_prover.

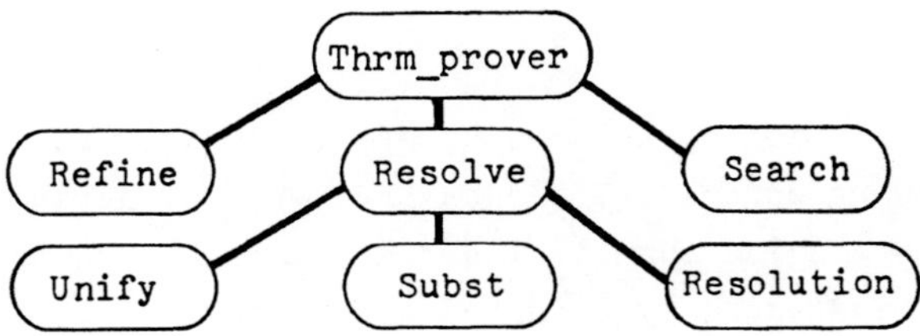

Figure 1. A sample system tree.

Our guideline for the rough decomposition of the project into a tree is
that each node should finally encompass an intellectually manageable
part of the whole problem, assuming that adequate support is provided
by the other nodes. Conceptually, there is for each subsystem (i.e.
system tree node) a designer who is responsible for the programming and

testing associated with this node, and who supervises the designers of
its children.

Definition: A "system tree" is a triple $T = (S, Pa, t)$ where
(1) S is a finite set of "subsystems" or "system tree nodes";
(2) t is a distinguished member of S called the "system" or "root";
(3) Pa: $(S-\{t\}) \rightarrow S$ is a total function, called the "parent function",
     such that for any $s_1 \in S$ $(s \neq t)$ there is a sequence $s_1, s_2, \ldots s_k$
     $(k \geq 1)$ with $s_k = t$ and $Pa(s_i) = s_{i+1}$ $(1 \leq i < k)$.
     The terms "child", "sibling", etc. are defined in the obvious way.

When pre-existing subsystems are used in a new system, the uniqueness
of the subsystem names may be difficult to achieve. Therefore, the
syntax of MIL 75 allows "qualified names" (e.g. Resolve.Unify) for un-
ambiguity and "aliases" for renaming.

2.2 Provided and derived resources

The next decisions to be made presumably concern the function of each
subsystem. As the function of a subsystem can be described in terms of
the resources it uses and provides, we now consider the association of
resources with system tree nodes (i.e. subsystems). Ultimately, resources
will originate in the LPS modules. Pursuing a top-down approach, however,
the designer of any subsystem p states the set of resources _provided_
by p. Then, the question is where these resources come from. Some might
originate in a module later to be attached to the node p, and thus are
the direct responsibility of the designer of p. All other resources
must come from the children of p. Therefore, the designer of p states
the set of resources each child q of p _must_ _provide_. This statement
specifies the desired function of q, provided that all resources are
adequately specified.

As seen from the node p, the resources it demands from its children are
called "derived resources". The subsystem p may derive resources from
a child q and provide them to its own parent, in turn. In diagrams,
such a case is indicated by a dotted arrow from q to p (see Fig. 2
below; the dotted arrow indicates that some resources provided by Search
are also provided by Thrm_prover).

Definition: A "resource-augmented system tree" is a quadruple
$T_R = (T, R, Pr, Mp)$ where
(1) $T = (S, Pa, t)$ is a system tree;
(2) R is a finite set of "resources";
(3) Pr: $S \rightarrow 2^R$ is a total function (2^R is the powerset of R);

we say that "s provides r" if $r \in Pr(s)$;

(4) Mp: $S \rightarrow 2^R$ is a total function;

we say that "s must provide r" if $r \in Mp(s)$;

(5) $Mp(s) \subseteq Pr(s)$ for all $s \in S$; and

(6) $Mp(p) \cap Mp(n) = \phi$ for all pairs of siblings $p, n \in S$.

Naturally, it is a task of the compiling system to check that condition (5) is satisfied, i.e. that the bottom-up flow of derived resources is consistent. We allow set inclusion in (5) for facilitating the use of pre-existing subsystems in a new parent system.

2.3 Accessibility

The next refinement is concerned with the interaction between siblings. The power and the responsibility to establish channels for transmitting names of resources between siblings rests solely with their parent. Here we follow Parnas's policy of a "designer controlled information distribution" (Parnas 1971). Consider Figure 2, where the "sibling accessibility links" are drawn as solid arrows between siblings.

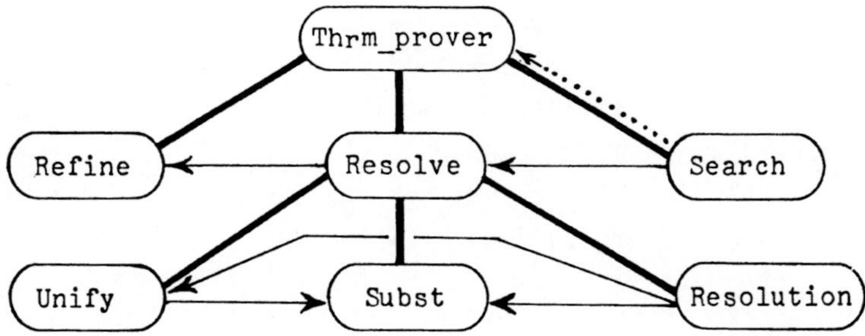

Figure 2. Sibling accessibility links.

These links do not represent individual connections between modules and resources. Rather, they allow the sibling at the tail of the arrow to access any resource provided by the sibling at the arrow head. In Figure 2, for example, Search has access to (any resource provided by) Resolve. For reliability reasons, access rights between siblings are not transitive; for instance, Search has no access to Refine. Also, the children of Resolve are invisible to Search. Thus, Search can access a resource provided by Unify if and only if this resource is also provided by Resolve. In short, the substructure of one sibling is not apparent to another. The accessibility links between a set of siblings may form any directed graph. Thus, the parent may allow mutual recursion between resources (e.g. procedures, coroutines, or data structures) of its children.

<u>Inherited access</u>. Typically, the access rights granted to a subsystem are also useful for most of its children. In MIL 75, a child inherits <u>by default</u> all access rights that have been granted to its parent. In Figure 2, Resolution inherits access to its "uncle" Refine by default. Alternatively, any parent may "will" a child nothing or an explicitly specified subset of its own access rights, thus formally asserting that the child and its descendants cannot exploit or disturb certain resources. If a child is to be partially disinherited, the parent must list all access rights left to the child. Thus, if the parent later obtains additional access rights, they do not inadvertently shine through to the less privileged child.

<u>Derived access</u>. Naturally, a parent has access to the resources that it demands from any of its children. However, all descendants of its children are invisible to the parent. Thus, we can build layers of virtual machines with the most privileged subsystems at the bottom.

<u>Definition</u>: An "access-augmented system tree" is a triple
$T_A = (T, Sac, Iac)$ where
(1) $T = (S, Pa, t)$ is a system tree;
(2) Sac and Iac are binary relations on $S-\{t\}$;
(3) $p\ Sac\ q$ ("p has sibling-access to q") implies that p and q are siblings;
(4) $p\ Iac\ q$ ("p inherits access to q") implies that either $Pa(p)\ Sac\ q$ or $Pa(p)\ Iac\ q$.

<u>Definition</u>: A subsystem p "has access to" a subsystem q iff either $p\ Sac\ q$ or $p\ Iac\ q$ or $p = Pa(q)$.

<u>2.4 Module placement</u>
We proceed to place modules into the system tree. With each node, we may associate at most one LPS module, as indicated by the following.
(1)   With each leaf of the system tree, we must associate a module.
(2)   A module associated with a non-leaf s may act as a driver or monitor of the subsystem s. Such a "root module of s" must define all resources in $Pr(s)$ that are not derived from the children of s.
(3)   A non-leaf without root module serves as a structural entity only.
Different modules might be programmed in different LPSs. The site of the modules is primarily determined by their intellectual manageability, vis-a-vis programming-in-the-small. In Figure 3, modules are denoted by the boxes attached to the system tree nodes.

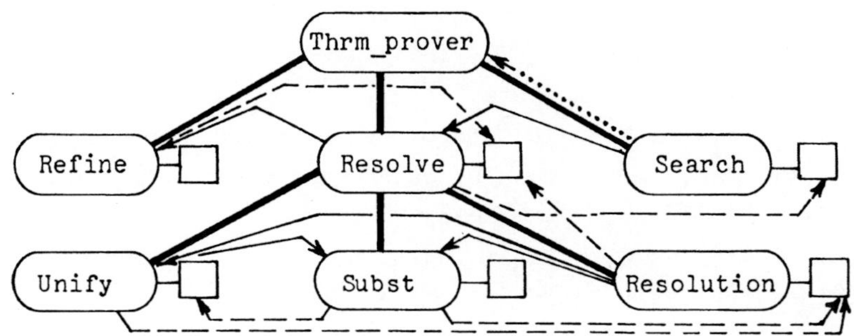

Figure 3. Module placement and usage links.

Origin and usage of resources. For each module m at a node s, there
must be two statements in the MIL 75 program:
(1)   the statement of origin, a list of the resources defined in m; and
(2)   the statement of usage, a list of the resources that are used,
      but not defined, in m.
For clarity, the latter statement is divided into a list of the "derived resources" provided by the children of s, and a list of all
others, i.e. those obtained through sibling or inherited access.

The compiling system must check that the actual usage of resources by
module m conforms to the access rights granted to subsystem s, and
that any resource provided by s either comes from a child of s or
originates in m. No subsystem may provide a resource that is obtained
through sibling access or inherited access; such a flow of resources
would have deleterious effects on reliability.

Usage links. The compiling system can now derive and graphically display
the "usage links", drawn as dashed arrows in Figure 3 above. If a subsystem n has access to a subsystem p, and the module m attached to
n uses a resource provided by p, then a usage link points from the
node p to the module m. Figure 4 shows the three possible cases.
Recall that the resources provided by p might not originate in the
module attached to p, if there is one at all. However, this is irrelevant to, and hidden from, the designer of n and m.

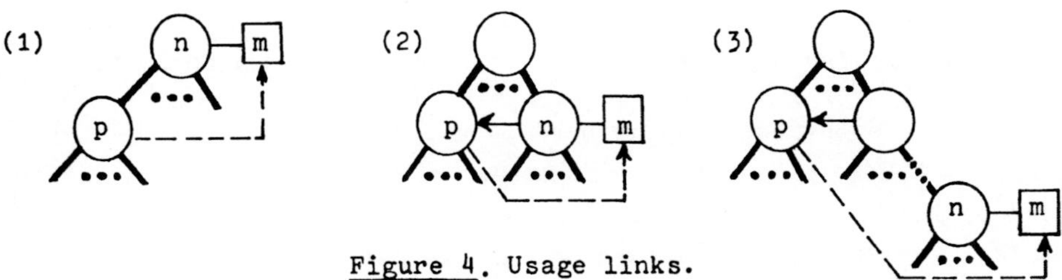

Figure 4. Usage links.

<u>Definition</u>: A "module interconnection structure" is a tuple
T_M = (T, T_R, T_A, M, Mod, Or, Ud, Und)   where
(1)   T = (S, Pa, t)   is a system tree,
      T_R = (T, R, Pr, Mp)   is a resource-augmented system tree, and
      T_A = (T, Sac, Iac)   is an access-augmented system tree;
(2)   M   is a finite set of "modules";
(3)   Mod: S → M   is a partial, injective function, such that Mod(s) is
      defined for every leaf s of the system tree;
(4)   Or, Ud, and Und   are total functions   S → 2^R, such that   Or(s) =
      Ud(s) = Und(s) = ϕ if   Mod(s)   is undefined; we say that
      r ε Or(s)   is a resource "originating in Mod(s)",
      r ε Ud(s)   is a "derived resource used in Mod(s)", and
      r ε Und(s) is a "non-derived resource used in Mod(s)";
(5)   for all   p, n ε S: Or(p) ∩ Or(n) = ϕ;
(6)   if we define for all   p ε S   the set of "derived resources"
      D(p) = { r ε R | Pa(q) = p   and   r ε Mp(q)   for some   q ε S },
      then for all   p ε S:
(7)   Pr(p) ⊆ Or(p) ∪ D(p),
(8)   Ud(p) ⊆ D(p), and
(9)   r ε Und(p)   implies   ((p Sac n   or   p Iac n) and r ε Mp(n)) for
      some   n ε S.

3. Programming in MIL 75

A complete MIL 75 program consists of a sequence of one-level "system
descriptions". Each is assumed to be (re-)compilable alone, or with
others. Put together, they can be translated into a module interconnection structure T_M. A system description for a subsystem p consists
of statements specifying
(1)   p, the designer's name, and a relevant date (etc.);
(2)   Pr(p);
(3)   Mod(p), Or(p), Ud(p), and Und(p);
(4)   for each child   q   of   p:
(4.1)   q, Mp(q), and   { n ε S | q Sac n };   and
(4.2)   the set   Will = { n ε S | q Iac n } either by enumeration
        (such that   Will ⊆ I) or by default (then Will = I), where
        I = { n ε S | p Iac n   or   p Sac n }.
Phrases specifying empty sets in (3) and (4) above may be omitted.

<u>Outlook</u>. It is obvious that we need languages for programming-in-the-
large. An MIL is but a first approximation to such a language, since it
does not include facilities for the specification of the <u>function</u> of
modules. An MIL may be regarded as only a "language feature" in the

sense of Hoare (Hoare 1973). It seems, however, powerful enough to increase software reliability, even in the absence of other needed extensions to current languages.

Acknowledgements

We are grateful to Frank Frazier, Nico Habermann, Jim Horning, Jean Ichbiah, Bernard Lorho, Bill McKeeman, Doug Michels, Dan Ross, Sharon Sickel, and Bill Wulf for many helpful comments and stimulating discussions.

References

Clark, B.L., and Horning, J.J. "The system language for project SUE."
    SIGPLAN Notices 6, 9 (October 1971).

Dijkstra, E.W. "Notes on structured programming." In: Dahl, O.J.,
    Dijkstra, E.W., and Hoare, C.A.W. "Structured Programming."
    Academic Press, London, New York, 1972.

George, J.E., and Sager, G.R. "Variables--Bindings and protection."
    SIGPLAN Notices 8, 12 (December 1973).

Hoare, C.A.R. "Hints on programming language design." Memo AIM-224,
    Computer Science Dept., Stanford University (1973). Also in:
    Proc. Symposium on Principles of Programming Languages, Boston, 1973.

Ichbiah, J.D. "Visibility and separate compilations." Proc. of IFIP
    WG 2.4, La Grande Motte, France (May 1974).

Liskov, B.H., and Zilles, S. "Programming with abstract data types."
    Proc. Symposium on Very High Level Languages, SIGPLAN Notices 9, 4
    (April 1974).

Mills, H.D. "Chief programmer teams: Techniques and procedures." IBM
    Internal Report (January 1970).

Parnas, D.L. "Information distribution aspects of design methodology."
    Technical Report, Dept. Computer Science, Carnegie-Mellon Univ.(1971).

Presser, L., and White, J.R. "Linkers and loaders." ACM Computing Surveys 4, 3 (September 1972).

Weinberg, G.M. "The Psychology of Computer Programming." Van Nostrand
    Reinhold Co., New York, 1971.

White, J.R., and Presser, L. "A tool for enforcing system structure."
    Report CS-11, Dept. of E.E., U. of California, Santa Barbara (1972).

Wulf, W., and Shaw, M. "Global variable considered harmful." SIGPLAN
    Notices 8, 2 (February 1973).

Professor Franklin L. DeRemer   and   Hans H. Kron
Information Sciences, University of California at Santa Cruz,
Santa Cruz, California 95064, USA

EINIGE EIGENSCHAFTEN DER PROGRAMMIERSPRACHE
BALG

Gerhard Goos
Fakultät für Informatik der Universität Karlsruhe

1. Einleitung

Die Programmiersprache BALG [Go75] ist der Versuch eine Systemprogrammiersprache ausgehend von den Charakteristiken höherer Programmiersprachen zu schaffen. Systemprogrammieren ist die Konstruktion von Programm-
systemen, welche den Rahmen, die Umgebung, für die Lösung von Anwendungs-
problemen abgeben (vgl. [Sa71]). Programmiersysteme bauen diese Umgebung
stufenweise auf, indem sie Eigenschaften der zugrundeliegenden Maschine
verdecken und durch neue, "höhere" Konstruktion ersetzen, welche sich
besser als Grundlage für die weitere Programmierung eignen.

Von einer Systemprogrammiersprache wird man daher erwarten, daß sie neben den "üblichen" Ablauf- und Datenstrukturen vor allem Hilfsmittel für
diese stufenweise Schichtung von Programmteilen, für die Modularisierung
und die Kontrolle der Modulschnittstellen anbietet. Solche Hilfsmittel
zur Beherrschung der Programmstruktur unterstützen den Systemprogram-
mierer auch im Hinblick auf den nicht unerheblichen Umfang und die Komplexität seiner Aufgaben, die besondere Anstrengungen auf dem Gebiet der
Programmorganisation erforderlich machen.

Viele bisherige Systemprogrammiersprachen sind als Vorläufer und unter
dem Zeitdruck größerer Systemprogramme, namentlich Betriebssysteme, entstanden (vgl. etwa PL360 [Wi68], PS440 [Go70], System SUE Sprache [CI74]).
Dies hatte zur Folge, daß die Probleme der untersten Schichten von Betriebssystemen: Beherrschung von Spezialbefehlen, namentlich für die
E/A- und Unterbrechungsbehandlung, absolute Adressierung, maschinenab-
hängige Speicherzuteilungsmethoden, fehlendes Laufzeitsystem, usw. im
Vordergrund des Interesses standen. Obwohl bekannt ist, daß Probleme
dieser Art vielleicht 5-10% des gesamten Betriebssystems ausmachen, ver-
drängte doch die Beschäftigung mit diesen Fragen vielfach die Lösung von
Problemen der Programmorganisation, der Sicherung der Integrität von Daten und Programmabläufen und der Bereitstellung höherer sprachlicher
Ausdrucksmittel. Charakteristisch ist die Verwendung typfreier Sprachen,
bei denen wie im Assembler der Typ der Datenobjekte nur implizit aus den
ausgeführten Operationen hervorgeht. Ein anderes Beispiel liefert Burroughs' Implementierungssprache ESPOL [Bu72], ein ALGOL60-Dialekt, in

welchem erst kürzlich die gut ausgebauten E/A-Möglichkeiten des Systems
in der auch dem Anwender verfügbaren Schreibweise zugänglich gemacht
wurden; bis dahin wurde der Schluß gezogen, daß eine Sprache keine prob-
lemorientierte Schreibweise der E/A erlauben könne, wenn in ihr zugleich
die Teile des Betriebssystems geschrieben sind, welche die Ein/Ausgabe
implementieren.

Erfahrungen mit Burroughs-Systemen und mit PASCAL [Wi74] legen schließlich den Versuch nahe, wesentlich mehr Zugriffsbeschränkungen bereits
durch den Übersetzer kontrollieren zu lassen und dadurch die Laufzeit
zu entlasten. Ein wesentliches Hilfsmittel bilden dabei die aus dem
CLASS-Konzept von SIMULA [Da67] hergeleiteten Strukturmoduln, die vor
allem der Definition von Datenstrukturen samt der auf ihnen erklärten
Operationen dienen.

Diese Überlegungen führten zu folgenden Entwicklungszielen für BALG:

- höhere Programmiersprache, in der zusätzlich niedere Spracheigenschaften in speziell gekennzeichneten Programmoduln zugänglich sind;

- Verallgemeinerung des Modulbegriffs zu hierarchisch geschachtelten,
  funktionalen Programmoduln, welche sowohl Strukturmoduln als auch
  Prozeduren einschließen;

- Verallgemeinerung des Variablenbegriffs zu einem Objektbegriff, der
  neben der unbeschränkten Weitergabe der Zugriffsrechte auf das Objekt
  an andere Moduln auch eine eingeschränkte Weitergabe (z.B. nur Lesen
  erlaubt) gestattet;

- Explizite Kontrolle der Schnittstellen zwischen Moduln mit der Möglichkeit, den Zugriff einzuschränken;

- Kellerorientierte Speicherorganisation, welche in vom Programmierer
  gesteuerter Form verschiedene Formen der Freispeicherorganisation
  einschließt.

Zur Erreichung dieser Ziele gehen wir von den Datentypen PASCALs [Wi74]
aus. Die Ablaufsteuerung für sequentielle Abläufe sowie viele Schreibweisen sind ALGOL68 [Wi69] entnommen. Die Steuerung paralleler Abläufe
soll mithilfe von Monitoren [Ho74] erfolgen; Prozesse und Ein/Ausgabe sollen mittels spezieller Strukturmoduln dargestellt werden. Diese Teile fehlen bisher noch; ebenso ist die Bereitstellung der notwendigen Informationen für die Speicherbereinigung durch den Übersetzer noch nicht ganz ge-
klärt.

Wir gehen im folgenden nur auf einige wenige Spracheigenschaften ein,
darunter die Situationsklausel, funktionelle Programmoduln, die Grund-
ideen der Speicherverwaltung und Schnittstellenbeschreibungen. Die Grund-
überlegungen, die dem Objektbegriff zugrundeliegen, wurden in [Go74] er-
klärt.

2. Situationsklauseln

Zu den Abläufen, die mangels besserer Ausdrucksmöglichkeiten in den
meisten Programmiersprachen mit Sprunganweisungen umschrieben werden
müssen, gehört der folgende: Gegeben sei ein Programmstück p, vorzüg-
lich eine Schleife, durch dessen Ausführung man eine der "Situationen"
s_1, ..., s_n erreicht; die Ausführung einer situationsabhängigen Anweisung A_1 oder die Berechnung eines entsprechenden Ausdruckes beendigt
dann die Ausführung von p und führt zum gewünschten Ergebnis. Das ein-
fachste Beispiel eines derartigen Ablaufs ist die sequentielle Suche
mit nachfolgendem Eintrag (zunächst in ALGOL68-Notation):

```
        begin
            for i to n
            do if x = a [i] then index := i; goto gefunden fi
            od;
            index := n := n+1;
            a [index] := x
    gefunden : index
        end
```

Knuth [Ku74] diskutiert zahlreiche Formulierungsmöglichkeiten für dieses
Beispiel. Die eleganteste Formulierung liefert wohl die von Zahn [Za74]
eingeführte Situationsklausel (hier in etwas fortentwickelter Schreibweise):

```
        until gefunden, nicht_gefunden:
            for i to n
            loop if x = [i] then gefunden (i) fi
            repeat;
            nicht_gefunden
on gefunden (int:j) : index := j
on nicht_gefunden : begin index := n := n+1;
                          a [index] := x;
                          index
                    end
end
```

Die "Situationsanweisungen" A_i, welche bei Eintreten einer der Situationen "gefunden" oder "nicht_gefunden" ausgeführt werden sollen, werden hier in prozedurähnlicher Schreibweise formuliert und können auch mit Parametern versehen sein. Aufgefaßt als Ausdruck liefert die Situationsklausel das Ergebnis einer der Anweisungen A_i als Gesamtergebnis.

Situationsklauseln können mit Vorteil auch zum Abfangen impliziter Fehlersituationen eingesetzt werden. BALG kennt eine Reihe von Standard-Fehlersituationen, darunter z.B. overflow und invalid_index, deren Eintreten implizit festgestellt wird (durch Hardware-Reaktion oder durch vom Übersetzer erzeugte Tests). Die Behandlung erfolgt jedoch explizit durch Situationsklauseln wie

```
until overflow :
      Programm
on overflow : A
end .
```

Auch die Schachtelung, welche in verschiedenen Programmteilen unterschiedliche Fehlerbehandlungen erlaubt, ist möglich:

```
until overflow :
      Hauptprogramm 1. Teil;
      until overflow :
          Teilprogramm
      on overflow : A_TP
      end ;
          Hauptprogramm 2. Teil
on overflow : A_HP
end .
```

Schließlich lassen sich Prozeduren und andere Programmoduln so parametrisieren, daß bei Eintreten einer Situation die an der Aufrufstelle gültige Situationsanweisung anstelle der an der Vereinbarungsstelle gültigen Situationsanweisung ausgeführt wird (und damit zugleich der Modul verlassen wird).

3. Funktionale Programmoduln

Für den Begriff Programmodul finden sich verschiedenartige Definitionen, z.B.

- Moduln als getrennt übersetzbare Programmeinheiten,

- Moduln als Programmteile mit "minimalen" Querbezügen,

- Moduln als logisch in sich abgeschlossene und zusammenhängende Programmeinheiten (funktionale Modularität)

Diese Definitionen betrachten entweder nur die äußere Form oder stellen auch inhaltliche Anforderungen. In BALG gehen wir von der dritten Möglichkeit, der funktionalen Modularität aus. Das schließt natürlich nicht aus, daß die resultierenden Moduln zugleich getrennt übersetzbar sind oder Schnittstellen geringeren Umfangs besitzen (vgl. auch [Go74a] für weitere Bemerkungen zum Modulbegriff).

Sprachlich betrachtet ist ein Programmodul entweder eine Prozedur, welche einen einzelnen Algorithmus wiedergibt, oder eine Datenstruktur, eventuell zusammen mit weiteren Prozeduren, welche die Operationen mit dieser Datenstruktur definieren. Letztere Klasse von Moduln nennen wir in BALG Strukturmoduln. Prozeduren in BALG haben die in ALGOL-ähnlichen Sprachen üblichen Eigenschaften; zusätzlich kann verlangt werden, daß eine Prozedur offen anstelle ihres Aufrufs eingebaut wird.

Als Beispiel geben wir die Definition eines Kellers an:

```
external situation : stack_overflow, stack_underflow ; (*externe
                                                  Parameter*)
public proc (type) : push ; (*von außen zugängliche Operationen
                                              und Objekte*)
            proc : pop ;
            proc type : value ;
            const int : depth #
    (*bis hierher geht die Schnittstellenbeschreibung. Jetzt folgt der
      Modul:*)

    module: stack (int : max_depth) type =
        begin
            var array [1:max_depth] type : a
              & int : depth ;
            proc : push (const type : x) =
                if depth ≥ max_depth then stack_overflow
                else depth :+ 1 ; a [depth] := x fi;
            proc : pop =
                if depth ≥ 1 then depth :- 1
                else stack_underflow fi;
            proc : value type =
                if depth ≥ 1 then a [depth]
                else stack_underflow fi;
```

```
    initialize:
         depth := O
     end (*module stack*)
```

Aufrufe von Strukturmoduln sind nur in Form von Strukturvereinbarungen
möglich, z.B.

```
         struct stack (27) real : s
```

Strukturvereinbarungen rufen den angegebenen Strukturmodul auf und hinter-
lassen die Parameter und die im Rumpf vereinbarten lokalen Prozeduren und
Datenobjekte als Datenstruktur. Diese wird durch den definierten Bezeichner benannt und existiert bis zum Verlassen des Blocks, der die Struktur-
vereinbarung enthält. In diesem Zeitraum können Operationen mit der Datenstruktur ausgeführt werden.

Strukturmoduln können mit einem Datentyp parametrisiert werden; im vorliegenden Beispiel ist "type" ein formaler Datentyp, im Aufruf ersetzt
durch den aktuellen Typ real. Mit dieser Parametrisierung wird dem Be-
dürfnis nach "Struktur-Konstruktoren" Rechnung getragen, das sind Strukturmoduln, deren Aufbau weitgehend unabhängig ist vom Typ der Elemente
der resultierenden Datenstrukturen. Der Elementtyp wird daher erst bei
der aktuellen Bildung der Struktur ergänzt. Wie aus dem Beispiel ersichtlich, kann man in einem Modul Objekte eines formalen Datentyps bilden,
zuweisen oder als Prozedurergebnisse abgeben; weitere Operationen sind
nicht zulässig.

Monitore im Sinne von [Ho74] sind Strukturen in einer nicht-sequentiellen
Programmumgebung. Sie lassen zu einer Zeit nur die Ausführung einer Operation zu. Auch andere Typen von Programmoduln wie etwa Koroutinen lassen
sich auf Strukturmoduln zurückführen.

4. Speicherorganisation

Bei der Konzeption von BALG wurde davon ausgegangen, daß nur in beschränk-
tem Maße Speicher absolut adressiert zugeteilt wird. Überwiegend soll
Speicher im Rahmen einer einheitlichen Kellerorganisation vergeben werden. Dieses Prinzip sollte auch aufrechterhalten werden, wenn für kollaterale Prozesse oder für haldenartige Organisation Speicher bereitgestellt werden soll. Die Begrenzung der Lebensdauer von Strukturen auf
den Block, in dem sie geschaffen wurden, und die Festlegung, daß Strukturen nur durch Vereinbarungen geschaffen werden, ist Ausfluß des Keller-
prinzips.

Um haldenähnliche Organisationsformen im Rahmen der Kellerorganisation
bereitzustellen, fassen wir die Halde als eine Datenstruktur auf, die
mithilfe eines entsprechenden Strukturmoduls gebildet wird. (Es könnte
mehrere Halden geben!) Globale Generatoren im Sinne von ALGOL68 werden
zusätzlich mit der Benennung der Halde gekennzeichnet, von der der Speicher bezogen wird. Diese bestimmt auch die Lebensdauer des generierten
Objekts. Auch der Typ von Verweisen auf Objekte in einer solchen Halde
wird zusätzlich mit der Haldenbenennung gekennzeichnet. Diese Regelung
erlaubt bei Verweisen eine sehr einfache Prüfung der Lebensdauerregeln
zur Übersetzungszeit statt -wie in ALGOL68 vielfach nötig- zur Laufzeit.
Die Kennzeichnung globaler Generatoren mit der entsprechenden Halde erlaubt es, den Generator zur Übersetzungszeit umzusetzen in einen Prozeduraufruf einer Speicherzuteilungsprozedur allocate, welche der Halden-
modul zur Verfügung stellen muß. Der Aufruf wird intern mit der Anzahl
von Speichereinheiten (Zellen) parametrisiert, welche für das unterzu-
bringende Objekt benötigt werden. Das Schema eines Haldenmoduls ist dem-
nach:

```
public proc (int) ref cell : allocate #
unsafe module : haldenmodul (int : länge) =
begin
      var array [1:länge] cell Haldenspeicher ; (*der eigentliche
                                        Haldenspeicher*)
      proc : allocate (int : umfang) ref cell =
            (*bringe <umfang> Zellen im Speicher, vorzugsweise im Hal-
            denspeicher, unter. Das Ergebnis des Typs ref cell wird
            extern als Referenz auf ein Objekt des gewünschten Typs
            aufgefaßt.*);
            .
            .
            .

      end
```

Der Aufruf des Haldenspeichers kann durch

```
      struct Haldenmodul (n) : Halde
```

erfolgen. Danach ist im Kontext

```
      var ref halde int : xx
```

die Zuweisung

```
      xx := new halde int
```

mit der Bedeutung

        xx := halde.allocate (<Länge von int>)

möglich. Wie ersichtlich ist der Modul Haldenspeicher primär für die
Speicherzuteilungsprozedur zuständig. Den benötigten Speicher kann er
aus einer eigenen einstufigen Reihung beziehen, er kann aber die Objekte
auch in anderen Speicherbereichen unterbringen, zu denen er Zugang besitzt.

Das Verfahren demonstriert ferner eine Spracheigenschaft, die ich als
semantische Erweiterbarkeit bezeichnen möchte: Für Sprachkonzepte wie
globale Generatoren und Referenzen ist der syntaktische Rahmen vorgegeben. Die semantische Interpretation dieser syntaktischen Konzepte wird
durch die Prozedur allocate und deren Ergebnis festgelegt und wird damit
durch den Programmierer, nicht durch die Sprache, bestimmt. Dabei müssen
allerdings gewisse, eventuell sogar implementierungsbedingte Beschrän-
kungen eingehalten werden; z.B. muß der Inhaltsoperator cont auf die resultierenden Referenzen anwendbar sein.

5. Schnittstellenbeschreibungen

Das Prinzip üblicher blockstrukturierter Sprachen, den Gültigkeitsbereich
einer Größe, die in einem äußeren Block vereinbart ist, automatisch auf
innenliegende Blöcke zu erweitern, sofern dort keine gleichbenannte Größe
definiert ist, wird in BALG bei der Schachtelung von Moduln nicht angewandt: Globale Größen sind in innenliegenden Moduln im allgemeinen unzugänglich. Sie werden nur zugänglich, wenn sie explizit als externe Größen
in einer Schnittstellenbeschreibung für den Modul aufgeführt sind. Umgekehrt können Bezeichner lokaler Größen eines Strukturmoduls nur dann außer-
halb des Moduls als Selektoren zusammen mit der Benennung einer Struktur
benutzt werden, wenn sie als Eingänge des Moduls in der Schnittstellenbeschreibung genannt sind. Die Forderung nach expliziter Kennzeichnung
der Eingänge und externen Größen ist aus dem Prinzip des "information
hiding" von Parnas abgeleitet: In der Kommunikation zwischen einem Modul
und seiner Umgebung sollen nur Größen vorkommen, die relevant für die
Funktion des Moduls sind; Größen, die implementierungsbezogene Einzelhei-
ten des Moduls oder seiner Umgebung betreffen, sollen nicht zur Schnittstelle gehören. Daher taucht die Reihung a unseres Moduls stack nicht in
der Schnittstelle auf. Die Zugriffsbeschränkung für externe Größen ist
außerdem nützlich, weil der Übergang Modulumgebung → Modul häufig den
Übergang zwischen einer tieferliegenden und einer höherliegenden Schicht
in einer Programmhierarchie entspricht. Die Zugriffsbeschränkung ist dann
Ausdruck der Abschirmung zwischen den Programmschichten.

Aus Gründen der Ausgewogenheit (eine Schnittstellenbeschreibung soll nicht länger als der zugehörige Modul sein) kann bei Moduln, die im Kontext ihrer Umgebung übersetzt werden, die Spezifikation der externen Größen weggelassen werden. Davon haben wir bei den Prozeduren unseres Moduls stack Gebrauch gemacht. Hingegen muß bei getrennter Übersetzung die Schnittstellenbeschreibung sogar zweimal angegeben sein: Im Text der Umgebung des Moduls werden die externen Größen aufgeführt, welche dem Modul zur Verfügung gestellt werden, und die Eingänge, welche in der Umgebung benötigt werden. Als Vorspann des Moduls erscheinen die externen Größen, welche der Modul benötigt, und die Eingänge, welche der Modul bereitstellt. Diese Doppelspezifikation erlaubt (und verlangt) dem Übersetzer die Prüfung der Konsistenz der beiden Angaben (benötigte Grössen bilden Teilmenge der bereitgestellten Größen). Dies erscheint angemessen, da die Modulschnittstelle im Programmierteam häufig auch den Wechsel der Zuständigkeit der Programmierer kennzeichnet. Der Übersetzer prüft also zugleich die richtige Verzahnung der Produkte mehrerer Programmierer, zumindest was Bezeichnung und Typ der Größen angeht.

Schließlich kann durch eine Schnittstellenbeschreibung auch das Zugriffsrecht auf Variable eingeschränkt werden. In unserem Modul stack ist beispielsweise die Tiefe des Kellers von außen nur als unveränderliche Grösse zugänglich, während sie im Modul natürlich eine Variable darstellt. Bei zusammengesetzten Objekten wie zum Beispiel Verbunden lassen sich die Zugriffsrechte "variabel", "unveränderlich", "unzugänglich" nicht nur für das Objekt als Ganzes, sondern sogar für die Glieder einzeln bestimmen.

6. Zusammenfassung

Wir haben in dieser Arbeit einige Eigenschaften der in Entwicklung befindlichen Programmiersprache BALG dargestellt. Bevor die noch ausstehenden Ergänzungen und Glättungen vorgenommen werden, soll die Sprache -überwiegend mithilfe von Diplomarbeiten- implementiert werden.

Für zahlreiche Diskussionen und wertvolle Hinweise bei der Entwicklung von BALG danke ich den Herren U. Kastens, H. Neugebauer, H. Rohlfing und H. Santo.

Literatur

Bu72   Burroughs Corporation: Burroughs B6700 ESPOL Language Infor-
        mation Manual, Burroughs Corporation Form 5000094, Detroit,
        1972

CL74   Clark, B.L., Ham. F.J.B.: The project SUE System Language
        Reference Manual Computer Systems, research group, Universi-
        ty of Toronto, report no. 42, 1974

Da67   Dahl, O.J., Myhrhaug, B., Nygaard, U.: SIMULA 67, Common Base
        Language, Norwegian Computing Center, Oslo, 1967

Go70   Goos, G., Lagally, K., Sapper, G.: PS440 - Eine niedere Pro-
        grammiersprache, Rechenzentrum der Technischen Hochschule
        München, Bericht 7002, 1970

Go74a   Goos, G.: Systemprogrammiersprachen und Strukturiertes Pro-
        grammieren, LNCS 23, 203-224, Springer: Berlin-Heidelberg-
        New York, 1974

Go74b   Goos, G.: Some Thoughts on Variables, Fakultät für Informatik,
        Universität Karlsruhe, Bericht 19/74, 1974

Go75   Goos, G.: Die Programmiersprache BALG - vorläufige Fassung
        Fakultät für Informatik, Universität Karlsruhe, Bericht 6/75,
        1975

Ho74   Hoare, C.A.R.: Monitors: An Operating System Structuring Con-
        cept, Comm. ACM 17, 549-557, 1974

Kn74   Knuth, D.E.: Structured Programming with goto Statements,
        Computing Surveys 6, 261-302, 1974

Sa71   Sammet, H.E.: A brief survey of languages used in systems
        implementation SIGPLAN Notices 6, no. 9, 1971

Wi68   Wirth, N.: PL360: A Programming Language for the 360 Computers,
        Journal ACM 15, 37-74, 1968

Wi74   Wirth, N.: The Programming Language PASCAL (Revised Report),
         LNCS 18, Springer: Berlin-Heidelber-New York, 1974

Wi69   Wijngaarden, A.v. (ed.): Report on the Algorithmic Language
         ALGOL 68, Num. Math. 14, 79-218, 1969

Za74   Zahn, C.T.: A Control Statement for natural top-down structu-
         red programming, LNCS 19, 170-180. Springer: Berlin-Heidelberg-
         New York, 1974

Anschrift des Verfassers: Prof. Dr. G. Goos
                          Fakultät für Informatik
                          Universität Karlsruhe
                          Postfach 6380
                          D-7500 Karlsruhe 1

SLAN - EINE ERWEITERBARE SPRACHE ZUR UNTERSTÜTZUNG DER STRUKTURIERTEN
UND MODULAREN PROGRAMMIERUNG

Günter Hommel, Stefan Jähnichen, Wilfried Koch

Informatik-Forschungsgruppe Programmiersprachen und Compiler 2
- Forschungsbereich Schulsprache -
Technische Universität Berlin

(Dieses Projekt wird von der Deutschen Forschungsgemeinschaft
unter Nr. Ko 588/2 gefördert)

1.   Entwurfsziele

Beim Entwurf der Programmiersprache SLAN wurde der gezielte Versuch unternommen, eine
Sprache für den Ausbildungssektor zu schaffen, welche allgemein anerkannte Anforderungen an eine solche Sprache berücksichtigt.

SLAN soll in folgenden Bereichen eingesetzt werden:
- Schule (school language)
- Grundausbildung in der Universität (student language)
- Software Engineering - Systemimplementierung im weitesten Sinn (system language).

1.1. Unterstützung strukturierter Programmierung /2/

Die systematische Konstruktion eines Algorithmus erfolgt (jedenfalls im Kleinen /3/)
top-down, wobei die Methode der schrittweisen Verfeinerung /4/ solange angewandt wird,
bis eine dem Problem und dem Programmierer angemessene primitive Abstraktionsebene erreicht ist. Die Sprache muß diese Art des Problemlösungsvorgangs unterstützen, wobei
das Programm eine möglichst genaue Abbildung des Lösungsweges sein soll.

Die Sprache muß das prozedurale Denken und die Zergliederung des Problems in Definitionen und Applikationen von Algorithmen, Objekten und Typen fördern.

Die Sprache muß die Verbalisierung von Verfeinerungsschritten, Objekten, Datentypen
und Operatoren unterstützen und erzwingen.

Die Sprache muß eine möglichst kleine Anzahl voneinander unabhängiger Konzepte enthalten. Barocke und der strukturierten Programmierung abträgliche Sprachelemente dürfen
nicht Bestandteil der Sprache sein, so daß Termination und Korrektheit von Programmen
nachgewiesen werden können.

Die Deklaration aller Objekte ist unerlässlich, wegen der Möglichkeit problembezogene

Datentypen zu benutzen.

Die Festlegung der Lebensdauer von Objekten muß einfach sein, hierzu genügen zwei Namensräume.

1.2. Unterstützung modularer Programmierung

Die schrittweise Verfeinerung eines Algorithmus endet auf einer Abstraktionsebene, die für das Problem oder den Programmierer als primitiv bezeichnet werden kann. Diese Abstraktionsebene entspricht einer abstrakten Maschine (Gedanken-machine /1/), die je nach Problem, Ausbildungs- und Kenntnisstand des Programmierers beliebig maschinennah oder besser maschinenfern sein kann. Sie ist weiterhin auch von den zur Verfügung stehenden Algorithmen einer Bibliothek abhängig. Die Sprache muß eine einfache Möglichkeit bieten, diese Abstraktionsebenen einzuführen und zu benutzen. Die Einführung dieser Abstraktionsebenen ist nicht nur für Algorithmen sondern auch für Datenobjekte notwendig. Die unterste Abstraktionsebene ist also nicht von der Sprache fest vorgegeben, sondern beliebig an das jeweilige Problem anzupassen. Dies geschieht durch eine bottom-up Konstruktion von geeigneten Typen und Grundalgorithmen.

Die Datenabstraktion ist genau so wichtig wie die algorithmische Abstraktion. Beide können nicht voneinander getrennt werden, da die Definition von Objekten nur zusammen mit der Definition von Zugriffsalgorithmen auf Objektkomponenten sinnvoll ist. Die Feinstruktur der Objekte, d.h. ihre maschinennahe Repräsentation, muß ebenso versteckt werden wie die algorithmische Komplexität der Zugriffsoperationen und weiterer Operationen zwischen den definierten Objekten. Die Definition dieser Feinstruktur von Objekten soll von deren Benutzung, wie Generierung, Änderung und Löschung getrennt werden. Diese Forderungen können nur mit Hilfe eines Modulkonzeptes realisiert werden, das die Kommunikation zwischen Moduln nur durch genau festgelegte Schnittstellen ermöglicht. Das Modulkonzept entspricht der intuitiven Idee einer black box.

1.3. Erweiterbarkeit und Downward Compatibility

Um eine Implementierung der Sprache auf Kleinrechnern zu ermöglichen, muß der Sprachkern klein sein. Dieser Sprachkern kann nur einfache Datentypen und Kontrollstrukturen enthalten. Für viele Anwendungsbereiche muß die Sprache erweiterungsfähig sein. Eine syntaktische Erweiterung um eine beschränkte Anzahl neuer und voneinander unabhängiger Konzepte kann dem Benutzer nicht zugemutet werden. Vielmehr sollte der maximale Sprachumfang von vornherein beim Entwurf in der Sprachbeschreibung festgelegt werden. Die Definition des Sprachkerns erfolgt dann durch Streichung von Sprachelementen. Die Reduzierung des Sprachumfangs erfolgt in verschiedenen Stufen, die dem jeweiligen Anwendungsbereich entsprechen. Bei dieser Einschränkung dürfen die Prinzipien der strukturierten und modularen Programmierung nicht verletzt werden. Insbesondere enthält der Sprachkern die Möglichkeit zu beliebiger Verbalisierung, zur Verfeinerung und zur Benutzung abstrakter Datentypen und Algorithmen. Die Reduzierung des Sprachumfangs beeinträchtigt also lediglich die Möglichkeit, selbst Datentypen, Operatoren und spezielle Algorithmen zu definieren, nicht jedoch, sie zu benutzen. Dieses Prinzip der downward compatibility erleichtert:

1. eine einfache Programmierung durch geringe Anzahl von Sprachkonzepten

2. die Verfügbarkeit einer mächtigen Sprache auf kleinen Systemen durch Benutzung von Moduln, die durch Precompilation oder eventuell Crosscompilation auf anderen Analgen zur Verfügung gestellt werden.

Die Sprache soll hauptsächlich mit Hilfe der folgenden Mechanismen erweiterbar sein:

1. Ein mächtiges Modulkonzept zur Realisierung der algorithmischen Abstraktion und der Daten-Abstraktion

2. Sprachmittel zur Definition beliebiger Datentypen

3. Sprachmittel zur Definition von Operatoren

4. Generische Algorithmen und Operatoren, d.h. die Identifizierung von Algorithmen und Operatoren erfolgt nicht nur durch ihren Namen sondern auch durch Anzahl und Typ der Parameter.

5. Sprachmittel zur semantischen Entleihung fehlender Elemente aus einer Zielsprache mittels Macros.

2. Realisierung in SLAN

2.1. Pakete

Ein SLAN-Programm ist eine Folge von Moduln, die Pakete genannt werden. Eines dieser Pakete ist dadurch ausgezeichnet, daß von ihm aus die Ausführung des gesamten Programms gestartet wird (Hauptprogramm). Pakete kommunizieren untereinander über festdefinierte Schnittstellen. Die Kommunikation besteht in der gegenseitigen Benutzung von Algorithmen, Typen, Operatoren und Konstanten. Jedes Paket definiert nach außen, welche dieser Größen allen anderen Paketen zur Verfügung gestellt werden. Dieses Konzept erzwingt keine hierarchische Anordnung von Paketen. Eine Hierarchisierung kann vielmehr vom Problem her erfolgen. Ein oder mehrere Pakete bilden je nach Problemstellung eine Abstraktionsebene. (siehe Abb. 1).

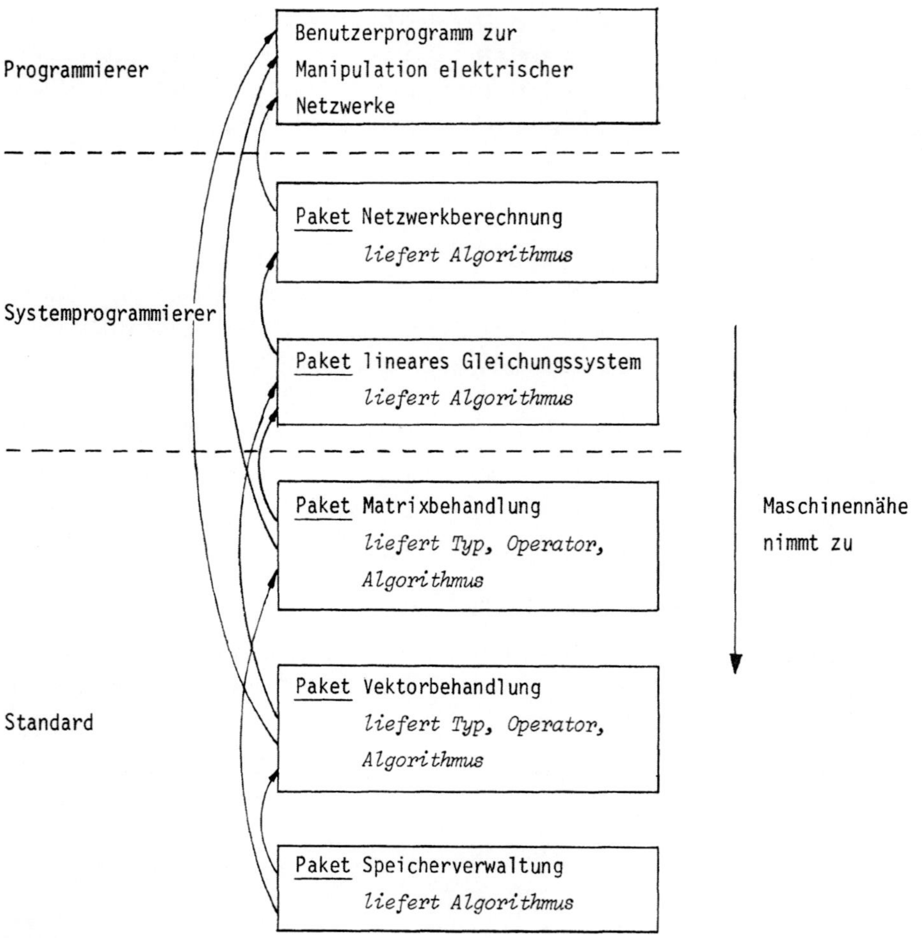

<u>Abb.1</u>: Beispiel zur Benutzung von Paketen

Die Pfeile im Bild bezeichnen die Sichtbarkeit von Objekten für andere Pakete

2.2. Algorithmen und Operatoren

Algorithmen-Definitionen sind die Grundbausteine jedes Paketes. Sie bestehen aus der Angabe des Algorithmen-Namens, der Spezifikation möglicher Parameter und des Ergebnisses und dem Rumpf.

Jeder Algorithmus definiert seinen eigenen Datenraum (lokal), der in den Datenraum des Paketes (global) eingebettet ist. Eine weitere Schachtelung von Datenräumen ist nicht notwendig. Der Rumpf besteht aus dem Anweisungsteil, gefolgt von Refinement-Definitionen. Operator-Definitionen haben die gleiche Struktur.

2.3. Refinement

Das Refinement ist das auffälligste Sprachelement, mit dessen Hilfe eine dem Problem angemessene Verbalisierung von algorithmischen Teilschritten erzwungen wird. Die beim Lösungsvorgang eingeführten Teilschritte bleiben im Programm stehen und müssen nicht an der Applikationsstelle substituiert werden. Das Refinement ist die syntaktische Realisierung der in der strukturierten Programmierung geforderten schrittweisen Verfeinerung. Entsprechend der top-down-Vorgehensweise bei der Konstruktion von Algorithmen, sind Refinements Bestandteile von Algorithmen-Definitionen und stehen im Rumpf des Algorithmus hinter dem Anweisungsteil. Refinements haben keinen eigenen Datenraum und keine Parameter.

2.4. Deklaration von Datenobjekten

Datenobjekte in SLAN bestehen aus einer Adresse, einem Typ, einem Wert, einem Akzess-Attribut und dem Existenzbereich. Jedes Datenobjekt muß deklariert werden. Die Deklaration enthält neben dem Namen das Akzessattribut (Konstante oder Variable) und den Typ. Datenobjekte können an beliebiger Stelle im Anweisungsteil des Algorithmus und innerhalb eines Refinements deklariert werden. Der Gültigkeitsbereich der entsprechenden Deklaration ist dann jeweils der Algorithmus.

Außerdem können Datenobjekt-Deklarationen Bestandteil eines Paketes sein. Ihr Gültigkeitsbereich ist dann das Paket. Deklarationen dürfen nicht innerhalb von Kontrollstrukturen auftreten.

2.5. Typen

Typ-Deklarationen legen Bezeichnung und Feinstruktur von Datentypen fest. Es gibt die Grundtypen <u>int</u>, <u>real</u>, <u>bool</u> und <u>set</u>. Aus ihnen können mittels Verbundbildung und Reihung andere Typen aufgebaut werden. Typ-Deklarationen können nur auf Paketebene auftreten. Sie sind ein Mittel zur Realisierung der Datenabstraktion.

SLAN kennt drei Arten von Operationen auf Datenobjekten:

- primitive arithmetische Operationen, beschränkt auf die Grundtypen _int_, _real_, _bool_ und _set_.

- Selektionsmechanismen zum Zugriff auf Objekt-Komponenten bei Kenntnis der Feinstruktur (Selektion von Komponenten von Verbunden, Indizierung eindimensionaler Felder).

- Operationen mit Objekten, deren Feinstruktur verborgen ist (z.B. Generierung und Initialisierung einer Einheitsmatrix).

2.6. Kontrollstrukturen

In SLAN gibt es einfache und zusammengesetzte Operationen. Einfache Operationen sind Assignationen, Ausdrücke, insbesondere der Aufruf von Algorithmen und Refinements, sowie Selektion und Indizierung. Eine einfache Operation ist auch die Leave-Anweisung, die das beliebige Verlassen eines Abschnitts ermöglicht. Dabei wird ein Ergebniswert entsprechend der Deklaration des Algorithmus angegeben. Kompositionsregeln für Operationen in SLAN sind die Aneinanderreihung, die Auswahl (Abfrageketten mit _if_-Konstruktion und Mehrfach-Auswahl mit _select_-Konstruktion) und die Wiederholung. Schleifen können mit Hilfe der _for_-Option und _while_ oder _until_ Endebedingungen konstruiert werden. SLAN kennt keine Sprunganweisung.

3.   Beispiel

Das folgende Beispiel zeigt die Struktur eines SLAN Programms. Dieses Beispielprogramm verwaltet eine Schülerdatei; es ist wegen seines großen Umfangs nicht voll ausgeführt, läßt sich aber durch Hinzufügen weiterer Algorithmen und Pakete leicht vervollständigen. Folgende Pakete auf verschiedenen Abstraktionsebenen sind angegeben:

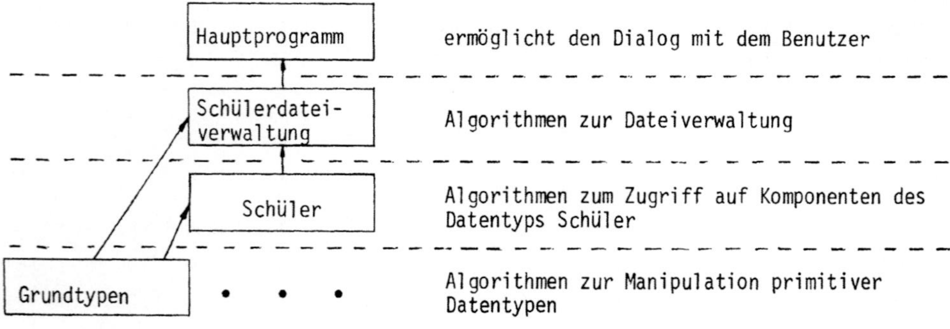

Hauptprogramm	ermöglicht den Dialog mit dem Benutzer
Schülerdatei-verwaltung	Algorithmen zur Dateiverwaltung
Schüler	Algorithmen zum Zugriff auf Komponenten des Datentyps Schüler
Grundtypen	Algorithmen zur Manipulation primitiver Datentypen

```
PACKET grundtypen
   DEFINES DATUM, NOTEN, SEX, put, get, durchschnitt, zensuren, maennlich,
      weiblich, ... :
      TYPE DATUM = STRUCT (INT tag, monat, jahr);
      ...
      TYPE NOTEN = STRUCT (REAL deutsch, englisch, suaheli, ...);
      ...
      TYPE SEX = COUNT 2;
      SEX CONST maennlich = 1, weiblich = 2;
      ...
END PACKET grundtypen;


PACKET schueler
   DEFINES SCHUELER, hole vornamen, hole nachnamen, hole adresse, hole geburtsdatum,
      hole klasse, hole geschlecht, hole noten, erzeuge schueler, ERHAELT, put, get,
      trage englischnote ein, ... :
      TYPE SCHUELER = STRUCT (TEXT vorname, nachname, adresse, DATUM geburtsdatum,
         INT klasse, SEX geschlecht, NOTEN noten);
      ALGORITHM hole vornamen (SCHUELER CONST pennaeler) TEXT CONST:
         pennaeler.vorname
      END ALG hole vornamen;
      ...
      ALGORITHM hole geburtsdatum (SCHUELER CONST pennaeler) DATUM CONST:
         pennaeler.geburtsdatum
      END ALG hole geburtsdatum;
      ...
      ALGORITHM erzeuge schueler (TEXT CONST vorname, nachname, adresse,
         DATUM CONST geburtsdatum, SEX CONST geschlecht) SCHUELER CONST:
         SCHUELER (vorname, nachname, adresse, geburtsdatum, 0, geschlecht,
            zensuren (0.0, ... 0.0))
      END ALG erzeuge schueler;
      ...
      OPERATOR ERHAELT (SCHUELER CONST pennaeler, TEXT CONST adresse):
         pennaeler.adresse := adresse
      END OP ERHAELT;
      OPERATOR ERHAELT (SCHUELER CONST pennaeler, INT CONST klasse):
         pennaeler.klasse := klasse
      END OP ERHAELT;
      ...
   END PACKET schueler;
```

```
PACKET schuelerdateiverwaltung
   DEFINES trage schueler ein, loesche schuelereintrag, aendere, lies schuelerdatei,
      speichere schuelerdatei ab, ... :
      TYPE INDEX = COUNT 200;
      ROW 200 STRUCT (SCHUELER pennaeler, INT freizeiger, vorgaenger, nachfolger)
         VAR penne;
      INT CONST nil = 0;
      INT VAR beginn freiliste, beginn der kette := nil, ende der kette := nil,
         anzahl freier elemente := 200;
      INDEX VAR index;
      FOR index REPEAT
         penne (index).freizeiger := index + 1
      END REPEAT;
      penne (200).freizeiger := nil;
      beginn freiliste := 1;
      ALGORITHM trage schueler ein (TEXT CONST vorname, nachname, adresse,
         DATUM CONST geburtsdatum, SEX CONST geschlecht):
         INDEX VAR eintragstelle;
         IF anzahl freier elemente > 0
         THEN eintragstelle := beginn freiliste;
            hole element aus freiliste;
            haenge in kette ein
         ELSE put ("penne voll"); stop
         END IF.
         hole element aus freiliste:
            beginn freiliste := penne (beginn freiliste).freizeiger;
            anzahl freier elemente MINUS 1.
         haenge in kette ein:
            penne (eintragstelle).pennaeler := erzeuge schueler (vorname, nachname,
               adresse, geburtsdatum, geschlecht);
            penne (eintragstelle).vorgaenger := ende der kette;
            penne (eintragstelle).nachfolger := nil;
            IF beginn der kette = nil
            THEN beginn der kette := eintragstelle;
               ende der kette := beginn der kette
            ELSE penne (ende der kette).nachfolger := eintragstelle;
               ende der kette := eintragstelle
            END IF
      END ALG trage schueler ein;
      ALGORITHM loesche schuelereintrag (TEXT CONST vorname, nachname):
      ...
```

```
      END ALG loesche schuelereintrag;
      ...
END PACKET schuelerdateiverwaltung;



                    #  Hauptprogramm Schuelerdatei  #

put ("Wollen Sie Informationen ueber die Programmbenutzung?");
TEXT VAR antwort, vorname, nachname, adresse;
DATUM VAR geburtstag;
INT VAR klasse;
SEX VAR geschlecht;
NOTEN VAR noten;
get (antwort);
IF antwort = "ja" THEN drucke programm informationen END IF;
lies schuelerdatei;
REPEAT
    put ("Bitte gewuenschte Aktion angeben");
    get (antwort);
    IF antwort = "ende" THEN ende
        ELIF antwort = "eintrag" THEN schueler eintragen
        ELIF antwort = "austrag" THEN schueler austragen
        ELIF antwort = "adresse" THEN adressaenderung

        ...
    END IF
END REPEAT.
drucke programm informationen:
    put ("...

    ...


ende:
    speichere schuelerdatei ab;
    stop.
schueler eintragen:
    put ("Vorname, Nachname"); get (vorname); get (nachname);
    put ("Adresse"); get (adresse);
    put ("Geburtsdatum"); get (geburtsdatum);
    put ("Geschlecht"); get (geschlecht);
    trage schueler ein (vorname, nachname, adresse, geburtsdatum, geschlecht).
 schueler austragen:
    put ("Vorname, Nachname"); get (vorname); get (nachname);
    loesche schuelereintrag (vorname, nachname).
```

```
adressaenderung:
   put ("Vorname, Nachname"); get (vorname); get (nachname);
   put ("neue Adresse"); get (adresse);
   aendere (vorname, nachname, adresse).
```

L I T E R A T U R

/1/ Bauer, F.L.:   Top-down teaching of informatics in secondary school.
                             IFIP 2nd World Conference Computers in education,
                             September 1975

/2/ Dijkstra, E.W.:   Structured Programming.
                             Academic Press

/3/ DeRemer,F.L.; Kron,H.: Programming in the Small versus Programming in the
                             Large.
                             SIGPLAN notices Vol. 10,6, 1975

/4/ Wirth,N.:   Program development by stepwise refinement.
                             CACM 14

/5/ van Wijngaarden,A. ed.: Revised Report on the Algorithmic Language ALGOL 68.
                             erscheint bei Springer-Verlag

/6/ Koster, C.H.A.:   Provisional Description of SLAN.
                             Arbeitspapier, TU Berlin, November 1974

CONS-FREIES PROGRAMMIEREN IN LISP UNTER DELETION-STRATEGIE

Friedemann Simon

Institut für Informatik und Praktische Mathematik der Universität Kiel

1. Einleitung

Eine wesentliche Eigenschaft der Sprache ALGOL 60 ist, dass zur Laufzeit eines Programmes für die Speicherung aller auftretenden Variablen ein Keller (stack) benutzt werden kann, wodurch eine relativ einfache Art der Speicherverwaltung möglich wird [1]: Beim Eintritt in einen Block bzw. eine Prozedur wird der notwendige Speicherplatz für lokale Variablen vom Laufzeitsystem auf dem stack angelegt und beim Verlassen nach dem Prinzip "last in - first out" wieder freigegeben. Dieses Vorgehen wird auch als "deletion-Strategie" [2],[3] bezeichnet. ALGOL 60 garantiert, dass nach dem Verlassen eines Blocks bzw. einer Prozedur keine Zugriffe auf die lokalen Objekte mehr erfolgen und deshalb die deletion-Strategie korrekt ist.

In anderen Sprachen, wie z. B. LISP, gibt es Möglichkeiten, auf Variable, die in einem inneren Block (λ-Ausdruck) an einen Wert gebunden sind, von aussen her zuzugreifen, so dass Variablenbindungen auch über das Verlassen des betreffenden Blocks (λ-Ausdruck) hinaus erhalten bleiben müssen; korrekte Behandlung verlangt daher sogenannte "retention-Strategie" [2],[3]. Diese von ALGOL 60 abweichende Situation beruht darauf, dass in LISP Prozeduren (functions) andere Prozeduren als Werte haben können.

Beispiel:
```
    begin
    s-expr proc proc p(a);value a;s-expr a;
        { s-expr proc q( ); {q:=a} ;
          p:=q} ;
    out p('A') ()
    end
```

In diesem auf ALGOL-artige Form umgeschriebenen Programm ist die Ausgabe bei deletion-Strategie undefiniert; bei retention-Strategie ist sie der atomare Wert A. Für die retention-Strategie ist eine Speicherorganisation des Laufzeitsystems in Form der üblichen ALGOL 60-stack-

Implementierung nicht ausreichend [4]; man benötigt einen heap als
Speicher für Variablenbindungen, was garbage collecting zur Speicherbereinigung impliziert. Eine weitere Unverträglichkeit mit einer stack-
Implementierung ergibt sich aus den Daten von LISP, den s-Ausdrücken,
die binären Bäumen entsprechen. Durch Anwendung der Operation cons
können s-Ausdrücke unbeschränkt wachsen, so dass sich die Speicherung
von s-Ausdrücken im stack des Laufzeitsystems praktisch verbietet; man
benutzt stattdessen Verweise auf s-Ausdrücke. Die s-Ausdrücke selber
werden in einem zusätzlichen Speicher aufgenommen, der durch Anwendungen
von cons beliebig wachsen kann.

Unter diesen Umständen erhebt sich das Problem, ob LISP dank der
retention-Strategie die Formulierung einer echt grösseren Klasse von
Programmen erlaubt als die Teilsprache derjenigen Programme, die mit
deletion-Strategie auskommen.

M. J. Fischer [5] hat bewiesen, dass deletion- und retention-Strategie
in einem starken Sinne äquivalent sind:

- Für jedes LISP-Programm π kann effektiv ein Programm π' konstruiert werden, das dieselbe n-stellige Funktion
  $f_\pi \equiv f_{\pi'} \mid E^n \longrightarrow E$ unter der deletion-Strategie berechnet
  (deletion tolerant). E ist die Menge aller s-Ausdrücke.

- Die Operation cons wird zur Dekodierung des Endresultats von π'
  in Form eines s-Ausdrucks genau so oft aufgerufen, wie es zu
  dessen Konstruktion aus den jeweiligen Atomen notwendig ist.
  Das Programm π' ist somit im wesentlichen cons-frei.

Der Beweis wird für eine Verallgemeinerung von LISP (lambda calculus
schemata) geführt, indem eine Reihe von Transformationen auf Programmen
definiert werden, für die dann ausgehend von expliziten Definitionen
der Programmausführung unter deletion- bzw. retention-Strategie umfangreiche, nicht triviale Lemmata bewiesen werden müssen.

Die Gleichwertigkeit von deletion- und retention-Strategie soll im
folgenden auf einfachere und elementare Weise einsichtig werden: Für
jedes LISP-Programm π gibt es einen effektiv angebbaren 2-Band-Keller-
automaten $\check{\mathcal{A}}_\pi$, der dieselbe Funktion f_π berechnet. Dieser Automat
wird als ein LISP-Programm $\pi_{\check{\mathcal{A}}}$ dargestellt, das, versehen mit einem
Vorspann zur Kodierung der Eingabedaten und einem Nachspann zur Deko-
dierung des Resultats, ebenfalls $f_\pi = f_{\pi_{\check{\mathcal{A}}}}$ berechnet und das in einer
deletion-toleranten Teilsprache von LISP programmiert ist. Ferner tritt

cons nur im Nachspann auf, so dass $\overline{\Pi_{\tilde{A}}}$ die gleichen Bedingungen erfüllt wie das Programm $\overline{\Pi}$' bei M. J. Fischer.

2. Definition von LISP

Die Sprache wird in ALGOL-ähnlicher Notation unter Einführung von geeigneten neuen Werten und Standardfunktionen zunächst so definiert, dass man Programme in dieser Teilsprache von LISP als ALGOL 60 Programme verstehen kann; Konzepte, die zwar zur Sprache gehören [*], in ALGOL 60 jedoch nicht definiert sind, wie z. B. Prozeduren als Werte, treten später hinzu. Die Übertragung eines Programmes aus der ALGOL-ähnlichen Notation in die übliche LISP-Notation als s-Ausdruck ist evident durchführbar.

2.1. Werte

Als Werte gibt es nur s-Ausdrücke. Atomare s-Ausdrücke sind endliche Folgen von Ziffern und Grossbuchstaben, die mit einem Grossbuchstaben anfangen. Sind s_1 und s_2 s-Ausdrücke, dann ist auch $s_3=(s_1 \cdot s_2)$ ein s-Ausdruck. Weiterhin gilt folgende als Listenschreibweise bezeichnete, abkürzende Konvention

$$(s_1 \cdot (s_2 \cdot \ \ldots \ \cdot (s_n \cdot NIL) \ \ldots)) = (s_1, s_2, \ldots, s_n) \quad n \geqslant 1$$

mit der Erweiterung ( ) = NIL für die leere Liste.

2.2. Standard-Funktionen auf s-Ausdrücken

Es sind 5 Funktionen definiert:

$$car(s) \ := \ \begin{cases} s_1 \text{ falls } s=(s_1 \cdot s_2) \\ \text{undefiniert sonst} \end{cases}$$

$$cdr(s) \ := \ \begin{cases} s_2 \text{ falls } s=(s_1 \cdot s_2) \\ \text{undefiniert sonst} \end{cases}$$

$$cons(s_1, s_2) \ := \ (s_1 \cdot s_2)$$

$$atom(s) \ := \ \begin{cases} T \text{ falls } s \text{ atomar} \\ F \text{ sonst} \end{cases}$$

$$eq(s_1, s_2) \ := \ \begin{cases} T \text{ falls } s_1, s_2 \text{ atomar und } s_1 = s_2 \\ F \text{ falls } s_1, s_2 \text{ atomar und } s_1 \neq s_2 \\ \text{undefiniert sonst} \end{cases}$$

---

[*] vergl. [6] S. 1 - 13 zur Definition von LISP

Die Atome NIL, T, F existieren standardmässig, wobei T bzw. F den Wahr-
heitswerten <u>true</u> bzw. <u>false</u> entsprechen. Es können durch Standard-
Funktionen keine weiteren Atome, die nicht in Argumenten auftreten,
erzeugt werden.

2.3. <u>Struktur von Programmen</u>

Programme sind stets als eine Hierarchie von (meist rekursiven) Funk-
tionsaufrufen aufgebaut, die jeweils einen s-Ausdruck als Wert besitzen
und wobei zusätzlich bedingte Ausdrücke zulässig sind [6]. Versteht man
LISP-Programme in der ursprünglichen Weise als Funktionen von s-Ausdrücken, d. h. mit getrennter Daten- und Programmstruktur [*], so treten
die folgenden Situationen nicht auf:
- Eine Funktion ist Wert einer anderen,
- eine Funktion wird wie ein s-Ausdruck, d. h. als Datum behandelt,
- während der Programmausführung werden Funktionen konstruiert und
  ausgeführt, die im Programmtext nicht explizit auftreten.

Wie sich zeigen wird, bedeuten diese Einschränkungen gegenüber üblichen
LISP-Implementationen jedoch keinen Verlust hinsichtlich der Menge der
in LISP programmierbaren Funktionen.

LISP-Programme lassen sich nun in ALGOL 60-ähnlicher Weise darstellen
als Hierarchie von Deklarationen und Aufrufen von Funktionsprozeduren
zum Typ s-Ausdruck mit s-Ausdrücken als Parametern; dabei werden in
Anlehnung an LISP-Konventionen Typangabe, Spezifikationsteil, value-
Angaben und die explizite Wertzuweisung an den Prozeduridentifikator
weggelassen.

Beispiel:

$$\underline{\text{proc}} \; f \; (x_1, \ldots, x_n); \; \{ \; \langle \text{function proc. declarations} \rangle; \; \langle \text{expr} \rangle \}$$

Parameterlose Prozeduren sind mit g( ) bezeichnet. Als ⟨expr⟩ ist jeweils ein wie in ALGOL 60 aufgebauter arithmetischer Ausdruck mit den
folgenden Operatoren zulässig:
- car, cdr, cons, atom, eq
- <u>if</u> ... <u>then</u> ... <u>else</u> ... (Bedingter Ausdruck)

und den Operanden:
- Konstante, d. h. s-Ausdrücke, die zur Kennzeichnung in '' eingeschlossen sind, z. B. '(A . B)'

---

[*] vergl. mit der m-notation

- formale Parameter, z. B. x_1, x_2,...,x_n

- Funktionsprozeduraufrufe mit <expr> als Parametern, z. B.

   $f('A', x_2, car(x_3))$

Der einfache Aufbau der Prozeduren ist durch das Fehlen von expliziten
Wertzuweisungen an Variable, von bedingten Anweisungen und von Sprüngen
zu erklären. Ein Programm für eine n-stellige Funktion $f \mid E^n \longrightarrow E$
hat dann die Struktur:

begin
proc $f(inp_1, inp_2, ..., inp_n)$; $\{ ... \}$;
comment Es folgen eventuell weitere Prozedurdeklarationen;
  ⋮
out $f(\underline{in}, \underline{in}, ..., \underline{in})$
end

Die Wortsymbole **in** bzw. **out** bezeichnen Standardoperationen für die Ein-
bzw. Ausgabe von s-Ausdrücken.

3. Transformation von Programmen in eine deletion-tolerante Form

Geht man von einem LISP-Programm Π aus, so ist dadurch eine berechenbare Abbildung $f_\Pi \mid E^n \longrightarrow E$ definiert und im Resultat treten nur
solche Atome auf, die bereits in der Eingabe für das Programm oder unter
den konstanten s-Ausdrücken des Programms aufgetreten sind oder zu den
Atomen T, F, NIL gehören. Aus diesem Grunde sind nicht alle berechenbaren Abbildungen $E^n \longrightarrow E$ exakt als LISP-Programm zu schreiben.
Beispiel:

$$g \mid E \longrightarrow E \quad \text{mit} \quad g(\underbrace{'AA...A'}_{n \geqslant 1 \text{ mal}}) := \underbrace{'BB...B'}_{n \geqslant 1 \text{ mal}}$$

(Unter Einführung geeigneter Kodierungen kann jedoch bekanntlich jede
partiell rekursive Funktion als LISP-Programm dargestellt werden).

Für die gewünschte cons-freie Berechnung der durch das gegebene Programm
definierten Abbildung ist die Simulation durch einen Automaten von der
Mächtigkeit einer Turingmaschine erforderlich. Mit Hilfe der Theorie
der Stackautomaten lässt sich zeigen, dass man ohne cons und ohne functional arguments keine universelle Umschreibung der Programme in eine
consfreie, deletion-tolerante Form erreichen kann. Es werden deshalb
in der in Abschnitt 2. definierten Sprache formale Prozeduraufrufe und
Prozedurnamen als aktuelle Parameter zugelassen, so dass mit diesen
Erweiterungen über einen 2-Band-Kellerautomat $\breve{A}_\Pi$ ein Programm $\overline{\Pi}_{\breve{A}}$ kon-

struiert werden kann, das atomwertige Funktionen consfrei berechnet.
Offensichtlich wird cons aber zur Erzeugung nichtatomarer Resultate
benötigt, da diese s-Ausdrücke i. a. weder in der Eingabe noch unter
den Programmkonstanten auftreten; jedoch beschränkt sich die Anwendung
von cons auf eine deletion-tolerante Dekodierung der Ausgabe des Automaten in einen s-Ausdruck, bei der cons genau so oft angewendet wird,
wie das Symbol "." in dem s-Ausdruck auftritt.

Betrachtet man nun die in Abschnitt 2.3. genannten üblichen Erweiterungen
zum vollen Sprachumfang von LISP, für die retention-Strategie erforderlich wird, so wird durch ein Programm $\overline{\Pi}$ auch weiterhin eine berechenbare
Abbildung f_{Π} definiert, für deren Werte die obigen Einschränkungen hinsichtlich der zulässigen Atome genauso gelten. Da 2-Band-Kellerautomaten
wie Turingmaschinen universell sind, und ALGOL 60-Programme keine retention-Strategie benötigen, ist gezeigt, dass f_{Π} in LISP unter deletion-
Strategie und consfrei bzw. mit restriktivem Gebrauch von cons programmiert werden kann.

4. Konstruktion von $\tilde{\mathcal{R}}_{\Pi}$ ausgehend von $\overline{\Pi}$

Wir betrachten 2-Band-Kellerautomaten $\tilde{\mathcal{R}}_{\Pi}$ mit dem folgenden Aufbau [7]:

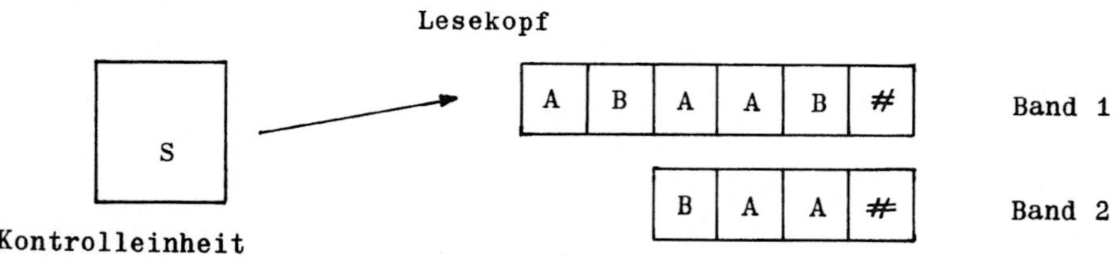

Die Automaten arbeiten mit den 11+n Symbolen des Alphabets
$$\Sigma = \left\{ A,B,\#,\#',*,*',H,T,C,\mathcal{L},\overline{\#},I_1,\ldots,I_n \right\},$$ wobei das Randsymbol $\#$
beide Bänder begrenzt und weder geschrieben noch gelöscht wird und wo-
bei die letzten 5+n Symbole nur auf das erste Band geschrieben und nie
gelöscht werden. Jeder Automat $\tilde{\mathcal{R}}_{\Pi}$ hat eine endliche, nicht leere Menge γ
von Zuständen S und einen ausgezeichneten Startzustand $\hat{S} \in \gamma$. Weiterhin
hat er ein Programm mit $|\gamma| \cdot 2 \cdot (11+n)$ Befehlen von der folgenden Form:

I. $(S,i,Z) \longrightarrow$ push down (S',i',Z') $\qquad Z' \neq \#$

$i = 2 \Rightarrow Z \in \{A,B,\#,\#',*,*'\}$, $\quad i' = 2 \Rightarrow Z' \in \{A,B,\#',*,*'\}$

Wenn der Automat im Zustand S das Symbol Z auf dem Band i liest, dann wird Z' auf dem Band i' gekellert, der Zustand S' angenommen und der Lesekopf zum Band i' bewegt.

II. $(S,i,Z) \longrightarrow$ erase(S') $\qquad Z \in \{A,B,\#',*,*'\}$

Wenn etc., dann wird das linke Symbol Z auf dem Band i gelöscht und der Zustand S' angenommen. Der Lesekopf bleibt auf Band i.

III. $(S,i,Z) \longrightarrow$ stop

Wenn etc., dann hält der Automat für $i = 1$ und $Z \neq \#$ regulär an, in allen anderen Fällen irregulär.

Es wird gefordert, dass alle Tripel (S, i, Z) paarweise verschieden sind (deterministisch). Die Menge aller Konfigurationen von $\breve{R}_{\pi}$ besteht aus den Quintupeln

$$K = (S,i,Z,X^{n_1} \ldots X^1, Y^{n_2} \ldots Y^1) \text{ mit}$$

$$S \in \Upsilon, \quad i \in \{1,2\}, \quad Z \in \textstyle\sum$$

$$X^{n_1}, \ldots, X^2 \in \textstyle\sum \backslash \# \quad, X^1 = \#, \quad n_1 \geqslant 1$$

$$Y^{n_2}, \ldots, Y^2 \in \{A,B,\#',*,*'\} \quad, Y^1 = \#, \quad n_2 \geqslant 1$$

$$Z = \begin{cases} X^{n_1} & \text{falls } i = 1 \\ Y^{n_2} & \text{falls } i = 2 \end{cases}$$

Die Konfiguration zu obiger Skizze ist

$$K = (S,1,A,ABAAB\#,BAA\#).$$

Es ist offenbar, wie man definiert, wann eine Konfiguration K' aufgrund einer der Befehle I oder II aus K resultiert ($K \longmapsto K'$).

Man erhält die Abschlüsse $\overset{+}{\longmapsto}$ und $\overset{*}{\longmapsto}$ von $\longmapsto$ in der Menge der Konfigurationen. Jede Konfiguration K hat höchstens einen unmittelbaren Nachfolger $K \longmapsto K'$. $K = (S,i,Z,x,y)$ ist genau dann maximal, wenn in $\breve{R}_{\pi}$ ein Haltebefehl $(S,i,Z) \longrightarrow$ stop existiert.

Vor dem Start des Automaten sind die Liste $\mathcal{C} = ('T','F','NIL',\ldots)$ der Standardatome und der in π explizit auftretenden Atome sowie die n s-Ausdrücke der Eingabe $inp_1, \ldots, inp_n$ in der Form

$$inp_{n_{Kod}} * \ldots * inp_{1_{Kod}} * \mathcal{C}_{Kod} \# \text{ auf das erste Band geschrieben,}$$

wobei für die auftretenden Atome nur festgehalten wird, welche untereinander gleich sind. Die Startkonfiguration ist

$$(\hat{S}, 2, \#', \quad inp_{n_{Kod}} * \ldots * inp_{1_{Kod}} * \mathcal{C}_{Kod} \#, \#)$$

Bei regulärem Halt des Automaten steht das Resultat durch die letzten 5+n Symbole von Σ in Postfixnotation kodiert auf dem ersten Band. Atome sind dabei ähnlich wie in der Eingabekodierung jeweils durch ihre Position in einem der s-Ausdrücke $\mathcal{C}, inp_1, \ldots, inp_n$ charakterisiert.

5. Konstruktion von $\overline{\Pi_{\breve{\mathcal{A}}}}$

In den folgenden Prozeduren treten, in "<" und ">" eingeschlossen, sogenannte Parameter neuer Art [7] auf. Sie werden dazu benutzt, Prozeduren f, die durch formale Prozeduranweisungen aufgerufen werden, bereits beim Auftreten von f als aktueller Parameter eines vorangegangenen Prozeduraufrufs, f mit Parametern zu versorgen.

Die Prozeduren von $\overline{\Pi_{\breve{\mathcal{A}}}}$ lassen sich zwar so umschreiben, dass keine Parameter neuer Art benutzt werden; allerdings wird durch sie erst die Simulation einsichtig, bei der die Bänder des Automaten $\breve{\mathcal{A}}_{\Pi}$ in $\overline{\Pi_{\breve{\mathcal{A}}}}$ durch "dicke" aktuelle Parameter neuer Art dargestellt sind. $\overline{\Pi_{\breve{\mathcal{A}}}}$ hat u. a. $|\mathcal{Y}| \cdot 2 \cdot (n+11)$ Funktionsprozeduren S_{iZ} mit $(S,i,Z) \in \mathcal{Y} \times \{1,2\} \times \Sigma$, wobei S_{iZ} als Prozeduridentifikatoren zu verstehen sind.

I. Für jeden Befehl der Form

$$(S,1,Z) \longrightarrow \text{push down } (S',i',Z') \qquad Z,Z' \neq \#$$

wird folgende Prozedur konstruiert:

$$\underline{\text{proc}} \ S_{1Z}(x,y); \ \left\{ \ S'_{i'Z'}(Z \langle x \rangle, y) \right\};$$

und entsprechend für die übrigen Befehle:

$$(S,2,Z) \longrightarrow \text{push down } (S',i',Z') \qquad Z,Z' \neq \#$$

$$\underline{\text{proc}} \ S_{2Z}(x,y); \ \left\{ \ S'_{i'Z'}(x, Z_2 \langle y \rangle) \right\};$$

$$(S,1,\#) \longrightarrow \text{push down } (S',i',Z') \qquad Z' \neq \#$$

$$\underline{\text{proc}} \ S_{1\#}(y); \ \left\{ \ S'_{i'Z'}(\#, y) \right\};$$

$$(S,2,\#) \longrightarrow \text{push down } (S',i',Z') \qquad Z' \neq \#$$

$$\underline{\text{proc}} \ S_{2\#}(x); \ \left\{ \ S'_{i'Z'}(x, \#_2) \right\};$$

II. $\quad\quad\quad\quad (S,1,Z) \longrightarrow$ erase (S') $\quad Z \in \{A,B,\#',*,*'\}$

$\quad$ **proc** $S_{1Z}(x,y)$; $\{ x(y,S'_{1A},S'_{1B},S'_{1\#'},S'_{1*},S'_{1*'},S'_{1\#}) \}$;

$\quad\quad\quad\quad (S,2,Z) \longrightarrow$ erase (S') $\quad Z \in \{A,B,\#',*,*'\}$

$\quad$ **proc** $S_{2Z}(x,y)$; $\{ y(x,S'_{2A},S'_{2B},S'_{2\#'},S'_{2*},S'_{2*'},S'_{2\#}) \}$;

III. $\quad\quad\quad\quad (S,1,Z) \longrightarrow$ stop $\quad Z \neq \#$

$\quad$ **proc** $S_{1Z}(x,y)$; $\{ x(\overline{\#},\text{'NIL'}) \}$;

$\quad\quad\quad\quad (S,2,Z) \longrightarrow$ stop $\quad Z \neq \#$

$\quad$ **proc** $S_{2Z}(x,y)$; $\{ car(\text{'T'}) \}$;

$\quad\quad\quad\quad (S,i,\#) \longrightarrow$ stop

$\quad$ **proc** $S_{i\#}(z)$; $\{ car(\text{'T'}) \}$;

Durch car('T') wird ein irreguläres Programmende erzwungen.

Die S_{iZ} benutzen erstens die 10 Prozeduren

$\quad$ **proc** $Z\langle x\rangle$ $(y,u_A,u_B,u_{\#'},u_*,u_{*'},u_\#)$; $\{ u_Z(x,y) \}$;

$\quad$ **proc** $Z_2\langle y\rangle(x,u_A,u_B,u_{\#'},u_*,u_{*'},u_\#)$; $\{ u_Z(x,y) \}$;

$\quad$ für $Z \in \{A,B,\#',*,*'\}$, zweitens die beiden Prozeduren

$\quad$ **proc** $\#(y,u_A,u_B,u_{\#'},u_*,u_{*'},u_\#)$; $\{ u_\#(y) \}$;

$\quad$ **proc** $\#_2(x,u_A,u_B,u_{\#'},u_*,u_{*'},u_\#)$; $\{ u_\#(x) \}$;

und drittens die 5+n Prozeduren $H,T,C,\mathcal{L},\overline{\#},I_1,\ldots,I_n$, deren genaue Gestalt erst im endgültigen $\overline{\Pi_{\tilde{R}}}$ interessiert.

Die genannten Prozeduren haben die interessante Eigenschaft, dass ihre Rümpfe jeweils aus genau einem Prozeduraufruf bestehen und dass im Falle

$$(S,i,Z,X^{n_1}\ldots\#,Y^{n_2}\ldots\#) \overset{+}{\longmapsto} (\tilde{S},\tilde{i},\tilde{Z},X^{\widetilde{n_1}}\ldots\#,Y^{\widetilde{n_2}}\ldots\#)$$

ein Aufruf

$$S_{iZ}(X^{n_1}\langle\ldots\langle\#\rangle\ldots\rangle, Y_2^{n_2}\langle\ldots\langle\#_2\rangle\ldots\rangle)$$

zu einem Aufruf

$$\tilde{S}_{\tilde{i}\tilde{Z}}(X^{\widetilde{n_1}}\langle\ldots\langle\#\rangle\ldots\rangle, Y_2^{\widetilde{n_2}}\langle\ldots\langle\#_2\rangle\ldots\rangle)$$

führt. Dies geschieht insbesondere in deletion-Strategie ohne Verwendung von cons!

Die Idee für das weitere Vorgehen ist es nun, einen cons-freien Vorspann zu konstruieren, der von den eingegebenen s-Ausdrücken
$inp_1, \ldots, inp_n$ ausgehend zu einem Prozeduraufruf führt, der der in Abschnitt 4. genannten Startkonfiguration entspricht. Ferner wird ein
Nachspann angegeben, der ausgehend von einem Aufruf

$$X^{n_1} \langle \ldots \langle \# \rangle \ldots \rangle \ (\overline{\#}, \text{'NIL'})$$

den Wert $f_{\pi}(inp_1, \ldots, inp_n)$ als s-Ausdruck ausgibt und dazu cons nur in
geringem Umfang benutzt.

Das vollständige Programm $\overline{\pi}_{\hat{A}}$ lautet nun:

<u>begin</u>
<u>proc</u> $f(inp_1, inp_2, \ldots, inp_n)$;
<u>comment</u> Die Prozeduren $1, w_1, \ldots, w_n$ organisieren das Kodieren von
$\quad\quad \mathcal{A}, inp_1, \ldots, inp_n$;
$\quad \Big\{$ <u>proc</u> $w_1(x)$;
$\quad\quad \big\{ \ \vdots$
$\quad\quad\quad$ <u>proc</u> $w_{n-1}(x)$;
$\quad\quad\quad\quad \big\{$ <u>proc</u> $w_n(x)$; $\ \big\{ \ 1(inp_n, \widehat{\widehat{S}}, *\langle x \rangle) \big\} \ $;
$\quad\quad\quad\quad\quad 1(inp_{n-1}, w_n, *\langle x \rangle) \big\} \ $;
$\quad\quad\quad \vdots$
$\quad\quad\quad 1(inp_1, w_2, *\langle x \rangle) \ \big\} \ $;

<u>proc</u> $1(i, f, x)$;
<u>comment</u> Der s-Ausdruck i wird in Parameterposition x kodiert und danach
$\quad\quad$ die Prozedur f aufgerufen;
$\quad \big\{$ <u>if</u> $atom(i)$ <u>then</u> $id(i, f, x)$ <u>else</u> $1(car(i), r\langle i, f \rangle, A\langle x \rangle)$<u>fi</u> $\big\} \ $;
<u>proc</u> $r\langle i, f \rangle(x)$; $\ \big\{ \ 1(cdr(i), r_1\langle f \rangle, A\langle B \langle x \rangle \rangle) \big\} \ $;
<u>proc</u> $r_1\langle f \rangle(x)$; $\ \big\{ \ f(B\langle x \rangle) \big\} \ $;

<u>proc</u> $id(i, f, x)$;
<u>comment</u> Die Prozeduren $1', w_1', \ldots, w_n'$ organisieren das Identifizieren
$\quad\quad$ von i in $\mathcal{A}, inp_1, \ldots, inp_n$. Danach wird f aufgerufen;
$\quad \big\{$ <u>proc</u> $w_1'(x)$;
$\quad\quad \big\{ \ \vdots$

```
     proc w_{n-1}'(x);
        { proc w_n'(x);  { l'(inp_n, S⃗, *'<x>) } ;

          l'(inp_{n-1}, w_n', *'<x>) } ;
          .
          .
        l'(inp_1, w_2', *'<x>) } ;

   proc l'(i', f', x');
   comment Es wird das Atom i im s-Ausdruck i' gesucht. Bei Erfolg
           wird anschliessend f aufgerufen, andernfalls f';

      { if atom(i') then
            if eq(i,i') then f(#'<x'>) else f'(x') fi
         else l'(car(i'), r'<i',f'>, A<x'>) fi } ;
      proc r'<i',f'>(x'); { l'(cdr(i'), r_1'<f'>, A<B<x'>>) } ;
      proc r_1'<f'>(x'); { f'(B<x'>) } ;
   l'(Λ, w_1', #'<x>) } ;

   proc S⃗(x); { Ŝ_{2#}(x, #_2) } ;

   comment Es folgen die Prozeduren S_{iZ},A,B,#',*,*',A_2,B_2,#_2',*_2,*_2',#,#_2
           als Hauptteil des Programmes;
        .
        .
   S_{1Z}(x,y); { x(#̄, 'NIL') } ;

   comment Bei der Dekodierung bedeuten:
            i   s-Ausdruck, in dem ein Atom bestimmt werden soll
            x   Kodierung des Restresultats
            f   Keller für die Zwischenresultate
          val   letztes Zwischenresultat
            i'  vorletztes Zwischenresultat;

proc H<x>(i,f,val);
   { if atom(car(i)) then x(V<f,val>,car(i)) else x(cdr(i),f,val) } ;
proc T<x>(i,f,val);
   { if atom(cdr(i)) then x(V<f,val>,cdr(i)) else x(cdr(i),f,val) } ;
proc C<x>(f,val); { f(x,val) } ;
proc V<f,i'>(x,val); { x(f,cons(i',val)) } ;
proc Λ<x>(f,val); { x(Λ,f,val) } ;
proc I_1<x>(f,val);
   { if atom(inp_1) then x(V<f,val>,inp_1) else x(inp_1,f,val) } ;
      .
      .
```

$\underline{\text{proc}}\ I_n\langle x\rangle(f,\text{val});$

$\qquad\big\{\ \underline{\text{if}}\ \text{atom}(\text{inp}_n)\ \underline{\text{then}}\ x(V\langle f,\text{val}\rangle,\text{inp}_n)\ \underline{\text{else}}\ x(\text{inp}_n,f,\text{val})\ \big\}\ ;$

$\underline{\text{proc}}\ \overline{\#}\langle x\rangle(f,\text{val});\ \big\{\ \text{val}\ \big\}\ ;$

$1(\mathcal{L},w_1,\#)\ \big\}\ ;$

$\underline{\text{out}}\ f(\underline{\text{in}},\underline{\text{in}},\ldots,\underline{\text{in}})$

$\qquad\qquad\text{n-mal}$

$\underline{\text{end}}$

6. Bemerkungen zum Programm

Der Parameter inp_5 habe den s-Ausdruck $s = (K.(L.L))$ als Wert. Der Einfachheit halber sollen die Atome K und L nur in s auftreten.

6.1. Kodierung der Eingabe

Der zu s gehörige binäre Baum wird vollständig durchlaufen und dabei der Weg durch die Symbole A (ahead) und B (back) vom Randsymbol $\#$ ausgehend angegeben.

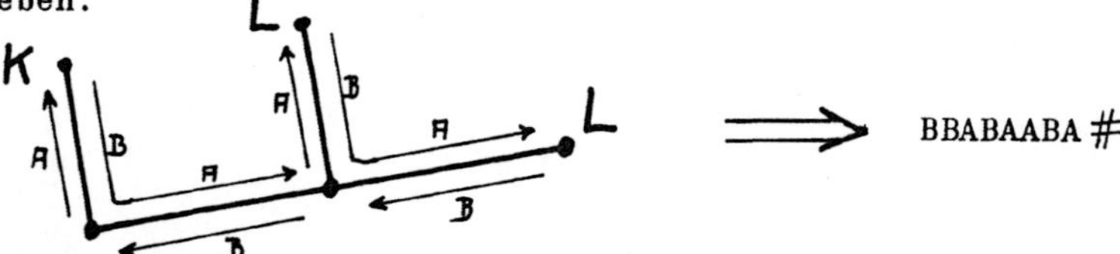

In diese Beschreibung der Struktur von s werden Kodierungen der Atome eingefügt, indem ein Atom durch den Weg zu seinem ersten Auftreten in s charakterisiert ist, z. B. L durch #'AABA #'. Die Kodierung von s ist somit: BB#'AABA#'AB#'AABA#'AAB#'A#'A# oder als Ergebnis des Aufrufs $1(\text{inp}_5,\hat{S},\#)$:

$$\hat{S}(B\langle B\langle\#'\langle A\ldots\langle A\langle\#'\langle A\langle\#\rangle\rangle\rangle\ldots\rangle\rangle\rangle).$$

6.2. Kodierung der Ausgabe

Der Aufbau des Resultats aus Atombeschreibungen und cons (C) ist auf Band 1 bzw. im Parameter x in Postfixnotation angegeben. Eine Atombeschreibung besteht aus der Angabe des Eingabeparameters (I_j bzw. $\mathcal{L}$), in dem das Atom auftritt sowie einer Folge von Operationen car (Head) und cdr (Tail), die zu dem gewünschten Atom führen. Durch einen Aufruf $x(\overline{\#},'\text{NIL}')$ mit

$$x = \underbrace{I_5\langle H\langle I_5}_{K}\langle T\langle H\langle C\underbrace{\langle I_5}_{L}\langle T\langle H\langle C\underbrace{\langle\overline{\#}\langle\#\rangle\rangle}_{L}\ldots\rangle}$$

werden die angegebenen Prozeduren bis auf die Kellerung von Zwischen-
resultaten der Reihe nach ausgeführt und das Ergebnis ((K.L).L) der
Dekodierung als Wert von $\overline{\overline{H}}$ und somit von f erzeugt.

Literaturverzeichnis

[1] Grau, A. A., Hill, U., Langmaack, H.: Translation of ALGOL 60.
    Handbook for Automatic Computation. Vol. I, Part b. Springer 1967

[2] Johnston, J. B.: The Contour Model of Block Structured Processes.
    SIGPLAN Notices 6 (2) 55 - 82 (1971)

[3] Berry, D. M.: Introduction to Oregano.
    SIGPLAN Notices 6 (2) 171 - 190 (1971)

[4] Berry, D. M.: Block Structure: Retention or Deletion.
    Proceedings of the Third Annual ACM Symposium on
    Theory of Computing (1971)

[5] Fischer, M. J.: Lambda Calculus Schemata.
    SIGPLAN Notices 7 (1) 104 - 109 (1972)

[6] McCarthy, J. et. al.: LISP 1.5 Programmer's Manual. MIT Press,
    Cambridge Mass., 1966

[7] Langmaack, H.: On Procedures as Open Subroutines II.
    Acta Informatica 3, 227 - 241 (1974)

ÜBER DIE ENTSCHEIDBARKEIT DER FORMALEN ERREICHBARKEIT

VON PROZEDUREN BEI MONADISCHEN PROGRAMMEN

Wolfram-Manfred Lippe

Institut für Informatik und angewandte Mathematik
Christian-Albrechts-Universität, D-23 Kiel

1. Einleitung

Beim Bau von Übersetzern für ALGOL-ähnliche Programmiersprachen erfordert die
Behandlung von Prozeduren einen besonderen Aufwand. Deswegen ist es wünschens-
wert, Algorithmen zu besitzen, die gewisse Eigenschaften von Programmen mit
Prozeduren bereits zur Übersetzungszeit entscheiden können, um so durch eine
differenziertere Behandlung der Prozeduren unnötigen Aufwand einzusparen und
effizientere Zielprogramme zu erzeugen. Zu diesen Eigenschaften gehören z.B.

    1) die formal korrekte Parameterübergabe in einem Programm
       mit Prozeduren,

    2) die formale Erreichbarkeit einer Prozedur,

    3) die formale Rekursivität einer Prozedur,

    4) die formal starke Rekursivität einer Prozedur,

    5) die Makro-Programm-Eigenschaft eines Programms mit Prozeduren.

Bei Programmen mit formal korrekter Parameterübergabe braucht zur Laufzeit
nicht geprüft zu werden, ob aktuelle und formale Parameter zueinander passen.
Nicht formal stark rekursive Prozeduren und erst recht nicht formal rekursive
Prozeduren dürfen wie Blöcke behandelt werden, d.h. ihre Festspeicher können
innerhalb der Festspeicher der kleinsten umfassenden Prozeduren untergebracht
werden, und eigene Display- (Index-) Register sind unnötig. Programme mit der
Makro-Programm-Eigenschaft benötigen zur Laufzeit überhaupt keine Prozeduror-
ganisation, was die Laufzeit erheblich verkürzt. Gewiß kann die makroartige
Expansion des Originalprogramms zu unerträglichen statischen Programmlängen
führen, in der Systemprogrammierung, insbesondere beim Compilerbau, wird man
den erhöhten Speicherbedarf trotzdem in Kauf nehmen, weil sonst wegen der
häufigen Prozeduraufrufe ein relativ großer Zeitverlust eintritt.

Für ALGOL 60 sind die Eigenschaften 1)-5) unentscheidbar, ebenso 2)-5) für
ALGOL 68, selbst wenn nur Identifikatoren als aktuelle Parameter zugelassen
sind [5,6].
Die bis jetzt bekannten Resultate bzgl. der formalen Erreichbarkeit von Prozeduren in generellen Programmen lassen sich durch folgendes Diagramm reprä-

sentieren, das die Programme nach maximaler Parameterzahl P pro Prozedur und
nach maximaler Prozedurschachtelungstiefe S einteilt:

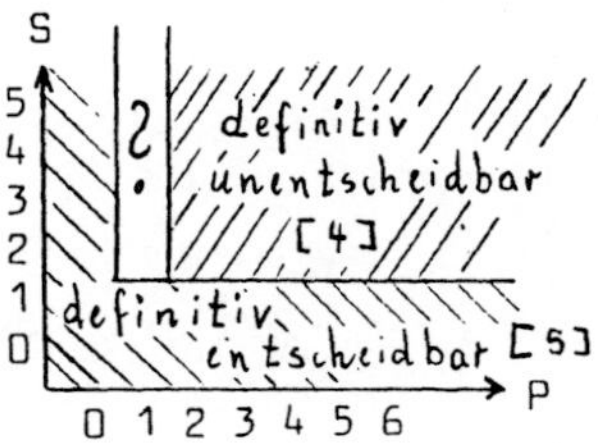

Wir wollen jetzt eine umfangreiche Programmteilklasse definieren, und für sie
die Entscheidbarkeit nachzuweisen versuchen. Der definitive Entscheidbarkeitsbereich sollte natürlich möglichst weit über den obigen hinausragen.

Zum Beweis der Unentscheidbarkeit der formalen Erreichbarkeit von Prozeduren
wird in [5] für jedes Post'sche Korrespondenzsystem $\mathcal{L}$ ein Programm π_2 mit einer Prozedur M1 effektiv konstruiert, so daß $\mathcal{L}$ genau dann eine Lösung hat,
wenn M1 in π_2 formal erreichbar ist. Es fällt auf, daß in π_2 die entscheiden-
den Prozeduranweisungen $a_0(a_1,\ldots,a_n)$ von der Art sind, daß alle formalen Identifikatoren a_i paarweise verschieden sind. Wenn wir nun ein Programm monadisch
nennen, falls in jeder Prozeduranweisung $a_0(a_1,\ldots,a_n)$ für die formalen Identifikatoren a_i,a_j $a_i=a_j$ ist, so führt der zitierte Beweis zu der Vermutung, daß
die formale Erreichbarkeit von Prozeduren für monadische ALGOL 60-Programme
entscheidbar ist.

Diese Vermutung kann noch nicht vollständig bewiesen werden. Der Beweis ist jedoch für zwei große Teilklassen monadischer Programme möglich, erstens für monadische Programme mit maximaler Prozedurschachtelungstiefe 2 und maximaler
Parameterzahl 2 pro Prozedur, zweitens für monadische Programme mit maximaler
Prozedurschachtelungstiefe 3 und maximaler Parameterzahl 1 pro Prozedur. Aus
dem Beweis des ersten Falls ist ersichtlich, daß die Beschränkung der Parameterzahl im Grunde unerheblich ist. Im ersten Fall benutzen wir als Hilfsmittel
Baumsysteme [8], im zweiten Fall Stacksysteme [1]. Von beiden Systemen ist bekannt, daß das Zustandserreichbarkeitsproblem algorithmisch lösbar ist.
Der Einfachheit halber beschränken wir uns auf die Sprache ALGOL 60-P (P=pure),
die gegenüber ALGOL 60 folgende hauptsächlichen Einschränkungen und Veränderun-
gen besitzt:

    a) keine Funktionsprozeduren,

    b) kein "call by value",

    c) nur Identifikatoren als aktuelle Parameter von Prozeduranweisungen,

    d) alle Prozedurrümpfe sind in Rumpfklammern eingeschlossen,

    e) leerer Spezifikationsteil im Prozedurkopf.

Für eine vollständige Definition von ALGOL 60-P siehe [5].

2. Definitionen

Ein formales Algol 60-P-Programm π ist eine Zeichenkette aus Grundsymbolen,
die durch die formalen Regeln der kontextfreien Grammatik $\mathcal{G}_P$ für ALGOL 60-P
auf das Axiom $\langle$program$\rangle$ reduziert werden kann und für die die folgende Eigenschaft gilt: Zu jedem auftretenden Identifikator gibt es genau ein zugehö-
riges definierendes Auftreten. Ein formales Programm heißt übersetzbar, falls
jedes Auftreten einer Konstanten oder eines Identifikators gemäß seiner Definition vernünftig erfolgt. Zwei formale Programme heißen identisch, falls sie
sich nur durch eine zulässige Umbenennung von Identifikatoren unterscheiden,
und wir wollen in Zukunft nicht zwischen identischen Programmen unterscheiden.
Ein formales Programm heißt ausgezeichnet, falls verschiedene definierende Vorkommen von Identifikatoren durch verschiedene Identifikatoren bezeichnet sind.
Ein formales Programm heißt partiell übersetzbar, falls nach dem Ersetzen aller
Prozedurrümpfe durch leere Rümpfe das sich so ergebende Programm übersetzbar
ist.

<u>Definition</u>: Sei π partiell übersetzbar. Ein Programm π' heißt <u>Ergebnis aus π</u>
<u>durch Anwendung der Kopierregel</u> ($\pi \longmapsto \pi'$) falls gilt:
Sei $f(a_1,\ldots,a_n)$ eine Prozeduranweisung im Hauptprogramm von π. Sei ferner
<u>proc</u> $f(x_1,\ldots,x_n);\{\sigma\}$ die zugehörige Prozedurdeklaration. Die partielle Über-
setzbarkeit von π garantiert, daß die Anzahl der aktuellen und formalen Parameter übereinstimmt. Sei ferner π o.B.d.A. ausgezeichnet. Dann wird $f(a_1,\ldots,a_n)$
durch einen modifizierten Rumpf $\{\sigma'\}$ ersetzt, indem die formalen Parameter x_i,
die in $\{\sigma\}$ auftreten, durch die entsprechenden aktuellen Parameter a_i ersetzt
werden.

$$\pi : \quad \ldots \underline{proc}\ f(x_1,\ldots,x_n);\{\sigma\}\ ;\ \ldots\ ;f(a_1,\ldots,a_n);\ \ldots$$
$$\pi': \quad \ldots \underline{proc}\ f(x_1,\ldots,x_n);\{\sigma\}\ ;\ \ldots\ ;\quad \{\sigma'\}\quad ;\ \ldots$$

Durch Umbenennung aller Identifikatoren in σ', die in σ' selbst gebunden sind
(lokal), wird π' ausgezeichnet. $\{\sigma'\}$ heißt <u>erzeugter Block</u>; die Klammern $\{\ \}$
bei $\{\sigma'\}$ heißen <u>Aufrufklammern</u> im Gegensatz zu den <u>Rumpfklammern</u> $\{\ \}$ bei $\{\sigma\}$.
$\overset{+}{\longmapsto}$ und $\overset{*}{\longmapsto}$ sollen die transitive bzw. transitive reflexive Hülle von $\longmapsto$
bezeichnen. Ein formales Programm π heißt <u>original</u>, falls $\{\ \}$ nur als Rumpf-
klammern auftreten.

<u>Definition</u>: Sei π original. Die Menge T_π mit
$$T_\pi := \{\pi'/\ \pi \overset{*}{\longmapsto} \pi',\ \pi'\ \text{besitzt höchstens einen innersten}$$
$$\text{erzeugten Block}\}$$
heißt <u>Ausführungsbaum</u> von π.

Mit IGB(π') bezeichnen wir den innersten erzeugten Block von π'. Entfernen wir
bei einem Programm $\pi' \in T_\pi$ alle Prozedurdeklarationen, so erhalten wir das zugehörige Hauptprogramm π'_m. Ersetzen wir alle Prozeduranweisungen in π'_m durch
ein Sonderzeichen, z.B. <u>call</u>, so erhalten wir das reduzierte Hauptprogramm π_r

von γ.

Definition: $T_{r\,\gamma} := \{ \gamma'_r / \gamma' \in T_\gamma \}$ heißt <u>reduzierter Ausführungsbaum</u> von γ.

Definition: Zwei originale Programme heißen <u>formal äquivalent</u>, falls ihre reduzierten Ausführungsbäume identisch sind.

Definition: Eine Prozedur in einem originalen Programm γ heißt <u>formal erreich-bar</u>, falls ein Programm $\gamma' \in T_\gamma$ ex., so daß IGB(γ') ein modifizierter Rumpf einer Kopie dieser Prozedur ist.

Im folgenden werden wir uns mit der formalen Erreichbarkeit bei einem besonde-ren Typ von Programmen, den monadischen Programmen, beschäftigen.

Definition: Ein Programm γ heißt <u>monadisch</u>, wenn in jeder Prozeduranweisung $a_o(a_1,\ldots,a_n)$ für die formalen Identifikatoren a_i, a_j gilt $a_i = a_j$.

Um die Beweise zu vereinfachen, machen wir ferner die unerhebliche Einschrän-kung, daß es neben Prozedurdeklarationen keine weiteren Deklarationen und neben Prozeduranweisungen keine weiteren Anweisungen geben soll.

Zum Beweis, daß die formale Erreichbarkeit von Prozeduren bei monadischen Pro-grammen entscheidbar ist, führen wir unsere ALGOL 60-P-Programme in formal äquivalente Programme der modularen Programmiersprache ALGOL 60-P-G (closure-Sprache) über. Prozedurdeklarationen in ALGOL 60-P-G haben die Form

$$(*) \qquad \underline{proc}\ f\ \langle y_1,\ldots,y_{m_f}\rangle\ (x_1,\ldots,x_{n_f});\ \{\S\}\ ;$$

Die Identifikatoren $y_1,\ldots,y_{m_f}$ heißen formale Parameter neuer Art, $x_1,\ldots,x_{n_f}$ sind die formalen Parameter alter Art. Die Klammern fallen weg, falls m_f bzw. n_f Null ist. Alle übrigen Deklarationen sehen wie in ALGOL 60-P aus. Ein Term ist eine endliche Zeichenreihe, die nach folgenden Regeln gebildet wird:

    1. Identifikatoren sind Terme.

    2. Wenn γ Identifikator ist und $\tau_1,\ldots,\tau_m$, $m \geq 1$, Terme sind, dann ist auch $\gamma\langle\tau_1,\ldots,\tau_m\rangle$ ein Term. τ_i heißt aktueller Parameter neuer Art.

Aus einem formalen ALGOL 60-P-Programm γ' entsteht ein formales ALGOL 60-P-G-Programm γ dadurch, daß die Prozedurköpfe in γ' durch neue Köpfe der Form $(*)$ ersetzt werden und daß man in γ' angewandt vorkommende Identifikatoren durch Terme auswechselt, so daß jeder Identifikator genau eine Definition besitzt. Auch alle übrigen Begriffe lassen sich ohne Schwierigkeiten auf ALGOL 60-P-G ausweiten.

Der Unterschied zwischen den beiden Sprachen liegt in der Methode, wie man Pro-zeduren f, die durch formale Prozeduranweisungen aufgerufen werden, durch aktu-elle Parameter versorgt. In ALGOL 60-P werden alle aktuellen Parameter im Moment des Aufrufs übergeben. In ALGOL 60-P-G werden die aktuellen Parameter alter Art ebenfalls im Moment des Aufrufs übergeben, während die aktuellen Parameter neu-er Art so betrachtet werden können, als ob sie bereits vorher übergeben worden wären, als der Prozeduridentifikator f als aktueller Parameter eines vorangegangenen Aufrufs auftrat. Auf Grund dieser Wirksamkeit der formalen Parameter neuer Art ist es möglich, jedes originale ALGOL 60-P-G-Programm in ein formal äquivalentes ALGOL 60-P-G-Programm ohne Prozedurschachtelung (modular) effektiv umzuformen.

3. Baumsysteme

Betrachtet man nur Programme mit maximaler Parameterzahl 1 und maximaler Prozedurschachtelungstiefe 2, so besitzen alle Terme, die bei den Prozeduranweisungen des Ausführungsbaumes auftreten können, die Form einer linearen Zeichenkette. Dieser Spezialfall wurde bereits in [7] untersucht, und die Entscheidbarkeit der formalen Erreichbarkeit mit Hilfe von regulären kanonischen Systemen gezeigt. Erhöht man bei den Programmen die Parameteranzahl, bzw. die Prozedurschachtelungstiefe, so besitzen die einzelnen Terme eine baumartige Struktur. Im Gegensatz zu den Baumautomaten, wie sie von Brainerd, Doner usw. betrachtet wurden, benötigen wir jedoch Systeme, die eine Modifikation des Eingabebaums durch Veränderung der Wurzel erlauben. Deswegen benutzen wir Baumsysteme, wie sie von Rounds [8] eingeführt wurden.

Definition: Ein markiertes Alphabet ist ein Paar (Σ, r), wobei Σ eine endliche Menge und $r: \Sigma \longrightarrow \mathbb{N}$ eine Abbildung ist. Sei ferner Σ_n durch

$$\Sigma_n := \{ \sigma \in \Sigma / r(\sigma) = n \}$$

definiert.

Hiermit lassen sich nun Σ - Terme (Bäume) definieren:

Definition: Sei (Σ, r) ein markiertes Alphabet. Die Menge $\mathcal{T}_\Sigma^o$ ist die kleinste Menge, derart daß

   (a) $\Sigma_o \subsetneq \mathcal{T}_\Sigma^o$

   (b) falls $t_o, \ldots, t_{n-1} \in \mathcal{T}_\Sigma^o$ und $\sigma \in \Sigma_n \succ \sigma \langle t_o, \ldots, t_{n-1} \rangle \in \mathcal{T}_\Sigma^o$

Was ein Unterterm eines Terms ist dürfte klar sein. Die t_i, $0 \leqslant i \leqslant n-1$, in $\sigma \langle t_o, \ldots, t_{n-1} \rangle$ bezeichnen wir auch als unmittelbare Unterterme, t_o als unmittelbaren linken Unterterm und t_{n-1} als unmittelbaren rechten Unterterm. Um Terme miteinander vergleichen zu können, benötigen wir noch

Definition: Zwei Σ-Terme $\sigma \langle t_o, \ldots, t_{n-1} \rangle$ und $\sigma' \langle t_o', \ldots, t_{k-1}' \rangle$ heißen fastidentisch, falls $n=k$ und $t_i = t_i'$ für $i = 0, \ldots, n-1$.

Definition: Seien $\sigma \langle t_o, \ldots, t_{n-1} \rangle$ und $\sigma' \langle t_o', \ldots, t_{k-1}' \rangle$ zwei Σ-Terme. Dann heißt $\sigma' \langle t_o', \ldots, t_{k-1}' \rangle$ Fastunterterm von $\sigma \langle t_o, \ldots, t_{n-1} \rangle$, falls ein Unterterm $\bar\sigma \langle \bar t_o, \ldots, \bar t_{k-1} \rangle$ von $\sigma \langle t_o, \ldots, t_{n-1} \rangle$ ex., so daß $\bar\sigma \langle \bar t_o, \ldots, \bar t_{k-1} \rangle$ und $\sigma' \langle t_o', \ldots, t_{k-1}' \rangle$ fastidentisch sind.
Ist $\bar\sigma \langle \bar t_o, \ldots, \bar t_{k-1} \rangle$ unmittelbarer Unterterm von $\sigma \langle t_o, \ldots, t_{n-1} \rangle$, so bezeichnen wir $\sigma' \langle t_o', \ldots, t_{k-1}' \rangle$ als unmittelbaren Fastunterterm von $\sigma \langle t_o, \ldots, t_{n-1} \rangle$.

Es sei A eine endliche Menge mit $A \cap \Sigma = \emptyset$. Wir erweitern Σ zu Σ' mit $\Sigma' = A \cup \Sigma_o$ und $\Sigma_n' = \Sigma_n$. Statt $\mathcal{T}_{\Sigma'}^o$ schreiben wir auch $\mathcal{T}_\Sigma^o(A)$.

Definition: Sei Q eine Menge sog. Zustände und $q,q' \in Q$. Dann heißt ein Paar $(q, \sigma \langle x_0,\ldots,x_n \rangle) \rightarrow (q',u)$ mit $\sigma \in \Sigma_n$, $u \in \mathcal{T}_\Sigma(\{x_0,\ldots,x_n\})$, $n \geq 0$, eine __Baumproduktion__. Die x_i bezeichnen wir als Variablen.

Definition: Ein __Baumsystem__ G über Σ ist ein 4-tupel $(\Sigma,Q,S,\mathcal{T})$ mit einer endlichen Menge Q von Zuständen, einer endlichen Menge $\mathcal{T}$ von Baumproduktionen über Q und Σ, und S einer endlichen Untermenge von $Q \times \mathcal{T}_\Sigma^0$ (Startkonfigurationen).

Die Wirkungsweise eines solchen Baumsystems ist gegeben durch:

Definition: Sei $(q,t),(q',t') \in Q \times \mathcal{T}_\Sigma^0$. (q',t') wird aus (q,t) __direkt erzeugt__ $((q,t) \Rightarrow (q',t'))$, falls gilt:

(a) $t = \sigma \langle t_0,\ldots,t_{n-1} \rangle$, $n \geq 0$

(b) es gibt eine Baumproduktion $(q, \sigma \langle x_0,\ldots,x_{n-1} \rangle) \rightarrow (q',u)$

(c) t' geht aus u dadurch hervor, daß die x_i in u durch t_i ersetzt werden.

Mit $\overset{*}{\Rightarrow}$ bezeichnen wir die reflexive transitive Hülle von $\Rightarrow$.

4. Programme mit zweiparametrigen Prozeduren und Prozedurschachtelungstiefe ≤ 2

Im folgenden beschäftigen wir uns mit Programmen, die nach der Umformung in ALGOL 60-P-G-Programme und der Beseitigung der Prozedurschachtelungen die allgemeine Gestalt

$$\pi_1 = \underline{begin} \quad \underline{proc}\ g_1(x_1^1,x_1^2); \{ \ldots \};$$

$$\vdots \quad \text{Hauptteil von } g_1$$

$$\underline{proc}\ g_n(x_n^1,x_n^2); \{ \ldots \};$$

$$\underline{proc}\ f_{11}\langle \bar{x}_1^1,\bar{x}_1^2 \rangle\ (y_{11}^1,y_{11}^2); \{ \ldots \};$$

$$\vdots \quad \text{Hauptteil von } f_{11}$$

$$\underline{proc}\ f_{1m_1}\langle \bar{x}_1^1,\bar{x}_1^2 \rangle\ (y_{1m_1}^1,y_{1m_1}^2); \{ \ldots \};$$

$$\vdots$$

$$\underline{proc}\ f_{n1}\langle \bar{x}_n^1,\bar{x}_n^2 \rangle\ (y_{n1}^1,y_{n1}^2); \{ \ldots \};$$

$$\vdots$$

$$\underline{proc}\ f_{nm_n}\langle \bar{x}_n^1,\bar{x}_n^2 \rangle\ (y_{nm_n}^1,y_{nm_n}^2); \{ \ldots \};$$

$$\vdots \quad \left.\begin{array}{c} \\ \\ \end{array}\right\} \text{Hauptprogramm}$$

$$\underline{end}$$

besitzen.

Im Hauptprogramm können nur Anweisungen der Art $g_i(g_{i'},g_{i''})$, $1 \leq i,i',i'' \leq n$ auftreten.

Bei den Anweisungen $a_0(a_1,a_2)$, die im Hauptteil von g_i (i fest, $1 \leq i \leq n$) auftreten, kann a_k, $k=0,1,2$, ein formaler Identifikator x_i^1 bzw. x_i^2, ein globaler Identifikator $g_{i'}$ ($1 \leq i' \leq n$) oder ein Term $f_{ij}\langle x_i^1,x_i^2 \rangle$ ($1 \leq j \leq m_i$) sein.

Bei den Anweisungen $a_0(a_1,a_2)$, die im Hauptteil von f_{ij} (i,j fest, $1 \leq i \leq n$, $1 \leq j \leq m_i$) auftreten, kann a_k, $k=0,1,2$, ein formaler Identifikator y_{ij}^1 oder y_{ij}^2 oder $\bar{x}_i^1$ oder $\bar{x}_i^2$, ein globaler Identifikator $g_{i'}$ ($1 \leq i \leq n$) oder ein Term

$f_{ij'}\langle \bar{x}_i^1, \bar{x}_i^2 \rangle$ $(1 \leqslant j' \leqslant m_i)$ sein.

Die durch die Kopierregel entstehenden Terme im Hauptprogramm besitzen nun offensichtlich die Gestalt binärer Bäume, deren Blätter aus Identifikatoren g_i bestehen. Den Zusammenhang zwischen den einzelnen Termen einer Anweisung zeigt

Satz 1: Bei allen Prozeduranweisungen $a_o(a_1, a_2)$, die in Hauptteilen von Programmen π_1' des Ausführungsbaumes T_{π_1} des ALGOL 60-P-G-Programms π_1 auftreten gilt: Bei je zwei Untertermen t_1, t_k von a_i, a_j ist einer der t_1, t_k Fastunterterm des andern.

Dies bedeutet insbesondere für die Terme a_i, a_j, daß einer stets Fastunterterm des andern ist. Beschränken wir uns auf monadische Programme, so lassen sich die Aussagen über den Zusammenhang zwischen den einzelnen Termen weiter verschärfen:

Satz 2: Bei allen Prozeduranweisungen $a_o(a_1, a_2)$, die in Hauptteilen von Programmen $\widetilde{\pi}_1'$ des Ausführungsbaumes $T_{\widetilde{\pi}_1}$ eines monadischen ALGOL 60-P-G-Programms $\widetilde{\pi}_1$ auftreten, gilt für je zwei Terme a_i, a_j, $0 \leqslant i, j \leqslant 2$, eine der folgenden drei Eigenschaften:

> a) $a_i = g_{i'}$ oder $a_j = g_{i'}$, $1 \leqslant i' \leqslant n$,   oder
>
> b) a_i und a_j sind fastidentisch   oder
>
> c) a_i ist unmittelbarer Fastunterterm von a_j oder umgekehrt.

Dieser Satz zeigt, daß sich die einzelnen Terme nur in dem unmittelbaren Bereich um die Wurzel unterscheiden. Durch das Notieren der Unterschiede zwischen den einzelnen Termen in einem Index an der Wurzel, lassen sich die einzelnen Terme der Prozeduranweisungen $a_o(a_1, a_2)$ zu einem Term zusammenfassen. Somit läßt sich zu unserem Programm $\widetilde{\pi}_1$ ein Baumsystem $G_{\widetilde{\pi}_1}$ konstruieren mit der Eigenschaft

Satz 3: Eine Prozedur p in $\widetilde{\pi}_1$ ist genau dann formal erreichbar, falls es in $G_{\widetilde{\pi}_1}$ eine Startkonfiguration s und es eine durch p bestimmte Konfiguration S_p gibt, so daß $s \overset{*}{\Longrightarrow} S_p$.

Da letzteres jedoch entschieden werden kann [8], erhält man unmittelbar

Satz 4: Es ist entscheidbar, ob eine Prozedur in einem monadischen ALGOL 60-P-Programm mit höchstens zweiparametrigen Prozeduren und Prozedurschachtelungstiefe < 2 formal erreichbar ist.

5. Programme mit einparametrigen Prozeduren und Prozedurschachtelungstiefe $\leqslant 3$

Im folgenden beschäftigen wir uns mit Programmen, die nach der Umformung in ALGOL 60-P-G-Programme und der Beseitigung der Prozedurschachtelung die allgemeine Gestalt

$$\Pi_2 = \underline{begin} \quad \underline{proc}\ g_1(x_1); \{ \dots \};$$
$$\vdots$$
$$\underline{proc}\ g_n(x_n); \{ \dots \};$$
$$\underline{proc}\ f_{11}\langle \bar{x}_1\rangle\ (y_{11}); \{ \dots \};$$
$$\vdots$$
$$\underline{proc}\ f_{1m_1}\langle \bar{x}_1\rangle\ (y_{1m_1}); \{ \dots \};$$
$$\vdots$$
$$\underline{proc}\ f_{n1}\langle \bar{x}_n\rangle\ (y_{n1}); \{ \dots \};$$
$$\vdots$$
$$\underline{proc}\ f_{nm_n}\langle \bar{x}_n\rangle\ (y_{nm_n}); \{ \dots \};$$
$$\underline{proc}\ p_{111}\langle \bar{x}_1,\bar{y}_{11}\rangle\ (z_{111}); \{ \dots \};$$
$$\vdots$$
$$\underline{proc}\ p_{111_{11}}\langle \bar{x}_1,\bar{y}_{11}\rangle\ (z_{111_{11}}); \{ \dots \};$$
$$\vdots$$
$$\underline{proc}\ p_{nm_n1}\langle \bar{x}_n,\bar{y}_{nm_n}\rangle\ (z_{nm_n1}); \{ \dots \};$$
$$\vdots$$
$$\underline{proc}\ p_{nm_n1_{m_n}}\langle \bar{x}_n,\bar{y}_{nm_n}\rangle\ (z_{nm_n1_{m_n}}); \{ \dots \};$$
$$\vdots$$
$$\underline{end}$$

besitzen.

Bei einem solchen Programm können im Hauptprogramm nur Anweisungen der Art $g_i(g_{i'})$, $1 \leqslant i, i' \leqslant n$, stehen.

Bei den Anweisungen $a_0(a_1)$, die im Hauptteil von g_i (i fest, $1 \leqslant i \leqslant n$) auftreten, kann a_k, $k=0,1$, ein formaler Identifikator x_i, ein globaler Identifikator $g_{i'}$ ($1 \leqslant i' \leqslant n$) oder ein Term $f_{ij}\langle x_i\rangle$ sein ($1 \leqslant j \leqslant m_i$).

Bei den Anweisungen $a_0(a_1)$, die im Hauptteil von f_{ij} (i,j fest, $1 \leqslant i \leqslant n$, $1 \leqslant j \leqslant m_i$) auftreten, kann a_k, $k=0,1$, ein formaler Identifikator alter Art y_{ij}, ein formaler Identifikator neuer Art $\bar{x}_i$, ein globaler Identifikator $g_{i'}$ ($1 \leqslant i' \leqslant n$), ein Term $f_{ij'}\langle \bar{x}_i\rangle$ ($1 \leqslant j' \leqslant m_i$) oder ein Term $p_{ijl}\langle \bar{x}_i,y_{ij}\rangle$ ($1 \leqslant l \leqslant l_{ij}$) sein.

Bei den Anweisungen $a_0(a_1)$, die im Hauptteil von p_{ijl} (i,j,l fest, $1 \leqslant i \leqslant n$, $1 \leqslant j \leqslant m_i$, $1 \leqslant l \leqslant l_{ij}$) auftreten, kann a_k, $k=0,1$, ein formaler Identifikator alter Art z_{ijl}, ein formaler Identifikator neuer Art $\bar{x}_i$ bzw. $\bar{y}_{ij}$, ein globaler Identifikator $g_{i'}$ ($1 \leqslant i' \leqslant n$), ein Term $f_{ij'}\langle \bar{x}_i\rangle$ ($1 \leqslant j' \leqslant m_i$) oder ein Term $p_{ijl'}\langle \bar{x}_i,\bar{y}_{ij}\rangle$ ($1 \leqslant l' \leqslant l_{ij}$) sein.

Beschränkt man sich nun auf monadische Programme, so läßt sich zeigen

__Satz 5:__ Für alle Prozeduranweisungen $a_0(a_1)$, die in Programmen Π_2 des Ausführungsbaumes T_{Π_2} eines monadischen ALGOL 60-P-G-Programms auftreten können, gelten die folgenden beiden Eigenschaften:

Eigenschaft a:

1) $a_0=g_i$ oder $a_1=g_i$, $1 \leqslant i \leqslant n$, oder

2) a_0 und a_1 sind fastidentisch oder

3) a_0 besitzt nur einen einzigen unmittelbaren Unterterm
und λ ist linker unmittelbarer Unterterm von a_1
oder umgekehrt oder

4) a_0 besitzt einen unmittelbaren Unterterm λ und λ und
a_1 sind fastidentisch oder umgekehrt oder

5) a_0 besitzt nur einen einzigen unmittelbaren Unterterm λ
und λ ist linker unmittelbarer Unterterm eines unmittelbaren
Unterterms von a_1 oder umgekehrt.

Eigenschaft b:

Bei allen Termen a_i, $i=0,1$, der Art $a_i = \propto \langle \beta_1, \beta_2 \rangle$ gilt für die unmittelbaren
Unterterme β_1, β_2 stets

1) $\beta_2 = g_i$, $1 \leqslant i \leqslant n$, oder

2) β_1 und β_2 sind fastidentisch oder

3) β_2 besitzt nur einen einzigen unmittelbaren Unterterm λ
und λ ist linker unmittelbarer Unterterm von β_1 oder

4) β_1 ist einziger oder linker unmittelbarer Unterterm
von β_2 oder

5) β_2 besitzt einen unmittelbaren Unterterm λ und β_1
ist einziger oder linker unmittelbarer Unterterm von λ.

Dieser Satz zeigt, daß auch in diesem Fall sich die einzelnen Terme nur in einem engen Bereich an der Spitze unterscheiden und sich somit zu einem einzigen Term zusammenfassen lassen. Eigenschaft b) zeigt darüberhinaus, daß, falls ein Term zwei unmittelbare Unterterme besitzt, diese Unterterme sich ebenfalls nur unwesentlich unterscheiden. Dies ermöglicht uns die Codierung eines Terms in eine lineare Zeichenkette. Somit läßt sich in diesem Fall die Entscheidbarkeit der formalen Erreichbarkeit einer Prozedur über Stacksysteme zeigen.

<u>Definition</u>: Ein <u>Stack-System</u> ist ein 4-tupel $\gamma = (\mathfrak{N}, \mathfrak{t}, S, \mathfrak{T})$ mit

(i) $\mathfrak{N}$ ist eine endliche nicht leere Menge (nicht terminale Symbole),

(ii) $\mathfrak{t}$ ist eine endliche nicht leere Menge (terminale Symbole) mit
$\mathfrak{N} \wedge \mathfrak{t} = \emptyset$,

(iii) $S \subset \mathfrak{t}\,\mathfrak{N}$ (Startworte),

(iv) $\mathfrak{T}$ ist eine endliche Menge von Produktionsregeln der Formen
(mit $S', S'' \in \mathfrak{N}$; $A, B \in \mathfrak{t}$; Q, Q_1, Q_2 Variablen über $\mathfrak{t}^*$):

1) $QAS' \longrightarrow QABS''$

2) $QAS' \longrightarrow QAS''$

3) $QAS' \longrightarrow QS''$

4) $Q_1 AS' Q_2 \longrightarrow Q_1 AS'' Q_2$

5) $Q_1 AS' Q_2 \longrightarrow Q_1 S'' AQ_2$

$$6) \quad Q_1 A S B Q_2 \longrightarrow Q_1 A B S'' Q_2$$

Die Arbeitsweise eines Stack-Systems ist gegeben durch

Definition: $x \Longrightarrow y$ mit $x,y \in \mathbf{4}^* \, \mathbf{\Pi} \, \mathbf{4}^*$

         $\divideontimes$: falls $x = \omega y$, $y = \omega y'$ mit $\omega \in \mathbf{4}^*$, $y,y' \in \mathbf{4}\,\mathbf{\Pi}$ ist und in $\mathbf{\Pi}$ eine

         Produktion $Qy \longrightarrow Qy'$ ex. oder falls $x = \omega y \omega'$, $y = \omega y' \omega'$ mit

         $\omega, \omega' \in \mathbf{4}^*$, $y,y' \in \mathbf{4}\,\mathbf{\Pi}\,\mathbf{4}$ ist und in $\mathbf{\Pi}$ eine Produktion

         $Q_1 y Q_2 \longrightarrow Q_1 y \, Q_2$ ex..

Mit $\overset{x}{\Longrightarrow}$ bezeichnen wir die transitive reflexive Hülle von $\Longrightarrow$.

Es läßt sich nun zeigen:

Satz 6: Zu $\widetilde{\mathbf{\Pi}}_2$ läßt sich ein Stack-System $\mathbf{\Upsilon}_{\widetilde{\mathbf{\Pi}}_2}$ konstruieren mit der Eigenschaft: Eine Prozedur q in $\widetilde{\mathbf{\Pi}}_2$ ist genau dann formal erreichbar, falls es in
$\mathbf{\Upsilon}_{\widetilde{\mathbf{\Pi}}_2}$ ein Startwort s und ein durch q bestimmtes Wort $t\omega \in \mathbf{4}^*\mathbf{\Pi}$ gibt, so daß
gilt $s \overset{*}{\Longrightarrow} t\omega$.

Da letzteres jedoch entscheidbar ist [1], erhält man

Satz 7: Es ist entscheidbar, ob eine Prozedur in einem monadischen ALGOL 60-
P-Programm mit höchstens einparametrigen Prozeduren und Prozedurschachtelungstiefe ≤ 3 formal erreichbar ist.

6. Schlußbemerkungen

Für monadische Programme haben wir also folgendes Diagramm

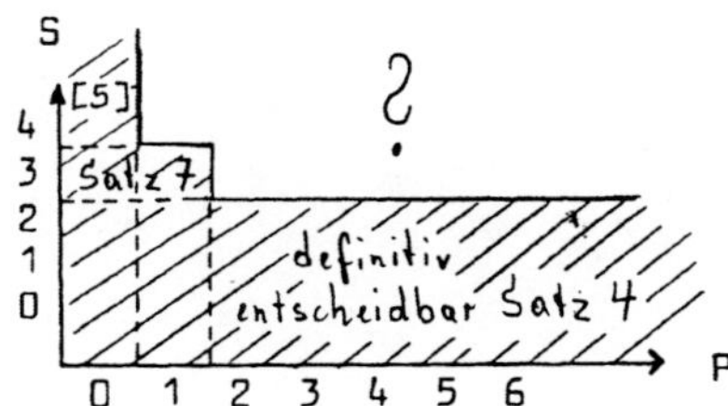

dessen definitiver Entscheidbarkeitsbereich über den früheren hinausragt.

Bei höherer Schachtelungstiefe als 3 im einparametrigen monadischen Fall wird
die formale Erreichbarkeit von Prozeduren wohl auch noch entscheidbar sein.
Bei höherer Parameterzahl und Schachtelungstiefe ≥ 3 wagen wir im Moment noch
keine Prophezeiung.

Literatur:

[1] Ginsburg,S.,Greibach,S.A. und Harrison,M.A.:
     Stack automata and compiling, J.ACM. 14,1 (Jan.67), 172-201

[2] Brainerd,W.: Tree generating regular systems,
     Information and Control 14 (1969), 217-231

[3] Doner,J.: Tree acceptors and some of their applications,
     Journal of Computer and System Sciences 4 (1979), 406-451

[4] Kaufholz,G.,Lippe,W.M.: A note on a paper of H. Langmaack
     about procedure parameter transmission, Bericht A 74/06
     des Fachbereichs Angewandte Mathematik und Informatik der
     Universität des Saarlandes (1974)

[5] Langmaack,H.: On correct procedure parameter transmission in
     higher programming languages, Acta Informatoca Vol.2,(1973)

[6] Langmaack,H.: On procedures as open subroutines I,II
     Acta Informatica Vol.2, 1973 und Vol.3,(1974)

[7] Lippe,W.M.: Entscheidbarkeitsprobleme bei der Übersetzung
     von Programmen mit einparametrigen Prozeduren,
     Lecture Notes in Computer Scince Nr.7, Springer Verlag (1974)

[8] Rounds,W.C.: Mappings and grammars on trees,
     Mathematical systems theorie, Vol. 4, Nr.3, 257-287

ON THE IMPLEMENTATION OF DATA GENERALITY *

Arndt von Staa

and

Carlos J. Lucena
Departamento de Informática
Pontifícia Universidade Católica
Rio de Janeiro/Brasil

ABSTRACT: Data generality is the property through which program modules are able to communicate via arbitrary data structures. Since the design of module interfaces is a very difficult and error prone activity in systems design, the implementation of data generality is a very desirable goal in programming. The present work describes one approach to the implementation of data generality and sketches the algorithm for its implementation.

KEYWORDS: Data Generality, Data Types, Classes, Clusters, Modularity.

1. INTRODUCTION

A very comprehensive definition of program modularity has been proposed by Dennis in [1]. According to his definition, a program segment written in a given programming language can be called a module if it follows the properties of syntactic non-interference, semantic context independence and data generality. Syntactic non-interference accounts for the possibility of combining program segments without having to make syntactic changes in any of the segments. Semantic context independence assures that a given segment cannot cause side-effects and cannot be affected by side-effects. In other words, its output assertion (specification) remains invariant no matter where the segment is used within a programming system. The property of data generality requires that modules be able to communicate via arbitrary data structures. Data generality allows for the full application of Parnas' "hiding principle" [2] through which each module's programmer needs to know only about another module's specification and not about its internal implementation.

Difficulties arise in practice with respect to the implementation of the concept of data generality. A software module specification language as proposed by Parnas [3] still requires a reference to the module's internal data structures in the assertions that describe the module. The classical programming solution of care-

---

* This research was partially supported by the Brazilian Government Agency FINEP under contract nº 244/CT.

fully planning the module interface data structures is but a distant managerial approximation of the data generality concept (see [4] for a well-designed example of the principle).

Two approaches, by v. Staa [5] and Lucena [6], have been proposed for the full application of the concept of data generality. Both approaches are based on the concept of abstract data types (or simply a data type). For the purpose of this introduction an abstract data type can be thought of as a heterogeneous algebra (defined over more than one set of objects) that can be specified by giving the family of sets or domains and the operations defined on them. A data type can be specified formally through, for instance, the algebaic theory developed by Zilles [7]. They can be implemented through programming features such as classes [8] or clusters [9].

In the approach by Lucena [6], the issue of data generality arises when clusters are used to model data types used in the context of a very high level language. The same data types, say SET, can be associated to different variables and yet be implemented differently for each variable. If these variables need to interact within the program, the standard compiler representation is used to effect the conversions during execution time.

In the approach by v. Staa [5], the module writers know the specification of a type T whose meaning is global to a program. Each module writer may implement T in a different way and yet he may transfer variables of abstract type to another module without knowing the other modules internal representations. In this paper we discuss the underlying ideas of this proposal and present an outline of an algorithm that describes how data transmition can be achieve with generality.

2. BASIC CONCEPTS

An abstract data type, or simply a type, is an algebra $T = (V,0)$ where V is a set* of values and 0 is a set of operators defined over these values. Types are used to model data abstractions of the kind used in connection with very high level languages. Algorithms expressed in terms of variables with associated abstract types are often called a program specification. A specification can be transformed into a program either by the automatic compilation of a type into a standard data representation or by the possibly automatic substitution of a type by a valid representation selected from a set of possible representations.

A data representation τ of an abstract data type is a triple $\tau = (V',0',D)$ where $V' \subseteq V$, 0' is a set of constructive models of the operators in the set 0(programs that implement the definitions of the operations in 0 —the set of axioms that define 0 and 0' are equivalent and D is the description of a particular representation for

---

* For simplicity of notation and without loss of generality we will overlook the fact
that types are, in fact, heterogeneous algebras.

the elements of V' for a given base machine (a set data declarations on a given programming language).

Let Φ be a special element of V and V' called the undefined value, and let g be a function[*] from V to V'. We say that a data representation represents (<u>rep</u>) a data type T, if the following diagram commutes for every o ϵ 0 and corresponding o' ϵ 0'

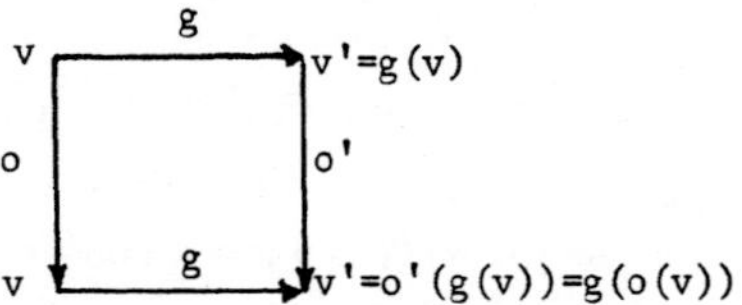

if τ <u>rep</u> T and additionally for every vϵV, such that v $\neq$ Φ, g(v) = v' and v' $\neq$ Φ, we say that data representation represents exactly the abstract data type.

Let $A \subseteq V$ be the set of the values in the domain of g such that g(a) = Φ and a ϵ A, for a given data representation τ and relation <u>rep</u>. The cardinality of A, $|A|$, is called the degree of approximation of the abstract data type by a data representation. The smaller the cardinality, the better the approximation.

We will call $B \subseteq V$ a set such that $\forall b \epsilon B$, g(b) and g(o(b)) are defined and the "values" o'(g(b)) that correspond to the g(o(b)) are error messages. The cardinality of B, $|B|$, reflects the restrictions that occur in practice in the implementation of the operation o'.

To illustrate the above notions we can use as an example the type INTEGER. INTEGER can be defined by the pair:

$$\text{(set of integer numbers, } \{+,-,*,/\})$$

Let us call INT a possible representation of INTEGER. INT will be defined as follows:

$$(\{i \mid -2^{-16} \leq i < 2^{16}\}, \{+,-,*,/\}, \text{ stored as a 16-bit word in two's complement notation)}$$

INT is an approximation of INTEGER because while $v_1 * v_2$ is always defined for INTEGER it may be undefined for INT (provoking an overflow): INT is clearly a <u>simulation</u> of INTEGER.

A type can be represented in a variety of ways. We will call

$$IS_T = \{\tau_1, \tau_2, \ldots, \tau_n\}$$

the <u>implementation set</u> of a type T. The representations $\tau_1, \ldots, \tau_n$ simulate the type T with different degrees of approximation.

For example, let us assume that the abstract type T models the concept of

---

[*] In some works about the correctness of data representation g is defined from V' to V. The way we formulated the definition will help presenting our forthcomming ideas.

stack. A stack can be characterized, for instance, by the well-known operations: _empty_, _pop_, _push_, etc. In this case τ_1 could be a list implementation of T, τ_2 an array implementation etc.

Let F be a function with $n \geq 0$ arguments of type T to some domain D.

$$F: TxTx...xT \to D$$

To achieve data generality we want to be able to use the function F within a program module, using τ_i as an approximation for T $(\tau_i \in IS_T)$ in the case where the argument of F were passed as parameters from a module that used τ_j as an approximation of T.

In the appendix we illustrate a programming mechanism which incorporates this concept. We left this example to the appendix in order not to interfere with the central ideas of this work.

Before discussing alternative solutions to the data generality problem we need to introduce another definition.

A _conversion_ is a function from a data representation to another data representation. We will write $x:\tau_i$ to mean that x is a variable of representation (type) τ_i, that is, x takes its values from the domain D_{τ_i}. A conversion C_{ij} is then specified as

$$C_{ij} : D_{\tau_i} \to D_{\tau_j}$$

Where $\tau_i, \tau_j \in IS_T$. A conversion is said to be meaning preserving if $\forall v$, $v \in V$ and for the function g_{τ_i} from T to the ith representation τ_i:

$$a) \quad g_{\tau_i}(v) = \Phi \iff C_{ij}(g_{\tau_i}(v)) \doteq \Phi$$

$$b) \quad g_{\tau_i}(v) \neq \Phi \supset C_{ij}(g_{\tau_i}(v)) \neq \Phi \quad \text{and}$$

$$g_{\tau_j}(v) = C_{ij}(g_{\tau_i}(v))$$

3. SELECTION OF DATA REPRESENTATIONS

We are interested in the alternative approaches to choose the representation into which parameters should be converted when passing the approximation of a type from one module to another. One possible choice would be to choose a standard representation and use it as a default option. The approach we will favor later on will be motivated by efficiency considerations. We will sketch an algorithm through which a systematic selection of representations can be made.

The standard representation approach can be carried out along the following lines. Let us define for each type a canonical implementation (representation) $\tau_c \in IS_T$, such that parameters of type T, being shipped from another module, would always be converted into τ_c . This operation implies that

$$C_{ic} : D_{\tau_i} \rightarrow D_{\tau_c} \qquad \text{and}$$

$$C_{ci} : D_{\tau_c} \rightarrow D_{\tau_i}$$

are defined (if we want the modules to be able to communicate). Several objections can be raised with respect to this approach. For one thing, τ_c can lead to an inefficient execution of a given critical (executed often) operation of T. Besides, C_{ic} may not be definable, in the sense that τ_c is not a meaning preserving representation of τ_i , or may be a very costly operation.

To overcome these difficulties, we propose a method which is presently being considered as a basis for a language being designed at PUC[*].

We start by defining a set of meaning preserving conversions

$$C_{ij} : D_{\tau_i} \rightarrow D_{\tau_j}$$

for significant pairs of implementations τ_i , $\tau_j \in IS_T$. As a next step we associate a cost function k_{ij} with each c_{ij} . We foresee the mechanism being described, used in connection with a language with a strong typing capability. That is, the language is capable of knowing the actual type τ_i and formal type τ_j at parameter association time.

When converting from τ_i to τ_j we may not find a conversion function C_{ij} that performs the operation. Instead, we may need to look for a sequence of conversions whose composition produces the same effect of C_{ij}. That is, we need to be able to detect a sequence of conversions such that:

$$C_{ij} = C_{12} \circ C_{23} \circ \ldots \circ C_{n-1\ n}$$

Where

$$\tau_i = \tau_1 \ , \ \tau_j = \tau_n \quad \text{and } 1 \leq n, \text{ and such that}$$

---

[*] Pontifícia Universidade Católica do Rio de Janeiro

$$C_{r\ell} \text{ exists for all the pairs } (r=1,\ \ell=2),$$
$$(r=2,\ \ell=3)\dots,\ (r=n-1,\ \ell=n)$$

Additionally, the $C_{r\ell}$ are required to be meaning preserving and the sum

$$\sum_{(r=1,\ \ell=2)}^{(r=n-1,\ \ell=n)} K_{r\ell}$$

needs to be minimal over the set of defined conversions.

Graphically this sequence can be visualized as follows

$$\overset{C_{12}}{\underset{\tau_i=\tau_1}{\circ\!-\!\!\longrightarrow\!\circ}} \overset{C_{23}}{\underset{\tau_2}{}} \underset{\tau_3}{\longrightarrow\!\circ} \cdots\cdots \overset{C_{n-i\ n}}{\underset{\tau_{n-1}}{\longrightarrow\!\circ}} \underset{\tau_n=\tau_j}{\longrightarrow\!\circ}$$

If such a path choice exists within the library of conversions, we can achieve data generality and portability as a byproduct.

It needs to be stressed that if we want to achieve intercommunication between modules it is required that another sequence of conversions C_{ji} also exists, possibly the inverse of C_{ij} , that allows the conversion from τ_j to τ_i.

In a network environment a programming system with the described capability should be able to go back to the user and interact with him in the case of impossibility of accomplishing a particular conversion. In this case the system should describe the environmental contraints (size of words in each machine etc), that were responsible for the problem. The user in such a situation should be able to reply and propose some "roundings" that would weaken the requirement of meaning preservation so that the processing could seccessfully terminate.

A number of interesting features can be stressed in the method outlined. It follows directly from the above that the method is very general and oriented to the achievement of maximum efficiency.

The method could be implemented by means of THUNKS [1] and occurs in an incomplete form in ALTRAN [10]. The method also suggests a new direction to the open problem of generating efficient code for very high level languages.

It can be proved without too much effort that if we have a library of conversions, all that is required of its structure in order to be able to produce every possible conversion, is that it forms a strongly connected directed graph of conversions.

In a very high level language all implementation details (in particular data structures that are oriented towards the base machine) are hidden from the user. As a result of that, a general purpose·compiler that compiles directly from the abstract data types used by the language (e.g. general sets and sequence) have to be general enough to allow for the implementation of the typically associative operations used at the language level (usually called specification level). This fact has led in all reported experiences to the generation of prohibitively expensive object code. The approach suggested in this paper induces a technique through which a compiler can select the best representation (from an existing repertoire) for a particular application of a type and, also, allows for the selection of paths of transformations that enable adjustments in the form of implementations for very different uses of the same data type.

Following this suggestion when defining a very high level language, an abstract type needs to be specified through the following tuple

$$T = (0, IS_T, CS)$$

The meaning of each element can be illustrated through an example:

0 is the set of operations which defines the type; e.g. $\{+,-,*,/,:=\}$ for fixed binary;

IS_T is the implementation set of this type; e.g. precisions (15,0), (12,3), (31,0) for fixed binary ; and

CS is the set of conversions

$$C_{ij}: x:\tau_i \to x:\tau_j \quad \text{where} \quad \tau_i, \tau_j \in IS_T$$

4. CONCLUSIONS

In the present paper we attempt to contribute to the better understanding of the problems of communication between program modules. We outlined one approach to data transmission that can help bridge the gap between the goals of ease of programming and program efficiency. We are aware that a number of issues remain to be investigated in this realm and that we will be raising a number of important problems as we proceed with the implementation of the method described here.

APPENDIX

In figure 1 we show the function <u>concat</u>. This function receives parameters and type descriptors associated with these parameters. We also show the minimum set of operators that have to be provided in order for the function to be used.

```
ref type_1 function concat (type type_1 contains(integer size;
          ref type_1 function obtain (integer length);
          type type_2; type_2 elem[*]; ref type_1 a,b);
   begin concat;
       integer length = a->size + b->size;
       concat:=obtain(length);
       for i:=1 until a->size do
         concat->elem[i]:=a->elem[i]; od;
       for i:=a->size+1 until length do

         concat->elem[i]:=b->elem[i-a->size]; od;

   end concat;
```

The following parameters were made explicit:

```
ref type_1: obtain(length);

integer /*fetch function*/  size;

type_2      /* access function*/elem[*];
```

Fig.1 Example of a function which accepts types as parameters

In figure 2 we illustrate the definition of a type which will be transmited
to concat.


```
type string (integer string_size)=
   begin string;
      outside scope scope;
         integer fetch function string_length=string_size;
         bit(2) string_elem[string_size];
         ref string function get (integer length)=
           get:=new string(length);
         ref string function constructor(bit(2) vector[*])=
          begin constructor;
             integer length=upper bound(vector),
             constructor:=get(length);
             for i:=1 until length do
                constructor->string_elem[i]:=vector[i];
             od;
          end constructor;
      end scope;
   end string;
```

Fig. 2 Definition of the type "string of bit (2)"

Figure 3 shows how the transmission is accomplished·

```
ref string a,b,c;
a:=constructor(array('01'B, 10'B));
b:=constructor(array('11'B));
c:=concat(type_1::string(elem::string_elem,size::string_length,obtain::get,
                type_2::bit(2)), a::a, b::b);
```

Fig. 3 Use of concat with the type "string"

Note that in figure 1 the operation contains (...) makes explicit the parameters that are transfered when "string" is used. In figure 3 the type "string" is
transmited to concat. The names defined by "string" and the names expected by concat
are different. This difficulty is overcome through the association of the parameter
names.

The sintax used is:

<name of the formal parameter>::<actual parameter>

The symbol <name of the formal parameter> stands for the textual name of the
formal parameter that will be associated with the value of <actual parameter>. The
construct array(...) in figure 3 defines a function which creates an array of as many
elements as the actual parameters in the list. The elements of array will be initia-
lized to the actual values of the parameters.

REFERENCES

[1] Dennis, J.B., 'Modularity'; in Bauer, F.L. ed; Springer Verlag; 1973

[2] Parnas, D.F., 'Information Distribution Aspects of Design Methodology'; IFIP
      Congress Proceedings; 1971

[3] Parnas, D.F.; 'A Technique for Software Module Specification with Examples';
      Communications of the ACM Vol. 15, nº 5; May 1972

[4] Mc Keeman, W.; 'Compiler Structure'; Proceedings of the First USA - Japan
      Computer Conference; 1972

[5] Staa, A.v.; Data Transmission and Modularity Aspects of Programming Languages;
      Research Report CS-74-17, Department of Computer Science, Univ. of Waterloo;
      1974

[6] Lucena, C.J.; <u>On the Synthesis of Reliable Programs</u>; Technical Report, Computer Science Department, Univ. of California, Los Angeles; 1975

[7] Liskov, B.H.; Zilles, S.N.; 'Specification Techniques for Data Abstractions'; <u>IEEE Transactions on Software Engineering</u>, Vol. 1, nº 1; 1975

[8] Hoare, C.A.R.; 'Proof of Correction of Data Representations' <u>Acta Informatica</u> Vol. 1, fasc 4; 1972

[9] Liskov, B.H.; Zilles, S.N.; 'Programming with Abstract Data Types'; <u>SIGPLAN Notices</u> Vol. 9; 1972

[10] Brown, W.S.; <u>ALTRAN User's Manual</u>; Bell Telephone Labs., Murray Hill, N.J.; 1973

[11] Ingerman, P.Z.; 'THUNKS a Way of Compiling Procedure Statements with Some Comments on Procedure Declarations'; <u>Comunications of the ACM</u> Vol. 4, nº 4;April 1961

[12] Bauer, F.L. ed; <u>Advanced course on Software Engineering</u>; Series: Lecture Notes in Economics and Mathematical Systems nº 81, Springer Verlag; 1973

PROMID - EINE PROBLEMBEZOGENE PROGRAMMIER-
SPRACHE FUER DIE MITTLERE DATENTECHNIK

Rudolf Marty
Institut für Informatik der Universität Zürich

1. Die Mittlere Datentechnik (MDT)

Der enorme Preiszerfall auf dem Hardwaremarkt für Zentraleinheiten und
Peripheriegeräte verhelfen in neuester Zeit Computer der Klasse der
"Mittleren Datentechnik" zu einem noch vor wenigen Jahren nicht geahn-
ten Durchbruch: Für Monatsmieten von 5000 DM sind Kleincomputer mit
Bildschirmen und Direktzugriffspeicher mit mehreren Megabyte Speicher-
grösse erhältlich. Solche Systeme lösen heute mehr und mehr die Ende
der Sechzigerjahre gross aufgekommenen Magnetkontencomputer ab.

Das hervorstechende Merkmal der MDT-Computer ist der hohe Grad der
Interaktion zwischen Bedienungskraft und Maschine:

- Ein beträchtlicher Teil der Problemdaten, welche in typischen
  MDT Programmen gebraucht werden, wird direkt durch die Bedienungskraft eingetippt.
- Gewisse Klassen von externen Speichermedien (z.B. Magnetkonten)
  werden durch die Bedienungskraft verwaltet und dem Computer
  zugeführt.
- MDT-Anlagen besitzen eine Reihe zusätzlicher Ein-/Ausgabe-
  einheiten wie Funktionstasten, Lampen usw. Diese erlauben
  einerseits der Bedienungskraft dem Programm bestimmte Entschei-
  de mitzuteilen, und geben andererseits dem Programm die Möglichkeit, der Bedienungskraft spezielle Zustände anzuzeigen.

Andere Eigenheiten von MDT-Computer sind:

- Relativ kleiner Zentralspeicher.
- Sehr elementarer Instruktionssatz, und meist recht primitive
  Adressiermechanismen und keine logischen und Zeichenketten-
  operationen.
- Keine Interruptmechanismen.
- Kein Betriebssystem und kein "Data Management", wie man
  es von Grosscomputer kennt.

2. Anforderungen an eine problembezogene Programmiersprache für die Mittlere Datentechnik

Basierend auf den vorgängig erwähnten Charakteristiken muss eine problembezogene Programmiersprache für Anlagen der MDT folgende Möglichkeiten bieten:

- Syntaktisch einfache und effiziente Konstruktionen, um alle Bedienungskraft-Computer Interaktionen zu kontrollieren, unter Umständen einen Fehler zu signalisieren und die falsche Aktion wiederholen zu lassen.
- Flexible Behandlung aller Dateitypen, insbesondere auch der Tastaturen, Bildschirme, Magnetkonten u.a.m.
- Spezielle Typen von Namen für Funktionstasten, Lampen, usw.
- Sprachelemente zur Ausführung und Kontrolle aller Ein-/Ausgabeoperationen (wie erwähnt hat man auf MDT-Anlagen üblicherweise kein eigentliches Betriebssystem zur Verfügung).

Neben diesen zielcomputerorientierten Anforderungen sollte die Programmiersprache ...

- ... eine Blockstruktur aufweisen und damit einen hierarchischen Gültigkeitsbereich von Variablen bieten.
- ... anweisungsorientiert sein.
- ... nur eine strikt hierarchische Programmstruktur ohne allgemeine GOTOs erlauben.
- ... problemorientiert und bis zu einem hohen Grad maschinenunabhängig sein.
- ... numerische logische Datentypen, Zeichenketten sowie die Datenstrukturen Datenbaum (structure) und Datenfeld (array) enthalten.

3. Die Sprache PROMID

Analysiert man die hardwaremässigen Gegebenheiten der MDT einerseits und die postulierten Anforderungen andererseits, so ergibt sich, dass keine bekannte höhere Programmiersprache für den anvisierten Einsatzbereich in die nähere Wahl kommt. Es drängten sich derart umfangreiche und grundlegende Aenderungen am Sprachgefüge von beispielsweise PL/I, PASCAL oder COBOL auf, dass das entstehende Produkt seinen Ahnen kaum noch ähnlich sähe. Deshalb wurde beschlossen, eine neue Sprache zu definieren, die den gestellten Anforderungen und Restriktionen gerecht wird.

Um den Forderungen nach einfacher Programmierung und kleinen Maschinen-
programmen nachzukommen, zeigte es sich als unumgänglich, einige zielcomputerabhängige Konstruktionen in die Sprache aufzunehmen. Diese
Konstruktionen (resp. Syntaxdiagramme) sind klar von den zielcomputer-
unabhängigen getrennt und deshalb auch in einer anderen Darstellung in
die Diagramme aufgenommen (siehe Anhang A).

Alle in einem PROMID Programm verwendeten Namen müssen in einer DCL-
Anweisung deklariert werden. Die einzige Ausnahme hievon bilden die
als Prozedur- und BEGIN-Block-Namen verwendeten Bezeichner. Als Datentypen sind dezimale, binäre Zeichenketten und logische Variablen eingeführt. Mögliche Datenstrukturen sind skalare Variable, Datenfelder
und Datenbäume. Letztere können sich rekursiv enthalten. Durch eine aus-
geklügelte und einfache Art der Deklaration von Datei-, Tasten- und
Lampennamen, sind programmtechnische Anpassungen an Peripherieände-
rungen leicht vorzunehmen, da im Programm nur die betreffende Deklaration, nicht aber Ablaufsbefehle verändert werden müssen. Als besonderes
Problem bei der Sprachdefinition zeigte sich die logisch-syntaktisch
saubere Behandlung von Magnetkontendateien, die einerseits eine magne-
tisch lesbare Direktzugriffsdatei, andererseits eine Druckdatei darstellen, sowie der Druckdateien im allgemeinen, da bei der MDT häufig
der Fall auftritt, dass mehrere logische Druckdateien von ein und
derselben physischen Druckeinheit beschrieben werden.

Die Regeln der Prozedurbildung sowie des Gültigkeitsbereiches von
Variablen entsprechen im grossen und ganzen denjenigen von PL/I, ALGOL
und PASCAL. Eine Prozedur wird durch CALL aufgerufen.

Innerhalb von Prozeduren werden mit den BEGIN- und END-Anweisungen
Programmblöcke gebildet, die sich, wie aus den Syntaxdiagrammen ersichtlich, auch rekursiv enthalten können.

Die IF-, ELSE-, REPEAT- und CASE-Konstruktionen werden "Anweisungspräfixe" genannt und enden im Unterschied zu normalen Anweisungen,
die alle mit einem Semikolon abgeschlossen werden, mit einem Doppel-
punkt. Anweisungspräfixe können sich entsprechend dem Syntaxdiagramm
"Anweisung" im Anhang A rekursiv enthalten. Auf eine Erklärung der
Präfixe IF-, ELSE- und REPEAT kann hier wohl verzichtet werden. Sie
sind hinlänglich von PL/I (REPEAT entspr. DO ....), PASCAL, ALGOL usw.
bekannt. Zum CASE-Präfix bleibt ergänzend zu sagen, dass, ähnlich wie

in PASCAL, jeder in der CASE-Konstruktion enthaltenen Anweisung ein
oder mehrere Selektoren vorangestellt werden müssen, die den Wert angeben, für den die zugehörige Anweisung durchgeführt werden soll. Dies
ergibt im Unterschied zur streng ordinalen Anweisungsauswahl, wie sie
von einigen Sprachen bekannt ist, eine bessere Anpassungsfähigkeit der
Programme.

Die GET-, PUT- und SET-Anweisungen werden für die Ausführung aller
Ein-/Ausgabeoperationen sowie zur Steuerung von Peripheriegeräten verwendet. Eine Reihe von Optionen ermöglichen die effiziente und einfache Programmierung von Eingabekontrollen, Ein- und Ausgabesteuerungen,
Vorschub-, Tabulations- und Editierungsanweisungen usw. Die GET-, PUT-
und SET-Anweisungen erlauben dem Programmierer die Ein-/Ausgabeeinhei-
ten ohne spezifische Hardwarekennntnisse auszusprechen, was bei den
heute für die MDT verwendeten Assemblersprachen noch weit weniger der
Fall ist als bei Grosscomputer mit Betriebssystemen.

Die QUIT- und SKIP-Anweisungen ersetzen in PROMID die allgemeine GOTO-
Anweisung. Im Gegensatz zum GOTO erlauben sie nur einen Sprung an das
Ende eines umgebenden BEGIN-Blockes oder an das Ende der umgebenden
Prozedur. Die Wirkung von SKIP und QUIT ist nur verschieden, falls das
angesprochene END zu einem BEGIN-Block gehört, dem ein oder mehrere
REPEAT-Präfixe vorangestellt sind. In diesem Fall....

 ... springt SKIP über den Rest der aktuellen Repetition.
  Die Repetition geht entsprechend dem REPEAT Präfix weiter.
  In anderen Worten erlaubt SKIP einen Sprung auf ein END.
 ... springt QUIT über den Rest der aktuellen Repetition und bricht
  alle verbleibenden Repetitionen ab. In anderen Worten erlaubt
  QUIT einen Sprung hinter ein END.

Diese Restriktionen der Programmverzweigungen führen zu einer sehr
viel einfacheren Programmstruktur verglichen mit üblichen "GOTO-
Programmen". Graphentheoretisch gesehen, ist es damit nur möglich,
einen Programmbaum zu codieren, während sich bei der Verwendung von
GOTO beliebige Programmgraphen erstellen lassen. Die Resultate einer
Restriktion auf Programmbäume sind:

 - Selbstdokumentierende Programme (keine Blockdiagramme).
 - Weniger logische Fehler und weniger vergessene Programmpfade.
 - Einfache Programmwartung.
 - Verbesserte Durchführungseffizienz in virtuellen Speichersystemen.

Nach Böhm und Jacopini wäre es möglich, beliebige PROMID-Programme auch
ohne die Anweisungen SKIP und QUIT zu schreiben. Trotzdem erleichtern
diese zwei Anweisungen die Programmierung erheblich, ohne die Grundge-
danken der strukturierten Programmierung aufzugeben.

4. Die Implementation NIXDORF 820

Um Anhaltswerte für einen Wirtschaftlichkeitsvergleich zu erhalten,
schrieb ich einen Compiler für die Sprache PROMID, der auf dem
NIXDORF System 820 als Zielcomputer basiert. Der Compiler ist in PL/I
geschrieben und umfasst insgesamt etwa 6300 Anweisungen in Quellen-
code. "Cross Compiling" drängte sich wegen der elementaren Hard- und
Software der meisten MDT Computer auf.

Der Compiler produziert Quellprogramm-, Pseudo-Assembler-, Attribut-,
Cross-Reference- und Fehlerlisten und stanzt NIXDORF 820 Objektprogramm-
karten, welche direkt auf dem System verwendet werden können.

Hinsichtlich der Uebersetzungskosten zeigte sich, dass gemäss den zur
Zeit üblichen Ansätzen die Uebersetzung eines PROMID Programmes auf
einem IBM System/370 auf etwa einen Viertel bis einen Drittel der
Kosten zu stehen kommt, die für die Assemblierung des äquivalenten
Assembler Programmes auf einer MDT Anlage einzusetzen wären.

Die Programmerstellungs- und -Unterhaltskosten liegen bei der Verwendung von PROMID bei rund einem Drittel der Kosten für die Erstellung und den Unterhalt des entsprechenden Assemblerprogrammes.

Der erstellte PROMID Compiler für die NIXDORF 820 generiert einen
Maschinencode, wie er für das selbe Problem in ähnlichem Umfang von
einem mittelmässigen Assembler Programmierer erstellt würde.

Anhang A   Syntaxdiagramme der Sprache PROMID

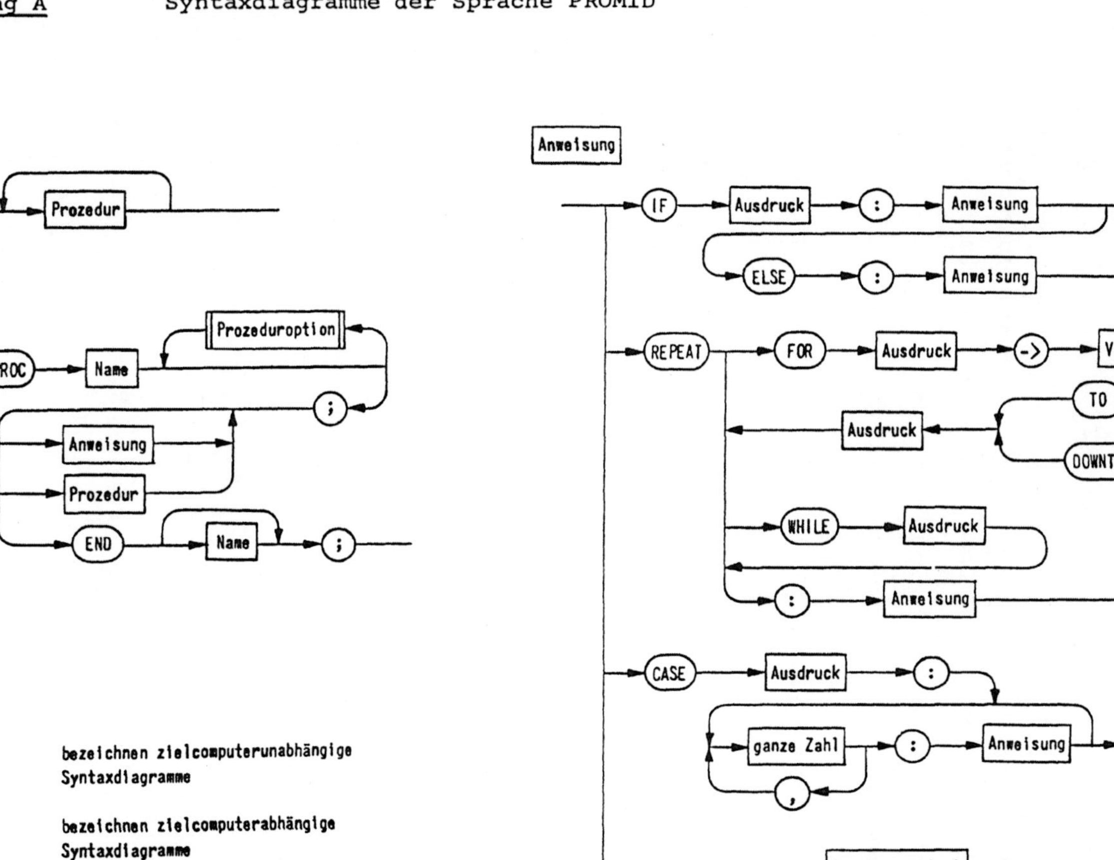

151

einfache Anweisung
Ausdruck -> Variable ;
CALL Name
DCL Deklaration ,
GET Name -> Variable Getoption
PUT Ausdruck -> Name Putoption
QUIT Name
SET Name Setoption
SIGNAL Name
SKIP Name
STOP
WAIT Ausdruck

Anweisungsblock
BEGIN Name ;
Anweisung
Prozedur
END Name ;

Deklaration
ganze Zahl Name Dimension
Attribut DEFINED

Dimension
(Grenze : Grenze) ,

Grenze
+ - ganze Zahl

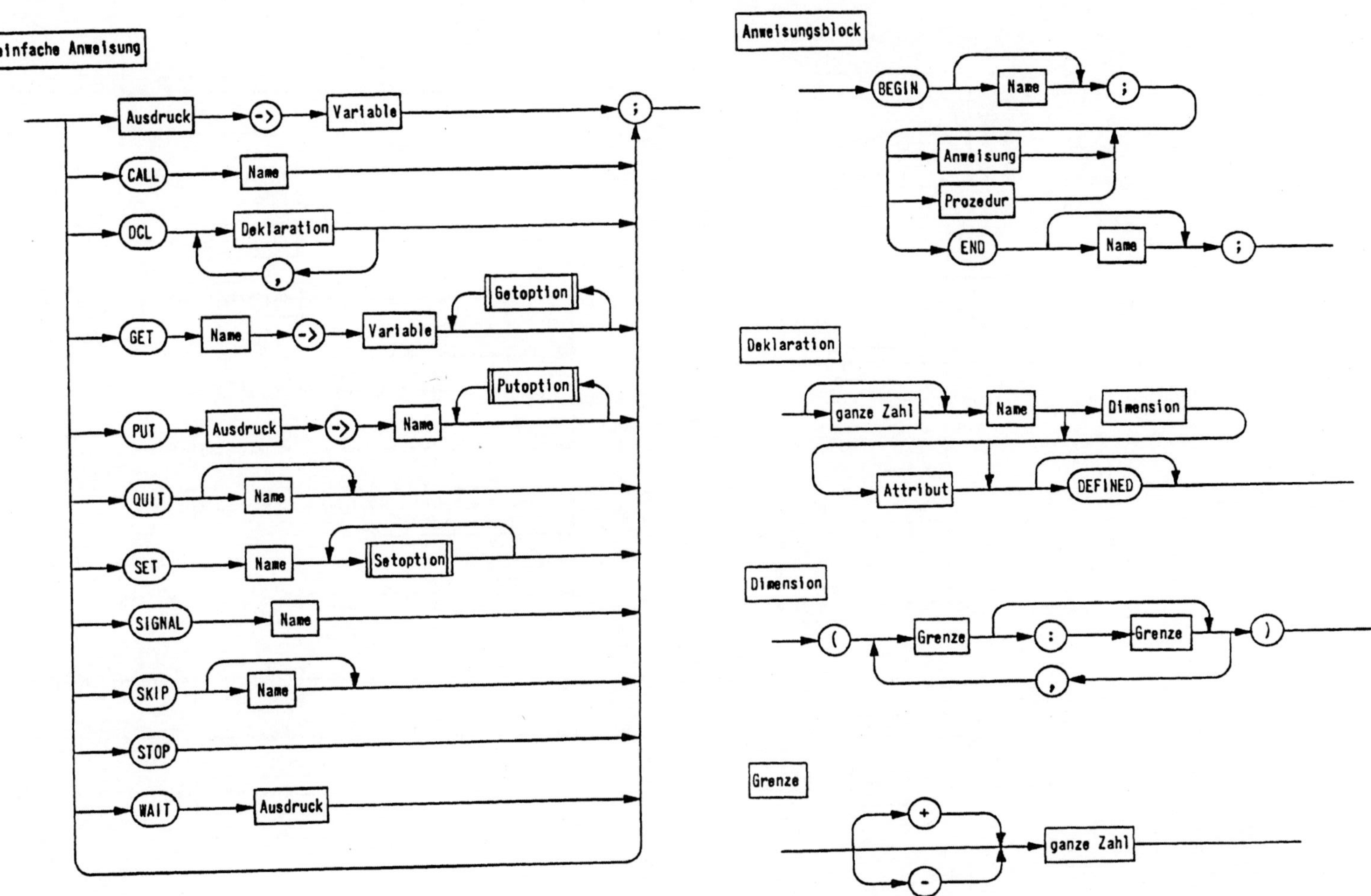

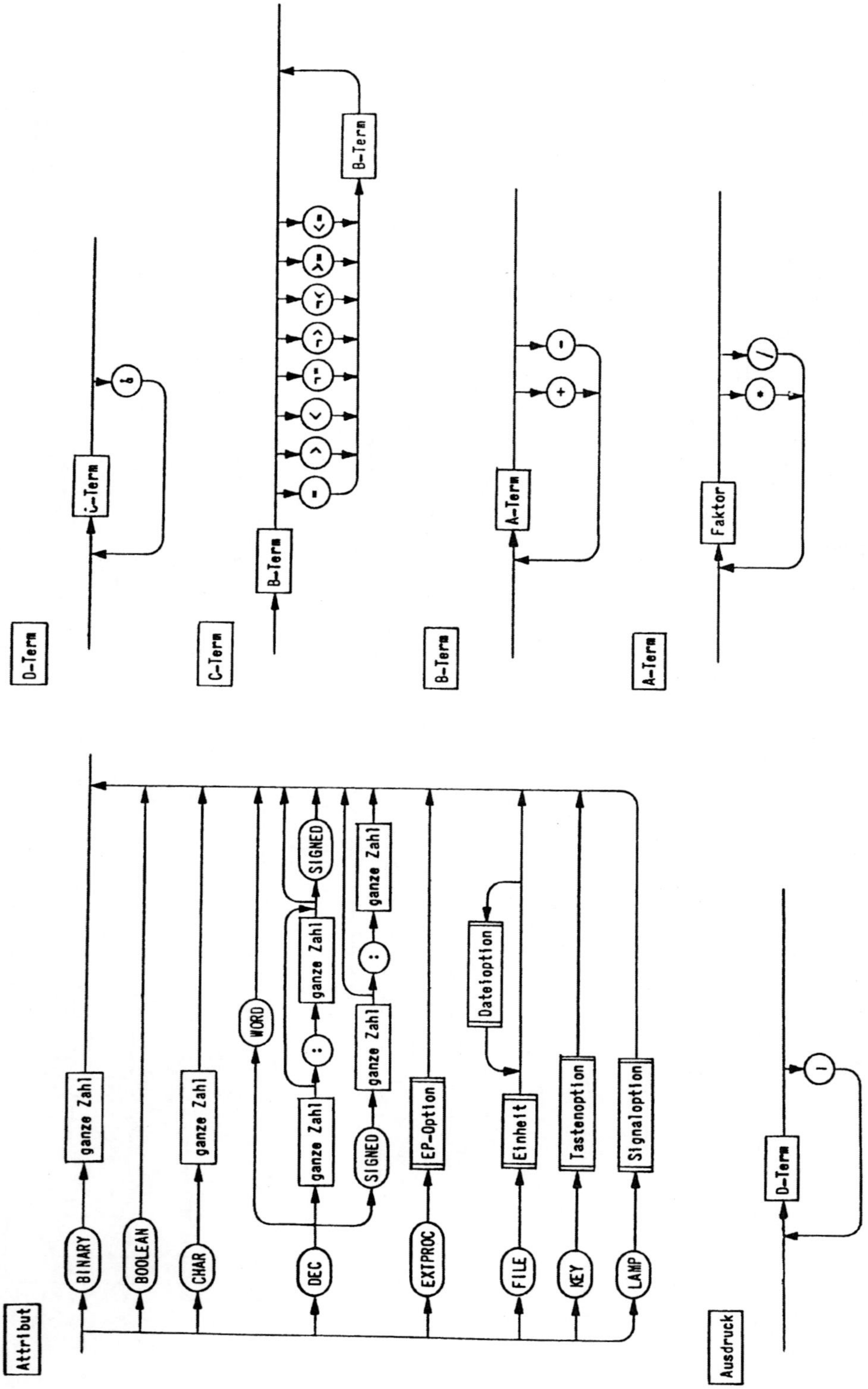

Attribut
BINARY
ganze Zahl
BOOLEAN
CHAR
ganze Zahl
DEC
WORD
ganze Zahl
:
ganze Zahl
SIGNED
SIGNED
ganze Zahl
:
ganze Zahl
EXTPROC
EP-Option
FILE
Einheit
Dateioption
KEY
Tastenoption
LAMP
Signaloption
Ausdruck
D-Term
D-Term
C-Term
C-Term
B-Term
B-Term
B-Term
A-Term
A-Term
Faktor
152

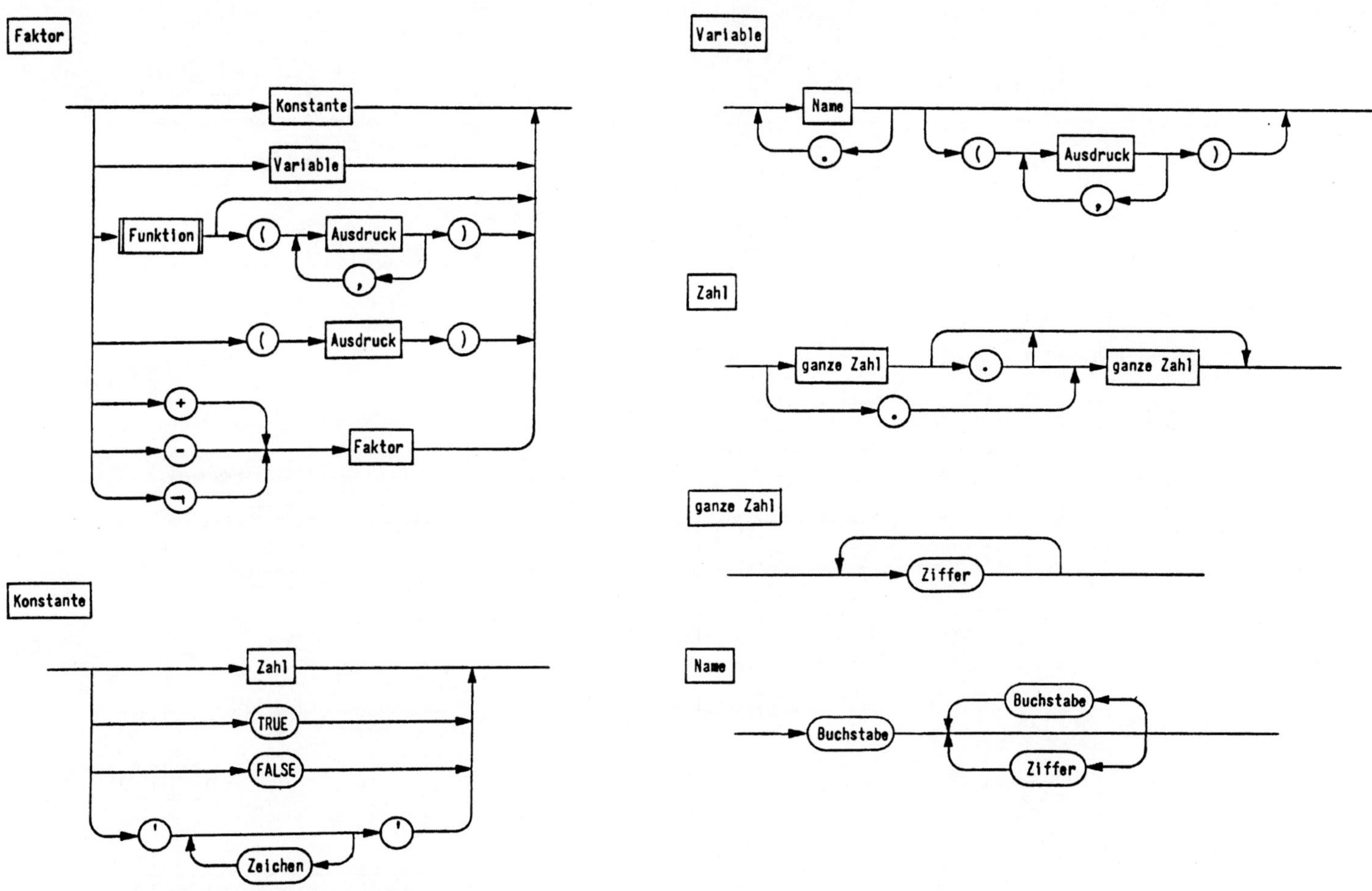

Faktor
Konstante
Variable
Funktion
Ausdruck
Ausdruck
Faktor
Variable
Name
Ausdruck
Zahl
ganze Zahl
ganze Zahl
ganze Zahl
Ziffer
Konstante
Zahl
TRUE
FALSE
Zeichen
Name
Buchstabe
Buchstabe
Ziffer

Zielcomputerabhängige Syntaxdiagramme für die Implementation NIXDORF 820

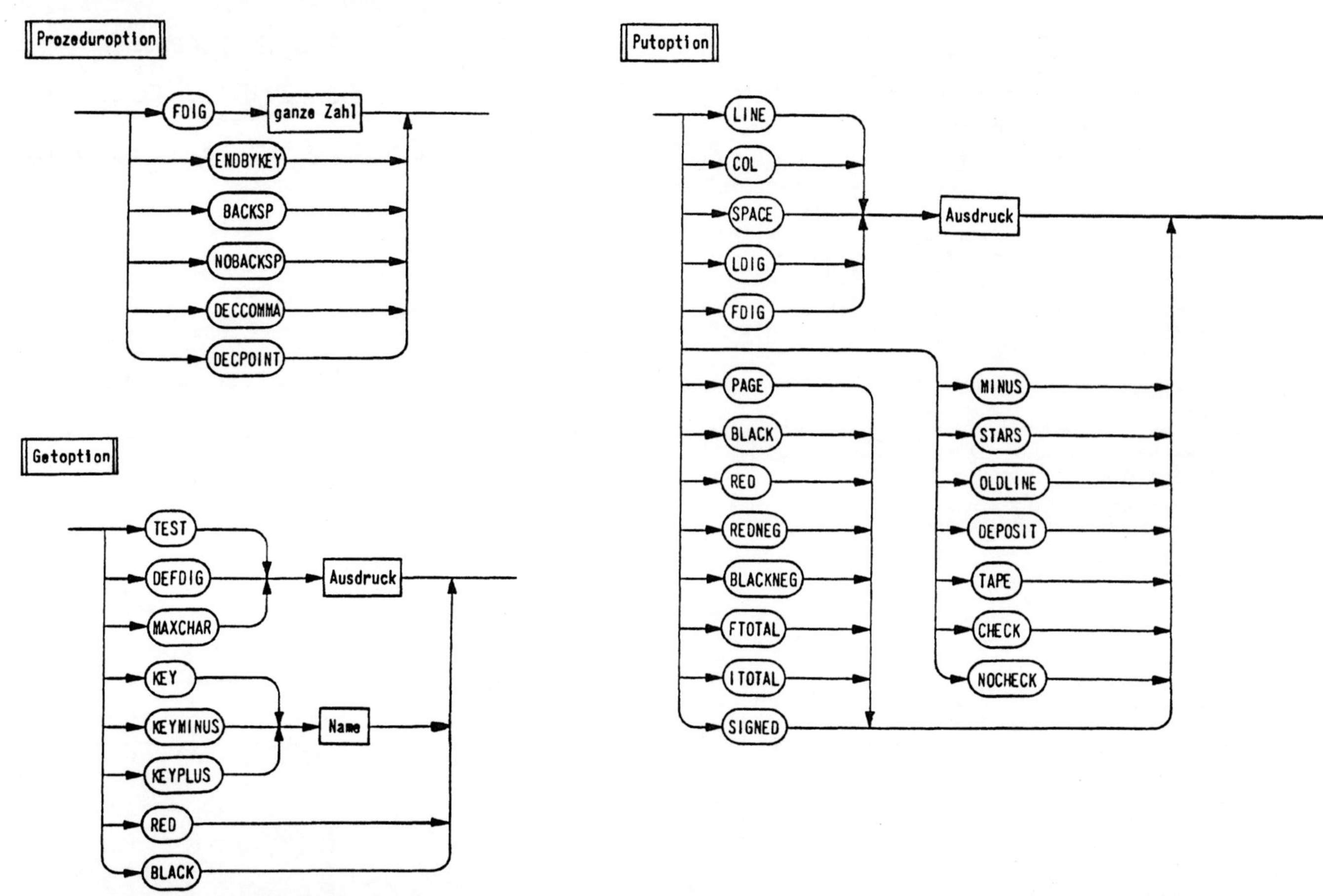

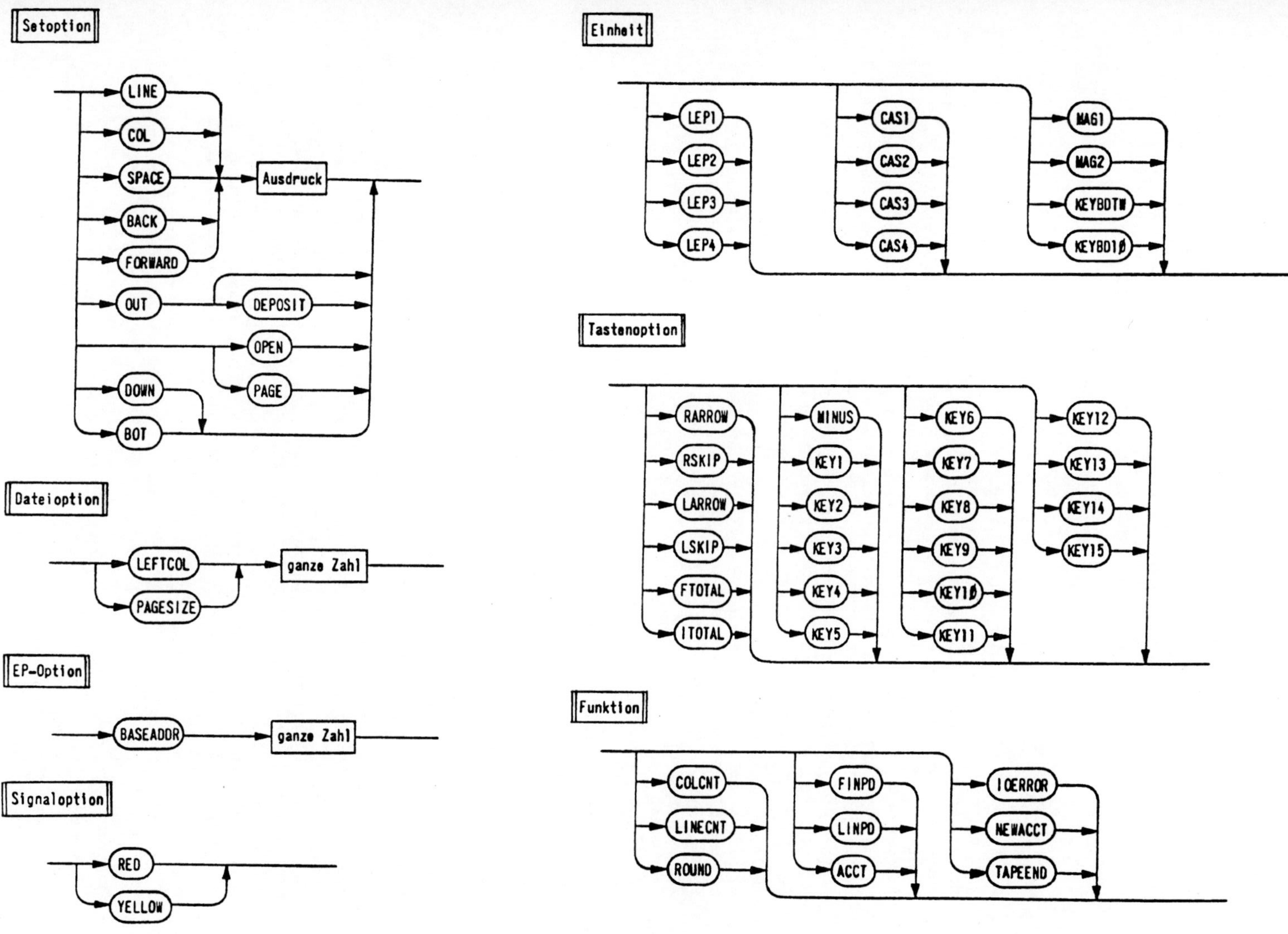

Setoption
LINE
COL
SPACE
BACK
FORWARD
Ausdruck
OUT
DEPOSIT
OPEN
DOWN
PAGE
BOT
Dateioption
LEFTCOL
PAGESIZE
ganze Zahl
EP-Option
BASEADDR
ganze Zahl
Signaloption
RED
YELLOW
Einheit
LEP1 LEP2 LEP3 LEP4
CAS1 CAS2 CAS3 CAS4
MAG1 MAG2 KEYBOTW KEYBOT1Ø
Tastenoption
RARROW RSKIP LARROW LSKIP FTOTAL ITOTAL
MINUS KEY1 KEY2 KEY3 KEY4 KEY5
KEY6 KEY7 KEY8 KEY9 KEY1Ø KEY11
KEY12 KEY13 KEY14 KEY15
Funktion
COLCNT LINECNT ROUND
FINPO LINPO ACCT
IOERROR NEWACCT TAPEEND

EHBIS: HIGH LEVEL PICTURE PROGRAMMING

Hans-Werner Brügmann, Alfons Rudert[+], Heinz Lehr[+]

Institut für Mathematische Maschinen und Datenverarbeitung II

der Friedrich Alexander Universität Erlangen-Nürnberg

1. MOTIVATION AND AIMS

In many areas of application, such as computer aided education, design and construction or process control, the graphical dialogue with the computer has become a base
for effective work and control. Essential hereby is a variety of pictures and graphic
representations. Designing the EHBIS (Erlanger Höhere Bildsprache) we tried to
create a language, which allows simple and effective handling of complete pictures,
not only of single elements e.g. lines, points and arcs. We also wished to supply
evident operation with pictures viz. a variety of transformations and combinations.

Neither did we wish to produce tools for programming of pictures on assembler level
- better done by compilers -, nor did we want to create another graphic package.
The latter method seemed to us not to be comfortable enough.

EHBIS was implemented on a PDP-15/VT-15 configuration with interactive display. Now
we have a high level picture programming language and, in addition, FORTRAN for
arithmetic and control in EHBIS programs. Construction of graphic sequences, like a
row of windows in the picture of a house for example, is done by means of loops
very easily.

2. THE EHBIS LANGUAGE

2.1 THEORETICAL BASE

The basic work, done by A.C. Shaw /3/, was published back in 1969. His formalism
serves as a base for picture analysis and also for picture synthesis and presents
a language (PDL), describing pictures by formal expressions very similar to arithmetic expressions. PDL emphasizes the structure of pictures and suggests "calculation"
of pictures.

2.1.1 PRIMITIVE PICTURES

While decomposing pictures stepwise one stops at some level and denotes the obtained
atoms "primitives". Each primitive represents a whole class of pictures, for example
all lines or all arcs, among others, in our implementation. The complexity of chosen
primitives is arbitrary. The kind of primitives is suggested by the actual application e.g. electrical engineering, control theory, flow charts. Each class of primitive
pictures is realized by a code generator yielding the desired representations.
EHBIS has 6 classes: LINIE, DLINIE, BOGEN, TEXT, FUNKT, PFUNKT (LINIE = line,
DLINIE = dark line, which establishes connection of unconnected pictures, BOGEN = arc,
TEXT = text line, FUNKT = ordinary function like $y = f(x)$, PFUNKT = parameter function
like $(x(p), y(p))$). These class names denote objects, which have a zero degree of

---

[+] graduates

reference in the sense of ALGOL 68.

In each class there are two points defined for every object, arbitrarily chosen
but suited for picture connection. These points are tail and head of a vector,
called abstract arrow or abstract picture. How is the abstract arrow located in
primitive pictures? For lines and arcs just as one would suppose. By texts it is
the unvisible underline, by functions it is the defined (FUNKT) or resulting (PFUNKT)
intervall of the abscissa.

While producing picture code at runtime, the class name selects the code generator
and the abstract arrow supplies for it the local geometry of a primitive picture.
Global coordinates of a whole picture are normally treated by the system, putting
it at the middle of the display, but also explicit positioning by the user is
possible.

2.1.2 CONNECTION BY OPERATORS

We use the operators defined by SHAW /1/. Given two primitive pictures a, b represented by their abstract vector, we get:

notion: a + b   a # b   a - b

result:

The resulting arrow, represented by a wavy line, has always its tail from the tail
of the left operand and its head from the head of the right operand. Obviously it is
defined by both the operands (+), or only by the left (-) or right (#) called the
"relevant operand". Another operator (*) requires identification of the tail of a
with the tail of b and the head of a with the head of b:

a * b   What to do, when a and b do not fit together? In SHAW's formal
                        PDL such an expression has an empty semantic. In EHBIS fitting
                        is achieved by trimming the right operand.

There are two more unary operators:
←a   interchanges tail and head of a picture

/a   picks up only the abstract, invisible picture.

When gluing pictures, this is accomplished by using "*", and multiple drawing is
suppressed by using "/". Of course the resulting arrow of one operator can serve
as operand of another operator. Then execution of operators obeys to the priorities

        first ← , /
        then   *
        then   +, -, #

For changing the order of execution we use parentheses.

2.1.3 CONNECTED PICTURES

Now we have picture expressions with class names and operators, representing an
inherent hierarchical and binary tree structure. Primitive and connected pictures
we simply call "pictures", but we term any operand of an operator "picture part".
Pictures and parts of them may be referenced by picture names having degree one of
reference in the sense of ALGOL 68. A typical EHBIS statement (assignation) looks like

        PIC1 = LINIE * BOGEN + PART2

PIC1 and PART2 being picture names, the others being class names.

2.2 DATA STRUCTURE

The data base contains mainly the tree structures of all defined pictures with data
nodes for each picture, picture part and primitive picture. They all possess an abstract arrow, stored twice in the associated node, in polar and cartesian coordinates.
This is done to facilitate the computation of connected pictures and for code generation.

2.2.1 DATA NODES FOR PRIMITIVE PICTURES

```
mode PRIMBILD = struct

            (int   PBCODE,
             int   ANGABE1,
             int   ANGABE2,
             int   RUECKV,
             int   DELTAX,
             int   DELTAY,
             int   GROESSE,
             int   RICHTUNG,
             bool  BDISPLAY, ref string DISPLAYCODE,
             bits  BILDPARAMETER)
```

BOGEN
9∅
–
1∅∅
1∅∅
141
45
⋮

The first component contains the class name. Total definition of a primitive picture
is achieved by maybe two more items, invariant under affine transformations, e.g. the
center angle of an arc. Complex primitives, requiring more items, use pointers instead.
Complete descriptions of primitives in EHBIS are e.g.

```
BOGEN  (90)

TEXT   ('XXXX', 20)

FUNKT  (COS, -PI, PI)

PFUNKT (F1, F2, 0.0, 1.0)
```

Meaning of the remaining components:

RUECKV	link for tree traverse and picture part decision
DELTAX to	
RICHTUNG	abstract arrow
BDISPLAY, -CODE	code already generated?
BILDPARAMETER	beam intensity, line type, run time identification bits

Five components hereby are programmable: GROESSE, RICHTUNG, beam intensity (HELL),
line type (STRIC) and run time identification bits (NAM). The latter feature renders
quick and simple identification of primitive pictures with a display light pen. Explicit setting of these attributes is done by attribute lists e.g.

```
...+ LINIE [GROES = 100,
           RICHT =   45,
           HELL  =    3,
           STRIC =    1,
           NAM   =   99] + ...
```

or

```
...+ FUNKT(SQRT,1,2) [H=6, S=3, N=8 ]+...
```

When not specified, attributes are set to standard values.

2.2.2 DATA NODES FOR CONNECTED PICTURES

Connected pictures are represented in the data base by an operator node showing the
last executed operator of the whole picture expression.

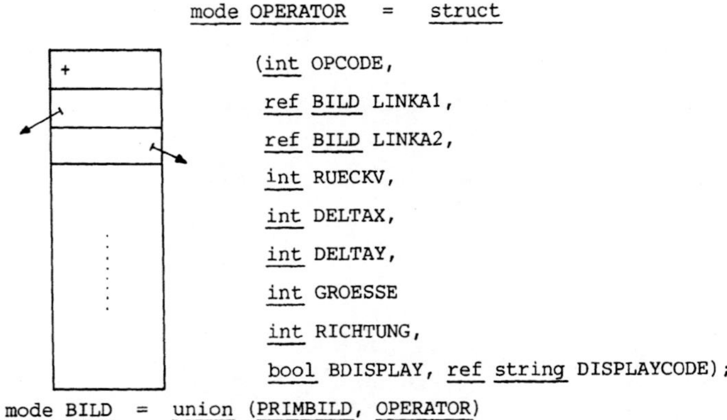


```
mode OPERATOR  =   struct

               (int OPCODE,

                ref BILD LINKA1,

                ref BILD LINKA2,

                int RUECKV,

                int DELTAX,

                int DELTAY,

                int GROESSE

                int RICHTUNG,

                bool BDISPLAY, ref string DISPLAYCODE);

mode BILD  =  union (PRIMBILD, OPERATOR)
```

The first component now contains the specification of an EHBIS-operator followed
by the pointers to one or two operands. The other components have the same meaning
as for primitive pictures. Component BILDPARAMETER is missing here, since explicit
changing of attributes HELL, STRIC and NAM results in an immediate change at all
subordinate primitive nodes. Explicit changing of GROESSE and RICHTUNG see section
2.4.2.

2.2.3 DATA STRUCTURE CONTROVERSY

An EHBIS-statement of the form A = B + B creates at runtime two identical subtrees
for B in the data base. Why should not one create such identical subtrees only once?
Then we would get a graph structured data base instead of a tree structured one.
This leads to the question of how to generate picture code from data structure. A
tree structure will be flatted to sequential code, but a graph structure to code
using subroutine techniques. This in turn asks the question about the performance
of the graphic processor. Consider a list, not necessary complete, of picture mani-
pulations and transformations:

> change of beam intensity
>
> change of line type
>
> translation
>
> rotation
>
> scaling, zooming
>
> windowing, clipping

Which one of them can the graphic processor perform by hardware? Pictures, subject
only to such transformations, may be coded as subroutines and the processor will be
put in the desired transformation before subroutine call.
But our configuration (PDP-15/VT-15) does not perform arbitrary rotation and zooming
by hardware. Another argument for a tree structured data base is the minimization of
side effects from implicit coercion of picture parts. Also subroutine techniques
are useless on some low level, when subroutine bodies are as small as subroutine
calls. So we have decided to use a tree structured data base in the first EHBIS implementation.

2.3 LANGUAGE CONSTRUCTS AND SEMANTICS

Picture construction is achieved by EHBIS statements of the general form
        <picture name> = <picture expression>
where picture names have to be declared before use in the form
        BILD: TEIL1, TEIL2, DETAIL(5), ...
with the reserved keyword BILD. The graphic output device is assumed to have a square
area. Relation between device coordinates and user coordinates is established by a

statemant
      MASS (50)
which prescribes the graphic area to be equivalent for example to 50 x 50 user units.
Now let us consider some aspects of data base management. After execution of

      A = ...

there will exist some tree structure A refers to. Further use of A, e.g. in

      B = C * A,

causes the tree of A to be incorporated in B. A was not part of any picture and therefore was not copied before use. Now we have
a situation like this:
But the semantic is
controversial, since
the contents of A may
be altered implicitly
during connection (*)

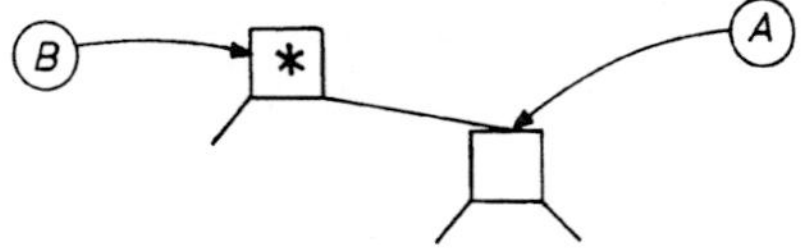

with C (see section 2.4.2) or later on by changes of B. To prevent this and to save
A, the user may prescribe

      B = C * KOPIE (A)

instead of B = C*A. Then A is copied first and then incorporated. The system always
takes a copy to work on, when a picture name refers to a picture part, e.g. C in

      D = C - E

or, when attributes of a picture are explicitly changed by an attribute list, the picture being referenced by a picture name e.g.

      ... = B [G = 20, R = 180]

Last not least, examination of constructed pictures is supplied by the EHBIS command

      DISPLAY (PIC27, STARTX, STARTY, TIME, LPEN)

which displays the desired picture some time or continuously and perhaps returns some
integer (contents of attribute NAM) in LPEN. Execution of such a statement may also
effect some changes of the data base (see section 2.4.1).

2.4 DIALOGUE FEATURES

So far described, EHBIS is also suited for passiv graphic devices. The only ballast
then would be the run time identification bits (attribut NAM) contained in the data
for primitive pictures. This information is recovered by interactive light pen picking
of picture parts and serves as a vehicle for programmed dialogues, controlled either
by the EHBIS run time system or by the FORTRAN and assembler run time system. Object
of a programmed dialogue is the user problem, treated throughout the whole EHBIS program. But also the spontaneous dialogue is possible in EHBIS, which deals with a picture or a picture part. The spontaneous dialogue takes place within the EHBIS command

      DISPLAY (PIC27, ..., TIME, LPEN)

cited above. It is finished by pressing some function pushbutton. But first the user
may initiate updating of the data structure and/or the generation and updating of
optimized display code for the shown picture by pressing function pushbuttons.

2.4.1 THE SPONTANEOUS DIALOGUE

At first the user identifies the whole picture or a certain picture part by direct
light pen picking of that part. Hereby the hierarchical structure of picture data
is very useful. The algorithm for picture part identification starts at the top node
associated with the named picture (e.g. PIC27) and makes the whole picture blink.
While the user continues light pen identification of his primitive picture, the algorithm descends through the data tree deciding at each stage, which of the two
operands caused a pen hit. Each pen hit is answered by successive restriction of picture blinking to the actual picture part. Identification stops, when further pen

hits fail to appear or when a primitive picture is reached.

Now the user specifies an action out of the following light pen menue:

- LOESCHE

- POSITION

- GROESSE

- WINKEL

- HELL

- STRICH

- GRO + WIN

        ALTER WERT (225)

        NEUER WERT (150)

The first action deletes the identified picture part. The other actions all require
input of some numbers, which is requested and issued on a teletype. The user sees
the old value and gives the new one. The second action changes the position of the
whole picture. The remaining actions from GROESSE to STRICH effect changes by the
identified picture part and also in the data base. Then the changed picture is shown
and the dialogue may go on.
To provide quick reactions of the system and a rapid regeneration of display code
for changed picture parts only, the code file is structured homomorphic to the data
base: Also connected picture nodes possess code portions containing subpicture calls
for the two operand pictures. The display code is patched locally.

2.4.2 PICTURE COERCION I TOP DOWN

Changing of primitive pictures is done very easily. The new attributes enter the
data base, and the pointer to the display code for that primitive is cleared. But
changing of connected pictures to new values of GROESSE and WINKEL must be done
consistently with picture connection. The need for change arises in the spontaneous
dialogue and in using picture names with attribut lists (see also section 2.3),
where new values are prescribed explicitly, and also on execution of the operator
"*" and trimming the right operand, where new values for size and direction are
given implicitly by the
left operand (section 2.1.2):
The whole subtree is changed,
and the changing starts at its
top node. Actual values for size
and direction to be changed and the
prescribed ones determine an angle
difference for rotation and a size
factor. Rotation and scaling now

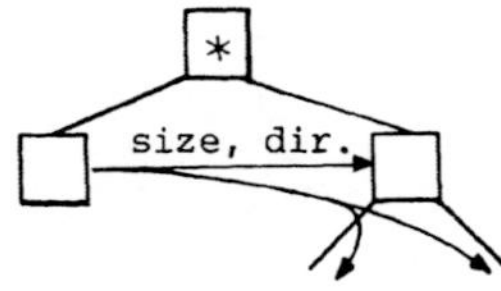

proceeds downward to <u>relevant operands</u> only (see section 2.1.2) preventing inclination
of texts or functions for example and stopping at primitive pictures.

2.4.3 PICTURE COERCION II BOTTOM UP

This kind of coercion is necessary only in the spontaneous dialogue when changing
picture parts. Connection of pictures must be preserved not only within some part,
but also to the surrounding picture. In data base, this may lead to correction of
size and direction attributes in the next higher node, the neighbouring node and
from there downward again. Consider an example:

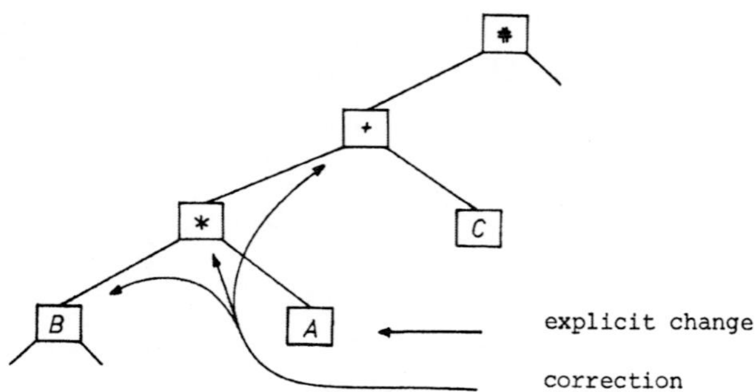

In the node "*" values for size and direction are changed to these of subtree A, A being a relevant operand of "*". The semantic of "*" also forces the subtree B to have the same values as A. Now "*" is a relevant operand of "+", causing the node "+" to be corrected. This does not affect subtree C, and correction stops at "+", because "+" is not a relevant operand of "#". In general, correction now proceeds to higher nodes, but only from relevant operands, stopping at the first irrelevant or the highest node.

3. FINAL REMARKS AND EXAMPLES

3.1 THE EHBIS PROGRAMMING SYSTEM

It was already mentioned, that for arithmetic and control EHBIS has adopted FORTRAN. This is realized by a precompiler, which accepts real picture lines and also FORTRAN lines. Picture lines are flagged with a B by the programmer and translated to some CALL statements calling the EHBIS run time system. FORTRAN lines are transfered to the output file unchanged. So the EHBIS precompiler produces a FORTRAN file for further compilation. The precompiler is written in FORTRAN and consists of about 2800 lines, the EHBIS run time system includes about 1500 FORTRAN lines and about as many assembler lines. For testing EHBIS programs, it is possible to dump the data structures of all constructed pictures and also some other lists. Garbage collection is done in data base after each assignation.
Additional software allows the spontaneous dialogue on updated pictures and use of EHBIS pictures in arbitrary programs (programmed dialogues).

3.2 EXAMPLES

EHBIS source:

```
 1   C       WURZEL-SCHNECKE
 2   C
 3   B       BILD: A, B, C
 4   B       A = (LINIE + LINIE [R=9Ø]) * LINIE
 5           DO 1ØØ I = 1,5
 6   B       B = LINIE [R=9Ø]
 7   B       C = (/A [R=Ø] + B) * LINIE + DLINIE [R=27Ø]
 8   B       A = A * C + /B
 9      1ØØ  CONTINUE
1Ø   B       DISPLAY (A,5ØØ,5ØØ,Ø,LPEN)
11           CALL AUS
12           STOP
13           END
```

and picture:

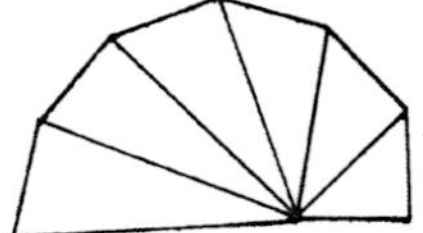

EHBIS precompiler output:

```
C     WURZEL-SCHNECKE
C
C
C ** GENERIERTER CODE VON ZEILE    3 **
      CALL INIT ( Ø.1ØØØØØE+Ø1)
      CALL NLIST('A     ',  1)
      CALL NLIST('B     ',  1)
      CALL NLIST('C     ',  1)
C
C
C ** GENERIERTER CODE VON ZEILE    4 **
      CALL PRIM ('LINIE',Ø, 1Ø2.Ø,Ø,4,Ø,Ø)
      CALL PRIM ('LINIE',Ø, 1Ø2.Ø,9Ø,4,Ø,Ø)
      CALL BINOP(1,'$     ',  Ø,'$     ',  Ø)
      CALL PRIM ('LINIE',Ø, 1O2.Ø,Ø,4,Ø,Ø)
      CALL BINOP(4,'$     ',  Ø,'$     ',  Ø)
      CALL ASSIG('A     ',  1,'$     ',  Ø)
C
      DO 1ØØ I = 1,5
C
C ** GENERIERTER CODE VON ZEILE    6 **
      CALL PRIM ('LINIE',Ø, 1Ø2.Ø,9Ø,4,Ø,Ø)
      CALL ASSIG('B     ',  2,'$     ',  Ø)
C
C
C ** GENERIERTER CODE VON ZEILE    7 **
      CALL ANPAS(1,   1,-2,-1.Ø,Ø,-1,-1,-1)
      CALL BLANK('$     ',  Ø)
      CALL BINOP(1,'$     ',  Ø,'B     ',  2)
      CALL PRIM ('LINIE',Ø, 1Ø2.Ø,Ø,4,Ø,Ø)
      CALL BINOP(4,'$     ',  Ø,'$     ',  Ø)
      CALL PRIM ('DLINI',Ø, 1Ø2.Ø,27Ø,Ø,Ø,Ø)
      CALL BINOP(1,'$     ',  Ø,'$     ',  Ø)
      CALL ASSIG('C     ',  3,'$     ',  Ø)
C
C
C ** GENERIERTER CODE VON ZEILE    8 **
      CALL BINOP(4,'A     ',  1,'C     ',  3)
      CALL BLANK('B     ',  2)
      CALL BINOP(1,'$     ',  Ø,'$     ',  Ø)
      CALL ASSIG('A     ',  1,'$     ',  Ø)
C
  1OO CONTINUE
C
C ** GENERIERTER CODE VON ZEILE   1Ø **
      CALL BZEIG('A     ',  1,5ØØ.Ø,5ØØ.Ø,Ø,LPEN )
C
      CALL AUS
      STOP
      END
```

part of picture data:

STRUKTURBAUM

NR.	ART	L.OP	R.OP	RK	X	Y	GROES	RICHT	PAR.	DISPLAY
175	*	173	174	177	-27Ø	-14	27Ø	183	ØØØØØØ	-1
176	DLINI	Ø	Ø	177	33	96	1Ø2	71	ØØØØØØ	-1
177	+	175	176	178	-236	81	25Ø	161	ØØØØØØ	-1
178	*	125	177	18Ø	-236	82	25Ø	161	ØØØØØØ	-1
179	/	Ø	Ø	18Ø	-33	-96	1Ø2	251	ØØØØØØ	-1
18Ø	+	178	179	Ø	-269	-14	269	183	ØØØØØØ	-1

NAMENLISTE:

NR.	NAME	KNOTENNR
1	A	18Ø
2	B	126
3	C	177

one more EHBIS source:

```
 1   C      KREISBOEGEN UND TEXTE
 2   C
 3   C      BILD: U, R, UR, EI
 4   B      U  = LINIE [R=45,S=1] + LINIE [R=315,S=2]
 5   B      U  = (( TEXT('...IN',15) # U )
 6   B    C    * BOGEN(9Ø) ) [G=3ØØ]
 7   B      U  = U - ◄TEXT('..OUT',15)
 8   B      R  = (/U) [G: Ø.5,R=9Ø] * BOGEN(9Ø)
 9   B      UR = U + R
1Ø   B      EI = UR * ◄UR
11   B      DISPLAY (EI,2ØØ,2ØØ,Ø,LPEN)
12          STOP
13          END
```

and picture:

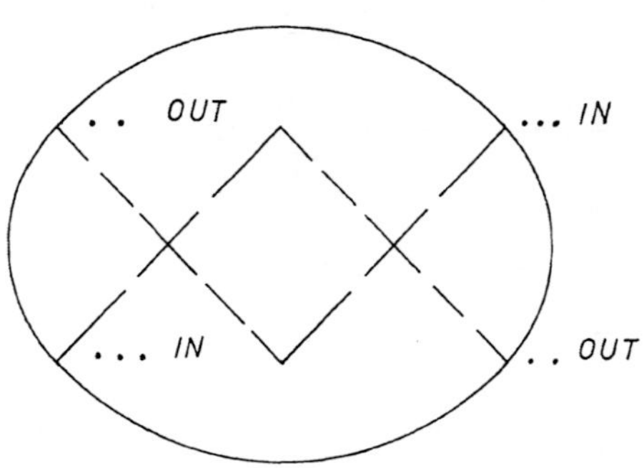

3.3 ACKNOWLEDGMENT

I should like to thank Prof. Schneider for remarks about this paper, Mr. Göttler, who has smoothed my English, Mrs. Bischoff for her careful typing of the manuscript, and Mr. Wanninger for the drawings.

LITERATURE

/1/ Brügmann, H.-W.

     SIDIPRO: Dialog-Sprache und Echtzeit-Über-
     setzer für die Programmierung eines Hoch-
     leistungs-Sichtgerätes,
     Fachtagung Computer Graphics, Berlin
     GI-Bericht Nr. 2 (1971).

/2/ Lehr, H.

     Ein Programmpaket zur interaktiven Defini-
     tion und Manipulation von strukturierten,
     dialogfähigen Bildern zweidimensionaler Ob-
     jekte,
     Diplomarbeit am Lehrstuhl für Informatik II
     FAU Erlangen-Nürnberg (1975).

/3/ Shaw, A.C.

     A Formal Picture Description Scheme as a
     Basis for Picture Processing Systems,
     Information and Control 14, 9-52 (1969).

/4/ Rudert, A.

     Ein Präcompiler für EHBIS, eine höhere
     Sprache zur Programmierung von Bildern
     und Bildschirmdialogen,
     Diplomarbeit am Lehrstuhl für Informatik II
     FAU Erlangen-Nürnberg (1975).

COMSKEE - Eine Sprache für Linguisten

Eberhard Bertsch und Angelika Mueller-von Brochowski
Sonderforschungsbereich "Elektronische Sprachforschung"
Universität des Saarlandes

1. Einleitung

Die algorithmische Sprache COMSKEE (COMputing and String-KEEping
language) wurde im SFB "Elektronische Sprachforschung" der
Deutschen Forschungsgemeinschaft an der Universität des Saarlandes
entwickelt. Anregungen dazu kamen von Linguisten und Philologen des
SFB, die ihre Programmieraufgaben bisher mit FORTRAN und Assembler-
Sprachen lösten. COMSKEE soll ihrem Wunsch nach einem leicht zu
beschreibenden textorientierten Programmiersystem entgegenkommen.
Dabei wurde der Versuch unternommen, ein ausgewogenes Verhältnis
zwischen algebraischer und mnemotechnischer Notation zu erreichen.
Das in vielen höheren Programmiersprachen verwirklichte Prinzip der
Schachtelung von arithmetischen Ausdrücken und Zugriffsoperationen -
wie beispielsweise bei

$$t-a(3+b(i)/r)+j$$

- wurde auf Stringausdrücke und Teilstringzugriffe ausgedehnt.
Ein weiterer Vorteil - verglichen mit Systemen wie COMIT und SNOBOL -
ist mit der Möglichkeit der Programmstrukturierung durch Blöcke und
Prozeduren gegeben.

Zur Beschreibung der Sprachkomponenten stellen wir zunächst die
Bedürfnisse der Linguisten den daraus entstandenen Datenstrukturen
gegenüber. Es folgt ein Abschnitt über die elementaren Datentypen
und die auf ihnen definierten Operationen. Der Stringmanipulation
mithilfe spezieller Anweisungen ist ein weiterer Abschnitt gewidmet.
Schließlich zeigen wir anhand eines Beispiels das Zusammenwirken
verschiedener Sprachmerkmale.

2. Bedürfnisse der Linguisten

Die folgenden Aspekte wurden als wesentlich für die sprachwissenschaft-
lich orientierte Programmierung erkannt. Die Reihenfolge ihrer
Priorität mag dabei von der speziellen Problemstellung eines Projekts
abhängen.

(a) Verarbeitung von (Teil-)Zeichenketten zur Erkennung von Endungen
    und zur Synthese von Ausgabedaten

(b) Setzen, Vergleichen und Abfragen von Masken zur Kennzeichnung von
    verschiedenartigen Mustern

(c) Herstellen von Bezügen zwischen Daten unterschiedlichen Typs
    in Wörterbucheinträgen

(d) Tabellen- und Kellerverwaltung, insbesondere zur syntaktischen
    und semantischen Analyse

(e) Arbeiten mit und in Bäumen - der Zugriff auf einzelne Knoten muß
    leicht möglich sein -

(f) Übersichtliche Darstellung von Regelgrammatiken für alle Arten
    von "rewrite"-Systemen

(g) Sammeln von Daten gleichen Typs in einer Menge und Abfragen auf
    Enthaltensein

3. Realisierung der Strukturen in COMSKEE

Zu den angegebenen Punkten (a)-(g) beschreiben wir nun in knapper
Form die entsprechenden Möglichkeiten im Rahmen der linguistisch
orientierten Programmiersprache:

(a) Dynamische Strings sind als elementare Größen deklarierbar und
    erlauben eine Reihe aufeinander abgestimmter Operationen und
    Zugriffsmechanismen.

(b) Bitketten fester Länge, bei denen auf Teilketten und auf einzelne
    Bits zugegriffen werden kann, bieten sich für binäre Operationen
    an.

(c) Es ist möglich, Records zu deklarieren, deren Komponenten Strings,
    Bitketten, Zahlen oder andere Records sein können. Zwischen gleich
    aufgebauten Records lassen sich Zuweisungen durchführen.

(d) Dynamische Arrays im Sinne von ALGOL können elementare Daten oder
Records als Komponenten enthalten. Für eindimensionale Felder sind
Standardprozeduren (push,pop) zur Kellertechnik vorgesehen.

(e) Bäume werden als endliche Mengen von Knoten aufgefaßt, zwischen
denen Nachfolgerelationen bestehen können. Die Knoten sind mit
elementaren Werten besetzt. Zugriff geschieht mit Standardprozeduren

(f) Grammatiken sind spezielle Arrays. Sie dienen als Parameter für
Analyse- und Syntheseprozeduren, deren Ausgabe im allgemeinen
Strukturbäume sind.

(g) Die Datenstruktur "Menge" ist dadurch gekennzeichnet, daß auf ihre
Elemente nicht einzeln zugegriffen werden kann. Operationen sind
Durchschnitt, Vereinigung, Komplement sowie gewisse Abfragen.

In stark vereinfachter Form können wir nun angeben, welche Strukturen
welche anderen Strukturen als Komponenten enthalten dürfen:

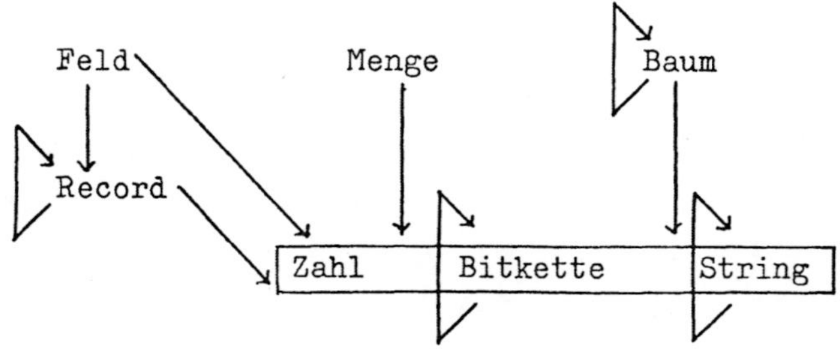

4. Die elementaren Datentypen

Wir stellen nun die auf den elementaren Datentypen Zahl, Bitkette und
String möglichen Operationen und Zugriffsmechanismen im einzelnen vor.

4.1 Rationale Zahlen

Sie sind unstrukturiert und über ihren Identifikator referierbar.
Zwischen ihnen sind die üblichen arithmetischen Operationen definiert.
Rationale Konstanten können als Dezimalbrüche, gemischte Zahlen und
ganze Zahlen im Programm vorkommen.

4.2 Zeichenketten

Zeichenketten bestehen aus einer (evtll. leeren) Folge von Symbolen
aus einem Zeichenvorrat. Durch **string** s wird eine Stringvariable
mit Identifikator s deklariert, der im Laufe des Programms verschiedene

und verschieden lange Zeichenketten als Werte zugewiesen werden können.
Die aktuelle (current) Länge der Zeichenkette, auf die s gerade referiert
, erhält man durch $\#$ s.

Teilstringzugriff über die Position:

s(i:j)   s ist Bezeichnung für eine Stringvariable, i und j sind
arithmetische Ausdrücke. Für die Werte muß sein
$1 \le i \le j \le \#$ s. s(i:j) bezeichnet den Teilstring von s,
der vom i-ten bis zum j-ten Zeichen reicht. Nach
s := 'erlangen'; s := s(3:6) enthält s das Wort 'lang'.

Teilstringzugriff über den Inhalt:

s(s':s")   s ist wie oben, s' und s" sind Stringausdrücke.
s(s':s") liefert den Teilstring, der zwischen dem ersten
Vorkommen von s' in s und dem ersten darauf folgenden
Vorkommen von s" liegt. Nach s := 'erlangen'; s':='er';
s":='en' liefert s(s':s") wiederum 'lang'.

Teilstringzugriff über Position und Inhalt:

s(i:s")   Hiermit ist es möglich, beide Zugriffsarten gemischt
s(s':j)   anzuwenden. So blenden zum Beispiel nach s := 'ankommen'
die Ausdrücke s('an':$\#$ s) und s(1:'en') Präfix und
Suffix jeweils alleine aus.

Die Teilstringzugriffe liefern Wortsegmente, die addressierbar sind,
sodaß also auch Zuweisungen der Art s(i:j) := s' formuliert werden
können. Das Segment verhält sich in solchen Fällen in gleicher Weise
dynamisch wie ein String: Bei verschiedener Länge der rechten und
linken Seite erfolgt kein Auffüllen oder Abschneiden, sondern ein
Anpassen der Segmentumgebung an den neuen Teilstring. Nach s := 'ankam';
s':= 'abkommen' liefert s'(3:6):=s(3:5) den Wert 'abkamen' und
s'('ab':'k'):='ge' den Wert 'abgekommen'.

Positionsoperator:

s.s'   s und s' sind Stringausdrücke. Falls s' Teilwort von s
ist, liefert s.s' die Anfangsposition des ersten
Vorkommens von s' in s, andernfalls den Wert 0.

Umkehroperator:

←s   ←s liefert die rückläufige Form von s.
←'leben' = 'nebel'. Falls s kein Identifikator oder
Konstante ist, muß ←(s) geschrieben werden.

Binäre Operationen auf Strings:

s __cat__ s'   Hiermit wird die Konkatenation von Zeichenketten
(s + s')   formuliert. s und s' können beliebige Stringausdrücke
                    sein.

s __tct__ s'   Falls s' Endzeichenkette von s ist, wird der um s'
(s - s')   verkürzte (trunkierte) Teilstring von s' gebildet,
                    andernfalls s. 'er'+'lang'+'ende'-'de' = 'erlangen'

4.3 Bitketten

Bitkettenvariablen werden durch __bits__ b deklariert und haben Werte
fester Länge von 24 Bits. Der Zugriff auf Bitketten geschieht über
den Identifikator b, der Zugriff auf Teilketten über Positionsangaben
$b(i:j)$.Eine Zuweisung an Teilketten ist nicht möglich; sie läßt sich
aber leicht durch Boole'sche Operationen ersetzen. Dabei hat man sich
Bitkettenkonstanten rechts mit Nullen ergänzt zu denken, sodaß mit
$b(1:1)$ stets das 1.Bit einer an b zugewiesenen Konstante gemeint ist.
Beispielsweise wird eine Zuweisung von 1001 an $b(3:6)$ durch

$$b := b \wedge (\neg\, 001111) \vee 001001 \text{ bewirkt.}$$

5. Stringmanipulation mit expliziten Anweisungen

Da für Benutzer aus nichtnumerischen Anwendungsgebieten die algebraische
Notation oft schwer zugänglich ist, soll es auch möglich sein, gängige
Zeichenkettenveränderungen mit in natürlicher Sprache formulierten
Anweisungen zu veranlassen. Wir unterscheiden hierbei fünf Bereiche:

    (a) Teilstring Ersetzen
    (b) Teilstring Ausschneiden
    (c) Teilstring Löschen
    (d) Teilstring Einfügen
    (e) Teilstring Ausblenden

(a)   __in__ svar __replace__ s __by__ s' [__success__ b] ;
    Falls s Teilstring der Stringvariablen svar ist, entspricht dies
    $svar(svar.s : svar.s + \#s-1) := s'$ bzw. der "Markov"-Ersetzung.
    Ist s kein Teilstring von svar, wird nur die Bitkette b auf
    0 gesetzt, andernfalls auf 1. Varianten zum __replace__-Befehl sind
    __replace last__ und __replace all__. Ihre Bedeutung ist anschaulich klar.

(b) $\underline{\text{move}}$ svar$\left[\underline{\text{from}} \left\{\frac{\text{position } i}{s}\right\}\left[\underline{\text{until}} \left\{\frac{\text{position } j}{s'}\right\}\right]\right] \left[\underline{\text{into}} \text{ svar}'\right]$;

Durch diesen Befehl wird ein durch seine linke und rechte
Begrenzung gekennzeichneter Teilstring ausgeschnitten und einer
Variablen svar' zugewiesen. Es handelt sich hierbei um keine echte
Zuweisung, da auch der Ursprungsstring verändert wird. Fall der
gesuchte Teilstring nicht gefunden wird, erhält svar' Länge O.

(c) $\underline{\text{delete}} \left[\left\{\frac{\underline{\text{last}}}{\underline{\text{all}}}\right\}\right]$ s $\underline{\text{in}}$ svar $\left[\underline{\text{success}} \text{ b}\right]$;

Die Bedeutung dieser Anweisungen ist anschaulich klar.(Bei
Auslassung von $\underline{\text{last}}$ und $\underline{\text{all}}$ wird der erste Teilstring s gelöscht.)
Der Leser kann sich leicht davon überzeugen, daß sich die Vari-
anten $\underline{\text{last}}$ und $\underline{\text{all}}$ nur sehr umständlich in algebraischer Schreibweise formulieren lassen.

(d) $\underline{\text{insert}}$ s $\underline{\text{in}}$ svar $\left\{\frac{\underline{\text{after}}}{\underline{\text{before}}}\right\} \left\{\frac{\text{position } i}{s'}\right\} \left[\underline{\text{success}} \text{ b}\right]$;

Auch hier ist die Bedeutung anschaulich klar. Ein Vergleich mit
der Komplexität der algebraischen Formulierung fällt (trotz deren
Kompaktheit) zugunsten des $\underline{\text{insert}}$-Befehls aus:
$\underline{\text{insert}}$ s_1 $\underline{\text{in}}$ svar $\underline{\text{before}}$ s_2 ;   ist äquivalent zu der Zuweisung
svar(svar.s_2) := s_1 $\underline{\text{cat}}$ svar(svar.s_2) ;

(e) $\underline{\text{mask}}$ s $\underline{\text{by}}$ b $\underline{\text{into}}$ svar ;
s ist Stringausdruck, b ist Bitkettenausdruck. Nach Ausführung
des Befehls enthält svar einen String, der sich aus der Anein-
anderfügung solcher Zeichen von s ergibt, deren Position in b
eine 1 enthält.
$\underline{\text{mask}}$ 'nürnberg' $\underline{\text{by}}$ 010011 $\underline{\text{into}}$ str; ergibt str='übe'.

In einem späteren Stadium soll COMSKEE mit einer Vielzahl von textorientierten Standardprozeduren der Form p(arg_1,...,arg_n) ausgestattet
werden.Damit bestehen drei Bearbeitungsmöglichkeiten für Textdaten,
nämlich über Infix-Operatoren($\S4$ oben), Prozeduraufrufe und explizite
Anweisungen ((a)-(e)).Wir möchten erwähnen, daß die Sprache ALGOL60
eben diese Möglichkeiten für numerische Werte anbietet. Beispiele sind

$\quad$ a+b-(c/d-e)   ,   arctan(1)   , $\underline{\text{for}}$ v:= e_1 $\underline{\text{step}}$ e_2...

6. Strukturen

COMSKEE erlaubt die Zuweisung kompletter Strukturen. Voraussetzung
für die syntaktische Korrektheit solcher Anweisungen ist die
komponentenweise Übereinstimmung der Datentypen. Da Strukturen selbst
als Komponenten von Strukturen auftreten können, ergibt sich somit
eine Vielfalt an knapp formulierbaren Transportbefehlen. Dabei können
auch Struktur-"Konstanten" verwendet werden, die durch Klammerung
elementarer Konstanten entstehen.

Eine durch
        struct satz (struct subjekt
        (string artikel, string nomen),

deklarierte Größe   string verb, number buchseite);

läßt sich durch   satz := (('der','mann'),'kommt',25);
initialisieren

und durch   subjekt := ('die','frau') ;
      buchseite := 28;

verändern.

An eine durch   struct nominalgruppe
      (string wort1, string wort2);

spezifizierte Struktur kann die Zuweisung erfolgen

      nominalgruppe := subjekt ;

Dies läßt sich bildlich folgendermaßen darstellen:

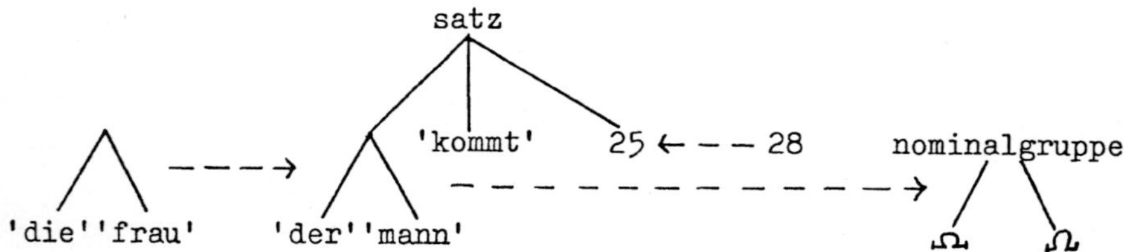

Die Verwendung von Strukturen lohnt sich vor allem bei umfangreichen
Wörterbucheinträgen. Das in Saarbrücken erstellte Shakespeare-
Wörterbuch enthält beispielsweise pro Eintrag etwa zwei Dutzend
verschiedene Angaben .

7. Beispiel

Wir geben nun eine in COMSKEE geschriebene Prozedur an, die einer im
Teilprojekt "Germanistik" des SFB verwendeten FORTRAN-Prozedur entsprich

```
 1    PROC UNTERSUCHEFORM;
 2        STRING  WORTFORM;
 3        STRUCT  (STRING  ENDUNG,
 4                 STRUCT EINTRAG (STRING STAMM,
 5                                 NUMBER WORTKLASSE,
 6                                 BITS DECLMASKE )
 7                 ) ARRAY FUNDLISTE [1:#WORTFORM]);
 8    BEGIN STRING KOPF; STRING SCHWANZ; NUMBER I;
 9        STRING SET ENDUNGEN; ENDUNGEN:=('EN','E','STES'));
10        KOPF:=WORTFORM; SCHWANZ:=''; I:=1;
11        REPEAT UNTIL #KOPF = 0
12        BEGIN IF SCHWANZ IN ENDUNGEN THEN
13                   CALL WOBUSUCHE(KOPF,EINTRAG[I]);
14                   IF STAMM[I] ¬= '' THEN ENDUNG[I]:=SCHWANZ;
15                                          I:=I+1
16                   FI
17              FI
18              SCHWANZ := KOPF(#KOPF) + SCHWANZ;
19              KOPF(#KOPF) := ''
20        END
21    END
```

Es handelt sich um eine Rahmenprozedur für die Wörterbuchsuche.
Zu einer im Text vorkommenden Wortform werden alle möglichen Endungen
abgetrennt und die so entstandenen hypothetischen Stämme im Wörterbuch
gesucht. Findet man einen entsprechenden Eintrag, der neben dem Stamm
auch Wortklasse und Deklinationsmaske enthält, wird er mit der
abgetrennten Endung in eine Fundliste eingetragen, die über einen
Parameter von der Prozedur zurückgegeben wird.
Im einzelnen ist die Prozedur folgendermaßen aufgebaut:
Eingangsparameter ist die Zeichenkette WORTFORM, Ausgangsparameter ist
ein Feld, dessen Elemente aus einer Zeichenkette ENDUNG und einer
Struktur EINTRAG bestehen. Lokale Größen sind die Zeichenketten KOPF
und SCHWANZ, der Zeiger für die Fundliste I sowie eine Stringmenge,
die mögliche Endungen enthält.
Die Hauptschleife wird solange wiederholt, bis alle Zeichen der Wort-
form als Endung abgetrennt sind. Falls der abgetrennte Teil eine
Endung ist,wird der Kopf mit dem Wörterbuch verglichen. Die Prozedur
WOBUSUCHE gibt den gefundenen EINTRAG zurück, falls der KOPF als Stamm
im Wörterbuch auftritt, andernfalls den Wert ('',0,0)

8. Acknowledgements

Für das beim Entwurf der Sprache COMSKEE entgegengebrachte Interesse
möchten wir allen jetzigen und ehemaligen Mitgliedern des SFB 100
herzlich danken.
Insbesondere danken wir dem Leiter unserer Projektgruppe, Herrn Professor
Günter Hotz, sowie Herrn Professor Hans Langmaack, der bis Sommer 1974
an der Leitung des Projekts beteiligt war.
Wertvolle Anregungen kamen auch vonseiten der von der DFG beauftragten
Gutachter anläßlich einer Begehung des SFB.
Schließlich sind wir unseren Kollegen Heinz-Dieter Maas, Alfred Neisius,
Axel Pink und Claus Simon für lange Diskussionen über Fragen des
Sprachumfangs zu Dank verpflichtet.

9.Literaturangaben

F.L.Bauer,J.Eickel (ed.): Compiler Construction (Advanced Course),
Lecture Notes in Computer Science 21, 1974

E.Bertsch,A.Mueller-v.Brochowski,C.Simon: Vorentwurf für die linguistisch
orientierte Programmiersprache, Bericht
E-74-1 des SFB 100

O.-J.Dahl,C.A.R.Hoare: Hierarchical Program Structures, in: Dahl,
Dijkstra,Hoare: Structured Programming,
Academic Press 1972

A.A.Grau,U.Hill,H.Langmaack: Translation of ALGOL 60, Springer 1967

L.E.Griswold: String- and List-Processing in SNOBOL 4,
Prentice Hall, Englewood Cliffs 1975

C.A.R.Hoare: Notes on Data Structuring, in: Dahl,Dijkstra,
Hoare: Structured Programming, Academic Press
1972

R.J.W.Housden: On String Concepts and their Implementation,
Computer Journal 18 (1975), 150

R.Milner: String Handling in ALGOL, Computer Journal
10 (1967), 321

J.E.Sammet: Programming Languages: History and Funda-
mentals, Prentice Hall, Englewood Cliffs 1969

N.Wirth,H.Weber: Euler: A Generalization of ALGOL, and its
Formal Definition, Comm.ACM 9 (1966), 13

N.Wirth: On the Design of Programming Languages,
Proc. of the IFIP Congress 1974, 386

SYNTAX-ERROR RECOVERY IN LR-PARSERS

Johannes Roehrich

Fakultaet fuer Informatik der Universitaet Karlsruhe

Abstract

An efficient algorithm for error-recovery in LR-parsers is presented. The algorithm is capable of repairing all syntax errors without backtracking, in time proportional to the stack depth. It needs only a small table, a mapping from the states of the parser into the terminal symbols. The algorithm is very similiar to the parser itself. Thus, it has the same interface, and its correctness can be derived from that of the parser. It requires only trivial changes in the construction of the parse-tree and in the attribute handling during semantical analysis.

1. Introduction

Parsers for LR-grammars can be automatically generated as deterministic push-down automata interpreting a transition function. Such parsers have the useful property of detecting syntactical errors before the erroneous symbol has caused any parsing or semantical action. A systematic approach to recovery from "parser-defined" errors of this kind seems to be an important part in the design of a LR-based compiler-generating system.

Gries [Gr71] proposes to recover from a syntax-error by changing the source-text to the right of the last acceptable symbol in order to construct a new, longer prefix of a correct program. This method has several advantages. Backtracking is not required, and the partial syntax-tree constructed so far remains unchanged. Hence, the syntactical analysis of correct programs is not slowed down. The only change in the semantical analysis is that it has to be prepared to assign the source-dependent attributes to terminal symbols inserted by the recovery.

In this paper we describe a method for recovery from syntactical errors by means of a relatively small error-table. The method is efficient with respect to space and time. It is capable of repairing all syntax errors. Since it is based on the parsing algorithm itself, it requires no change in the interface of the parser.

In section 2 we develop the recovery-procedure for LR(0)-grammars. A complete algorithmic description is given. Section 3 is concerned with influences of the error recovery on the construction of the parse-tree and on semantical analysis. In section 4, space- and time-requirements of the method are briefly discussed. The extension to LR(1)- and LALR(1)-grammars is the subject of section 5.

2. Error Recovery in LR(0)-Parsers

In this section we describe the recovery from parser-defined errors for the LR(0)-case. An algorithm is developed which transforms every incorrect string into a correct one without backtracking. This is done by means of a preconstructed mapping from the set of parser-states into the set of terminal symbols, assigning to each state an acceptable symbol.

2.1. We start with a LR(0)-Grammar $G=(V,T,P,S)$; V is the vocabulary of the grammar, T the set of terminal symbols, P the set of productions and S the axiom.

Let L be the language generated by G. We assume that L is not the empty set. In addition, we require that L has an endmark $\#\in T$, defined by the following condition:

Every $x\in L$ is of the form $y\#$ with $y\in(T\backslash\{\#\})^*$.

Such an endmark is unique, e.g. L cannot have two different endmarks. Throughout this section we consider only strings $x\in(T\backslash\{\#\})^*\#$. Thus, # plays the role of the usual end-of-file.

If $xy\#\in L$, then x is said to be a prefix of L, and $y\#$ is called a postfix of L (with respect to x). The case where x is the empty word is included. A postfix, however, is never empty, since it consists at least of the endmark #.

Next, we consider a table-driven parser for G with an explicit stack as described in [Ah72]. The parser consists of a stack-alphabet Z, an initial state z0 and a transition function

$$u: ZxV \rightarrow \{shift\}xZ \cup \{shiftreduce\}xP \cup \{stop,error\} \quad .$$

The transition function is interpreted by the following

Algorithm 1 (LR(0)-Parser)

```
z:=initial_state; k:=0;
do begin
     stack[k:=k+1]:=z; s:=readsymbol;
transition:
     if u(z,s)=error then error_recovery;
     while u(z,s)=(shiftreduce,p) do
        begin
          z:=stack[k:=k+1-length_of_righthandside(p)];
          s:=lefthandside(p)
        end;
```

```
        if u(z,s)=(shift,zl) then z:=zl
     end
  until u(z,s)=stop
```

At the point "transition", the situation of the parser can be completely described by the stacked word z[1]...z[k] and the remainder sy of the input.

2.2. Assume we want to parse xsy where x is a prefix of L, but xsy∈((T\{#})*#)\L. Parsers of the type described above will scan x, halt in front of s and indicate an error on the first inspection of s, e.g. they will halt with stack-contents z[1]...z[k] such that sy is the remainder of the input and u(z[k],s)=error. For that reason, xsy is called a <u>parser-defined error</u> [Pe72].

The erroneous symbol s has not yet caused any parser actions, and, since x is a prefix, there is still a continuation z# such that xz#∈L. Therefore, we do not need to backtrack. Instead, we could try to handle the error as follows:

<u>Algorithm 2 (Recovery from a parser-defined error)</u>

(1)   Generate a mapping A:T -> T* such that, for every t∈Dom(A), xA(t)t is a prefix of L or xA(t)t∈L. Let H:=Dom(A).

(2)   Let sy=qhr be a decomposition of sy such that q∈(T\H)* and h∈H. Delete q to obtain hr as the remaining input.

(3)   Insert A(h) between x and hr.

(4)   Continue parsing.

This algorithm will work if H as defined in step (1) is not the empty set and if, in addition, the decomposition of sy in step (2) is possible, e.g. if at least one symbol of H occurs in sy. Since we have assumed xsy∈(T\{#})*#, both conditions will be satisfied if #∈H.

In the remainder of this section, we will develop algorithms refining step (1) and step (3) of the above algorithm.

2.3. We describe now the central idea of the proposed error-recovery method. If xsy is a parser-defined error, then there exists always a postfix z# such that xz#∈L. Let us assume, for the moment, that such a postfix z# is known. With z#, we simulate the continuation of the syntax analysis. For every symbol t∈T such that z#=utv, the parser will reach a situation with:

```
z[1]...z[k]        stack-contents
tv                 remaining input
```

Let h be a terminal symbol with $u(z[k],h) \neq$ error. If $A(h)$ is not yet defined, we set $A(h) := u$.

Let $H := Dom(A)$ after the parser has halted. It should be clear that $\# \in H$, and $xA(\#)\# \in L$. Moreover, for every $h \in H$ with $h \neq \#$, $xA(h)h$ is a prefix of L.

Example 1 outlines how algorithm 2 will repair a parser-defined error xsy using a postfix for x:

Example 1 (Construction of A and H using a postfix)

Let $G=(V,T,P,S)$ be a grammar with

$$V = \{S,E,T,a,(,),+,\#\}$$
$$T = \{a,(,),+,\#\}$$

P = {   (1)   S -> E#
          (2)   E -> E+T   (3)   E -> T
          (4)   T -> a   (5)   T -> (E)   }

G is LR(∅) and has the endmark #. A parser for G is defined by the following transition function:

	E	T	a	(	)	+	#
1	s 2	sr3	sr4	s 4	e	e	e
2	e	e	e	e	e	s 3	stop
3	e	sr2	sr4	s 4	e	e	e
4	s 5	sr3	sr4	s 4	e	e	e
5	e	e	e	e	sr5	s 3	e

where 1 is the initial state, "s i" is short for shift to state i, "srj" means shiftreduce with production j and "e" means error. Parsing the input a+(+a)# a parser-defined error xsy will be detected where

$$x = a+($$
$$s = +$$
$$y = a)\# \quad .$$

At that time, the stack contains the word 1234, and $u(4,+)$=error. As a postfix with respect to x we choose z# = a)#. From the current state 4 we obtain

$$A("a"):=A("("):= \epsilon \quad \text{(the empty word)} \quad .$$

Next, the parser will shiftreduce productions (4) and (3), then shift to state 5. Hence,

$$A("+"):=A(")"):= a \quad .$$

Finally, productions (5) and (2) are applied, the parser shifts
to state 2 and halts. Thus, we get in addition

$$A("\#") := a) \quad .$$

Since $H:=Dom(A)=\{a,(,+,),\#\}$, the decomposition of sy to qhr with
$q\in(T\backslash H)^*$ and $h\in H$ (step (2) of algorithm 2) yields:

$$q = \epsilon \qquad \text{(the empty word)}$$
$$h = +$$
$$r = a)\#$$

Clearly, "+" can be accepted after insertion of $A("+") = a$. Thus,
the erroneous input is repaired to $a+(a+a)\#$.

2.4. In the previous section we have seen that one can recover from
any parser-defined error provided one is able to construct for every
prefix x a corresponding postfix. For that end, we introduce termina-
tion-functions. A <u>termination-function</u> for a parser is simply a mapping

$$f: Z \rightarrow T \quad \text{such that} \quad u(z,f(z))\neq error \text{ for all } z\in Z \quad .$$

If the parser is in situation $z[1]...z[k]$ we can try to construct a
postfix w for all prefixes x which lead into that situation using a
termination-function f and the following

<u>Algorithm 3</u> (Construction of a postfix)

```
n:=0; k:=k-1;
do begin
     stack[k:=k+1]:=z; s:=f(z); q[n:=n+1]:=z;
     while u(z,s)=(shiftreduce,p) do
        begin
          z:=stack[k:=k+1-length_of_righthandside(p)];
          s:=lefthandside(p)
        end;
     if u(z,s)=(shift,z1) then z:=z1
   end
until u(z,s)=stop;
```

Let $w := f(q[1])...f(q[n])$.

Clearly, w is a postfix if this algorithm halts, since it it exactly
what the parser has parsed (note also that $f(q[n])$ must be #). It is,
however, not obvious whether, given a particular termination-function
f, algorithm 3 will halt for any situation $z[1]...z[k]$. To demonstrate
this difficulty, consider the following

<u>Example 2</u> (Termination-functions)

For the parser given in example 1, a termination-function might look like:

```
z         1    2    3    4    5
-----------------------------------
f(z)      a    #    a    a    +
```

By inspection, one can see that, being once in state 4 or 5, algorithm 3 would never halt (since it is not capable to insert the required right parenthesis). Now, let us change f(5) to ")". Clearly, starting from any situation z[1]...z[k], algorithm 3 will either halt or decrease the stack-level k by at least 1 before inserting the next symbol. The latter can occur at most k times.

The proof of the following proposition, although ommitted here, is based on an inductive argument very similiar to that.

<u>Proposition 1</u> (Termination of Algorithm 3)

Let f be an arbitrary termination-function. Then, it is decidable whether algorithm 3 will halt for every situation z[1]...z[k] of the parser or not.

Proposition 1 can be checked by an algorithm which is based on algorithm 3 itself. A concise description is omitted because of lack of space.

A particular termination-function will be choosen in accordance with heuristic requirements (such as bracketing structure) depending strongly on the language concerned. In practical cases we were always able to construct a feasible termination-function, and to produce reasonable results.

2.5. In an implementation of the error-recovery procedure described so far one is not interested in the construction of the whole postfix or of the mapping A. In order to see that, consider algorithm 2 again. What we really need is the set H in step (2), and the word A(h) in step (3). This information is contained in the vector $q[1],..,q[n]$ computed by algorithm 3. Let

$$H := \bigcup_{i=1}^{n} \{t \in T:\ u(q[i],t) \neq error\}$$

For every $h \in H$ there is, by definition, a (smallest) index i such that $u(q[i],h) \neq error$. Let

```
A(h):=f(q[1])..f(q[i-1]) .
```

Since $f(q[1])...f(q[n])$ is a postfix corresponding to x, xA(h)h is either a prefix of L or it belongs to L as required by step (1) of algorithm 2.

2.6. The computation of A(h) is, however, not necessary prior to execution of step (3) of algorithm 2. If h€H the following algorithm will insert A(h) properly:

Algorithm 4 (Insertion of A(h))

```
k:=k-1;
while u(z,h)=error do
   begin
      stack[k:=k+1]:=z; s:=f(z);
      while u(z,s)=(shiftreduce,p) do
         begin
            z:=stack[k:=k+1-length of righthandside(p)];
            s:=lefthandside(p)
         end;
      if u(z,s)=(shift,z1) then z:=z1
   end;
stack[k:=k+1]:=z
```

Algorithm 4 repeats the steps executed by algorithm 3 a second time, until A(h) has been inserted and the state q[i] accepting h has been reached.

2.7. We show now by a rather informal argument that the error-recovery algorithm as described in the previous subsections will in fact repair every string in $(T\setminus\{\#\})^*\#$, e.g. that it is correct. First, we must prove that no loops can occur.

Let xsy be any parser-defined error. The error-recovery procedure will repair xsy to xA(h)hr such that sy=qhr. Thereafter, at least the symbol h is consumed by the parser. Hence, the error-recovery can be invoked only finitely often.

In 2.3 we have seen that the endmark # will always belong to H. Thus, it will never be skipped.

Finally, the string produced belongs to L since it has been completely parsed.

2.8. To conclude this section we demonstrate how the error-recovery procedure works for the parser-defined error in example 1.

Example 3 (Error-recovery using Algorithms 2 to 4)

Consider the termination function of example 2. Algorithm 3 will run through the following states:

```
i        q[i]        f(q[i])
--------------------------------
1         4            a
2         5            )
3         2            #
```

From that, we obtain

$$H = \{a,(,+,),\#\} \quad .$$

Since $+ \in H$, $+$ is not skipped, and after insertion of $A(+)=a$ by algorithm 4 normal parsing can be resumed.

3. Construction of the Parse-Tree and Semantical Analysis

In this section, we will discuss the influence of the error-recovery procedure described in section 2 on the construction of the parse-tree and on the semantical analysis. It is a major advantage of the proposed method that the text to be semantically analysed is always syntactically correct.

3.1. When a parser-defined error xsy occurs, the erroneous symbol s has not yet caused any parsing actions. This implies that the syntax-tree constructed so far is still correct. Executing the insertion-step (3) of the recovery algorithm 2 as specified by algorithm 4 will cause leaves of the tree to be created and reductions to take place. All leaves should be marked so that they are recognizable to the semantical analysis as inserted by error recovery. Since algorithm 4 does normal parsing actions, the outcoming tree will always correspond to a syntactically correct string.

3.2. As semantical analysis proceeds to a leaf of the parse-tree it has to be prepared to find such an artificial symbol. Inserted symbols do not have a correspondence in the source-program. Thus, any attributes derived from there must be generated (entry in the symbol- or constant-table, coordinates etc.). Also, semantical errors caused by such symbols should be suppressed.

4. Time- and Space-Requirements

The overhead of the proposed error-recovery method with respect to time and space is relatively small. This is partly due to the fact that no backtracking occurs. Another important consideration is that the algorithms are short, simple, easy to implement, and that they require no cnange in the parser interface to other modules of the compiler.

4.1. Besides the algorithm itself, space is needed for a single table, a termination-function. With M states, N terminal symbols and one symbol per byte it occupies $M*N$ bytes.

4.2. As to the time-requirements, an analysis of the algorithms presented shows that they do mainly parsing actions. Hence, the time needed is proportional to the length of the postfix constructed by algorithm 3 plus the number of symbols inserted by algorithm 4. A worst-case analysis shows that these numbers, in turn, are not greater that $C*K$, where K is the stack-depth when the error occurs and C is a constant depending on the termination-function.

5. Application to LR(1)- and LALR(1)-Parsers

The error-recovery procedure as described in section 2 can easily be extended to LR(1)- and LALR(1)-parsing [Ah72]. We recall that in such parsers, the transition function may take a value of the form $u(z,s)=(reduce,p)$ where the current symbol s is used as a lookahead-symbol. The only problem is that s is not immediately consumed by the parser, and that when using optimized parse-tables s may not be acceptable at all. Thus, when a parser-defined error xsy occurs, s might well have caused parsing actions.

However, x will be still a prefix of the language, and by virtue of the LR(k)-property there is an acceptable symbol t which would have caused the same reductions as s if any.

Recall the vector $q[1],...,q[n]$ computed by algorithm 3 in section 2.4. Changing the definition of H to

$$H := \bigcup_{i=1}^{n} \{t \in T: u(q[i],t) \neq error \text{ and } u(q[i],t) \neq (reduce,p)\}$$

and accordingly changing the second line of algorithm 4 to

"while $u(z,h)=error$ or $u(z,h)=(reduce,p)$ do"

we obtain results similiar to those described in section 2.

It seems that modifications as above will render the proposed error-recovery concept applicable to a wide class of deterministic push-down automata.

References

[Ah72]   Aho   A.   V.,   Ullman J. D., <u>The Theory of Parsing, Translation and Compiling</u>, Volume I, Parsing, Englewood Cliffs, N.J. 1972

[Gr71]   Gries   D.,   <u>Compiler   Construction   for Digital Computers</u>, New York, N.Y. 1971

[Pe72]   Peterson   T.   G., <u>Syntax Error Detection, Correction and Recovery in Parsers</u>, Ph.D. Thesis 1972, Stevens Inst. of Tech., Hoboken, N.J. 1972

GENERATING ERROR RECOVERY IN A COMPILER GENERATING SYSTEM

Joachim Ciesinger
Institut für Informatik der TU München, 8 München, Arcisstr. 21

1. INTRODUCTION

One of the parts occurring in a compiler generating system is the parser generator module. Our approach to error recovery generation can be
considered as an extension of this module such that not only the tables
for the syntax analysis but also the tables for error handling are computed. These tables essentially consist of pairs of elements of the alphabet — called braces — which allow
— to select a program segment which contains the point of the error
  and
— to determine the reduction goal of the selected program segment.

The error recovery then can be considered as an extension of the parser
module in which a suitable program segment containing the error place
is selected and replaced by its reduction goal.

For example given an ALGOL 60 - like grammar and the partially reduced
string

$ <block head> ; <statement> ; x := x * (x + y) x END $
        syntax pushdown list   current input symbol

the syntax analysis proceeds to

$ <block head> ; <statement> ; <left part list> <term> x END $
                    syntax pushdown list   error point

when the error is encountered. Now the pair (; , END) of alphabet
elements could be used to select the program segment <left part list>
<term> x and to replace it by its reduction goal <statement> . After
that syntax analysis would proceed with

$ <block head> ; <statement> ; <statement> END $
              syntax pushdown list   current input symbol

This paper was sponsored by the Sonderforschungsbereich 49 - Elektronische Rechenanlagen und Informationsverarbeitung (Informatik) in Munich.

As in the compiler generating system attributed grammars [1] are used
for semantic definition, the information given to the semantic handling
part of the compiler consists essentially in denoting that the topsym-
bol <statement> of the syntax pushdown list has been introduced by
error recovery and that therefore a dummy value "erroneous" has to be
assigned to its attributes. For implementation details see [2].

Our error recovery method is applicable to all programming languages
which have a sufficiently large set of braces and is compatible with
all syntax analysis algorithms which provide for the left and right
context of the error place.

2. COMPUTATION OF THE SET OF BRACES

More formally we can describe the extension of the parser generator module as follows:

From the context-free grammar $G = (V,T,\Pi,Z)$ with alphabet V , set
T of terminals, set Π of productions, axiom Z and language $L(G)$
a set $B \subset V \times V \times \{1,2,3\}$ of "braces" together with a one-to-one correspondence $r : B \to V$ is computed such that the following statement
holds:
In a correct sentential form of $L(G)$ between two corresponding in-
stances of the first and the second component of a brace $b \in B$ one
can always find a string which is a sentential form of $r(b)$.

We denote with $\xrightarrow[G]{} \subset V^* \times V^*$ the relation "direct derivation" according to grammar G and as usual drop the subscript G , if it is
obvious which grammar we are talking about. With $\xrightarrow{+}$ ($\xrightarrow{*}$) we denote the transitive (transitive and reflexive) closure of $\longrightarrow$. Instead of G from now on we consider an augmented grammar G' with an
additional rule $Z' ::= \$ Z \$$ where $Z', \$ \notin V$.

We further define for all $x \in V$ the sets $\alpha(x), \omega(x) \subset V$ by
$$\alpha(x) := \{y \mid \exists u \in V^* : x \xrightarrow{*} yu\}$$
$$\omega(x) := \{y \mid \exists u \in V^* : x \xrightarrow{*} uy\}.$$

In our paper we will take our examples from the following grammar:
<program> ::= <block>
<block> ::= <block head> : <compound tail>
<block head> ::= BEGIN <declpart>

```
<compound tail> ::= <statement list> END
<statement list> ::= <statement> | <statement> ; <statement list>
<statement> ::= <assignment> | <conditional statement> |
                BEGIN <compound tail>
<conditional statement> ::= <if clause> <statement list> FI
<if clause> ::= IF <boolean expression> THEN
```

with additional rule $\langle program \rangle' ::= \$ \langle program \rangle \$$. A set $B(G)$ of braces for a given grammar G is computed in two steps. (As usual we write B instead of $B(G)$.)

FIRST STEP: Compute $B^1 := \bigcup_{v \in V} B^1(v)$, where $B^1(v)$ is the union of three sets $A_i(v)$ $(1 \le i \le 3)$ which are defined as follows: Let a,b,c,d be arbitrary elements of V^* and $z,u,s \in V$ then
$A_1(v) := \{[x,y,1] \mid \exists \pi_i \in \Pi : Y^i ::= a u v \text{ and } \exists \pi_j \in \Pi : Y^j ::= c z s d \text{ and } Y^i \in \omega(z) \text{ and } x \in \omega(u) \text{ and } y \in \alpha(s)\}$.

This means essentially that the triple $x v y$ appears in at least one sentential form of the grammar and that uv and s don't belong to one phrase.

Example: $A_1(\langle \text{statement list} \rangle) := \{[; , \text{END} , 1] , [; , \text{FI} , 1]\}$.

$A_2(v) := \{[x,y,2] \mid \exists \pi_i \in \Pi : Y^i ::= v s b \text{ and } \exists \pi_j \in \Pi : Y^j ::= c u z d \text{ and } Y^i \in \alpha(z) \text{ and } x \in \omega(u) \text{ and } y \in \alpha(s)\}$.
Here we have the case that u and vs don't belong to one phrase.

Example: $A_2(\langle \text{statement list} \rangle) := \{[: , \text{END} , 2] , [\text{BEGIN} , \text{END} , 2]\}$.

$A_3(v) := \{[x,y,3] \mid \exists \pi_i \in \Pi : Y^i ::= a u v s b \text{ and } x \in \omega(u) \text{ and } y \in \alpha(s)\}$.
In the last case the triple $u v s$ belongs to one phrase.

Example: $A_3(\langle \text{statement list} \rangle) := \{[\langle \text{if clause} \rangle , \text{FI} , 3] , [\text{THEN} , \text{FI} , 3]\}$.

Given a set B of braces for a grammar G we introduce a predicate $cor_B(x,z,y)$ called the correspondence of the first component x and the second component y of a brace $b = (x,y,j) \in B$ with intermediate text $z \in V^*$. The predicate $cor_B(x,z,y)$ is a slight generalization of the correspondence of the brackets "(" and ")" in arithmetic expressions.

Informally we can describe its meaning by saying that only between corresponding brace components of a brace b we can be sure to have a
sentential form of the symbol $r(b)$.
We have

Proposition 1: The predicate $cor_B(x,z,y)$ can be computed by a deterministic pushdown automaton.
Proof: omitted.

Example: Let B := {[; , ; , 2] ,[<if clause>,;,2], [; , FI , 1],
[<if clause> , FI , 3]} be a set of braces. Then we have cor_B(; , z , ;)
with intermediate texts z = <assignment> and
z = <if clause> { <assignment> ; }* <assignment> FI but not
cor_B(;, z,;) with the intermediate texts
z = <if clause> { <assignment> ; }* <assignment> .

As usual we drop the subscript B in $cor_B(x,z,y)$ if the set of
braces is obvious.

Now we introduce three properties which have to be fulfilled by a set
B^1 of braces for a given grammar G .

C1: If b_1 = [x,y,j] ϵ B^1 and b_2 = [x,y,j'] ϵ B^1 then we must have
j = j' and there is exactly one v ϵ V with b_1,b_2 ϵ $B^1(v)$.
i.e.: If two braces coincide in the first two components, then they
must also coincide in the third component and must be elements of exactly one $B^1(v)$.

Example: The property C1 is violated by b_1 = [BEGIN,END,1] and
b_2 = [BEGIN,END,2] with $r(b_2)$ = <statement list> and
$r(b_1)$ = <compound tail> .

C2: If [x,y,j] ϵ $B^1(v)$ then we have $\omega(x) \times \alpha(y) \times \{j\} \subset B^1(v)$. This
is a nontrivial condition if x and/or y are nonterminals.

Example: {[<if clause> , FI , 3] , [THEN , FI , 3]} $\subset$ B^1(<statement list>).

C3: Under the conditions [x,y,j] ϵ $B^1(v)$ and s = a x z y b is a correct sentential form such that z is most reduced and $cor_{B^1}(x,z,y)$
we can conclude z = v .
We have

Proposition 2: For each set B^1 of braces and for each element

$[x,y,j] \in B^1(v) \subset B^1$ the property $C3$ is decidable.

Proof: omitted.

Now we can formulate the second step in computing a set of braces for a given grammar.

SECOND STEP: a) Mark all elements of B^1 which violate one or more of the properties $C1$, $C2$, $C3$.

b) Remove all marked elements from B^1.

c) Repeat a) and b) until no more elements are removed.

We call the resulting set the set $B(G)$ of braces for a given grammar G and define $r : B(G) \to V$ by $r(b) = v$ iff $b \in B^1(v)$ for all elements of $B(G)$.

Example: $r([\ \text{<if clause>} , FI , 3]) = \text{<statement list>}$

We now can repeat the statement at the beginning of section 2 as

Proposition 3: Under the conditions a) B is a set of braces fulfilling $C1 - C3$ and $b = [x,y,j] \in B$ with $r(b) = v$ and

b) $s = a\,x\,z\,y\,b$ is a correct sentential form with $cor_B(x,z,y)$ we can conclude $s' = a\,x\,v\,y\,b$ is also a correct sentential form.

Proof: omitted.

Furthermore we have the

Corollary: Proposition 3 remains valid if we take instead of B any subset B' of B which fulfills $C1 - C3$.

Example: If we restrict B^1 to $\bigcup\limits_{v \in V \backslash T} B^1(v)$ we obtain the subset of B which consists of the braces of those program segments which reduce to the nonterminals of the language.

For our example grammar we now give a set B of braces.

symbol	braces
<program>	[$, $, 3]
<block head>	[$, : , 2]
<compound tail>	[: , $, 1] [BEGIN , FI , 1]
<declpart>	[BEGIN , : , 1]
<statement list>	[; , END , 1][: , END , 2][<if clause> , FI , 3][THEN , FI , 3] [; , FI , 1]
<statement>	[: , ; , 2][; , ; , 2][<if clause> , ; , 2][THEN , ; , 2]
<boolean expression>	[IF , THEN , 3]

3. CORRECTIONS ON THE BRACE STRUCTURE

The ideas presented so far would suffice if we could assume that we
have to perform error recovery on a string with correct brace structure.
But of course we have to provide for the case of an incorrect brace
structure. We will now outline a strategy which is restricted to local
corrections of the brace structure, well knowing that this restriction
might well give way to consecutive errors. Our justification for doing
so is that we hope to achieve greater efficiency than with a global error correction method.

We use the following denotations:
Let $BC := \{z \mid \exists b = (x,y,j) \in B$ and $z = x$ or $z = y\}$ be the set of
the brace components for a given set B of braces and
$h_{BC}: V \rightarrow BC \cup \{\varepsilon\}$ a homomorphism defined by $h_{BC}(x) := \begin{cases} x \text{ if } x \in BC \\ \varepsilon \text{ otherwise} \end{cases}$
with the usual extension $h^*_{BC}: V^* \rightarrow BC^*$. A string $x \in V^*$ is said to
have a correct brace structure denoted by $cbs(x)$ iff there exists a
correct sentential form s with $h^*_{BC}(s) = h^*_{BC}(x)$.
A generalized neighbourhood relation $\sim[BC] \subset BC \times BC$ is defined by
$\sim[BC] := \{(x,y) \mid \exists u,v \in V^*; w \in (V \backslash BC)^*; t \in T^*: Z' \xrightarrow{+} u\,x\,w\,y\,v \xrightarrow{*} t\}$
whereas the set LBE of local brace errors is the complement of $\sim[BC]$
in $BC \times BC$.

Example: We have $(\text{<if clause>},FI) \in \sim[BC]$ and $(\text{<if clause>} , END) \in LBE$
for the set B of braces given at the end of section two.

Correcting the brace structure we will consider the context of at
most say k_1 (k_2) brace components $x_{k_1} \ldots x_1$ ($y_1 \ldots y_{k_2}$) to the
left (to the right) of the local brace error (x,y). The local brace
error correction method lbc_{k_1,k_2} of degrees k_1 and k_2 then replaces the string $z = x_{k_1} \ldots x_1\,x\,y\,y_1 \ldots y_{k_2}$ by a string $z' \in BC^*$
which occurs as a brace substring in at least one string with correct
brace structure and which is obtained from z by less than a fixed
number of elementary corrections such as deleting, inserting or replacing an element.

Example: If we have $z =: \text{<if clause>}$ END; then all correct substruc-
tures z' which can be obtained from z by at most one elementary
correction are:
$z' =: \text{<if clause>}$ FI ; $\mid$: <if clause> ; $\mid$: <if clause> BEGIN END ; $\mid$
    : BEGIN END ;

The selection of one possible correction can be guided by heuristic
assumptions or by inspection of more context of the local brace error.

Furthermore we can at error recovery generation time compute the tables
which for each local error situation contains all possible corrections
which are derived by lbc_{k_1,k_2} for some fixed degrees k_1, k_2 such
that not more than a given number of elementary corrections are applied.

During error recovery we will apply an algorithm cb which, given
two strings $x_m \ldots x_1, y_2 \ldots y_n \in BC^+$ returns with a pair (i,j)
$(1 \le i \le m, 1 \le j \le n)$ such that the string $z = z_1 \ldots z_k \in BC^+$
which is equal to or derived from $x_i \ldots x_1 y_1 \ldots y_j$ by local
brace error corrections has the property $cor(z_1, z_2 \ldots z_{k-1}, z_k)$.

We denote the configuration of a (left-to-right) parser in an error
state by the pair $(\$ X_m \ldots X_1, a_1 \ldots a_n \$)$ where the first component represents the syntax pushdown list and the second component the
unused part of the input. If we have $cb(h^*_{BC}(\$ X_m \ldots X_1), h^*_{BC}(a_1 \ldots a_n \$)) =$
$= (i,j)$ where $1 \le i \le m+1$ and $1 \le j \le n+1$ the follow configuration
delivered by our error recovery method is given by
$(\$ X_m \ldots X_{s+1} X'_s X'_{s-1}, a'_p a_{p+1} \ldots a_n \$)$ where $z = z_1 \ldots z_k$ with
$z_1 = X'_s$ and $z_k = a'_p$ is the string derived from the brace component
string $last_i(h^*_{BC}(\$ X_m \ldots X_1)) \; first_j(h^*_{BC}(a_1 \ldots a_n \$))$ by local
brace error corrections such that $cor(X'_s, z_2 \ldots z_{k-1}, a'_p)$ holds and
(X'_s, a'_p, j) is a brace b with $r(b) = X'_{s-1}$. In that case X_s would
be the i-th (counted from right to left) brace component in $\$ X_m \ldots X_1$
and a_p the \j-th brace component (counted from left to right) in
$a_1 \ldots a_n \$$.

<u>Example</u>: Given the string
$ BEGIN <declpart> : IF <boolean expression> THEN <assignment> ;
<assignment> END ; <assignment> ; <assignment> FI ; <assignment> ;
<assignment> END $.

Syntax analysis proceeds to the configuration (ξ, α) with
$\xi = \$$ <block head> : <if clause> <compound tail> and

$\alpha = $; <assignment> ; <assignment> FI ; <assignment> ;
<assignment> END $

when an error state is reached.
We have $h^*_{BC}(\xi) = \$$: <if clause> , $h^*_{BC}(\alpha) = $; ; FI ; ; END $ and
$cb(h^*_{BC}(\xi), h^*_{BC}(\alpha)) = (1,1)$. As no local brace error occurs in the

brace string <if clause> ; and cor(<if clause> , ε , ;) is valid we
simply have to replace the top symbol <compound tail> of the syntax
pushdown list by r([<if clause> , ; , 2]) = <statement> . Thus the configuration (ξ',α') after error recovery is described by
ξ' = \$ <block head> : <if clause> <statement> and $\alpha' = \alpha$. The error
correction proposed by Lévy in [3] for a similar example would have the
same effect on the progress of syntax analysis. As we cannot go into
the details of the attribute handling we will now only give for the
example the information which after the error recovery has to be provided for the attribute handling module. It consists essentially of the
number of the actual production <statementlist> ::= <statement> ;
<statement list> , the position of the newly introduced nonterminal
<statement> in the right hand side of this production, as well as its
position in the syntax pushdown list. In our example these positions
are 1 and 5 respectively. At the same time we signal to the attribute
handling module that to all attributes of <statement> has to be giv-
en the dummy value "erroneous".

4. CONCLUSION AND FURTHER CONSIDERATIONS

The described error recovery method uses — as far as we have seen —
a new systematic approach for selecting a program segment containing
the point where the parser has been caused to stop by a syntax error.
Furthermore it allows to replace this program segment by its reduction
goal.
The method fits well into a compiler generating system for the following reasons
— its tables can be computed at the generation time of the system
— it is not restricted to a special class of programming languages or
   syntax analysis algorithms
— it has a clean interface to the semantic handling part of the generated compiler if attributed grammars are used for semantic definition.

The following extensions of the presented brace concept are now being
worked upon:
— Dispense from the conditions C1,C2 and try to solve the arising am-
   biguities by imposing restrictions on the left and right context
   and the intermediate text of the brace components.

- Compute braces for strings of length > 1 .
- Convert the error recovery method into an error correcting method
  by replacing the intermediate text s' of the brace components of
  a brace b by a "similar" sentential form s of r(b) .

In the above example we have s' = <compound tail> and
r(b) = <statement> . In this case s would be BEGIN <compound tail>
which would induce the correction of inserting a BEGIN after the
<if clause> .

LITERATURE

[1]   Koster, C.H.A.: A Compiler Compiler
                    Mathematisch Centrum Amsterdam
                    MR 127, 1971

                    AFFIX Grammars.
                    In Peck (Ed.), ALGOL68 Implementation,
                    North Holland 1971

[2]   Wilhelm, R.:   Syntax und Semantikspezifikation in der Eingabe-
                     sprache für einen Compiler Compiler.
                     Abteilung Mathematik an der Technischen Universi-
                     tät München, Bericht Nr. 7301

                     System documentation 3.6, Project MUG

[3]   Lévy, J.-P.:   Automatic Correction of Syntax Errors in
                     Programming Languages.
                     Acta Informatica 4, 271-292 (1975)

DARSTELLUNG DER ARTANPASSUNG IN HÖHEREN PROGRAMMIERSPRACHEN DURCH REPRÄSENTATIONEN VON GRUPPEN*

Harald Ganzinger
Institut für Informatik der TU München, 8 München 2, Arcisstr.21

1. EINLEITUNG

In höheren Programmiersprachen, wie z.B. ALGOL 68, wurde die Möglichkeit geschaffen, dem Benutzer eine Vielfalt von verschiedenen Klassen
von Datenstrukturen, die sogenannten Arten ("Modes"), zur Verfügung zu
stellen. Da die Operationen, die man auf den Datenstrukturen ausführen
möchte, die Einhaltung von vorgegebenen Operandenarten erfordern, war
es somit gleichzeitig nötig, einen nichttrivialen Mechanismus zur Artanpassung vorzugeben, damit der Programmierer von Einschränkungen weitgehend befreit werden konnte. Dieser Prozeß wurde in [A68] mit Hilfe
der zweistufigen ALGOL 68 - Syntax beschrieben, einen Vorschlag für
dessen praktische Realisierung als Teil eines ALGOL 68 - Übersetzers
findet man z.B. in [Scheidig 70].

Betrachtet man nun die Definition von Programmiersprachen unter dem Ge-
sichtspunkt des automatischen Generierens entsprechender Übersetzer im
Rahmen der Eingabesprache für ein übersetzererzeugendes System, so er-
kennt man die Notwendigkeit der Existenz sprachlicher Hilfsmittel, die
dem Sprachbeschreiber die Möglichkeit bieten, Mechanismen wie die Artanpassung bequem darzustellen. Voraussetzung dafür ist ein formales Mo-
dell für die Begriffe Art und Artanpassung. In diesem Papier soll nun
ein solches vorgeschlagen werden.

Nach begrifflichen und notationellen Vorbemerkungen im zweiten Abschnitt wird im dritten Abschnitt der Begriff der Art definiert. Daran
anschließend wird im vierten Abschnitt die Artanpassung auf das Wortproblem in Gruppen zurückgeführt. Wegen der Unlösbarkeit dieses Problems werden dann im fünften Abschnitt der Artanpassung sinnvolle Einschränkungen auferlegt, die zur Lösbarkeit des Problems führen. Beispiele zur Erläuterung des Modells sind aus einem ALGOL 68 Subset entnommen.

---

* Diese Arbeit ist im Sonderforschungsbereich 49 - Informatik - an der TU München
entstanden.

2. VORBEMERKUNGEN ZU BENUTZEN BEGRIFFEN UND NOTATION:

1. Ist A ein Alphabet, so bezeichne A^* das freie Monoid über A.
2. Ist $A = \{a_1, a_2, \ldots, a_n\}$ ein Alphabet, so bezeichne
   $A^{-1} = \{a_1^{-1}, a_2^{-1}, \ldots, a_n^{-1}\}$ die Menge der (formalen) Inversen zu A.
   Hierbei sei $A \cap A^{-1} = \emptyset$. Durch $\bar{A}$ sei $A \cup A^{-1}$ bezeichnet.
3. Sind $R_1, \ldots, R_n \in \bar{A}^*$, so sei durch $G = \langle A; R_1, \ldots, R_n \rangle$ die Gruppe
   G mit Erzeugenden aus A und definierenden Relatoren $R_1, \ldots, R_n$
   bezeichnet.
4. Seien $a_1 = a_{11}\ldots a_{1n_1}$, $a_2 = a_{21}\ldots a_{2n_2} \in \bar{A}^*$. Durch $=$ sei nachfolgend die graphische Gleichheit von a_1 und a_2 bezeichnet, d.h.
   $a_1 = a_2 \not\Leftrightarrow n_1 = n_2$ und $a_{1i} = a_{2i}$, $1 \leq i \leq n$.
5. Sei $a = a_1 a_2 \ldots a_n \in \bar{A}^*$. a^{-1} bezeichne das (formale) Inverse
   $a_n^{-1} \ldots a_2^{-1} a_1^{-1}$ von a. Hierbei gelte für jedes $a_i \in A$: $(a_i^{-1})^{-1} = a$.
6. Sei G wie in 3., a_1 und a_2 wie in 4. a_1 und a_2 repräsen-
   tieren dasselbe Element der Gruppe G, i.Z. $a_1 \equiv a_2$, falls a_1
   durch endlich viele Operationen $(*)$ und $(**)$ in a_2 überführt
   werden kann, wobei
   $(*)$ Einsetzen oder Löschen eines R_i oder R_i^{-1}
   $(**)$ Einsetzen oder Löschen von $a_i^{-1} a_i$ mit $a_i \in A$.
7. In G wird die Eins durch die leere Zeichenreihe ϵ und das Inverse eines durch $a \in \bar{A}^*$ repräsentierten Gruppenelementes durch a^{-1}
   repräsentiert.
8. Im übrigen sei für die gruppentheoretischen Grundlagen z.B. auf
   [Magnus 66] verwiesen.

3. ARTPRÄFIXE, RESTARTEN UND ARTEN

In ALGOL 68 kann man eine Art, was die Anpassung betrifft, in einen
Artpräfix und eine Restart aufspalten. Nachfolgend seien RA und AP
endliche Mengen und P eine reguläre Menge über AP, genannt Menge
der *Restarten*, *Artpräfixsymbole* und *Artpräfixe*. Dann definiert man

<u>Definition 1</u>. Eine *Art* ist ein Paar (p,r), wobei $p \in P$ ein Artprä-
fix und $r \in RA$ eine Restart ist. Es sei M die Menge aller Arten.

<u>Beispiel 1</u>.

RA = {<u>int</u>, <u>real</u>, <u>char</u>, <u>string</u>}

AP = .{<u>ref</u>, <u>proc</u>, <u>row</u>}

Hierbei stehe <u>ref</u> für Referenz., <u>proc</u> für eine parameterlose Prozedur und <u>row</u> für ein (eindimensionales) array.

P = AP*

Die ALGOL 68 - Art <u>ref</u> <u>row</u> <u>proc</u> <u>real</u> wird dann durch
(<u>ref</u> <u>row</u> <u>proc</u>, <u>real</u>) repräsentiert. In den nachfolgenden Beispielen be-
ziehe man sich auf die hier definierten Mengen RA, AP und P .

4. ARTANPASSUNG UND REPRÄSENTATIONEN VON GRUPPEN

Der nachfolgenden Definition der Artanpassung liegt folgendes Schema
zugrunde: Sind $m_1 = (p_1, r_1)$ und $m_2 = (p_2, r_2)$ zwei Arten, so erfolgt
die Anpassung von m_1 an m_2 in drei Schritten
a) Abbauen des Präfixes p_1
b) Anpassung von r_1 an r_2
c) Aufbauen des Präfixes p_2

So wird z.B. in ALGOL 68 die Art <u>proc</u> <u>proc</u> <u>int</u> an <u>proc</u> <u>real</u> durch
zweimaliges Deprozedurieren (= Elimination von <u>proc</u> <u>proc</u>), nachfol-
gendes Ausweiten von <u>int</u> zu <u>real</u> (= Restartenanpassung) und Pro-
zedurieren (= Aufbau des Präfixes <u>proc</u>) angeglichen.

Es seien nun PM und RAM endliche Mengen, die Menge der *Präfixmodifikatoren* und die Menge der *Restartenmodifikatoren*. Hierbei gelte
PM ∩ RAM = ∅ . Dann wird durch APW $\underset{df}{=}$ PM ∪ RAM die Menge der *Artan-
passungsworte* gegeben. Das Auf- und Abbauen von Artpräfixen beruht auf
folgender Definition:

<u>Definition 2</u>. Eine Abbildung η : AP → PM heiße *Präfixelemination*.

Nachfolgend bezeichne ebenfalls η die Fortsetzung dieser Abbildung
zu einem Homomorphismus zwischen den (freien) Gruppen <AP;> und
<PM;> .

Die Restartenanpassung kann wegen der vorausgesetzten Endlichkeit von
RA einfach dargestellt werden.

<u>Definition 3</u>. Eine Abbildung ρ : $RA \times RA \to P(\overline{PM}{}^* \, RAM^+ \, \overline{PM}{}^*) \cup \{\{\epsilon\}\}$
heißt *Restartenanpassung*, falls
1. $\forall r_1, r_2 \in RA$: $|\rho(r_1, r_2)| < \infty$
2. $\forall r_1, r_2 \in RA$: $\rho(r_1, r_2) = \{\epsilon\} \nmid r_1 = r_2$
3. $\forall r_1, r_2, r_3 \in RA$:
   $\rho(r_1, r_2) = \rho_1 \wedge \rho(r_2, r_3) = \rho_2 \wedge r_1 \neq r_3 \;)\; \rho(r_1, r_3) = \rho_1 \rho_2$

Die bisherigen Definitionen sollen an einem weiteren Beispiel verdeut-
licht werden.

<u>Beispiel 2</u>. Es seien RA und AP wie in Beispiel 1 und
PM = {rw, dp, pr, dr, rrw} ,   RAM = {kir, kchs, krchs, ksrch} . Durch
diese Symbole seien folgende ALGOL 68 - Artanpassungsoperationen bezeichnet:

rw	Reihung;		m ——>	<u>row</u> m
dp:	Deprozedurieren;	<u>proc</u> m ——>	m	
pr:	Prozedurieren;	m ——>	<u>proc</u> m	
dr:	Dereferenzieren;	<u>ref</u> m ——>	m	
rrw:	Referenzenreihung;	<u>ref</u> m ——>	<u>ref</u> <u>row</u> m	

kir:	Konvertierung	<u>int</u>	nach	<u>real</u>
kchs:	"	<u>char</u>	"	<u>string</u>
krchs:	"	<u>row</u> <u>char</u>	"	<u>string</u>
ksrch:	"	<u>string</u>	"	<u>row</u> <u>char</u>

Dann setzt man η und ρ wie folgt:
$\eta(\underline{ref})$ = dr
$\eta(\underline{proc})$ = dp
$\eta(\underline{row})$ = rw^{-1}
$\rho(r, r)$ = $\{\epsilon\}$, für alle $r \in RA$
$\rho(\underline{int}, \underline{real})$ = {kir}
$\rho(\underline{char}, \underline{string})$ = {kchs, rw krchs}
$\rho(\underline{string}, \underline{char})$ = {ksrch rw}
Für alle übrigen Fälle:
$\rho(r_1, r_2)$ = $\emptyset$

Der Grund dafür, daß man für zwei Restarten eine Menge möglicher Anpassungen definiert, liegt darin, daß man die Restartenanpassung von den
vorangestellten Präfixen abhängig machen will. So kann man, wie sich

aus der Definition 5 erkennen lassen wird, die Sequenz rw krchs aus
ρ(char, string) als Anpassung von row char an string durch die
Operation krchs deuten. Hat man nun z.B. m_1 = (proc ref, int)
m_2 = (proc ref row row, int) gegeben, so kann man sagen: Der Abbau
von proc ref geschieht durch η(proc ref) = dp dr . Die Restartan-
passung erfolgt durch $\varepsilon \in \rho$(int, int) . Den Aufbau von
proc ref row row bewerkstelligt $(\eta($proc ref row row$))^{-1}$ =
rw rw dr^{-1} dp^{-1} . Insgesamt ergäbe sich dp dr rw rw dr^{-1} dp^{-1} als
die Folge der auszuführenden Anpassungsoperationen.

Wie man an diesem Beispiel sieht, ist der bisherige Anpassungsbegriff
noch unzulänglich, denn was heißt es z.B. das Inverse einer Dereferen-
zierung dr^{-1} auszuführen und was geschieht, wenn dies gar nicht möglich sein soll? Andererseits wird man feststellen: Das Inverse einer
Deprozedurierung ist eine Prozedurierung oder die Folge der (Pseudo-)
Anpassungsoperationen dr rw dr^{-1} bewirkt dasselbe wie eine Re-
ferenzenreihung rrw . Allgemeiner soll es nun zusätzlich möglich
sein, "Gleichheitsbeziehungen" zwischen Folgen von Präfixmodifikatoren
zu definieren. Dies führt bei der bisherigen Begriffsbildung zu definierenden Relatoren in der Repräsentation von Gruppen.

Definition 4. Seien APW, PM und RAM wie früher. Weiter seien
$R_1, R_2, \ldots, R_k$, k $\geq$ 0 , Worte über $\overline{PM}$. Dann heißt die Gruppe
G = <APW ; $R_1, R_2, \ldots, R_k$> eine *Artanpassungsgruppe*.

Jetzt kann man die Begriffe Anpaßbarkeit und Anpassungssequenz wie
folgt erklären:

Definition 5. Sei G = <APW; $R_1, R_2, \ldots, R_k$> eine Artanpassungsgruppe
und η und ρ wie in den Definitionen 2 und 3. Eine Art $m_1 = (p_1, r_1)$
heißt an die Art $m_2 = (p_2, r_2)$ *anpaßbar*, falls
1. $\rho(r_1, r_2) \neq \emptyset$
2. es ein Wort as $\in$ APW* gibt, so daß as $\equiv \eta(p_1)$ ra $(\eta(p_2))^{-1}$ in
   G für ein ra $\in \rho(r_1, r_2)$.

Setzt man zusätzlich in APW eine Ordnung voraus, so heiße das kleinste[1] Wort as , das 2. erfüllt,die *Anpassungssequenz* von m_1 und m_2,
i.Z. as(m_1, m_2).

---

[1] Es gelte $W_1 < W_2 \Longleftrightarrow$
   $|W_1| < |W_2|$ oder $|W_1| = |W_2|$ und W_1 steht in alphabetischer Reihenfolge vor W_2

Bemerkung:
1. Nachfolgend soll, wenn $G = \langle E;R_1,\ldots,R_n\rangle$ eine Gruppe und $E_0 \subset \bar{E}^*$
   ist, für ein $e \in \bar{E}^*$ die Schreibweise $e \underset{=}{\in} E_0$ bezeichnen, daß es
   ein $e_0 \in E_0$ gibt, so daß $e \equiv e_0$ in G gilt.
2. Die Menge $\{a \in \overline{APW}^* \mid a \underset{=}{\in} \eta(p_1)\rho(r_1,r_2)\eta(p_2)^{-1}\}$ heiße die Menge
   PAS der *Pseudoanpassungssequenzen* von (p_1,r_1) und (p_2,r_2).

__Beispiel 3__. Seien PM, RAM, η und ρ wie in Beispiel 2. Setzt man
$R_1 = dp\ pr$ und $R_2 = rrw\ dr\ rw^{-1}\ dr^{-1}$ so ist $m_1 = (\underline{proc\ ref},\ \underline{int})$
an $m_2 = (\underline{proc\ ref\ row\ row},\ \underline{int})$ anpaßbar.

Aus $\eta(\underline{proc\ ref}) = dp\ dr$, $(\eta(\underline{proc\ ref\ row\ row}))^{-1} = rw\ rw\ dr^{-1}\ dp^{-1}$
und $\rho(\underline{int},\ \underline{int}) = \{\varepsilon\}$ erhält man wegen

$$
\begin{array}{llllll}
 & dp & dr & rw & rw & dr^{-1} & dp^{-1} \\
\underset{=}{R}2 & dp & rrw & dr & rw & dr^{-1} & dp^{-1} \\
\underset{=}{R}2 & dp & rrw & rrw & dr & dr^{-1} & dp^{-1} \\
\equiv & dp & rrw & rrw & dp^{-1} & & \\
\underset{=}{R}1 & dp & rrw & rrw & pr & & \\
 & dp & rrw & rrw & pr & \text{als Anpassungssequenz.} & \\
\end{array}
$$

Leider hat man nun folgendes Resultat:

__Satz 1__. Äquivalent sind folgende Aussagen:
(1) zu bel. AAP-Gruppe G ist die partielle Funktion as_G , die jedem
    Paar (m_1,m_2) aus $M \times M$ im Falle der Anpaßbarkeit deren Anpas-
    sungssequenz zuordnet, berechenbar.
(2) Das allgemeine Wortproblem für Gruppen ist lösbar und zu G , m_1
    und m_2 ist die Anpaßbarkeit von m_1 an m_2 entscheidbar und
    der Entscheidungsalgorithmus liefert im Falle der Anpaßbarkeit ein
    as , das die Bed. 2 in Def. 5 erfüllt.

Wegen der Unentscheidbarkeit des Wortproblems für Gruppen erhält man
dann das

__Korollar__. Die partielle Funktion as_G ist bei bel. vorgegebener Artanpassungsgruppe G nicht berechenbar.

Damit man sich wieder im Rahmen der Entscheidbarkeit bewegt, sind Einschränkungen nötig, die im nächsten Abschnitt dargelegt werden sollen.

5. ZIELARTEN UND ZIELFUNKTIONEN

In der Definition 5 wird davon ausgegangen, daß durch zwei Arten m_1 und m_2 eine Menge von Pseudoanpassungssequenzen und möglicherweise eine Anpassungssequenz gegeben ist. Umgekehrt soll nun sinnvollerweise durch m_1 und eine "geeignete" Pseudoanpassungssequenz a eindeutig eine "Zielart" m_2 spezifiziert werden, so daß $a \in PAS(m_1,m_2)$ ist.

PM, RAM, AP, RA, η und ρ seien wieder vorgegeben. Zur Vereinfachung sei angenommen, daß $P = AP^*$ gelte. $G = \langle APW; R_1,\ldots,R_k\rangle$ sei eine bel. aber feste Artanpassungsgruppe bzgl. dieser Größen.

<u>Definition 6</u>. Sei $\widetilde{M} = (\overline{AP})^* \times RA$. Eine partielle Abbildung
$\mathcal{Z} : \widetilde{M} \times (\overline{APW})^* \to \widetilde{M}$ heißt eine *Zielfunktion* bzgl. G , falls
1. $\mathcal{Z}((p_1,r_1), x) = (p_2,r_2) \Rightarrow x \in \eta(p_1)\rho(r_1,r_2) (\eta(p_2))^{-1}$
{Das bedeutet, wenn man speziell p_1 und p_2 aus P wählt, daß jede Pseudoanpassungssequenz, die man bei der Anpassung von (p_1,r_1) an (p_2,r_2) erhalten kann, (p_1,r_1) in (p_2,r_2) überführen soll und umgekehrt.}
2. $\forall a \in PM \; \exists p_1,p_2 \in P \; \forall r \in RA : \mathcal{Z}((p_1,r),a) = (p_2,r)$
{d.h. es soll keine überflüssigen Präfixmodifikatoren geben.}
3. $\forall a \in PM : \forall p_1,p_2 \in P : \mathcal{Z}((p_1,r_1),a) = (p_2,r_2) \Rightarrow r_1 = r_2$
{d.h. Präfixmodifikatoren lassen die Restarten invariant.}

<u>Beispiel 4</u>. Sei die Gruppe $G = \langle APW;\ dr\ rw^{-1}\ dr^{-1}\ rrw,\ dp\ pr\rangle$ aus Beispiel 3 gegeben. Setzt man $\mathcal{Z}$ folgendermaßen

$((\varepsilon , \underline{int}) , kir) \longmapsto (\varepsilon , \underline{real})$

$((\varepsilon , \underline{char}) , kchs) \longmapsto (\varepsilon , \underline{string})$

$((\varepsilon , \underline{string}) , ksrch) \longmapsto (\underline{row} , \underline{char})$

$((\underline{row} , \underline{char}) , krchs) \longmapsto (\varepsilon , \underline{string})$

und für $p \in (\overline{AP})^*$ und $r \in RA$

$((p,r) , dr) \longmapsto (\underline{ref}^{-1}p , r)$

$((p,r) , dr^{-1}) \longmapsto (\underline{ref}\ p , r)$

$((p,r) , rw) \longmapsto (\underline{row}\ p , r)$

$$((p,r)\,,\ rw^{-1})\ \longmapsto\ (\underline{row}^{-1}p\,,\ r)$$

$$((p,r)\,,\ dp)\ \longmapsto\ (\underline{proc}^{-1}p,\ r)$$

$$((p,r)\,,\ dp^{-1})\ \longmapsto\ (\underline{proc}\ p,\ r)$$

$$((p,r)\,,\ pr)\ \longmapsto\ (\underline{proc}\ p,\ r)$$

$$((p,r)\,,\ pr^{-1})\ \longmapsto\ (\underline{proc}^{-1}p,\ r)$$

$$((p,r)\,,\ rrw)\ \longmapsto\ (\underline{ref}\ \underline{row}\ \underline{ref}^{-1}p\,,\ r)$$

$$((p,r)\,,\ rrw^{-1})\ \longmapsto\ (\underline{ref}\ \underline{row}^{-1}\underline{ref}^{-1}p,\ r)$$

und

$$\zeta((p,r)\,,\ a_1\ldots a_n)\ =\ \begin{cases} (p,r)\,, & \text{falls}\ \ n = 0 \\ (\zeta((p,r),a_1)\,,\ a_2\ldots a_n)\,, & \text{sonst} \end{cases}$$

so ist ζ eine Zielfunktion bzgl. G.

Es ergibt sich dann die folgende Aussage

<u>Satz 2</u>. Sei G eine AAP-Gruppe. Existiert zu G eine Zielfunktion, so ist das Wortproblem in G entscheidbar.

<u>Beweisidee</u>. Sei ζ die Zielfunktion. Dann wird durch die Zuordnung

$a \mapsto a \quad \forall a \in RAM$

$a \mapsto p_1 p_2^{-1} \quad$ für $\quad a \in PM$,

falls $((p_1,r),a) = (p_2,r)$ für alle $r \in RA$ gilt, ein Isomorphismus von G auf die freie Gruppe $\langle AP \cup RAM\,;\,\rangle$ definiert.

Weitgehend kann man feststellen

<u>Satz 3</u>. Sei G eine AAP-Gruppe und ζ eine Zielfunktion bzgl. G. Dann ist die partielle Funktion as_G (vgl. Def. 5 und Satz 1) berechenbar.

6. SCHLUSSBEMERKUNGEN

Es wurde gezeigt, wie man die Artanpassung für Programmiersprachen mit nicht-endlicher Artenmenge algebraisch durch Erzeugende und definierende Relatoren in einer Gruppenrepräsentation darstellen kann. Wie man

aus den Beispielen erkennen kann, sind die "strong-coercions" aus AL-
GOL 68 (mit Ausnahme des "uniting") auf diese Weise einfach zu definieren. Der Begriff der Zielfunktion, der auch in [Scheidig 70] benutzt wird, liefert die Entscheidbarkeit der Anpaßbarkeit. Die Frage
nach der Entscheidbarkeit der Existenz einer Zielfunktion führt, wie
man aus der Beweisidee zu Satz 2 erkennen kann, auf einen bisher unge-
lösten Teilaspekt des Isomorphieproblems für endlich erzeugte Gruppen.
Weitere Arbeit wird zeigen, wie man die hier vorgestellten Begriffe
verfeinert, um z.B. wie in ALGOL 68 mehrere Typen von Artanpassungen
darstellen zu können. Dies könnte z.B. durch die Definition verschiedener regulärer Mengen von Artanpassungssequenzen geschehen. Es müßte
dann möglich sein, auch solche Dinge, wie z.B. das "mode-balancing",
einfach zu handhaben.

LITERATUR

[A 68]   A. van Wijngaarden (Ed.):
                Report on the Algorithmic Language ALGOL 68,
                Numerische Mathematik, 14, 79-218 (1969)

[Magnus 66]   W. Magnus, A. Karrass, D. Solitar:
                Combinatorial Group Theory: Presentation of Groups in
                Terms of Generators and Relations, J. Wiley & Sons
                (1966)

[Scheidig 70]   H. Scheidig:
                Anpassungsoperationen in ALGOL 68,
                Dissertation, Technische Universität München,
                (1969/70)

MATHEMATICAL THEORY OF SERIAL COMPUTERS

Karel Čulík, Brno, Czechoslovakia

0. Introduction

About 20 years ago (see e.g. [1]) the automation of programming started. Its aim was to facilitate the programming activity, and the direct
reason was the "difficulty" of learning and using machine codes.

In full accordance with human history one revolutionary attempt and
one evolutionary attempt was made in order to reach the aim.

The revolutionary attempt consisted in introducing - step by step -
the new "higher" programming languages (e.g. ALGOL 58 [3], ALGOL 60 [10],
ALGOL 62 [11], ALGOL 68 [12]). The revolutionary way led to new problems concerning grammars and compilers for these languages, but unfortunately - again in full accordance with the human history - the original aim was not reached, since who dares to say that ALGOL 68 is "easy"
to learn and to use and it is "difficult" to learn and to use machine
code.

The evolutionary attempt overcame all objections to machine code very
soon, when symbolic addresses (instead of binary numerals) and also
other mathematical symbols for operations and relations were admitted
in assembly languages. In addition, if we allow to use some micro-
instructions (e.g. three address instructions), we are getting a basic
computer language, which is as similar to the language of mathematics
as possible. This means that the maximum of intelligibility of any programming language was reached, and any further facilitation of programming activity consists in proper extensions of this basic computer language.

The basic computer language is introduced in Sect. 1 and 2, the theory of flow diagrams (or program schemes) is presented in Sect. 3, the
automodifying stored programs (which use routines and procedures) are
studied in Sect. 4, and finally the data structures are discussed in
Sect. 5. Let us remember that a natural extension of the basic computer language to parallel and precedence programs for parallel computers was done in [37].

All these extensions cover things which are well known and still used in all machine codes of all computers, to which all higher level programming languages must be translated. A great advantage of the basic computer language consists in its independence from any computer [36] and therefore in the possibility to be a base for any system programming within operational systems, being also very natural extensions of the basic computer language.

1. Basic concepts of a language theory

The study of syntax of languages is still preferred - first of all for historical reasons - although the kernel of each language is in its semantics, which is a function (in general multivalued) sem such that its domain Domain sem = Expr is the set of expressions, and its range Range sem = Mean is the set of meanings of the language under the consideration. If one uses a language then he is saying its expression $e \in$ Expr but he is thinking its meaning sem(e) $\in$ Mean, which is the basic language convention accepted by all of us almost always.

The simplest case of semantics is a naming function, when the inner structure of expressions need not have any connection with the structure of the corresponding meanings.

A relational structure <Obj,Opr,Rel> consists in the triple of sets of basic objects, operations, relations, respectively. Who wants to speak about the relational structure, needs to have the corresponding names. A naming function for basic objects is called denotation den, and Range den = Obj, Domain den = SymbObj is the set of symbols for objects (= object names). A naming function for basic operations and relations is called interpretation (or connotation) int, and Domain int = SymbOpr $\cup$ SymbRel is the set of symbols for operations and relations (which include an integer called the arity), Range int$|_{\text{SymbOpr}}$ = Opr and Range int$|_{\text{SymbRel}}$ = Rel.

If Obj $\cup$ Opr $\cup$ Rel $\subset$ Mean and SymbObj $\cup$ SymbOpr $\cup$ SymbRel $\subset$ Expr, then the denotation and interpretation are partial functions of the semantics, i.e. den = sem$|_{\text{SymbObj}}$ and int = sem$|_{\text{SymbOpr} \cup \text{SymbRel}}$. According to the basic language convention one is writing <SymbObj,SymbOpr,SymbRel> but he is thinking <Obj,Opr,Rel>, when den and int are assumed silently.

The basic elements of empirical knowledge concerning the structure

<Obj,Opr,Rel> are expressed by two sorts of atomic formulas. The <u>atomic relational formula</u>

(1.1) $r^{(n)}(x_1,\ldots,x_n) \in$ Expr, where $r^{(n)} \in$ SymbRel and $x_i \in$ SymbObj
for i = 1,2,...,n (n $\geq$ 1 is the arity),

means (or expresses)

(1.1)* (int $r^{(n)}$) (den $x_1,\ldots,$den x_n),

and the <u>atomic operational formula</u>

(1.2) $\left[f^{(n)}(x_1,\ldots,x_n) = x_0 \right] \in$ Expr, where $f^{(n)} \in$ SymbOpr and
$x_i \in$ SymbObj for i = 0,1,...,n (n $\geq$ i is the arity),

means

$(1.2)^*$ (int $f^{(n)}$) (den $x_1,\ldots,$den x_n) = den x_0

with respect to the semantics, i.e. to den and int.

Besides the symbols for objects, which are called <u>constants</u>, because

(1.3)(i) den x = den'x for each two denotations den and den', and for
each x $\in$ SymbObj,

a further set Var of names of objects is used such that

(1.3)(ii) SymbObj $\cap$ Var = $\emptyset$ and Var $\subset$ Domain den for each denotation den.

A name x $\in$ Var is called a <u>variable</u>, because it needs not to satisfy
(1.3)(i). In all atomic formulas the constants may be replaced by variables anywhere we want.

The operations, which are composed of the basic ones, are expressed by
terms over SymbOpr and Var (or SymbObj too). <u>The syntactical definition</u>
of a term t and of its set Inp(t) of <u>input variables</u> is inductive as
follows:

(1.4)(i) each x $\in$ Var is a term and Inp(x) = {x};
(ii) each x $\in$ SymbObj is a term and Inp(x) = $\emptyset$;

(iii) if $f^{(n)} \in$ SymbOpr and $t_1,\ldots,t_n$ are terms then the string $f^{(n)}(t_1,\ldots,t_n)$ is a term and $\mathrm{Inp}(f^{(n)}(t_1,\ldots,t_n)) = \bigcup\limits_{i=1}^{n} \mathrm{Inp}(t_i)$.

The term t means (or expresses or denotes)

$(1.4)*(i)$ if $t \in$ SymbObj $\cup$ Var then sem $t =$ den $t \in$ Obj;

(ii) if $t \notin$ SymbObj $\cup$ Var then $t = f^{(n)}(t_1,\ldots,t_n)$ and we can assume that sem $t_i \in$ Obj has been determined already for $i = 1,\ldots,n$; thus we put sem $t = (\mathrm{int}\ f^{(n)})(\mathrm{sem}\ t_1,\ldots,\mathrm{sem}\ t_n)$ which is the value of the operation int $f^{(n)}$ when applied to the n-tuple of arguments sem $t_1,\ldots,$ sem t_n.

This is the <u>semantical definition</u> of a term (again inductive) with respect to int and den, and it is a further step in definition of semantics sem, when $t \in$ Expr for each term t.

By an ordering of all input variables of $\mathrm{Inp}(t) = \{x_1,\ldots,x_n\}$ (and for a fixed interpretation int) each term t determines a <u>composed operation</u>, i.e. an n-ary function, the name of which is $[\lambda[x_1,\ldots,x_n];t]$, when the λ-notation [4] is used. If $F^{(n)}$ is a new symbol for operations, i.e. $F^{(n)} \notin$ SymbOpr or $F^{(n)}$ is not interpreted in int, then its meaning can be determined by the usual definition

$(1.5)\ (i)\quad F^{(n)} =_{df} [\lambda[x_1,\ldots,x_n];t]$

with respect to all possible denotations den, or directly and without using the λ-notation one can write

$(1.5)\ (ii)\quad F^{(n)}(x_1,\ldots,x_n) = t,$

where $F^{(n)}(x_1,\ldots,x_n)$ is used as an abreviation of the term t (and the ordering of variables is arbitrary but a fixed one).

The theoretical knowledge about the relational structure <Obj,Opr,Rel> concerns the <u>logical possibilities</u>, which appear if the <u>truth functions</u> $\wedge,\vee,\longrightarrow,\longleftrightarrow,\neg$ etc. of the <u>truth values</u> yes(= true) and no(= false) are introduced. The <u>composed relational formulas</u> (or the propositional schemas) are terms over the symbols of truth functions and atomic relational formulas as truth variables. E.g. if $R^{(3)}$ is a new symbol for relations i.e. $R^{(3)} \notin$ SymbRel or $R^{(3)}$ is not interpreted in int, then its meaning is defined either using the λ-notation or directly by precription of an ordering of all variables as follows

$$(1.5)\ (iii)\ R^{(3)}(x_1,x_2,x_3) =_{df} ((r^{(2)}(x_1,x_2) \wedge r^{(2)}(x_2,x_3)) \longrightarrow r^{(2)}(x_1,x_3))$$

with respect to all possible denotations den, where $r^{(2)} \in$ SymbRel and $x_1,x_2,x_3 \in$ SymbObj $\cup$ Var.

If we admit terms instead of variables in atomic and composed relational formulas, then we have all expressions available in recent mathematics and logic which are used in actual computations.

In practical computing and in numerical analysis the relational structure $\langle$Rational,$\{+,-,*,/,\uparrow\},\{=,\neq,<,\not<,\leq,\nleq\}\rangle$ of the usual arithmetics of rational numbers (with restricted length) was intensively used and studied long ago before the discovery of computers. Besides the usual sequencing of operations the crucial idea of <u>iteration a step</u> (which corresponds to the while-statement of programming languages) and also the crucial idea of <u>branching the computing proces</u> (which corresponds to the if-statement) were very well known and very often used. E.g. the prescription for the evaluation of the expression $|x|/y$ (where the absolute value is required) must have two branches in Fig. 2a) and it seems to be rather surprising that nobody came with the idea to combine operations and relations in a general way in order to get new composed operations, i.e. nobody passed over from Fig. 2a) to Fig. 2b), where is an usual flow diagram, the concept of which seems to be so clear and simple today.

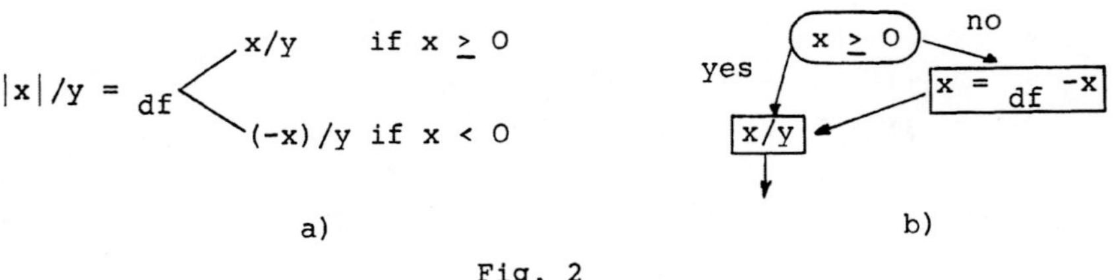

Fig. 2

This fact seems to be even more remarkable because within logic the theory of recursive functions was developed after the discoveries of K. Gödel [5], where an arbitrary combination of operations and relations is admitted implicitly.

Let us show the algorithmization of a relational structure $\langle$Obj,Opr,Rel$\rangle$ if we add the idea of flow diagram, as a way how to prescribe the computing activity, to the conceptual framework of recent mathematics and logic [6].

A <u>flow diagram</u> Fd = $\langle V, \rho, \lambda, \Lambda \rangle$ is a <u>directed graph</u> $\langle V, \rho \rangle$, where V is its set of <u>vertices</u>, the binary relation $\rho \subset V \times V$ is its set of <u>edges</u> and λ, Λ is the labelling of vertices, edges, respectively, such that [7]:

(1.6) (i)   there exists exactly one input vertex (i.e. no edge terminates in it);

     (ii)   there exists at least one output vertex (i.e. no edge starts in it);

   (iii)   in each vertex at most two edges start;

    (iv)   if only one edge (v,w) starts in $v \in V$ then $\lambda(v)$ is an atomic operational formula (1.2) and $\Lambda(v,w)$ is not defined;

    (v)   if two edges (v,v_1), (v,v_2) start in $v \in V$ then $\lambda(v)$ is an atomic relational formula (1.1) and either $\Lambda(v,v_1) =$ yes and $\Lambda(v,v_2) =$ no, or conversely $\Lambda(v,v_1) =$ no and $\Lambda(v,v_2)=$ yes.

Each flow diagram Fd together with an interpretation int and a denotation den of its atomic formulas, is a computing prescription which determines the following <u>computing activity</u> (or process) $\mathrm{Act}_{\mathrm{int}}(\mathrm{Fd,den}) =$ $= ((v_1,\mathrm{den}_0),(v_2,\mathrm{den}_1),\ldots,(v_i,\mathrm{den}_{i-1}),\ldots)$ which can be finite or infinite and which is defined inductively:

(1.7) v_1 is the input vertex of Fd and $\mathrm{den}_0 = \mathrm{den}$; if $i > 0$ and v_i, den_{i-1} have been defined already then
either $\lambda(v_i) = [f^{(n)}(x_1,\ldots,x_n) = x_0]$ and we define
a) v_{i+1} is the unique vertex in Fd such that $(v_i,v_{i+1}) \in \rho$, and
b) $\begin{cases} \mathrm{den}_i(x_0) =_{\mathrm{df}} (\mathrm{int}\ f^{(n)})(\mathrm{den}_{i-1}x_1,\ldots,\mathrm{den}_{i-1}x_n) \text{ so far as} \\ \qquad\qquad (\mathrm{den}_{i-1}x_1,\ldots,\mathrm{den}_{i-1}x_n) \in \mathrm{Domain}(\mathrm{int}\ f^{(n)}), \\ \mathrm{den}_i(z) =_{\mathrm{df}} \mathrm{den}_{i-1}(z) \text{ for each } z \in \mathrm{SymbObj} \cup \mathrm{Var} - \{x_0\}; \end{cases}$
or $\lambda(v_i) = r^{(n)}(x_1,\ldots,x_n)$ and we define
a) v_{i+1} is determined by the requirement $\Lambda(v_i,v_{i+1}) = (\mathrm{int}\ r^{(n)})$ $(\mathrm{den}_{i-1}x_1,\ldots,\mathrm{den}_{i-1}x_n)$ so far as $(\mathrm{den}_{i-1}x_1,\ldots,\mathrm{den}_{i-1}x_n) \in$ $\in \mathrm{Domain}(\mathrm{int}\ r^{(n)})$, and
b) $\mathrm{den}_i =_{\mathrm{df}} \mathrm{den}_{i-1}$.

The finite activity $\mathrm{Act}_{\mathrm{int}}(\mathrm{Fd,den}) = ((v_1,\mathrm{den}_0),\ldots,(v_N,\mathrm{den}_{N-1}))$ is called <u>stopped</u> (or completed) if its last vertex v_N is an output vertex of Fd. In this case the last denotation den_{N-1} is called the <u>result</u> and

denoted by Res den, which corresponds to the given _initial denotation_
den = den_o.

The sequence Compt_{int}(Fd,den) = $(\text{den}_o,\text{den}_1,\ldots,\text{den}_{N-1})$ is called the
computation and the sequence TrBr_{int}(Fd,den) = $(\lambda(v_1),\Lambda(v_1,v_2),\lambda(v_2),$
$\Lambda(v_2,v_3),\ldots,\Lambda(v_{N-1},v_N),\lambda(v_N))$ is called the _(truth) branch_ of the
activity Act_{int}(Fd,den), where $\lambda(v_{i+1})$ follows immediately $\lambda(v_i)$ if
$\Lambda(v_i,v_{i+1})$ is not defined.

If two sets of _input_, _output variables_ Inp(Fd) = $\{x_1,\ldots,x_n\}$, Outp(Fd) =
= $\{y_1,\ldots,y_m\}$, respectively, are prescribed, and $F_j \notin$ SymbOpr is a new
symbol for operations then the composed operation (which can be partial)

(1.8)(i) $F_j(\text{denx}_1,\ldots,\text{denx}_n) =_{df} \text{Resden } y_j$

is defined for each j = 1,...,m and each denotation den such that Resden
exists. Using the extended λ-notation, when also an ordering of output
variables is prescribed, we could define

(1.8)(ii) $[\lambda_j[x_1,\ldots,x_n;y_1,\ldots,y_m];Fd] =_{df} F_j$ for j = 1,...,m.

The composed operations $F_1,\ldots,F_m$ are said to be _computable_ (or evaluable) _by Fd with respect to int_.

Then one writes Fd = $_{int}\text{Fd}^*$ and says that Fd and Fd^* are _functionally_
equivalent in all interpretations int if

(1.9) $[\lambda_j[x_1,\ldots,x_n;y_1,\ldots,y_m];Fd_{int}] = [\lambda_j[x_1^*,\ldots,x_n^*;y_1^*,\ldots,y_m^*];Fd_{int}^*]$
        holds for each j = 1,...,m.

In a special case if $x_i = x_i^*$ for each i = 1,...,n, and $y_j = y_j^*$ for each
j = 1,...,m, then for den = den^* we have

(1.1o) Resden = $\text{Resden}^* \implies$ Fd = $_{int}\text{Fd}^*$.

On the other hand it is possible to differentiate the methods of evaluation (or computation) of F_j, $1 \leq j \leq m$, as follows. If $(\text{denx}_1,\ldots,$
$\ldots,\text{denx}_n) \in \text{DomainF}_j$ and TrBr_{int}(Fd,den) = $(\lambda(v_1),\Lambda(v_1,v_2),\lambda(v_2),\ldots$
$\ldots,\lambda(v_N))$ then there exists the maximal index k such that $\lambda(v_k) =$
= $[f^{(p)}(z_1,\ldots,z_p) = y_j]$ and therefore by supression of all members of
TrBr_{int}(Fd,den) which are not operational formulas and not precede the

member $\lambda(v_k)$, one gets a finite sequence $OpBr_{int}(Fd,den,j)$ called <u>oper-ational branch</u>. The mapping $Meth_{int}(Fd,j)$ of $(denx_1,...,denx_n)$ to $OpBr_{int}(Fd,den,j)$ is called the <u>algorithmic (operational) method of evaluation of F_j by Fd with respect to int</u> [6]. Obviously

$$(1.11) \quad Meth_{int}(Fd,j) = Meth_{int}(Fd^*,j) \implies F_j = F_j^* \text{ for } j = 1,...,m.$$

Let us stop with algorithmization of relational structures and let us show that this extension of the usual mathematical language can be used as a computer language directly.

2. The mathematization of computer field

From the user's point of view the most natural and convenient level of description of computer's activity consists in defferentiating two main parts of the computer: its functional unit and its storage (in the broadest sense of the word). This level is the nearest one to the user and its mathematical language of Sect. 1. Let us remind that there is no difficulty to replace this level by an other one which corresponds to micro-commands.

The <u>functional unit</u> is a relational structure <Obj,Opr,Rel> such that all its basic operations and relations can be evaluated within the computer directly, i.e. there are the corresponding commands available.

The <u>storage</u> (without any differentiation of its sorts and types as re-gisters, tapes, discs, their zones, etc.) is the set $Cont^{Loc}$ of all functions S, called <u>states</u> (of storage), where the elements of $DomainS = Loc$ are called <u>basic locations</u>, and the elements of $RangeS \subset Cont$ are called (possible) <u>contents</u> (of locations), and they will be specified consecutively. The concept of location replaces two known concepts namely that of <u>memory cell</u> and of its <u>address</u>, which is a clear and convenient simplification (and the locations are considered as symbols).

The only connection between the functional unit and the storage of the same computer concerns the fact the basic objects can be stored at the basic locations directly, and on the other hand that basic locations can be used as names for basic objects, i.e.

$$(2.1) \quad Obj \subset Cont \text{ (and Var} \subset Loc).$$

Then it is clear that if $x \in Loc$ and $S \in Cont^{Loc}$ then $S(x) = c \in Cont$, and the computer phrase "c is the content of (or c is stored at) the location x at the state S" says nothing else than the logical phrase "c is denoted by the object name x in the denotation S". Therefore states of storage can be considered as denotations of Sect. 1 and it is clear that the mathematical language of Sect. 1 can be directly used to the description of the activity of the computer itself, because all its activity consists in repeated evaluations of its basic operations and relations, and of repeated evalutations of its states of storage (together with their change). Thus the "distance" between the language of Sect. 1 and the computer is zero, at least here at the beginning, because after the replacing the logical terminology by the computer terminology, the definitions of flow diagram (1.6) and its activity (1.7) become perfect computing prescriptions for the computer under consideration, determined by the corresponding interpretation.

Therefore let us call the language of Sect. 1 <u>computer language</u> (after some conventional modifications). The level of the computer language corresponds to abstract assembly language [42] with macro-commands.

There is just custom instead of (1.2) to write the assignement statement, called here the <u>operational command</u>,

(2.2) (i) $f^{(n)}(x_1,\ldots,x_n) =: x_o$, where $x_i \in Loc$ for $i = 0,1,\ldots,n$, and $f^{(n)} \in SymbOpr$,

and an usual writing of the <u>assignement symbol</u> =: instead of the usual := agrees with [3] when procedures are concerned, and is justified by a simpler and more natural definition of scope in Sect. 3.

If we assume that $I^{(1)} \in SymbOpr$ and that $I^{(1)}$ always is interpreted as the unary identity operation then there is an other custom to write the <u>restoring command</u>

(2.2) (ii) x =: y, where $x,y \in Loc$,

instead of $I^{(1)}(x) =: y$.

Each occurence of a location on the right, left hand side of the assignement symbol =: is called the <u>defining, applied occurence of the location</u> within an operational (or restoring) command.

Almost at the very outset of the computer history there appeared [8] the requirement to store all the program in the computer storage. According to [9] the real inventors of this important idea were Eckert and Mauchly, the technical leaders of the project ENIAC during the last war, when J.v. Neumann [8] started his work in computer field. He is the inventor of flow diagram, although he did not give its mathematical definition. Nevertheless J.v. Neumann recognised the proper difficulty of passing from the pure mathematical and traditional solution of a numerical problem to its flow diagram. The further passing from the flow diagram to the stored program is relatively simple.

For the tutorial reasons let us differentiate two kinds of locations

$$(2.3) \qquad Loc = Var \cup Lab, \text{ where } Var \cap Lab = \emptyset.$$

Each element $x \in Var$ is a variable, which is in accordance (1.3) with the use of this term within mathematics and logic, and which corresponds to the term _identifier_ in higher level languages as [3,1o,11]. Each element $b \in Lab$ is called a _label_ in full accordance with the use of this term in higher level languages.

In order to be able to store a flow diagram $Fd = \langle V,\rho,\lambda,\Lambda\rangle$ at labels from Lab we assume $V \subset Lab$ and if $\lambda(v)$ is an operational formula (1.2) we store the operational command (2.2) at v. If $\lambda(v) = r^{(n)}(x_1,\ldots,x_n)$ and $\Lambda(v,w_1) = yes$, $\Lambda(v,w_2) = no$ then at v we store the _relational command_

$$(2.2)(iii) \quad r^{(n)}_{[w_1,w_2]}(x_1,\ldots,x_n) \text{ where } x_i \in Var \text{ for } i = 1,\ldots,n, \text{ but}$$
$$w_1,w_2 \in Lab \text{ and } w_1 \neq w_2,$$

instead of the relational formula (1.1). There is a convention that the order of labels $[w_1,w_2]$ in (2.2)(iii) corresponds to the order of truth values $[yes,no]$.

Finally new _starting_ and _stopping commands_

$$(2.2)(iv) \quad START \text{ and } STOP$$

are chosen in order to distinguish the input and output vertices of Fd (using the additional vertices at which these commands are stored).

The labels from Lab are usually natural numbers and from the point of
view of the command counter [21] of the control unit (which is not considered here) it is convenient to store Fd in such a way that

(2.4) (v,w) ϵ ρ and $\lambda(v)$ is an operational formula $\implies$ $w = v + 1$,

which can be satisfied only by such flow diagrams which satisfy the
following requirement

(2.5) w ϵ V $\implies$ there exists at most one vertex v ϵ V such that
             (v,w) ϵ ρ and $\lambda(v)$ is an operational formula.

Unfortunately (2.5) is not satisfied very often and therefore a new
auxiliary <u>GOTO-command</u>

(2.2)(v)   GOTOw where w ϵ Lab

is used and inserted where necessary in Fd in order to achieve the
satisfaction of (2.5) for a modified Fd* such that Fd* = $_{int}$Fd in all
interpretations int [7]. Therefore GOTO-commands are absolutely necessary in this lower level language.

If Comm is the set of all commands (2.2)(i)-(v) then

(2.6)(i)   Comm $\subset$ Cont,
    (ii)   Loc $\subset$ Cont,

are requirements which ensure the possibility of storing flow diagrams
(where in fact (ii) follows from (i) although it is not necessary now).

Let us introduce the concept of a (stored computer) program independently on the concept of flow diagram. A pair <b,C> where b ϵ Lab and
C ϵ Comm is called a <u>labelled command</u>; and a program P = $(K^0; K^1; \ldots; K^N)$
is an ordered set (which can be infinite too) of labelled commands
$K^i = \langle b^i, C^i \rangle$ such that [7]:

(2.7)(i) $i \neq j \implies b^i \neq b^j$ for all $i,j = 0,1,\ldots,N$;
    (ii) C^0 = START and $C^i \neq$ START for each $i = 1,2,\ldots,N$;
    (iii)   there exists at least one index i such that C^i = STOP
            and $1 \leq i \leq N$.

The concepts of activity, of computation, of labelled branch instead of truth branch, etc. are introduced in the same way as for flow diagrams in Sect. 1, and the translation of flow diagrams into (stored) programs is fully described [7].

Let us remind that (2.2)(iii), (2.2)(v) is the _conditional_, _unconditional jump_, respectively, because after it the command is executed which is stored at the corresponding label of it. All other commands, inclusively those which will be introduced later, are _regular_, i.e. after them their right neighbour in program should be executed as the next.

If P is a stored program then only such states S of storages are admissible which satisfy $S(b^i) = c^i$ for each $i = 0,1,...,N$, which means that the partial state $S|_{Lab}$ remains unchanged during all the computation, and therefore only the partial state $S|_{Var}$ is considered. This is the simplest case of program schemes and flow diagrams in Sect. 3.

Obviously, the reason why to store the program consists in a possibility to change it during its execution, by which J.v. Neumann [8] was fascinated so much. These changes are called _modifications_ from a new set Mod of operations and let SymbMod be the corresponding set of _symbols for modifications_ (SymbMod $\cap$ SymbOpr $= \emptyset$ although it does not exclude the possibility to use some operations as modifications). Let us restrict to the known "address modifications" only and let us use only the following three types of _modifying commands_:

(2.8)(i)   MODIF(c)b where b,c ε Lab and MODIF ε SymbMod;
    (ii)   LMODIF(z)b where z ε Var, b ε Lab and LMODIF ε SymbMod;
    (iii) RMODIF(z)b where z ε Var, b ε Lab and RMODIF ε SymbMod;

the meaning of which is as follows: all of them are regular and the current state S is changed in the new state S^* such that

(2.9)(i) $S(b) = GOTOa \implies S^*(b) = GOTOc$ and $S^*(p)=S(p)$ for each $p \neq b$;
    (ii) $S(b) = [x=:y] \implies S^*(b) = [z=:y]$ and $S^*(p)=S(p)$ for each $p \neq b$;
    (iii) $S(b) = [x=:y] \implies S^*(b) = [x=:z]$ and $S^*(p)=S(p)$ for each $p \neq b$.

Let MComm be the set of all modifying commands (2.8)(i)-(iii).

Till now no special commands have been introduced which required the evaluation of states of storage repeatedly, although (2.6)(ii) is a

sufficient assumption for an iteration of states as it is necessary for
"the address of the address", for pointers and ref-mechanism of ALGOL
68. Let us introduce only the following five sorts of <u>state commands</u>,
which are followed by the assumed state conditions concerning the current state S:

(2.1o) (i)   refx =: y where x,y ε Var : $S(x)$ ε Loc;

    (ii)   x =: refy where x,y ε Var : $S(y)$ ε Loc;

    (iii) x $\equiv$: y   where x,y ε Loc;

    (iv)   1GOTOx   where x ε Loc : $S(x)$ ε Lab;

    (v)   GOTOrefx where x ε Loc : $S(S(x))$ ε Lab.

The meanings of these commands are as follows: the first three commands
(2.1o) (i)-(iii) are regular and the remaining two (2.1o) (iv) and (v)
are jumps, which do not change the state, and the second parts of their
meanings are determined consecutively when S is the current state and
S^* is the next one :

(2.11) (i) $S(x)$ ε Loc $\Longrightarrow$ $\begin{cases} S^*(y) =_{df} S(S(x)); \\ S^*(z) =_{df} S(z) \text{ for each } z \neq y; \end{cases}$

    (ii) $S(y)$ ε Loc $\Longrightarrow$ $\begin{cases} S^*(S(y)) =_{df} S(x); \\ S^*(z) =_{df} S(z) \text{ for each } z \neq y; \end{cases}$

    (iii) $\begin{cases} S^*(y) =_{df} \text{"x" where the quotation name } [13] \text{ is used, i.e.} \\ \qquad\qquad \text{the symbol x itself is stored;} \\ S^*(z) =_{df} S(z) \text{ for each } z \neq y; \end{cases}$

    (iv) $S(x)$ ε Lab $\Longrightarrow$ the command stored at the label $S(x)$, i.e.
          the command $S(S(x))$, is executed as the next;

    (v) $S(x)$ ε Loc, $S(S(x))$ ε Lab $\Longrightarrow$ the command stored at the
          label $S(S(x))$, i.e. the command $S(S(S(x)))$,
          is executed as the next.

If we compare the three commands refx =: y, x =: y and x $\equiv$: y we are
geting $S^*(y) = S^2(x) = S(S(x))$, $S^*(y) = S^1(x)$ and $S^*(y) = S^o(x)$, respectively, where S^o is the identity state, which calls for writing
$S^o(x) = x$ without the quotation marks. Here, in the basic language convention, is the source of irregularities of ref-mechanism of $[12]$.

The possibilities of composition states of storage are discussed in details in $[14]$, where only one content function is admitted instead of
the huge number $|\text{Cont}^{\text{Loc}}|$ here. The command (2.9)(iii) corresponds to
the equality 7 = z where 7 ε SymbObj and z ε Var, which is not allowed

in [14]. Therefore in [14] all considerations are pushed one level
higher than necessary and variables are always considered as pointers
with very complicated structure.

At last let us differentiate one special part of storage called <u>stack</u>
(or push-down) of the <u>width</u> $r \geq 1$ and of the <u>depth</u> $s \geq 1$, which consists
in $r * s$ basic locations $u_j^i \in$ Loc where $1 \leq j \leq r$ and $1 \leq i \leq s$, which
are forbidden to write in the program. Instead there are r new <u>stack</u>
<u>locations</u> u_1, $u_2, \ldots, u_r$ which are used in programs and one special lo-
cation $dr \in$ Loc called the <u>depth register</u>. In each state S such that
$S(dr)$ is an integer and $1 \leq S(dr) \leq s$, the stack variable u_i stands for
the basic variable $u_i^{S(dr)}$ for each $i = 1,2,\ldots,r$, i.e. the stack mechanism works e.g. in the same way as the modifications of u_i into $u_i^{S(dr)}$.

<u>3. Flow diagrams (program schemes)</u>
Very often it is more convenient and more transparent to use and also
to study the flow diagrams (1.6) instead of stored programs (2.7).

The crucial consequence of the concept of activity (1.7) is the possibility to separate the truth branch from the computation. The truth branches can be studied independently on any interpretation and denotation,
i.e. their study belongs to the syntax of the language of flow diagrams.
Of course the main aim of such a study are assertions of the following
sort: from some syntactical properties of truth branches certain semantical properties of computations, and therefore of evaluated functions
(1.8), are deduced.

Let int be an interpretation of a flow diagram $Fd = \langle V,\rho,\lambda,\Lambda \rangle$ and let
S_o be the initial state (we always use states instead of denotations).
In [15] it was ascertained that each stopped truth branch $TrBr_{int}(Fd,S_o) =$
$= (C_1,t_1,C_2,t_2,\ldots,C_n)$ is <u>consistent</u>, i.e. it satisfies

(3.1) $i < j$, $C_i = C_j = r^{(m)}(x_1,\ldots,x_m)$ and C_h is no operational command
   for each h such that $i < h < j \implies t_i = t_j$.

Nevertheless for the sake of simplicity let us consider the set $TrBr_{Fd}$
of all possible stopped truth branches of Fd (if each branch of $TrBr_{Fd}$
is consistent then Fd is called <u>free</u> in [16]). Further let us write
$Fd \equiv_{s} Fd^*$ if $ResS_o = ResS_o^*$ holds in all interpretations int, where $S_o = S_o^*$
is the <u>initial state</u> and $ResS_o$, $ResS_o^*$ are the corresponding <u>result</u>
<u>states</u> (when denotations are replaced by states everywhere). Then one

sees that

(3.2) $\mathrm{TrBr}_{Fd} = \mathrm{TrBr}_{Fd^*} \implies Fd \underset{s}{=} Fd^* \implies Fd = {}_{int}Fd^*$ in all interpreta-
      tions.

An <u>Fd-homomorphism</u> is a mapping ϕ such that if $Fd^* = \langle V^*, \rho^*, \lambda^*, \Lambda^* \rangle$ then

(3.3) (i)   Domain $\phi = V$, Range $\phi = V^*$;
      (ii) $(v,w) \; \epsilon \; \rho \implies (\phi v, \phi w) \; \epsilon \; \rho^*$;
      (iii) $(v^*, w^*) \; \epsilon \; \rho^* \implies$ there are $v, w \; \epsilon \; V$ such that $(v,w) \; \epsilon \; \rho$ and
             $\phi v = v^*, \; \phi w = w^*$;
      (iv) $odv = od\phi v$ for each $v \; \epsilon \; V$, where the output degree odv of v
             is the number of edges which start in v;
      (v) $v \; \epsilon \; V$ is an input, output vertex in $Fd \implies \phi v \; \epsilon \; V^*$ is an in-
             put, output vertex in Fd^*, respectively;
      (vi) $\lambda(v) = \lambda^*(\phi v)$ for each $v \; \epsilon \; V$;
      (vii) $\Lambda(v,w) = \Lambda^*(\phi v, \phi w)$ for each $(v,w) \; \epsilon \; \rho$,

and one easy sees that each Fd-homomorphic image and pattern Fd^* of Fd
satisfies $\mathrm{TrBr}_{Fd^*} = \mathrm{TrBr}_{Fd}$, and therefore by (3.2) also $Fd^* \underset{s}{=} Fd$ in all
interpretations. Among the Fd-homomorphic patters of Fd are trees, which
are infinite if any cycle in Fd occurs.

An effective construction [17] of infinite many Fd-homomorphic patterns
Fd^* of Fd can be given such that Fd is an <u>almost tree</u>, i.e. the following requirement is satisfied:

(3.4) $v \; \epsilon \; V^* \implies$ there exists exactly one monoton simple (i.e. without
      repeated vertices) path in Fd^* $(v_1, v_2, \ldots, v_m)$ such that v_1 is the
      input vertex of Fd^* and $v_m = v$.

This requirement is equivalent to E. Engeler's [18] intuitive characteri-
zation of his <u>normal form</u>: "a program is in normal form if its flow
diagram has the form of a tree in which some leaves are bent back to
earlier nodes of the branch on which they sit".

According to the inductive definition of normal form [19] it follows
that normal form is a stronger requirement than a <u>well structured form</u>
[2o]. On the other hand any minimization of the number of vertices (i.e.
of the length of the stored program) leads neither to a normal nor to a
well structured form, and in addition the GOTO-commands are most conven-

ient means how to minimalize the number of vertices.

The arbitrary choice of input and output variables in Sect. 1 and also a fixed choice of them for all flow diagrams [16] should be replaced by reasonable and natural definitions. If $tb \in TrBr_{Fd}$ then $Inp(tb)$ is the set of all variables $x \in Var$ such that the first occurence of x in the string tb (from the left to the right) exists and is an applied occurence in a command, $Outp(tb)$ is the set of all variables $x \in Var$ such that the last defining occurence of x in tb exists and each further occurence of x, if any, belongs to a relational command. Such an occurence of an output variable is called the <u>output occurence</u>. Using the <u>input</u>, <u>output variables of tb</u> from $Inp(tb)$, $Outp(tb)$, respectively, we define

$$(3.5) \quad Inp(Fd) \underset{df}{=} \bigcup_{tb \in TrBr_{Fd}} Inp(tb) \quad \text{and} \quad Outp(Fd) \underset{df}{=} \bigcup_{tb \in TrBr_{Fd}} Outp(tb).$$

The flow diagram Fd is called <u>input</u>, <u>output homogeneous</u> if

$$(3.6) \quad Inp(tb) = Inp(tb^*), \quad Outp(tb) = Outp(tb^*), \text{ respectively, for all } tb, tb^* \in TrBr_{Fd}.$$

If <u>input commands</u> $=: x$ (or LOADx) and <u>output commands</u> $x =:$ (or STOREx and PRINTx), where $x \in Var$, are admitted (they are considered as parts of restoring commands), and if Fd is output homogeneous then the output commands can be inserted in Fd in such a way that

$$(3.7) \quad y \in Outp(tb) \iff \text{there is exactly one occurence of the output}$$
command $y =:$ in tb and this occurence is to the right of the output occurence of y in tb

holds for each $tb \in TrBr_{Fd}$.

In Fig. 3 a flow diagram Fd is shown, which is not output homogeneous and which does not allow any insertion of output commands according to (3.7) because $TrBr_{Fd}$ contains $tb_1 = (1,yes,2,4,yes,5,6)$, $tb_2 = (1,no,3,4,no,6)$ and $tb_3 = (1,yes,2,4,yes,5,6)$, but $Outp(tb_1) = Outp(tb_2) = \{t\}$ and $Outp(tb_3) = \{y\}$. The output command $t =:$ can be inserted neither between 5 and 6, nor between 4 and 6, thus nowhere.

If Fd is an almost tree then the insertion of output commands according to (3.7) is possible always.

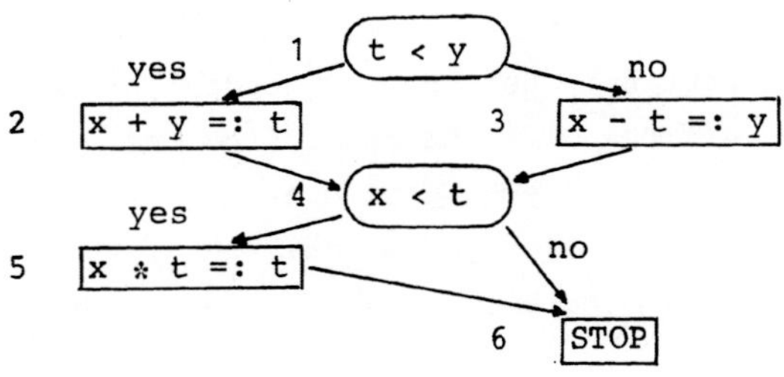

Fig. 3

Let us remind that an insertion of an output command in a cycle (in the
graph theoretical sense) leads to a new type of evaluated functions, because a sequence of output values is determined to one single input
value (see Sect. 5).

Let us distinguish the occurences of variables (of perticular commands)
within a truth branch tb, within a flow diagram Fd by the <u>left lower</u>,
<u>left upper</u> indeces, respectively, and let us add the new auxiliary
symbol $_o x$ as the <u>input occurence</u> of $x \in \text{Inp(tb)}$, which preceds all other
occurences of x, so far as no input commands are admitted.

If $pa = (v_1, \ldots, v_N)$ is a monoton path in Fd underlying the truth branch
$tb = (\lambda(v_1), \Lambda(v_1, v_2), \ldots, \lambda(v_N))$ then the <u>scope</u> $Sc_{tb}(_j x)$ and the vertex
scope $VerSc_{tb}(_j x)$ of $_j x$ in tb are defined as follows

(3.8) (i) $Sc_{tb}(_j x) =_{df} \{_h x; \; _h x$ is an applied occurence of x in tb being between $_j x$ and the next defining occurence of x, if any$\}$,
and

(ii) $VerSc_{tb}(_j x) =_{df} \{v_k; \; r < k \leq s$, where $_j x$ belongs to $\lambda(v_r)$ and
the most right occurence of x in $Sc_{tb}(_j x)$ belongs to $\lambda(v_s)\}$.

Now the <u>scope</u> and <u>vertex scope of an occurence</u> $^i x$ in Fd is defined as
follows

(3.9) (i) $Sc_{Fd}(^i x) =_{df} \{^p x; \;$ there exists a $tb \in TrBr_{Fd}$ and a defining
occurence $_j x$ in tb such that $_j x = {}^i x$ and an applied occurence
$_k x$ in tb such that $_k x \in Sc_{tb}(_j x)$ and $_k x = {}^p x\}$;

(ii) $VerSc_{Fd}(^i x) =_{df} \{w \in V; \;$ there exist a $tb \in TrBr_{Fd}$ and a defining occurence $_j x$ in tb such that $_j x = {}^i x$ and $w \in VerSc_{tb}(_j x)\}$.

Obviously the same "content" must be stored at all occurences of a scope
and therefore this "content" must not be changed during the execution
of all commands of vertices which belong to the corresponding vertex
scope. This gives us a sufficient knowledge for renaming variables in
order e.g. to economize the storage. A <u>renaming of Fd</u> is a mapping ν,
which is defined for all occurences of variables in Fd and such that

(3.1o) (i) ^ix and ^hy are the defining occurences such that $x \neq y$ and
$\qquad \text{VerSc}_{Fd}(^ix) \cap \text{VerSc}_{Fd}(^hy) \neq 0 \implies \nu(^ix) \neq \nu(^hy)$;

(ii) $^jx \in \text{Sc}_{Fd}(^ix) \implies \nu(^ix) = \nu(^jx)$;

(iii) if ^ix and ^hy are output occurence then: $x \neq y \Longleftrightarrow \nu(^ix) \neq \nu(^hy)$.

Flow diagrams Fd and Fd* are <u>similar</u> if one arises from the other by a
renaming of its variables. From the similarity the functional equivalence follows (with respect to the renaming of input and output variables) [22,33]. The number of different variables, which occur in Fd, is
called its <u>width</u> and the minimal width in the class of similar flow
diagrams is the chromatic number of the <u>scope graph of Fd</u>, the vertices
of which are maximal sets D_r of defining occurences in Fd such that

(3.11) (i) $^ix, ^jx \in D_r \implies$ there are scopes $R_1, R_2, \ldots, R_n$ of Fd such
$\qquad$ that $R_1 = \text{Sc}_{Fd}(^ix)$, $R_n = \text{Sc}_{Fd}(^jx)$ and $R_k \cap R_{k+1} \neq \emptyset$ for
$\qquad$ $k = 1, 2, \ldots, n-1$,

and two vertices D_r and D_s are connected by an (undirected) edge if

(3.11) (ii)   there are $^ix \in D_r$, $^jx \in D_s$ such that $\text{VerSc}_{Fd}(^ix) \cap$
$\qquad$ $\cap \text{VerSc}_{Fd}(^jx) \neq \emptyset$.

The assertion about the chromatic number of the scope graph generalizes
concrete combinatorial results of the sort in [24,25], which is visualized on the following figures 4, 5 and 6.

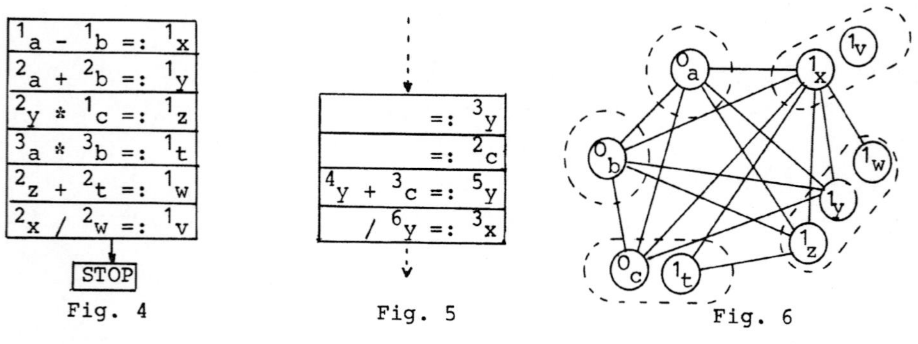

Fig. 4   Fig. 5   Fig. 6

In Fig. 4 a flow diagram of the arithmetic expression (a-b)/((a+b)*c +
+ (a * b)) is presented with the greatest possible width, because each
variable has exactly one defining occurence, and in Fig. 6 is the corresponding scope graph, which is represented in such a way that its chromatic decomposition of the smallest cardinality 5 is distinguished by
dotted lines. This decomposition allows to rename the Fig. 4 and to get
Fig. 5, where only the changed places are presented.

Using scopes we have a sufficient knowledge about all intermediate results, i.e. where they are stored and also how long it is necessary to
keep them, which can be used for clearing up the storage.

There are known many transformations of flow diagrams which keep the
functional equivalence in all interpretations but we would like to have
such transformations under which the structural equivalence or even the
method of Sect. 1 is invariant. An other point of view is the study of
transformations which keep the functional equivalence not in all interpretations but only in such interpretations which satisfy certain axioms
concerning the relational structure, i.e. the functional unit of the
computer.

Finally let us remind the crucial concept [22] of partial ordering relation $\leq_{int}$ among the flow diagram. One write $Fd \leq_{int} Fd^*$ if each function F_j which can be evaluated by Fd can also be evaluated by Fd^* under
the same interpretation int (but there can exist a function F_k^* evaluable
by Fd^* and not evaluable by Fd). Thus Fd^* is <u>an output extension of</u> Fd.
By inserting proper restoring commands (with new variables on their
right sides) all possible output extensions can be obtained. Thus there
exists the <u>output extension closure</u> of each flow diagram which is a
suitable concept for a mathematical study.

4. Automodifying stored programs (routines and procedures)

In this section a program will be understood according to (2.7), i.e.
as a stored program $P = (K^0;K^1;...;K^N)$ where $K^i = \langle b^i,c^i \rangle$ and $b^i \in$ Lab,
$c^i \in$ Comm, because the modifying commands (2.8)(i)-(iii) were formula-
ted for stored programs (and not for flow diagrams, where the labelling
λ of vertices would be modified). Therefore the general case of state
$S \in Cont^{Loc}$ is assumed.

The flow diagrams are more convenient for actual solving particular
mathematical problems, while stored programs are natural if several

problems have been solved already and the question arises how to compose the parts into the whole.

New problems arise when we have many (stored) programs and therefore a shortage of free labels, because in general two different programs must not have any label in common, although they could have common variables so far as their parallel execution is not allowed. If there are several "parts" of these programs, which are similar (3.9) each the other, then they can be taken off and replaced by side jumps to one of them, which is stored separately and provided at its "end" with a return jump. This is the "routine" and if its length is long enough and the number of similar "parts" sufficiently high then some labels are saved when routines are used.

We assume that essentially each program can be a routine, but we add the requirement (3.6) of output homogenity, because each program of this sort can be transformed into a new program P, which is functionally equivalent to the given one and which is <u>standard</u>, i.e.

(4.1) c^N = STOP and $c^i \neq$ STOP for i = 0,1,...,N-1,

which requires some GOTO-commands. In $\left[45\right]$ only flow diagrams with the unique stopping command are admitted.

An <u>open routine</u> R is a sequence of labelled commands over Comm, which arised from a standard program P = ($\langle b^0,$START$\rangle$;$\langle b^1,c^1\rangle$;$\ldots$;$\langle b^N,$STOP$\rangle$), where Inp(P) = $\{x_1,\ldots,x_n\}$ and Outp(P) = $\{y_1,\ldots,y_m\}$, by adding the <u>input</u> and <u>output segments</u> as follows

(4.2)(i)   (input segment)   R = ($\langle c_1^*,? =: x_1\rangle$;$\ldots$;$\langle c_n^*,? =: x_n\rangle$;

       (kernel) $\langle b^1,c^1\rangle$;$\ldots$;$\langle b^{N-1},c^{N-1}\rangle$;$\langle b^N,$EMPTY$\rangle$;

       (output segment) $\langle d_1^*,y_1 =: ?\rangle$;$\ldots$;$\langle d_m^*,y_m =: ?\rangle$)

where EMPTY is a new regular command which does not change the states of the storage and ? ε Var is an arbitrary variable.

A <u>closed routine</u> arises from an open one if we add at its end

(4.2)(ii) (return jump) $\langle e_1^*,$GOTO?$\rangle$

where ? ε Lab is an arbitrary label.

The input and output variables of the kernel are called the input and output variables of the routine, respectively.

Let MacrSymb be a new set of symbols, called <u>macro-symbols</u> and let the following string

(4.3)(i) $M(z_1,\ldots,z_n) =: (t_1,\ldots,t_m)$, where $M \in$ MacrSymb and z_i, $t_j \in$ Var,

be called a <u>macro-command</u>. The occurence of z_i, t_j in (4.3)(i) is called applied, defining, respectively, and the integer n, m is called the <u>input</u>, <u>output arity</u> of the macro-symbol M, respectively.

Each macro-command is considered as regular and its macro-symbol M will be not interpreted, but defined in its definition (or declaration)

(4.3)(ii) $M =_{df} [[x_1,\ldots,x_n;y_1,\ldots,y_m];Q]$ where Q is an arbitrary program such that $\text{Inp}(Q) = \{x_1,\ldots,x_n\}$, $\text{Outp}(Q) = \{y_1,\ldots,y_m\}$ and n, m is the input, output arity of M.

A <u>macro-program</u> is an ordered set of labelled commands or macro-commands, which otherwise satisfies (2.7), and the <u>computer macro-language</u>, i.e. the computer language with definitions, is the extension of the original computer language, when the macro-programs are admitted also. The meaning of a macro-program is determined by interpretation and by definitions of its macro-commands, which are translations into the original computer language (and therefore the compiler of computer macro-language into the computer language itself is clear and transparent).

Let Decl $=_{df} \{M_1 =_{df} [[x_1^1,\ldots,x_{n_1}^1;y_1^1,\ldots,y_{m_1}^1];Q_1],\ldots,M_r =_{df} [[x_1^r,\ldots\ldots,x_{n_r}^r;y_1^r,\ldots,y_{m_r}^r];Q_r]\}$ be the set of definitions of macro-symbols $M_1,\ldots,M_r$. A <u>macro-program MP</u> (of the computer macro-language) <u>with</u> <u>declaration Decl</u><MP,Decl> satisfies

(4.3)(iii)   to each macro-symbol M, which occurs in MP, there exists an integer i such that $M = M_i$, $1 \leq i \leq r$, and $|\text{Inp}(Q_i)|$, $|\text{Outp}(Q_i)|$ is the input, output arity of M, respectively, and

(iv) Q_i is a standard program for $i = 1,2,\ldots,r$.

The meaning of the macro-program MP with declarations Decl is defined as follows. Let Rout $= \{R_1,\ldots,R_r\}$ be a set of closed routines, which arised from the programs $Q_1, \ldots, Q_r$, such that they do not have any label (and if necessary also any variable) in common. The set Rout is a <u>routine library</u>. The <u>bearer program BP for Rout</u> is a program, which arises from the macro-program MP by replacing each occurence of a macro-command (4.3)(i) by the following sequence of labelled commands

$$(4.4) \quad \text{(input modif.)} \quad <c_1, \text{LMODIF}(z_1)c_1^*>; \ldots; <c_n, \text{LMODIF}(z_n)c_n^*>;$$
$$\text{(output modif.)} \quad <d_1, \text{RMODIF}(t_1)d_1^*>; \ldots; <d_m, \text{RMODIF}(t_m)d_m^*>;$$
$$\text{(return modif.)} \quad <e_1, \text{MODIF}(b)e_1^*>;$$
$$\text{(side jump)} \quad <e_2, \text{GOTO}c_1^*>,$$

where b is the next label after the macro-command under consideration, further c_i, d_j and e_k are new labels, and finally the corresponding declaration is (4.3)(ii).

Then the <u>routine program</u> $RP = (BP, R_1, \ldots, R_r)$, which is the ordered set of labelled commands from $BP, R_1, \ldots, R_r$, determines the meaning of the $<MP,$ Decl$>$. The routine program RP is called automodifying program because some modifying commands are used in it.

Obviously, if P^* arises from MP by replacing each occurence of a macro-command by the corresponding (with respect to Decl) open routine, which is properly renamed (3.9) and restored at new labels (and after the necessary adjustments of labels which belong to relational commands and to GOTOs), then $P^* = {}_{int}RP$ in all interpretations int and P^* is not an automodifying program, but usually essentially longer than RP.

Using the store commands (2.9)(i)-(v) instead of the modifying ones the same effect can be reached if the closed routine (4.2) is replaced by the following one

$$(4.5) \quad R^* = (<c_1^*, \text{ref } x_1^* =: x_1>; \ldots; <c_n^*, \text{ref } x_n^* =: x_n>;$$
$$<b^1, C^1>; \ldots; <b^{N-1}, C^{N-1}>; <b^N, \text{EMPTY}>;$$
$$<d_1^*, y_1 =: \text{ref } y_1^*>; \ldots; <d_m^*, y_m =: \text{ref } y_m^*>;$$
$$<e_1^*, 1\text{GOTO}x_o>)$$

and the modifying commands in (4.4) are replaced by

$$(4.6) \quad <c_1, z_1 =: x_1^{**}>; \ldots; <c_n, z_n =: x_n^{**}>;$$
$$<d_1, t_1 \equiv: y_1^* >; \ldots; <d_m, t_m \equiv: y_m^* >;$$
$$<e_1, b \equiv: x_o>;$$

$$\langle e_2, \text{GOTOc}_1^* \rangle$$

where the same conditions must be added as above, and in addition each state S must satisfy the following assumptions concerning the pointers x_i and y_j where $1 \leq i \leq n$, $1 \leq j \leq m$

$$(4.7) \qquad\qquad S(x_i^*) = x_i^{**} \text{ and } S(y_j^*) = y_j^{**}.$$

Thus the second sort of routine program $RP^* = (BP^*, R_1^*, \ldots, R_r^*)$ is defined and it holds $RP^* = {}_{int}RP$ in all interpretations int.

Within the computer macro-language a natural and important generalization consists in admission macro-commands in routines also, and therefore in admission of macro-programs in declarations. These macro-programs are called <u>procedures</u> and the occurences of the corresponding macro-commands are called <u>procedure calls</u>. The constructions (4.2) and (4.5) lead from procedures to <u>macro-routines</u>, i.e. it is allowed to use a side jump in any macro-routine and not only in the bearer program as before.

One says that the procedure declarations $\text{Decl} = \{MR_1 = {}_{df}[[x_1^1, \ldots, x_{n_1}^1; y_1^1, \ldots, y_{m_1}^1]; MQ_1], \ldots, MR_r = {}_{df}[[x_1^r, \ldots, x_{n_r}^r; y_1^r, \ldots, y_{m_r}^r]; MQ_r]\}$ require a <u>recursive call</u> if there exists a finite sequence of macro-symbols $MR_{i_1}, MR_{i_2}, \ldots, MR_{i_k}$ such that: (i) $1 < k$; (ii) $1 \leq i_j \leq r$ for each $j = 1, 2, \ldots, k$; (iii) the macro-symbol MR_{i_j} occurs in the procedure $MQ_{i_{j+1}}$ for each $j = 1, 2, \ldots, k-1$; and (iv) $MR_{i_k} = MR_{i_1}$.

In this case a new problem arises because before finishing the execution of MR_{i_1} the same MR_{i_k} should be started again. Within the computer language this conflict can be avoided either (I) by having more "exemplars" of the closed macro-routine MR_{i_1}, which all are similar each the other, but they are stored separately and therefore they are usable simultaneously (in addition a mechanism of counting the exemplares actually used is required), or (II) by using the mechanism of interruptions, or finally (III) by infinite insertions of the suitably modified exemplars of open macro-routines in the bearer macro-program, which corresponds to the "copy rule" of higher languages, and which can be admitted in the computer macro-language also.

Obviously the interruptions require a stack storage for the storing all intermediate results and other things, which must be saved for certain time, in order to be able to finish the interrupted activity under the original conditions.

(I) Let us consider the first possibility and let

$$(4.2^*) \qquad {}^s MR_i = (<{}^s c_1^i,? =: {}^s x_1^i>;\dots;<{}^s c_{n_i}^i,? =: {}^s x_{n_i}^i>;$$
$$<{}^s b_1^i,{}^s C_1^i>;\dots;<{}^s b_h^i,{}^s C_h^i>;\dots;<{}^s b_{N_i}^i,{}^s C_{N_i}^i>;$$
$$<{}^s d_1^i,{}^s y_1^i =: ?>;\dots;<{}^s d_{m_i}^i,{}^s y_{m_i}^i =: ?>;$$
$$<{}^s e_1^i,GOTO?>)$$

be the s-th exemplar of the i-th macro-routine MR_i, where $1 \le i \le r$, for $s = 1,2,\dots$ If in (4.2^*) the procedure call ${}^s C_h^i = \big[MR_j(z_1^j,\dots,z_{n_j}^j) =: =: (t_1^j,\dots,t_{m_j}^j)\big]$ of the j-th macro-routine occurs, where $1 \le j \le r$, then this call must be replaced by the following sequence of commands

$$(4.4^*) \qquad <{}^s b_h^i,EMPTY>;<hc_1^j,LMODIF(z_1^j)^{s+1}c_1^j>;\dots;<hc_{n_j}^j,LMODIF(z_{n_j}^j)^{s+1}c_{n_j}^j>;$$
$$<hd_1^j,RMODIF(t_1^j)^{s+1}d_1^j>;\dots;<hd_{m_j}^j,RMODIF(t_{m_j}^j)^{s+1}c_{m_j}^j>;$$
$$<he_1^j,MODIF({}^s b_{h+1}^i)^{s+1}e_1^j>;$$
$$<he_2^j,GOTO^{s+1}c_1^j>$$

and the same must be done also in MP, thus let us admit $i = 0$ and put $MP = MR_o$. Let ${}^s MR_i^*$ arise from ${}^s MR_i$ after all required replacements (4.4^*) and let MR_o^* arise from $MR_o = MP$ similary. Then the <u>procedure program</u> is the sequence of labelled commands $PP^* = (MR_o^*, {}^1 MR_1^*, {}^1 MR_2^*,\dots, {}^1 MR_r^*, {}^2 MR_1^*, {}^2 MR_2^*,\dots, {}^2 MR_r^*,\dots, {}^s MR_1^*, {}^s MR_2^*,\dots, {}^s MR_r^*,\dots)$ which can be infinite and which clearly defines certain functions evaluable by it, and they are the functional meaning of macro-program with procedures $<MP,Decl>$.

(II) In the second possiblity the interruptions will be used. Let each macro-routine MR_i have the following form

$$(4.2^{**}) \qquad MR_i = (<c_1^i,? =: x_1^i>;\dots;<c_{n_i}^i,? =: x_{n_i}^i>;$$
$$<b_1^i,C_1^i>;\dots;<b_h^i,C_h^i>;\dots;<b_N^i,EMPTY>;$$
$$<d_1^i,y_1^i =: ?>;\dots;<d_{m_i}^i,y_{m_i}^i =: ?>;$$
$$<e_1^i,GOTO?>,$$

where $i = 1,2,\ldots,r$, and let each procedure call $c_h^i = [MR_j(z_1^j,\ldots,z_{n_j}^j) =: (t_1^j,\ldots,t_{m_j}^j)]$, where $1 \leq j \leq r$, be replaced by the following sequence of labelled commands

$$
\begin{aligned}
(4.4^{**})\quad &<b_h^i,\text{EMPTY}>;<cf_1^i,c_1^i =: u_1>;\ldots;<cf_{n_i}^i,c_{n_i}^i =: u_{n_i}>; \\[4pt]
&<df_{n_i+1}^i,d_1^i =: u_{n_i+1}>;\ldots;<df_{n_i+m_i}^i,d_{m_i}^i =: u_{n_i+m_i}>; \\[4pt]
&<ef_{n_i+m_i+1}^i,e_1^i =: u_{n_i+m_i+1}>; \\[4pt]
&<f_1^i,w_1 =: u_{n_i+m_i+2}>;\ldots;<f_{p_i}^i,w_{p_i} =: u_{n_i+m_i+p_i+1}>; \\[4pt]
&<f_o^i,dr + 1 =: dr>; \\[4pt]
&<cc_1^j,\text{LMODIF}(z_1^j)c_1^j>;\ldots;<cc_{n_j}^j,\text{LMODIF}(z_{n_j}^j)c_{n_j}^j>; \\[4pt]
&<dd_1^j,\text{RMODIF}(t_1^j)d_1^j>;\ldots;<dd_{n_j}^j,\text{RMODIF}(t_{m_j}^j)d_{m_j}^j>; \\[4pt]
&<ee_1^j,\text{MODIF}(g_o^i)e_1^j>; \\[4pt]
&<e_2^j,\text{GOTO}c_1^j>; \\[4pt]
&<g_o^i,dr - 1 =: dr>; \\[4pt]
&<cg_1^i,u_1 =: c_1^i>;\ldots;<cg_{n_i}^i,u_{n_i} =: c_{n_i}^i>; \\[4pt]
&<dg_1^i,u_{n_i+1} =: d_1^i>;\ldots;<dg_{m_i}^i,u_{n_i+m_i} =: d_{m_i}^i>; \\[4pt]
&<eg_1^i,u_{n_i+m_i+1} =: e_1^i>; \\[4pt]
&<g_1^i,u_{n_i+m_i+2} =: w_1>;\ldots;<g_{p_i}^i,u_{n_i+m_i+p_i+1} =: w_{p_i}>; \\[4pt]
&<b_{h+1}^i,c_{h+1}^i>
\end{aligned}
$$

where $u_1,u_2,\ldots,u_{n_i+m_i+p_i+1}$ are stack variables, dr is the stack depth register, and $w_1,w_2,\ldots,w_{p_i}$ are all variables or labels at which are stored those contents, which must be saved. In the same manner the procedure calls in the bearer macro-program $MP = MR_o$ must be replaced.

Let MR_i^{**} arise from MR_i for $i = 0,1,\ldots,r$ by the replacement (4.4^{**}). Then the _procedure program_ is the following finite sequence of labelled commands $PP^{**} = (MR_o^{**}, MR_1^{**},\ldots,MR_r^{**})$, the latent infinity of which is in possible infinity of the used stack. Obviously $PP^{**} = {}_{int}PP^*$ in each int.

(III) The third possibility of using the copy rule is the most often

used in the higher level languages [1o,11,12,27,28,29] although it is
the least transparent one. In the higher level languages the copy rule
concern certain strings of symbols in the same way as the substitutions
are used in mathematics, without any connection to the computer storage.
But the concept of mathematical substitution does not satisfy the requirement of computer constructivism, according to which each intermediate result of the computing process must be stored at (or must be
denoted by) a concrete label or variable, and the different occurences
of the same symbol are considered as different things nearly always
(as it is necessary at any description on changes in time).

5. Types of problems. Structure of storage and data structures

If we assume that the only aim of computer consists in evaluation of
output values for the given input values, i.e. in evaluation of one or
more functions, then the types of problems (solved at computers) can be
classified according to the types of evaluated functions, where the
type of a function is determined by logical types [3o,2] of its domain
and range, or by logical types of composed objects, which are their
elements [31,32,33].

In the previous sections 3 and 4 only the n-ary functions $f^{(n)}$ were
considered, i.e. Domain$f^{(n)} \subset \text{Obj}^n$ and Range$f^{(n)} \subset \text{Obj}$, where $n \geq 1$
and Obj is the set of basic objects, which can be stored at the parti-
cular basic locations of the storage directly. The n-tuples $(a_1, a_2, \ldots$
$\ldots, a_n) \; \varepsilon \; \text{Obj}^n$ are composed objects for $n \geq 2$. It is possible to restrict
the considerations to the case $n = 2$, as it is done in [34]. The type
of an n-ary function $f^{(n)}$ can be $((\underbrace{*,*,\ldots,*}_{n \text{ times}}); (*))$.

With respect to Turing machine and its (one-sided) infinite tape a func-
tion F is called a tape function if Domain $F \subset \bigcup\limits_{n=1} \text{Obj}^n$ and Range $F \subset$
$\bigcup\limits_{m=1} \text{Obj}^m$, which cannot be evaluated by a computer without any structure
of storage. One possibility how to compare Turing machine with a com-
puter directly, i.e. without any mediating coding, consists in taking
locations as natural numbers and in admitting that each natural number
is a location [35], but computers are not used in this way. The second
possibility consists in accepting the assumption

(5.1) Loc $\times$ Loc $\subset$ Cont, i.e. at a location a pair of other locations
      can be stored.

In principle it is sufficient to have the possibility to store only the

pairs of locations, because their n-tuples, where n = 3,4,..., can always be defined by iterated evaluation of states of storage (in this way
also the lists are introduced by S-expressions in [34]). This concerns
also the translation of macro-commands, where the macro-symbols can have
an arbitrary high input and output arity.

E.g. the sorting problem has the type of a tape function, because it is
required to determine to a sequence of numbers of an arbitrary length an
other sequence of numbers (of the same length, i.e. it is a special tape
function). Further it is clear that the sorting problem cannot be even
formulated without a structure of storage, by which the ordering of natural numbers is representable. In addition nearly all standard problems
required in operating systems are of tape type and cannot be formulated
without assumed tape structure of storage.

There is a conceptual confusion in textbooks of operating systems when
data structures are introduced in general, i.e. there is no clear differentiation between a composed object, as a concept which is independent on the computer and its storage, and a composed location, which
must be heavily dependent on the computer and its storage [31].

Let Obj be the set of basic objects, which are considered as symbols
(i.e. objects are identified with their names of SymbObj), and let us
define the set of <u>structured objects</u> StrObj over Obj, their <u>rank</u> and
<u>arity</u> as follows

(5.2) (i) $A \in \text{Obj} \implies A \in \text{StrObj}$; $\text{rank}A = 0$ and $\text{arity}A = 1$;

   (ii) $A_i \in \text{StrObj}$ for $i = 1,2,\ldots,n$, where $n \geq 1 \implies (A_1,A_2,\ldots,A_n) \in$
         $\in \text{StrObj}$;

$$\text{rank}(A_1,A_2,\ldots,A_n) = \max_{1 \leq i \leq n} \text{rank}A_i + 1 \text{ and}$$

$$\text{arity}(A_1,A_2,\ldots,A_n) = \sum_{i=1}^{n} \text{arity}A_i,$$

which agrees with [31] and corresponds to the usual logical types [30,2],
but there is no more an agreement in the definition of the set StrLoc of
<u>structured locations</u> (or macro-locations) over the set of basic loca-
tions Loc

(5.3) (i) $L \in \text{Loc} \implies L \in \text{StrLoc}$; $\text{rank}L = 0$, $\text{base}L = \text{free}L = \{L\}$ and
         $\text{lead}L = L$;

(5.3)(ii) $L_i \in$ StrLoc and $baseL_i \cap baseL_j = \emptyset$, where $i \neq j$ for all

$i,j = 1,2,\ldots,n$ and $n \geq 1$; $L_o \in$ Loc and $L_o \notin \bigcup_{i=1}^{n} baseL_i \Longrightarrow$

$L = L_o(L_1,L_2,\ldots,L_n) \in$ StrLoc;

$rankL = \max_{1 \leq i \leq n} rankL_i + 1$;

$baseL = \{L_o\} \cup \bigcup_{i=1}^{n} baseL_i$; $freeL = \bigcup_{i=1}^{n} freeL_i$; $leadL = L_o$,

where simultaneously the <u>rank</u>, <u>base</u>, <u>leading location</u> lead and the <u>set of free locations</u> free of each structured location are defined.

One sees immediately that each $L' \in baseL$ is the leading location of exactly one <u>sublocation of L</u>. If $L = L_o(L_1,\ldots,L_n)$ then L_i is the <u>i-th main sublocation of L</u>, and the arity of L is defined as follows: $arityL = = |freeL|$.

A structured location $L \in$ StrObj belongs to a state of storage $S \in$ $\in$ Cont^{Loc} if

(5.4) $L_o' \in baseL - freeL$ and $L_o'(L_1',\ldots,L_m')$ is a sublocation of L, where L_o' is its leading location $\Longrightarrow S(L_o') = (leadL_1',\ldots,leadL_m')$, i.e. at the basic location L_o' the leading locations $leadL_i'$ of all main sublocations L of the sublocation $L_o'(L_1',\ldots,L_m')$ are stored in the same order as they occur in the sublocation itself,

which obviously assumes the following requirement concerning the storage

(5.5) $Loc^n \subset$ Cont for each $n = 1,2,\ldots$

As (5.5) is not acceptable for the computer language itself we introduce the second extension of the computer language, when besides the macro-commands also the macro-locations are admitted, together with the definitions (or declaration) of macro-locations themselves. The translation of this general computer macro-language, i.e. of macro-locations into sets of basic locations, is determined by the definitions of structured locations and is the same as the translation of the general list expressions of LISP into the original S-expressions in [34]. For the user the generality of structured locations and structured objects is very important and useful (because (5.1) is too restrictive for the usual mathematical thinking, which naturally requires (5.5)).

Using the graph representation of structured objects and structured locations, which are directed rooted trees with labelled vertices and edges, one can easily define that an $A \in$ StrObj <u>can be stored</u> at a $L \in$ StrLoc if

(5.6) the trees which represent A and L are isomorphic (and the label of corresponding edges are the same).

Then also arityA = arityL = $|$freeL$|$.

If (5.6) and also (5.4) holds, i.e. L belongs to the state S, then one says that <u>A is stored at L with respect to S</u> if

(5.7) in S at the i-th basic location $L_i \in$ freeL (from the left to right) the i-th basic object of A is stored for each i = 1,2,... ...,arityA.

The type of a structured object A arises from A by replacing each basic object of A by an auxiliary symbol * (according to [30]). If A' is a subobject of A then the type typeA' of A' is a subtype of the type typeA, and we write typeA' $\leq$ typeA. Each subobject A' of A is determined by its <u>tree coordinates</u> $(i_1, i_2, \ldots, i_k)$ uniquely, where i_j are labels of edges in the rooted path of the graph representation of A, which starts at the root of A and terminates at the root of A'.

A function F has the type (typeA,typeB) if typeA' $\leq$ typeA and typeB' $\leq$ $\leq$ typeB for each A' $\in$ DomainF and each B' $\in$ RangeF. If A,B is stored at the structured location L_A, L_B, respectively, and if freeL$_A$ = $\{x_1, \ldots, x_n\}$ and freeL$_B$ = $\{y_1, \ldots, y_m\}$, then it would be possible to use the macro-command $M(L_A)$ =: (L_B) within the computer macro-language also before we know the actual program for evaluating F (where L_A and L_B are ordered in a way), as it is meant in the heuristics of structured programming [20,47].

<u>References</u>
[1] Annual review in automatic programming I (ed.R.Goodman), Pergamon Press, New York-Oxford-London-Paris, 1960
[2] Kreisel, G. and J.-L. Krivine: Modelltheorie, Springer, Berlin-Heidelberg-New York 1972

[3] Perlis, A.J. and K. Samelson: Preliminary report of ACM-GAMM Committee
     on an International Algebraic Language, Annual review in automatic
     programming, vol. I, Pergamon Press, New York-Oxford-London-Paris
     1960, 268-290

[4] Church, A.: The Calculi of Lambda-Conversion, Princeton University
     Press, Princeton 1941

[5] Gödel, K.: Über formal unentscheidbare Sätze der Principia Mathe-
     matica und verwandter Systeme I, Monatshefte für Mathematik und
     Physik 38 (1931), 173-198

[6] Čulík, K.: Algorithmization of algebras and relational structures,
     Com. Math. Universitatis Carolinae 13, 3 (1972), 457-477

[7] Čulík, K.: Syntactical definitions of program and flow diagram,
     Aplikace matematiky 18 (1973), 280-301

[8] Neumann, J.v. Collected Works V: Design of computers, Theory of
     Automata and Numerical Analysis, Pergamon Press, Oxford-London-
     New York-Paris 1963

[9] Metropolis, N. and J. Worlton: A trilogy of errors in the history of
     computing, First USA-Japan Computer Conference Proceedings, AFIPS
     & IPSJ, Tokyo 1972, 683-691

[10] Naur, P. et.al.: Report on the algorithmic language ALGOL 60, Comm.
     ACM, vol. 3 (1960), 299-314

[11] Naur, P. et.al.: Revised report on the algorithmic language ALGOL 60,
     Comm. ACM, vol. 6 (1963), 1-17

[12] Wijngaarden, A.v. and B.J. Mailoux, J.E.L. Peck, C.H.A. Koster:
     ALGOL 68, Math. Centrum, Amsterdam 1968

[13] Tarski, A.: Wahrheitsbegriff in den formalisierten Sprachen, Studia
     Philosophica I (1935), Lwów, 261-405

[14] Bauer, F.L. and G. Goos: Informatik I, II, Springer, Berlin-Heidel-
     berg-New York 1971

[15] Luckham, D.S. and D.M.P. Park, M.S. Paterson: On formalized computer
     programs, Jour. of Computer and System Sciences 4 (1970), 220-249

[16] Manna, Z.: Program Schemas, in Currents in the Theory of Computing
     (editor A.V. Aho), Prentice Hall 1973, 90-142

[17] Čulík, K.: Extensions of rooted trees and their applications (in
     print in Discrete Mathematics), 26 p.

[18] Engeler, E.: Structure and Meaning of Elementary Programs, in Sym-
     posium on the Semantics of Algorithmic Languages (editor E. Enge-
     ler), Springer Lecture Notes in Math., vol. 188, 1971

[19] Engeler, E.: Introduction to the theory of computation, Academic
     Press, New York 1973

[20] Horejs, J.: Structured programming (Czech), Proceedings of Software

Seminar 1974, Research Comp. Centre of UN, Bratislava, Nov. 1974, 11-58

[21] Pawlak, Z.: Programmed Machines (Polish), Algorithmy V (1969), Polish Academy of Sciences, Warsow, 5-19

[22] Čulík, K.: Programming theories and languages (Czech), a textbook for graduated students, mimeographed in Research Institute for Mathematical Machines, Prague 1973, 143 p.

[23] Čulík, K.: Algorithmic algebras for computers, Proceedings of International Symposium and Summer School on Mathematical Foundations of Computer Science, Warsow, August 1972 (see also Czech. Math. Jour. 23 (98), 1973, 670-689)

[24] Sethi, R. and J.D. Ullman: The generation of optimal code for arithmetic expressions, Jour. ACM 17 (1970), 715-728

[25] Čulík, K.: A note on complexity of algorithmic nets without cycles, Aplikace matematiky 16 (1971), 297-301

[26] Čulík, K.: Structural similarity of programs and some concepts of algorithmic method, Proceedings of 1. Fachtagung über Programmiersprachen der Gesellschaft für Informatik, Lecture Notes in Economics and Mathematical Systems 75, Springer, Berlin-Heidelberg-New York 1972

[27] Langmaack, H.: On procedures as open subroutines I, Acta Informatica 2 (1973), 311-333

[28] de Bakker, J.W.: Recursive Procedures, Math. Centre Tracts 24, Math. Centrum, Amsterdam

[29] Scott, D. and J.W. de Bakker: A theory of programs, unpublished notes, IBM seminar, Vienna 1969

[30] Mostowski, A.: Mathematical Logic (Polish), University Press, Warszawa-Wroclaw 1948

[31] Walk, K.: Modelling of Storage Properties of Higher-Level Languages, Int. Jour. of Comp. and Inf. Sciences 2, March 1973, 1-24

[32] Čulík, K.: On logical types of structured individuals and their application in computer theory, submitted for IFIP WG 2.2 meeting in Rigi, January 1, 1975 (in print), 14 p.

[33] Čulík, K.: Logical analysis of the concept of data structure (Czech), (in print), 26 p.

[34] McCarthy, J. and P.W. Abrahams, D.J. Edwards, T.P. Hart, M.I. Levin: LISP 1.5 Programmar's Manual, MIT Press, Cambridge 1962, 2.ed.

[35] Čulík, K.: A note on comparison of Turing machines with computers, (in print), 18 p.

[36] Dömölki, B.: On the formal definition of assembly language, Proceedings of the Symposium on Mathematical Foundations of Computer Science, High Tatras, September 1973, 39-50

[37] Čulík, K.: The importance of formal methods for definition of programming languages and operating systems, the invited talk to
GAMM Tagung 1975 (in print)

[38] Dijkstra, E.W.: Co-operating sequential processes, in Programming
languages (editor F. Genuys), Academic Press 1968

[39] Petri, C.A.: Kommunikation mit Automaten, University of Bonn, 1962

[40] Petri, C.A.: Concepts of Net Theory, Proceedings of Symposium on
Mathematical Foundations of Computer Science, High Tatras, September 1973, 137-146

[41] Čulík, K.: Equivalence of parallel courses of algorithmic nets and
precedence flow diagrams, Proceedings of Symposium on Mathematical
Foundations of Computer Science, High Tatras, September 1973, 27-38

[42] Dömölki, B.: On the formal definition of assembly language, Proceedings of Symposium on Math. Found. of Comp. Science, High Tatras,
September 1973, 39-50

[43] McFarland, C.: A language-oriented computer design, AFIPS Conference
Proceedings 37 (1970), 629-640

[44] Meade, R.M.: On memory system design, AFIPS Conference Proceedings
37 (1970), 33-43

[45] Böhm, C. and G. Jacopini: Flow Diagrams, Turing Machines and Languages with only two Formation Rules, Comm. ACM 9, May 1966, 366-371

[46] Čulík, K.: Combinatorial problems in theory of complexity of algorithmic nets without cycles for simple computers, Aplikace matematiky 16 (1971), 188-202

[47] Knuth, D.E.: Structured programming with GOTO statements, Stanford
University, STAN-CS-74-416, May 1974, 98 p.

[48] Backus, J.: Reduction languages and variable-free programming,
IBM Research RJ 1010, Yorktown Heights, April 1972, New York

[49] Hewitt, C.: Description and theoretical analysis (using schemata)
of PLANNER: A language for proving theorems and manipulating models
in a robot, Artificial Intelligence Lab. MIT, Cambridge, April 1972

[50] Winograd, T.: Understanding Natural Language, Academic Press, New
York-London, 1972

[51] Floyd, R.W.: On the nonexistence of a phrase-structure grammar for
ALGOL 60, Comm. ACM 1962, 483-484

[52] Glassover, S.M. and K.V. Hanford, C.B. Jones: The syntax machine,
Techn. Rep. 12.077, IBM United Kingdom, 1968

[53] Čulík, K.: On conditional context-free grammars for programming
and natural language, in Automatentheorie und formale Sprachen
(editors J. Dörr and G. Hotz), Bibliographisches Institut, Mannheim 1970, 209-220

SOME COMMENTS ON
PROGRAMMING LANGUAGE DESIGN

David Gries
Cornell University and
Technical University Munich

I find myself in the awkward position of talking about programming language design, without ever having designed a language myself. True, I have thought about the design of various "features", but this is vastly different from designing a complete, unified language.

Nevertheless, I do feel I have some points to make on the subject. I should like to discuss who should design (or at least have the major responsibility for) a programming language. To back up my opinion that designing a good language is a difficult task, I will describe some areas in which the designer should be proficient, and discuss why these areas are important. I will also discuss extensible languages, and show that some initial thinking on the merits of extensibility could have helped reduce the amount of wasted research that has been done in this area over the past ten years. Of course, it is always easy to look back and say what could have been; the problem is to learn something from it which we can later put to use.

As you may know, I am deeply interested in programming methodology, in learning how to efficiently produce correct and efficient programs without having to test them, in learning how to prove programs correct in a practical manner. Unfortunately, the majority of the programming languages in use today actually hinder me in this task. This may be because the language is out of date, because the designers did not have the requisite knowledge, or because they didn't use the same criteria in designing the language that I would have chosen.

Belonging to the Dijkstra-Hoare-Wirth school of thought on programming methodology, I endorse Hoare's criteria for good programming language design [1,2]:

> utmost simplicity, efficient translation, efficient execution, security, and readability.

Wirth gave the following similar criteria, used as guidelines in developing PASCAL [7]:

> clarity and rigour of description, wide range of applica-
> bility, compile-time and runtime efficiency, reliability
> (which demands simplicity and regularity of structure),
> and machine independence.

It is difficult to argue against such criteria; one might only argue more strongly in favor of other criteria, but not against these. In the context of these criteria, let us now discuss who should be designing languages.

Who Should Design a Programming Language?

In a discussion of programming language design [4], my friend and colleague Bill McKeeman said that the major responsibility for computer language design should rest with the language user. I violently disagree and feel that

> the major responsibility for language design should rest
> with a professional computer scientist educated or ex-
> perienced in that profession.

Of course, every person is entitled to design, experiment with, and use his own language. But the design of a substantial language is much more than the typical or even educated user can handle. An analogy might be made with building houses. If I want to design and build a house, I hire an architect. As the ultimate user, I of course impress my ideas on the architect. With his much greater knowledge and experience in designing and building such objects, he can show me why some of my ideas won't work, massage others so that they will work, and so on. In short, he can massage my half baked ideas into a clean unified design.

I would like to tell a story, but I will change facts and figures to protect the guilty. Several years ago a project to design and implement a new language was started. The language was to be adopted and used exclusively by several firms and universities, and thus would have quite an influence. One of the firms sent as their representative on the committee to determine initial requirements, a physicist turned programmer, presumably because he was the only "software specialist" who was not overloaded with work at the time. This specialist, whose experience consisted of 1 1/2 years of PL/I programming, immediately wrote a report for all other committee members to read, extolling the virtues of PL/I-like languages. His only criticism was that PL/I lacked a few features.

One cannot blame the programmer for this; he was doing his job as best as he knew how. The blame must lie with his superiors, who felt that language design was so easy that any user could do it. Luckily for all, the project folded.

If I, a computer scientist, after one year of study at some nuclear physics laboratory, felt that I could design a newer, better particle accelerator, the physicists would laugh me right out of my job. The design of a good programming language is just as difficult, and re- quires prior knowledge and experience in several areas.

We must be careful in designing a language, for a language can have a negative as well as a positive effect. As an example, I cite BASIC, designed by an academic user with little knowledge of compiler design or programming language theory. In my opinion, it is worse than FORTRAN, which preceded BASIC by 10 years. (This phenomenon occurs often. I think it was Hoare who said that ALGOL was a great achieve- ment - - it was a significant advance over most of its successors!) The use of BASIC spread not because it was a good language, but be- cause it filled a much needed gap (sic) in software services, and cheaply. However, today thousands of teenagers in the US are having their first algorithmic thoughts polluted by this language.

As designers, we must take more time to think deeply about the practical and theoretical implications of our languages.

Areas of Proficiency for a Language Designer

I can determine four distinct areas in which the designer must have competence:

1. Programming
2. Compiler construction

3. Style, and his native tongue
4. Theory of programming languages.

Let us discuss each of these in turn.

<u>Programming</u>

It is of course not enough to know one language, or two, or three. One must have practised programming for some time, in real-world situations, in order to understand the practical problems that arise in developing large systems.

Just as important, or more so, is a firm grasp of the newest (and oldest) thoughts on programming methodology. This should not be just a reading knowledge, but a practical, working knowledge. One must try the proposed methods out on real, live problems.

This is a conference on programming languages, and thus on programming. You all probably consider yourselves good to expert programmers, and you teach programming courses. But how many of you have proved a program correct, and how many of you enforce good programming disciplines upon your students and colleagues? If you don't <u>practise</u> good programming methodology, you cannot expect to understand it.

Now, a language cannot help the programmer in his difficult tasks: it cannot tell him how to split a problem into smaller ones, it cannot help him manage a project, it cannot tell him which algorithm is more effective, and it cannot prevent him from making mistakes.

But a language <u>can</u> <u>hinder</u> the programmer, and indeed most programming languages do. Exceptions to rules, a high astonishment factor, awkward syntax, necessary inefficiency of a particular feature due to the complexity of its design, verboseness, disagreement with traditional conventions, all these can actually slow the programmer down in completing his task.

The goal of the language designer should be to make the language seem so simple, clear, and natural, that the programmer forgets that it is there, so that he isn't bothered by its inadequacies or mistakes. To achieve this, the designer must first have an extremely good understanding of and appreciation for the programming process and how it should be carried out.

Compiler construction

A compiler writer need not have designed a language, but a designer should have studied compiler construction. The reason is quite simple. The designer must be able to estimate the cost of each part of his language, in terms of implementation time, compile-time and runtime efficiency. He must be able to say: "that's a nice feature but it will double the size of the compiler", or "add this to your language at the sacrifice of the one-pass compiler you wanted".

One must of course have faith in a compiler, one must know that it is secure, error-free, efficient and so on. Only a compiler writer can really appreciate the fact that the necessary complexity of a compiler is directly proportional to the complexity of the language being compiled. If the language is simple and well-structured, with few exceptions to rules, then the compiler may be also.

Style, and the native tongue

This is an awfully difficult topic to discuss, but I feel it is important. A programming language is a tool for communicating algorithmic thoughts, and as such has a tremendous influence on how we think and express ourselves. If the language is simple and cleanly defined, has a pleasing syntax, is concise without being obscure, in short, if it has what I would call style, then we may hope to produce pleasing, readable programs. Beautiful algorithmic poems, if you will. On the other hand, this is impossible in an awkward, illdefined language. The importance of style in the language cannot be overestimated.

To produce a good language, the designer must combine a sense of simplicity with mathematical presision, expressiveness, and a mastery of grammar. ALGOL 68 (or at least its description) lacks the simplicity; PL/I lacks most of these qualities, as I will show in a moment.

Now I can't really define what I mean by style, and it is sometimes a matter of taste. I don't know where or how one learns it except by contact and experience. In my country, one rarely looks for style in solutions to general problems; the typical way to solve a problem is by brute force - - bury it in money. Translated into programming language terms, this means if there is a hole in the language, fill it with another feature.

I have trouble with English at times - - I interchange words,use the

wrong word, use bad grammar, and so on. But I am slowly learning to
appreciate well-expressed English, concise but clear definitions, and
elegant and simple descriptions.

I would like to discuss PL/I in this context, because I feel we can
learn something from it. PL/I was supposed to incorporate the best
from ALGOL, COBOL and FORTRAN. In my opinion, the prime reason for the
"downfall" of PL/I is that it failed to incorporate the most important
property of ALGOL, its style: its sense of elegance, its clean syn-
tyx, its respect for conventional grammar, its precise and concise
terminology. It just didn't occur to the PL/I designers that these
things were important.

In ALGOL, a statement is an entity to be executed, an operation.
The execution of a statement can be completely defined in terms of
the variables it uses, without discussing the context in which it
appears. A declaration on the other hand is just a descriptive mechanism to help both the reader and the compiler; a declaration is not
executed.

The designers of PL/I failed to realize the importance of these
clean definitions, of this effective separation of tasks, and called
everything a statement, including END;, BEGIN; and DO;.

Thus the END was no longer a syntactic delimiter, but a statement
to be executed, although it is impossible to tell how it is executed
without knowing the context in which it appears.

This lack of precise definition of terms can be seen as the reason
for many of PL/I's sore spots: the confusion of iteration and the compound statement with the single word DO; the use of the semicolon as
a terminator as a separator (in English and ALGOL, the semicolon is
used to separate adjacent clauses of the same weight); the use of a
label following END to terminate all enclosed "Do-groups" (which leads
to sloppy programming and many mistakes); the ON-condition, which has
properties of both the ALGOL declaration and statement; and the confusion of parameter specification with variable declaration.

Had the designers been forced to use BNF and to produce a mathema-
tically precise, clear language definition, many of PL/I's sore spots
would not have appeared. Perhaps they felt that the average programmer

couldn't understand such recursive language definitions. However the game WFF n PROOF shows that a 5 year old can understand and use such recursive definitions!

Given the chance, I think every intelligent programmer can learn to understand and appreciate (what I call) good style in programs and in programming languages, and he will then be a much better programmer.

Programming language theory

Computer science is young, but yet is growing so rapidly that it is often difficult to know what is important and what is just a passing fancy. Research has been performed in many areas: classification of various kinds of programming schemata, proofs of equivalence of programs, correctness proofs, development of program transformation algorithms (e.g. forms of code optimization, translation of recursion into iteration), classification of control structures, formal definitions of the semantics of languages, and so on. The designer must of course be aware of what has been done, but should determine what is pertinant to program language design and concentrate on that.

The designer must be familiar with many languages: ALGOL 60, FORTRAN, COBOL, PL/I, SIMULA, PASCAL, LISP, SNOBOL, and APL to name a few. He must be aware of their disadvantages and shortcomings as well as their good points. A knowledge of the history of the development of various languages might keep the designer from repeating past mistakes.

Formal methods for defining the semantics of a programming language have been developed: operational methods such as the Vienna Definition Language, GLOSS, and hierarchical graphs; mathematical methods such as Scottery; and methods developed with the aim of helping the programmer prove correctness of his program, such as Hoare's axiomatic method. The development of this latter formalism, which is based on an idea of Bob Floyd's on assigning meanings to programs, was a significant step forward for both programming methodology and programming language design. Hoare's axiomatic method is in my opinion the only formalism which warrants discussion in this talk, so let me explain it briefly.

Given a statement S and assertions P and Q (these are relations concerning the program variables), the notation {P}S{Q} informally means: if P is true before execution of S, then Q is true after execution.

Using this notation, the assignment statement <u>is</u> <u>defined</u> <u>as</u>

$$\{P^{x}_{(e)}\} \; x := e \; \{P\}$$

where P^{x}_{e} is the result of replacing all occurrences of x in P by e. As an application of this rule, we have $\{(x+2)>o\}$ x:=x+2$\{x>o\}$. Using the notation a/b to represent inference (<u>if</u> a holds, <u>then</u> so does b), we <u>define</u> the while loop as

(*)
$$\frac{\{P \wedge B\} \; S \; \{P\}}{\{P\} \; \underline{while} \; B \; \underline{do} \; S \; \{P \wedge \neg B\}}$$

Given such a set of axioms (definitions of the simple statements) and inference rules (among them the definitions of the compound statements), and given a program S with input relation I and output relation $\emptyset$, to prove correctness we need to develop a logical proof of the formula $\{I\}$ S $\{\emptyset\}$.

As a simple informal example we take Dijkstra's program to compute $z=a^{b}$ where a,b>o are integers:

```
{a,b integers; a,b>o}
 x := a; y := b; z := 1;
 while y>o do
     begin while even(y) do begin y := y/2; x := x*x end;
           y := y-1; z := z*x
     end
{z=a^b}
```

Now, we don't want to give a completely formal proof of correctness; we want to give that portion of the proof which lets the reader understand the program. In general this is the creative part of the proof, and for many programs, this turns out to be the <u>invariant</u> <u>relations</u> P of the loops defined by (*); all other parts of a proof can be generated mechanically from the input and output relations I and $\emptyset$, and these invariant relations. The above program becomes amazingly clear when we give the following loop invariant P (for both loops in this case) and appeal to definition (*):

$$P: \; y \geqslant o \wedge z \cdot x^{y} = a^{b}$$

This axiomatic method is important, and is revolutionizing the programming methods of those who are willing to try to understand and apply·it, for several reasons.

1. <u>The axiomatic method</u> points the way to proving programs correct. In doing so, the programmer learns to turn his attention away from the dynamic aspects of the program (how it gets executed) and towards more static objects - - the assertions which must hold at the various program points. We then look upon a statement as a <u>predicate-transformer</u>, which changes one predicate (assertion) into another. The method has taught us more about program documentation and definitions of program variables - - these definitions being nothing more than assertions.

2. <u>The axiomatic method</u> helps hide implementation details. This frees the programmer from thinking about how things get executed - - indeed it sometimes forces him away from it - - and lets him concentrate on correctness. The designer must of course be sure that each language feature can be implemented efficiently, but for both the programmer and designer, correctness and efficiency are two separate concepts which should be handled separately.

3. <u>The axiomatic method</u> helps in the design of programming languages. The complexity of a program is directly related to the ease of understanding - - that is to the length of a proof of correctness and the complexity of the inference rules used in the proof. The simplicity or ease of use of any programming language statement is directly related to the simplicity of its axiomatic definition. A difficult, subtle definition is sure to define a statement which the programmer will have trouble with. Hoare and his colleagues have written a number of papers concerning axiomatic definition of loops, procedures and parameters, functions, gotos, and the like. These papers shed some light on the relations between the programming language statements, their implementation, and their use in programming, and are <u>must</u> reading for every would-be designer.

4. <u>The axiomatic method</u> allows for a machine-independent description. Since the formal language description is essentially non-operational, there is little tendency for machine-dependent features to creep in. One can also give only a partial list of axioms, and leave the rest to the implementor. For example, for integer arithmetic one would give some necessary, useful axioms, say that = is transitive, etc., but

could leave undefined such actions as what happens on overflow. The implementor can then define these as he wishes, as long as the original list of axioms remains satisfied.

Extensibility

A programmer first clarifies his algorithmic ideas in a notation which suits his needs - - usually one which fits the problem. He then proceeds to describe these ideas in the programming language. Since the language is usually far removed from the initial notation, this requires a series of "refinements" each succeeding one being closer to the language and requiring more detail. For a class of problems, the process can be made more efficient by first extending the language upwards, towards a more suitable notation. Thus the language is extended into a special purpose language.

Such an extensible language consists of a base language, together with mechanisms for making extensions. The idea was quite popular in the late 1960's, and in 1971 a symposium was held on the subject (Schumann (71)). The preface of the proceedings stated that "extensible languages are currently considered to be one of the more promising directions of research...", while Tom Cheatham felt that "we have arrived - ... there exist langauges and host systems which fulfill the goals of extensibility...".

Yet one hears little about extensible languages today. People don't seem to be asking for and using these existing extensible languages as they do, say, PASCAL. From our vantage point as language designers who understand good programming methodology and the design criteria given at the beginning of this talk, let us discuss these extensible languages and try to understand the reason for this. It will be seen that much of the research "barked up the wrong tree", and could have been saved. Of course, we must remember that the extensible language researchers, and I and most of us here today, had a totally different view of programming and language design at that time.

A good part of the extension mechanisms allowed purely syntactic extensions; one defined a new notation in terms of old ones. Thus, each programmer could easily define his own control structures, he could do away with semicolons, he could change the precedence of operations, he could change, add and delete reserved words, and so on.

However,such uncontrolled syntactic extensions are against good
programming principles, because they lead to total confusion. Programs
are difficult enough to understand without having to worry about the
strange notational preferences of the programmer. I know a numerical
analyst, a good programmer, who spent at least 2 weeks finding an
error in his APL program, caused by the fact that 4-3-2 is 3, and not
-1, in APL. What chaos would result if each programmer could define
his own operator precedences?

Such uncontrolled extensions should be very <u>costly</u> to make rather
than cheap, so that they will be made only when really worthwhile.

As modern designers, we could see the weakness of such extension
mechanisms from another point: implementation. A satisfactory parsing
algorithm which can handle such extensions, especially when a number
of perhaps-conflicting extensions are piled up on one another, has
still not been published.

A second mechanism proposed was the semantic extension. Instead of
indicating what a new notation meant by associating with it a second,
known notation, one showed how the first notation was to be <u>executed</u>.
This idea fails our test of simplicity and transparency. It requires
the programmer (and every subsequent reader of the program) to know
far too much about either the compiler or the runtime execution of the
translated program.

On top of this, researchers found that no matter how hard they
tried, they could not develop extension mechanisms which were sufficient to allow one to extend the base language with some concepts (e.g.
block structure) if these concepts were not already in the base language. Thus their goal of complete flexibility with regard to extensions could never be reached.

We have attempted to argue that complete flexibility in extensions
is not worthwhile from the point of view of good programming methodology. However, we <u>do</u> need to be able to "extend" languages in some
fashion, in order to reduce our workload. It wouldn't be fair to cri-
ticize without presenting an alternative. Let me therefore discuss
what I think are viable extension mechanisms, but I hope you won't be

disappointed by my simplistic approach!

Any extension mechanism must be <u>controlled</u>. It must lead to clear, readable programs. It must be simple and efficient to implement.

We don't want the programmer to be able to introduce new statements, control structures, or syntax, for this would lead to confusion. The base language should contain enough simple control structures to sa- tisfy the programmers needs, suitably defined via Hoare's axiomatic method, of course. Those that we can understand with our mental aids of enumeration and mathematical induction are simple sequencing, al- ternation (e.g. <u>if</u> and <u>case</u> statements), and simple forms of iter- ation. Read Dijkstra's Notes on Structured Programming for more in- formation.

You might think at this point that I have by the whole preceding discussion completely outlawed every possible kind of extension, but I haven't. Every program defines sequences of operations on objects of certain kinds or types. I <u>don't</u> want the programmer to extend the notation used in defining the sequence of operations at all. However, he should have the ability to extend the language with new operations, and with new types of objects.

The procedure concept

The main extension mechanism used today is the procedure; it has been in use ever since the beginning of time (of computers). When I write

```
{sort array A}
procedure sort(A);
    begin ... end
```

I am actually extending my programming with a new operator. There- after, when I write sort(B) I look upon this as an <u>indivisible</u> <u>oper-</u> <u>ation</u> of my language, which is to be executed. In the same manner, for example, I never concern myself with how the operation a*b is executed.

The procedure should not be viewed as just an abbreviating device; it is a powerful but controlled extension device, which we understand using the mental aid called <u>abstraction</u>. After I have written procedure sort, I single out that property of the procedure which is most import- ant: <u>what</u> <u>it</u> <u>does</u>. And for purposes of understanding a program using

this new operation, this is the only property the reader need know. I
don't even care what language it is written in.

Now, in order not to hinder the programmer, this most powerful
mechanism must be implemented efficiently. If it is necessary to explain to the programmer how to get rid of his procedures to make his
program efficient, then the language is hindering the programmer; it
is rendering ineffective his most important tool, abstraction.

The macro

The macro definition has essentially the same form as the procedure
definition and serves exactly the same purpose: extension of a language through inclusion of a new operator. The difference is in implementation. The procedure call is implemented as a jump to a separate
piece of code forming the procedure body, while the macro call is
textually replaced by the macro body (with suitable argument-for-para-
meter substitution). Correct use of macros and procedures helps us get
each program unit to a reasonable size, say one or two pages, ending
up with a much more readable product.

One hears much about "flexible" macro processors which allow arbitrary textual substitution, and even some calculation during macro
processing. The PL/I preprocessor is a good example. While such macro
processors have their place in the computing world and can be useful,
they should not be used every day as an extension mechanism for a
programming language. The macro concept should be tied closely with
the language and should only allow restricted, controlled kinds of extensions.

Data types

The procedure has been the basic extension mechanism for over 25
years. The past several years have seen the gradual development of a
new kind of extension mechanism concerned with data types. The idea
stems from a mixture of Simula's classes, and Hoare's records which
have been implemented in PASCAL.

Previously, a type was considered to be a set of values (e.g. the
integers). PASCAL allows one to extend the language with new types - -
either scalar types like suit=(clubs, diamonds, hearts, spades) or records. A record value consists of a finite sequence of named values of
previously known types. An example of a record definition is complex =

<u>record</u> rpart:integer; ipart:integer <u>end</u>.

   Currently, a <u>type</u> is considered to be a set of values, <u>together</u> <u>with</u> <u>the</u> <u>operations</u> <u>to</u> <u>be</u> <u>performed</u> <u>on</u> <u>those</u> <u>values</u>. Thus, when one defines a new type one should define not only the set of values but also the operations. For example:

```
complex = type var rpart: integer;
               var ipart: integer;
               proc plus (x,y: complex) : complex;
                     begin plus.rpart := x.rpart + y.rpart;
                           plus.ipart := x.ipart + y.ipart
                     end;
               proc mult ...
          endtype
```

Thus, if one defines

```
var  a,b : complex;
var    c : integer;
```

one can then write

```
a := complex (2,0);   b := complex (5,10);
b := plus (a,b);      c := b.rpart
```

One might also allow the type-definer to associate plus with the symbol +, etc., so that one could write b := a+b in conventional notation (this <u>overloading</u> concept has been in use in MAD since around 1960). However, he should not be allowed to redefine the precedence of the operators; this would only lead to confusion.

   We have of course only outlined the basic idea behind this new, powerful but controlled extension mechanism. The idea is not yet ready to be incorporated in anything but an experimental language; development is being performed at a number of institutions around the world. We will briefly discuss problems to be solved shortly, but first let us turn to one further extension mechanism.

<u>Types as parameters</u>
   This mechanism of extending a language by adding new types can be

made more useful by allowing types of parameters of a procedure to be parameters. As an example, the function below returns the maximum value of the input array A of values. The parameter specification $\underline{array}^+\ \underline{of}\ <z>$ means that A has one or more dimensions, and that the base element type z depends on the particular input array argument. Note that the input argument then also determines the type of the result.

This procedure works correctly for any type z which consists of an ordered set of elements (for which < is correctly defined), and for which a minimum value exists. Min(z) returns the minimum value of the type z. Domain (A) is the set consisting of all possible subscript values of array A. Thus, if A is declared A[1:20, 1:30], domain (A) = {(i,j)|1≤i≤20, 1≤j≤30}. This finite set can be thought of as a type, and thus variable i can be declared with this type.

```
proc max(var A array+ of <z>) : <z>;
     var i : domain (A);
     var s : z;
     begin s := min(z);
          for i in domain(A)do
              if s<A(i) then  s := A(i);
          max := s
     end
```

This addition to the procedure concept as it appears in most languages is still quite controlled, and makes further use of abstraction. Thus we no longer need one procedure to sort an array of integers and another to sort an array of reals, we have a single operation sort(A) which will sort any one-dimensional array of elements, as long as the element type has a well-defined ordering on the type of the element values has been defined.

This new idea would make it easier to develop flexible "building blocks" - - operations and types which can easily be used by others. In practical terms, the library of subroutines would be much smaller. For the most part, such procedures can be used without loss of runtime efficiency and perhaps even with a gain in compile-time efficiency, if the subroutine library is kept in a symbolic but condensed form. When a procedure call max(b) is processed by the compiler, a conventional procedure max[1] for max is generated, with the type of b replacing the parameter type z, while the call max(b) is replaced by max^1(b). This of course means that max cannot be separately compiled. This is no problem; a good compiler for a well-structured language can compile into memory directly just as fast as the typical linkage-loader can link and load a relocatable object program. Thus, independent compilation becomes obsolete.

Discussion of proposed extension mechanisms

The ideas of data types and parameter types as parameters are certainly not fully developed, and don't yet belong in any but experimental languages. Several theoretical questions should and are being asked and answered: what really is a type? What operations should be automatically defined on any type (assignment, equality)? What is a subtype or supertype of a type? From a theoretical standpoint, should implicit conversion from a subtype to a supertype be allowed? How does (or should) a subtype inherit its supertype's operations?

Once these kinds of questions are answered satisfactorily there are practical considerations to take into account, from the standpoint of good programming methodology (ease of proof of program correctness, for example) and efficiency. Should a type's operations be implemented as procedures or macros? Are implicit conversions from a subtype to its supertype efficient enough to be allowed? Is the notation simple, elegant and convenient? What about initialization of variables of a programmer-defined type? And so on, and so on.

It is not an easy task to imbed such ideas conveniently and cleanly in a language!

Special purpose languages

No matter how good a general purpose language is, there will always be areas where it is not really suitable, where it just does not fit. In some cases it may actually be necessary to design and implement a whole new, different language. However we must be wary in taking this route, for the following may happen. The new special purpose language incorporates several special mechanisms but strips the general purpose features to a bare-bones niminum. At a later stage, however, the users begin to feel that they really do need the more general features, and slowly the language and compiler are extended, in an ad hoc fashion, to include the users' desires. One ends up with a large, unwieldy, unstructured language and compiler.

If our general purpose language is simple and efficient enough, a much easier method for producing a special purpose language can be used. Just add the necessary special features (but as few as possible) to the general purpose language, taking care not to tread on the language design too much! Much of the special features can be added as new operations or types (as procedures, for example).

I know of one instance where this technique was successful. A company built a simple PASCAL compiler for the PDP-11/04, in order to be able to write a system for the production of hybrid laser-trimming systems. PASCAL programs were written to handle all real-time details - - the motion of the laser beam, power of the laser, etc. Only two additions to PASCAL were deemed necessary: (1) the ability to define the address of a variable, e.g. var PSW origin 177776B: integer; and (2) the ability to use octal constants, as in the above declaration. This allowed the system routines, programmed in PASCAL, to reference the hardware clock, the status of the laser beam positioning system, and so on. All special-purpose features were imbedded as new operations (procedures) or PASCAL types.

This project would not have been possible without a simple, well-structured, efficient, effective general purpose language. It could not have been possible to use FORTRAN or PL/I, or even a subset of PL/I, as the general purpose language.

Thus we see that the simplicity and efficiency of a language is an asset in more ways than one, and is far superior to a language which has more features but is ill-defined.

Conclusion

I have tried to present programming language design from a viewpoint that might not as yet have occurred to you. I have not presented anything new or deep or exciting, but I at least feel that what I have said is important. At the same time, I am able to stand back and laugh at myself preaching in this manner. One must always overemphasize a point in making it to make sure that it is noticed, and I have overemphasized style and elegance and simplicity because so few have noticed its importance in programming.

I can give you a few references on the subject of programming language design. First and foremost is the Infotech State of the Art Report 7 [72] on High Level Languages. Here you will find very interesting reading - - discussions of various languages, etc. - - with some conflicting views on what languages should look like. It also contains a large set of references. Besides this report, my list of references consists of a few other discussions of programming language design which have been useful to me in preparing this talk.

References

[1] Hoare, C.A.R. Prospects for a better programming language, in Infotech Limited [72], 328-343.

[2] Hoare, C.A.R. Hints on programming language design. Invited address, SIGPLAN/SIGACT Symposium on Principles of Programming Language, Boston, Oct. 1973.

[3] Infotech Limited: High Level Languages, Infotech State of the Art Report 7. Infotech Limited, Maidenhead, Berkshire, England. 1972.

[4] McKeeman, W.M. Programming language design. In: Bauer and Eickel (ed): Compiler Construction. Lecture Notes in Computer Science 21, Springer Verlag, 1974. 514-524.

[5] Schuman, S.A. (ed). Proceedings of the interntional symposium on extensible languages. SIGPLAN Notices 6, Dec. 1971.

[6] Wirth, N. On certain basic concepts of programming languages. CS 65, Stanford University, May 1967.

[7] Wirth, N. The programming language PASCAL and its design criteria. In: Infotech Limited [72], 450-473.

[8] Wirth, N. Programming and programming languages. ACM International Symposium, Bonn 1970.

ON GENERATING VERIFICATION CONDITIONS FOR CORRECTNESS PROOFS

James C. King
IBM T. J. Watson Research Center
Yorktown Heights, New York
USA

ABSTRACT: The generation of verification conditions is one of the basic steps in proving the correctness of programs. Alternative methods for generating verification conditions have been developed and used, each technique apparently quite different from the others. This paper presents three of the most well-known methods and shows how they relate to each other and to the basic program analysis task.

INTRODUCTION

Proving that a program is correct, using the method first introduced by Floyd [9] and Naur [16], involves four basic steps:

1) Supplying an *entry assertion* (predicate) and an *exit assertion* which define admissible program inputs and correct program results, respectively. Together these assertions give a complete formal specification of correct program behavior.

2) Supplying additional *inductive assertions* associated with points in the program such that at least one lies on every loop.

3) Generating a *verification condition* (VC) for every path in the program that goes from one assertion to another.

4) Proving that all of the VC's are *true* (theorems).

This presentation discusses and compares several ways to accomplish step 3. The processing performed in each method is quite different but the underlying concepts as well as the results produced are the same. This is brought out in detail.

The ALGOL procedure, Z, shown in Figure 1 is used for examples throughout the presentation. It computes $X \uparrow Y$, where X and Y are its two integer inputs. Examining the bit representation for Y, when considered as a binary number, the procedure multiplies together a subset of $\{X, X^2, X^4, X^8, \dots \}$ to form the proper result. (e.g., Y = 5 = $(101)_2$, $X^5 = X \times X^4$.) The method will only work for non-negative Y so the entry assertion is $Y \geq 0$ and is included in the procedure as line 4 using the syntax for a dummy built-in procedure call "entry." Since the initial values of X and Y must be referenced in the exit assertion (both values are changed by the program) the dummy statements at line 5 are included to save those values for verification purposes in A and B, respectively. Braces { } are used to indicate their use for verification only. The obvious exit assertion is $Z = A \uparrow B$ and is included as line 18, using dummy procedure "exit." The procedure's only loop is cut by an inductive assertion included at line 8, using dummy procedure "assert."

The placement of the inductive assertion allows the program to be considered as four segments, or paths, which "cover" the original program. They are listed in Figure 2 by giving the line numbers for all the statements along

```
1        integer procedure Z(X, Y);
2            value X, Y;  integer X, Y, YD;
3            begin
4                entry(Y≥0);
5                { A ← X;  B ← Y; }
6                Z ← 1;
7        LOOP:
8                assert( Z×(X↑Y) = A↑B ∧ Y≥0);
9                if Y≠0 then
10               begin
11                   YD ← Y÷2;
12                   if Y≠2×YD then
13                           Z ← Z×X;
14                   X ← X×X;
15                   Y ← YD;
16                   go to LOOP;
17               end;
18               exit(Z = A↑B);
19           end;
```

Figure 1. ALGOL Procedure Z (to a power)

each path. Each path starts and ends at an assertion. A path is said to be verified with respect to its assertions if *for any* values which satisfy the assertion at the beginning of the path, the values resulting at the end of the path satisfy the assertion there. A general inductive argument shows that if all of the covering paths are verified, then so is the program. (See [9], [8], [12], or [15] for details.) In this example, one can see that if all four of the paths listed in Figure 2 are verified, then so is the complete program. The verification of path 1 would show that if the procedure's entry assertion is satisfied by the procedure inputs (i.e., if $Y≥0$), then the inductive assertion is satisfied at the first entrance to the loop. The verification of paths 2 and 3, the alternative paths around the loop, would show that if the inductive assertion is satisfied at line 8, it is again satisfied after traversing the loop once. The verification of path 4 would show that if the inductive assertion is satisfied at line 8 and the execution exits the procedure, then the exit assertion holds. Note that this form of inductive proof does not guarantee that program execution will always terminate. What is proved is: if the program terminates, the exit assertion is satisfied.

PATH	Line Numbers From Figure 1.
1	4, 5, 6, 7, 8.
2	8, 9, 10, 11, 12, 13, 14, 15, 16, 7, 8.
3	8, 9, 10, 11, 12, 14, 15, 16, 7, 8.
4	8, 9, 18.

Figure 2. Covering Paths for the Procedure of Figure 1.

PATH SEQUENCES

The basic features of an algebraic language are the ability to compute and save new values, for example, by assignment statements, and the ability to follow alternative paths through a program, for example, by use of **if** statements. The following discussion is confined to these two simple constructs. For our purposes, assignment statements will be of the general form:

$$x_i \leftarrow f(x_1, x_2, ..., x_n) \tag{1}$$

where there are n program variables $x_1, x_2, ..., x_n$, f is some total function (e.g., arithmetic expression) over the program variables, and x_i (for some i, $1 \leq i \leq n$) is the variable receiving a new value computed according to f. For simplicity, assume that f does not involve function calls nor any operations not primitive in the programming language. Similarly, assume that no side effects occur while evaluating f.

Since a path through the program is determined by a set of assumptions as to the alternatives taken at **if** statements, it is convenient to introduce a new statement of the form:

assume(<Boolean expression>)

to use in place of **if** statements when considering any particular path. A program path can then be described by a sequence consisting of assignment statements and **assume** statements and will be called a *path sequence*. The assignment statements are those encountered along the path, in order. Whenever an **if** statement (testing a <Boolean expression>, say B) is encountered along the program path, an **assume** statement is included in the path sequence and takes the form **assume**(B) or **assume**($\neg$(B)). The choice of B or $\neg$(B) is determined by the path being followed; the first form is used along all paths for which B is assumed to evaluate to *true* and the second whenever B is assumed to evaluate to *false*. (Assume that B is also a total function.) The fact that a particular path will be followed only under certain conditions (determined by **if** statements) is often essential to the proof of the path. This information is conveniently provided in the path sequence by the **assume** statements.

To verify a program path the assertion associated with the beginning of the path is assumed to be *true* over the values of the variables at that point. Otherwise, the path is trivially verified. This initial assertion has the same meaning as, and can be written in the same way as, the **assume** statement introduced above. The assertion associated with the end of the path is included in the path sequence by use of a **prove** statement and always occurs as the final statement of the path sequence. It has the form:

prove(<assertion>).

To summarize, a *path sequence* is a sequence of three types of statements, assignment statements, **assume** statements, and a final **prove** statement. The first statement in the sequence is always an **assume** statement and exactly one **prove** statement occurs and it occurs last. For notational convenience, the statements in a path sequence of length m are numbered from 1 to m. There is the obvious correspondence between statements in the program and statements in a path sequence. The following discussion uses path 3 from Figure 2, as an example and it is written as a path sequence in Figure 3.

```
1      assume(Z×(X↑Y) = A↑B ∧ Y≥0);
2      assume(Y≠0);
3      YD←Y÷2;
4      assume(Y=2×YD);
5      X←X×X;
6      Y←YD;
7      prove(Z×(X↑Y) = A↑B ∧ Y≥0);
```

Figure 3. Path Sequence for Path 3 of Figure 2.

GENERATING PATH VERIFICATION CONDITIONS

Four methods for verifying a program path as represented by a path sequence are discussed next. They all generate a *verification condition*, or VC, from the path sequence. A verification condition is a predicate which is a theorem if an only if the program path is correct with respect to its associated initial and final assertions. Generating verification conditions, VC-generation, is the final step in reducing the program verification problem to a theorem proving one. Note that, in this presentation, VC-generation is not involved with procedure termination (execution, once started on a path, will always reach its end).

The methods are called simply A, B, C, and D to avoid naming problems. Floyd's early terminology had been keyed to the direction in which the path sequence is traversed while generating the VC. The two methods known to him at that time (A and B) were simply dubbed "going forward" and "going backward". With the introduction of method C (symbolic execution), the binary direction-oriented terminology associated with path traversal became inadequate. The verification conditions are predicates over the program variables (which are the free variables in the predicate) and can be thought of as describing the values of the program variables at the beginning of the path or at the end of the path. This property, together with the direction of traversal, distinguishes four methods as shown pictorially in Figure 4. The vertical lines represent the path sequence, the arrows represent the direction the path sequence is traversed and the bullet symbols ● denote with which end of the path the verification condition variables are associated.

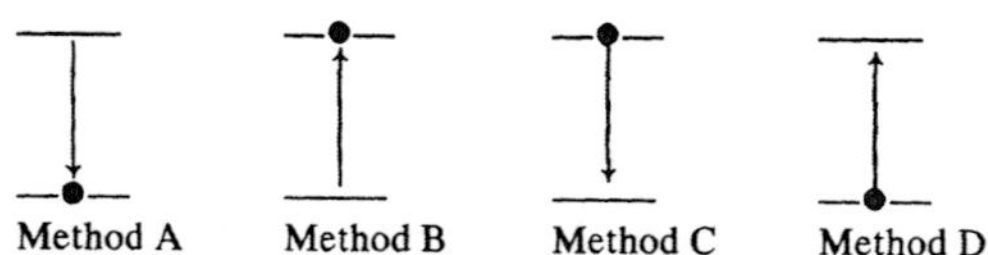

Figure 4. Distinguishing Four VC-generation Methods

Method A. Floyd forward or *strongest post condition* method. This is the method introduced by Floyd in his first paper on the subject [9]. It traverses the path in the forward direction and the free variables in the VC are associated with the program variables at the end of the path. This method associates a sequence of assertions (predicates) $\{P_1, P_2, ..., P_m\}$ with the path sequence $S = \{s_1, s_2, ..., s_m\}$. Assertion P_1 is identically *true*. Each P_{i+1} for $i = 1, 2, ..., (m-1)$ is derived so as to follow from P_i and the execution of statement s_i. Using a notion introduced by Hoare [11], this can be written as: $P_i \{s_i\} P_{i+1}$. Assertion P_i is claimed to hold over the program state between statements s_{i-1} and s_i.

Having derived assertions P_i for $i = 2, 3, ..., j$, P_{j+1} is derived as follows:

a) If s_j is **assume**(Q) then $P_{j+1} \equiv (P_j \wedge Q)$, or using Hoare's notation:

$$P_j \{assume(Q)\} (P_j \wedge Q).$$

The intuitive meaning of this operation should be clear: the assertion which holds for the current state (P_j) *and* the new assumptions being made (Q) result in the new assertion $(P_j \wedge Q)$. The initial assertion, *true*, is the most general starting condition which is required in the overall program correctness induction proof. If an assertion should ever become identically *false* as a result of **assume** statement processing, the path sequence is inconsistent and represents a path in the program which can never be traversed during any legal program execution. In this case, the path verification process stops; the path is vacuously verified to be correct.

b) If s_j is an assignment statement of the form shown in (1) above, and the dependence of P_j on the program variables is made explicit as $P_j(x_1, x_2, ..., x_i, ..., x_n)$, then the new assertion is:

257

$$\exists x_i'\ (P_j(x_1, x_2, ..., x_i', ..., x_n) \wedge x_i = f(x_1, x_2, ..., x_i', ..., x_n)),$$

where x_i' is a new variable name not used in the program and not occurring in P_j. Note that this variable name is *bound* in the expression by the existential quantifier ($\exists$). This derivation can be written in Hoare's notation as:

$$P_j(x_1, x_2, ..., x_i, ..., x_n)\ \{x_i \leftarrow f(x_1, x_2, ..., x_n)\}$$
$$\exists x_i'\ (P_j(x_1, x_2, ..., x_i', ..., x_n) \wedge x_i = f(x_1, x_2, ..., x_i', ..., x_n)),$$

The intuitive meaning of this expression is: there did exist a value ($\exists x_i'$) for which P_j held, and in terms of which the current value of x_i was computed. That *old value* of x_i is no longer available in the program as the value of some program variable, so the hypothetical existence of such a variable is claimed, since it *could* be available if the assignment statement were changed to two:

$$x_i' \leftarrow x_i$$
$$x_i \leftarrow f(x_1, x_2, ..., x_i', ..., x_n)$$

and the variable x_i' were a program variable.

The processing of **assume** and assignment statements in the path sequence proceeds in this way until the final **prove** statement, s_m, of the form **prove**(Q). The verification condition for the path sequence using Method A is then:

$$P_m \supset Q.$$

The current assertion always represents the *strongest post condition* derivable from the previous assertion, and accounting for the behavior of the statement. The verification condition simply presents the question: does the final assertion follow as a consequence of what is known to hold at this point (P_m).

Generating the verification condition for the path sequence of Figure 3 using Method A is shown in Figure 5A. The assertions are shown on the right between the statements of the path sequence. Whenever two assertions occur in sequence the first is that obtained from direct application of the method and the second is an equivalent one, simplified for subsequent use.

Method B. Backward substitution method. While this method was never published by Floyd it was to this author's knowledge invented by him. This method has been commonly used in automated program verifiers ([13], [18]) and is, perhaps the best known method. In some recent work ([1], [7]), this method has been called the method of *weakest pre-condition*. With this method the path sequence is traverse backward from last statement to first. The free variables in the resulting VC are associated with the program variables at the beginning of the path. (See Figure 4.)

As with Method A, this method associates a predicate sequence with the path sequence, but this time the process starts at the final statement, **prove**(Q), by establishing $P_m \equiv Q$. Having derived P_i for $i = m-1, m-2, ..., j+1$, P_j is derived as follows:

a) If s_j is **assume**(Q) then $P_j \equiv (Q \supset P_{j+1})$, or using Hoare's notation:

$$(Q \supset P_{j+1})\ \{s_j\}\ P_{j+1}.$$

The intuitive meaning is: the assertion P_{j+1} need hold only under the condition that the assumption which determines the path (Q) holds.

b) If s_j is an assignment statement as shown in (1) and P_{j+1} is written as $P_{j+1}(x_1, x_2, ..., x_i, ..., x_n)$, then $P_j \equiv P_{j+1}(x_1, x_2, ..., f(x_1, x_2, ..., x_n), ..., x_n)$, or written in Hoare's notation:

$$P_{j+1}(x_1, x_2, ..., f(x_1, x_2, ..., x_n), ..., x_n)\ \{x_i \leftarrow f(x_1, x_2, ..., x_n)\}\ P_{j+1}(x_1, x_2, ..., x_i, ..., x_n).$$

The intuitive meaning is: if P_{j+1} holds for $f(x_1, x_2, ..., x_n)$ before the assignment to x_i, then since x_i gets the value $f(x_1, x_2, ..., x_n)$, it must hold for x_i afterward.

Path Sequence	Assertion Sequence

                         ---- *true*

1   **assume**$(Z \times (X \uparrow Y) = A \uparrow B \wedge Y \geq 0)$;

                         ---- $Z \times (X \uparrow Y) = A \uparrow B \wedge Y \geq 0$

2   **assume**$(Y \neq 0)$;

                         ---- $Z \times (X \uparrow Y) = A \uparrow B \wedge Y \geq 0 \wedge Y \neq 0$

3   $YD \leftarrow Y \div 2$;

                         ---- $\exists YD'(Z \times (X \uparrow Y) = A \uparrow B \wedge Y \geq 0 \wedge Y \neq 0 \wedge YD = Y \div 2)$
                         ---- $Z \times (X \uparrow Y) = A \uparrow B \wedge Y \geq 0 \wedge Y \neq 0 \wedge YD = Y \div 2$

4   **assume**$(Y = 2 \times YD)$;

                         ---- $Z \times (X \uparrow Y) = A \uparrow B \wedge Y \geq 0 \wedge Y \neq 0 \wedge YD = Y \div 2 \wedge Y = 2 \times YD$

5   $X \leftarrow X \times X$;

                         ---- $\exists X'(Z \times (X' \uparrow Y) = A \uparrow B \wedge Y \geq 0 \wedge Y \neq 0 \wedge$
$$YD = Y \div 2 \wedge Y = 2 \times YD \wedge X = X' \times X')$$

6   $Y \leftarrow YD$;

                         ---- $\exists Y' \exists X'(Z \times (X' \uparrow Y') = A \uparrow B \wedge Y' \geq 0 \wedge Y' \neq 0 \wedge$
$$YD = Y' \div 2 \wedge Y' = 2 \times YD \wedge X = X' \times X' \wedge Y = YD)$$
                         ---- $\exists X'(Z \times (X' \uparrow (2 \times YD)) = A \uparrow B \wedge 2 \times YD \geq 0 \wedge 2 \times YD \neq 0 \wedge$
$$YD = (2 \times YD) \div 2 \wedge X = X' \times X' \wedge Y = YD)$$

7   **prove**$(Z \times (X \uparrow Y) = A \uparrow B \wedge Y \geq 0)$;

VC:
$$\{\exists X'(Z \times (X' \uparrow (2 \times YD)) = A \uparrow B \wedge 2 \times YD \geq 0 \wedge 2 \times YD \neq 0 \wedge YD = (2 \times YD) \div 2 \wedge X = X' \times X' \wedge Y = YD)\} \supset$$
$$\{Z \times (X \uparrow Y) = A \uparrow B \wedge Y \geq 0\}$$

Figure 5A. VC-generation Using Method A.

This processing continues following the path sequence in reverse order until the first **assume** statement (s_1) has been processed. The verification condition is just the assertion P_1, last derived. If it can be proved to be *true* for all values of the variables (i.e., a theorem) then the derived sequence of assertions all hold at their associated point in the path sequence. This includes the predicate of the **prove** statement which was P_m, the first assertion in the derivation. The use of Method B is shown for the path sequence of Figure 3 in Figure 5B. As was done in Figure 5A when two assertions occur in succession the first is produced directly from the rules and the next is equivalent but simplified.

Method C. Symbolic execution method. The path sequence is traversed in a forward direction under this method and the free variables in the VC are associated with the program variables at the beginning of the path. This method was used by Deutsch [6] in his program verifier, by Boyer and Moore in theirs [2], and has been explored in a variety of program analysis contexts by Burstall and his students [3, 5, 17]. This method exploits the fact that all computations along the path are some function of the values of the variables at the beginning of the path. Let x_i' for each i, $1 \leq i \leq n$, represent a new variable not used in the program and which has been set to the value that x_i had at the beginning of the path. That is, assume that the path begins with the n assignments:

$$x_i' \leftarrow x_i \ (1 \leq i \leq n).$$

During the forward traversal of the path, enough information about the current value of each variable (x_i) is maintained so that at any point an assignment statement, involving only the primed variables, could be produced to compute the current value of x_i.

For a path sequence $\{s_1, s_2, ..., s_m\}$, a sequence of sets of expressions, $\{ \{r_{i,1}\}, \{r_{i,2}\}, ..., \{r_{i,m}\} \}$, are determined which provide the right hand side of the assignment statements such that immediately before statement s_j the value of x_i could be obtained by:

$$x_i \leftarrow r_{i,j}(x_1', x_2', ..., x_n').$$

Path Sequence (Reversed)	Assertion Sequence
7 **prove**$(Z\times(X\uparrow Y)=A\uparrow B\wedge Y\geq 0)$;	
	---- $Z\times(X\uparrow Y)=A\uparrow B\wedge Y\geq 0$
6 $Y\leftarrow YD$;	
	---- $Z\times(X\uparrow YD)=A\uparrow B\wedge YD\geq 0$
5 $X\leftarrow X\times X$;	
	---- $Z\times((X\times X)\uparrow YD)=A\uparrow B\wedge YD\geq 0)$ ---- $Z\times(X\uparrow(2\times YD))=A\uparrow B\wedge YD\geq 0)$
4 **assume**$(Y=2\times YD)$;	
	---- $Y=2\times YD\supset(Z\times(X\uparrow(2\times YD))=A\uparrow B\wedge YD\geq 0)$
3 $YD\leftarrow Y\div 2$;	
	---- $Y=2\times(Y\div 2)\supset(Z\times(X\uparrow(2\times(Y\div 2)))=A\uparrow B\wedge Y\div 2\geq 0)$
2 **assume**$(Y\neq 0)$;	
	---- $Y\neq 0\supset\{Y=2\times(Y\div 2)\supset(Z\times(X\uparrow(2\times(Y\div 2)))=A\uparrow B\wedge Y\div 2\geq 0)\}$ ---- $(Y\neq 0\wedge Y=2\times(Y\div 2))\supset(Z\times(X\uparrow(2\times(Y\div 2)))=A\uparrow B\wedge Y\div 2\geq 0)$
1 **assume**$(Z\times(X\uparrow Y)=A\uparrow B)\wedge Y\geq 0)$;	
	---- $(Z\times(X\uparrow Y)=A\uparrow B\wedge Y\geq 0)\supset$ $\{(Y\neq 0\wedge Y=2\times(Y\div 2))\supset(Z\times(X\uparrow(2\times(Y\div 2)))=A\uparrow B\wedge Y\div 2\geq 0)\}$ ---- $(Z\times(X\uparrow Y)=A\uparrow B\wedge Y\geq 0\wedge Y\neq 0\wedge Y=2\times(Y\div 2))\supset$ $(Z\times(X\uparrow(2\times(Y\div 2)))=A\uparrow B\wedge Y\div 2\geq 0)$

VC:

$$(Z\times(X\uparrow Y)=A\uparrow B\ \wedge\ Y\geq 0\ \wedge\ Y\neq 0\ \wedge\ Y=2\times(Y\div 2))\ \supset\ (Z\times(X\uparrow(2\times(Y\div 2)))=A\uparrow B\ \wedge\ Y\div 2\geq 0)$$

Figure 5B.   VC-generation Using Method B.

Initially $r_{i,1}=x_i'$ for $i=1, 2, ..., n$. Assuming that the $r_{i,k}$ have been determined for all $k=1, 2, ..., j$ then $r_{i,j+1}$ can be determined as follows:

a) If s_j is an **assume** statement, then $r_{i,j+1}=r_{i,j}$ for all i, $1\leq i\leq n$. The **assume** statements in the sequence, or the corresponding **if** statements in the program have no affect on the values of program variables. However, separate processing of **assume** statements not affecting the r's is done as described later.

b) If s_j is an assignment statement as denoted in (1) then

$$r_{k,j+1}=r_{k,j}\ \text{for all }k,\ 1\leq k\leq n,\ k\neq i,$$

and

$$r_{i,j+1}=f(r_{1,j}, r_{2,j}, ..., r_{n,j}).$$

The intuitive justification is: the assignment only changes the value of x_i and if $\{r_{k,j}\}$ represent the expressions for computing the respective values of $\{x_k\}$ in terms of their initial values (in the primed variables), then composing them with f gives an expression for the new value of x_i strictly over the primed variables.

In a similar manner, the assumptions represented by **assume** statements can be rewritten to be conditions over the initial values $\{x_i'\}$. A sequence of predicates called *path conditions*, denoted PC_j, $j=1, 2, ..., m$, and similar to the assertions $\{P_j\}$ of Methods A and B, are also associated with the path sequence and used to record the assumptions made along the path. However, the PC_j is not called an assertion as in Methods A and B because it is *not* an expression over the current (j-th) values of the program variables. It is a condition on the primed (path begin) values, exclusively. The initial assertion, PC_1, is *true*. Since the predicates of **assume** statements are over the current values of the program variables the recording of the assumptions in the PC's must occur in sequence with assignment statement processing.

When an **assume** statement is encountered as statement s_j in the path sequence and has the form:

$$\textbf{assume}(\ Q(x_1, x_2, ..., x_n)\ )$$

then

$$PC_{j+1} \equiv (PC_j \wedge Q(r_{1,j}, r_{2,j}, ..., r_{n,j})\,). \tag{2}$$

The intuitive meaning is: the predicate Q is composed with the $\{r_{i,j}\}$ to produce an equivalent predicate over the $\{x_i'\}$ which is then added to the old PC_j. Assignment statements do not directly affect the sequence of PC's: if s_j is an assignment statement then $PC_{j+1} \equiv PC_j$. Encountering the final **prove** statement s_m, say

$$\mathbf{prove}(\, Q(x_1, x_2, ..., x_n)\,)$$

the VC is formed, for Method C, as:

$$PC_m \supset Q(\, r_{1,m}, r_{2,m}, ..., r_{n,m}\,).$$

The predicate PC_m is the summary of conditions over the $\{x_i'\}$ required for traversal of the path, and Q composed with the $\{r_{i,m}\}$, represents the desired output condition but converted to a condition strictly over $\{x_i'\}$.

The use of Method C on the path sequence of Figure 3 is shown in Figure 5C. The explanation of Method C was done in terms of fictitious variables x_i' in order to make the notation more uniform and subsequent comparisons of the various methods easier. Another way of describing the method is in terms of *symbolic values*. Instead of using the **variables** x_i', a corresponding set of **values** $\{\alpha_i\}$ is invented, symbolically representing the respective **values** of the variables $\{x_i\}$ at the beginning of the path. The right hand sides, $r_{i,j}$, become a, *value of*, function say *val*. Each program variable always has a current value $val(x_i)$ which is an expression over the initial values $\{\alpha_i\}$. The operations and overall effects are identical to before using values wherever r's were used. However, a caution must be issued not to confuse the basic concepts involved. The symbols x_i' are program variables which are assign values in the program just like the x_i's. The symbols α_i are strictly mathematical variables representing specific values and are outside the realm of the program. When more subtle issues are consider, such as procedure calls with side effects, the difference between the value of a variable, $val(x_i)$, and a symbolic value, α_i, may be quite critical.

The author has found the use of symbolic values (α_i's) preferable [14] and for that reason has included this brief digression and comparison. In addition, the Method C subtitle "symbolic execution method" becomes more meaningful when one considers "executing" the path sequence on a program domain which has been extended to include the symbols $\{\alpha_i\}$.

Method D. Backward symbolic execution method. This method is included to complete the four cases enumerated by the two binary properties. The path sequence is traversed in reverse order and the variables in the VC are associated with the program variables at the end of the path. There may be a *known* method that satisfies these properties but it is unknown to this author. The method described here is clumsy and impractical when compared with the previous three. However, it's discussion may contribute to understanding the other methods more fully by completing the set and, in fact, by its clumsiness.

The basic idea is to do Method C in a backward fashion. If assignment statements were "invertable" this method would follow that idea faithfully. Consider Method C (forward symbolic execution) applied to the assignment statement, s_j: $x_i \leftarrow x_i + 1$. Suppose $r_{i,j} = x_i'$. Then $r_{i,j+1}$ would be $(x_i'+1)$. Going *backward* over the same statement with $r_{i,j+1} = x_i'$ one should like to have $r_{i,j} = x_i'-1$. In this case, the right hand side of the assignment is invertable, but in general it is not. A simple example is: $x_i \leftarrow x_i \div 2$. For this example, if $r_{i,j+1} = x_i'$, $r_{i,j}$ could be either $2 \times x_i'$ *or* $2 \times x_i'+1$. "Unexecuting" assignment statements is just not easy. Method D's way to cope with this is discussed just after **assume** statement are covered.

Assume statements are handled as in Method C, by developing a sequence of path conditions $\{PC_m, PC_{m-1}, ..., PC_1\}$. However, the backward traversal forces the derivations to be formed with implications ($\supset$) as in the other backward Method B. That is, using the same notation as used for Method C in equation (2) above:

$$PC_j \equiv (Q(r_{1,j}, r_{2,j}, ..., r_{n,j}) \supset PC_{j+1}).$$

The initial PC, PC_m, is $Q(r_{1,m}, r_{2,m}, ..., r_{n,m})$ where s_m is **prove**$(Q(x_1, x_2, ..., x_n))$ and, analogous to Method C, $r_{i,m}$

Path Sequence	Right Hand Sides (r)				PC's
	$\underline{X}$	$\underline{Y}$	$\underline{Z}$	$\underline{YD}$	
	X'	Y'	Z'	YD'	*true*

1   **assume**$(Z\times(X\uparrow Y)=A\uparrow B\wedge Y\geq 0)$;

$$Z'\times(X'\uparrow Y')=A\uparrow B\wedge Y'\geq 0$$

2   **assume**$(Y\neq 0)$;

$$Z'\times(X'\uparrow Y')=A\uparrow B\wedge Y'\geq 0\wedge Y'\neq 0$$

3    $YD\leftarrow Y\div 2$;

$$Y'\div 2$$

4   **assume**$(Y=2\times YD)$;

$$Z'\times(X'\uparrow Y')=A\uparrow B\wedge Y'\geq 0\wedge Y'\neq 0\wedge$$
$$Y'=2\times(Y'\div 2)$$

5    $X\leftarrow X\times X$;

$$X'\times X'$$

6    $Y\leftarrow YD$:

$$Y'\div 2$$

7   **prove**$(Z\times(X\uparrow Y)=A\uparrow B\wedge Y\geq 0)$;

VC:

$$(Z'\times(X'\uparrow Y')=A\uparrow B \wedge Y'\geq 0\wedge Y'\neq 0 \wedge Y'=2\times(Y'\div 2)) \supset$$
$$(Z'\times((X'\times X')\uparrow(Y'\div 2))=A\uparrow B \wedge Y'\div 2\geq 0)$$

Figure 5C. VC-generation Using Method C.

is initially x_i', for i, $1\leq i\leq n$.

Fictitious variable names and the PC's can be used to handle the assignment statement problem. For the assignment statement s_j:

$$x_i \leftarrow f(x_1, x_2, ..., x_n)$$

a new unique variable name, x_i', is invented and $r_{i,j} = x_i'$ (the value destroyed by the assignment). Of course, the unaffected $r_{k,j}$ ($1\leq k\leq n$, $k\neq i$) remain the same: $r_{k,j} = r_{k,j+1}$. The PC is used to capture the relationship between $r_{i,j+1}$ and x_i' ($r_{i,j}$) by setting $PC_j \equiv (PC_{j+1} \wedge r_{i,j+1} = f(r_{1,j}, r_{2,j}, ..., r_{n,j})$).

The use of Method D on the standard path sequence is shown in Figure 5D.

COMPARISON OF METHODS

The basic issue with which all of these methods deal, is the difference between *program variables* and normal *mathematical variables*. At any single point in time, during the execution of a program, (a *point* being between two program statements) the program variables do follow the traditional mathematical rules. At a point, if X has value 3 then, certainly, $(X+1)$ has value 4. Of course, if claims are not qualified with respect to program execution time, the traditional assumptions collapse; X having value 3 at one point yields no information about the value of $(X+1)$ (or for that matter X itself) at some later point.

A beginning FORTRAN programmer learns this early when puzzled by the world's most common assignment statement:

$$I = I + 1.$$

The ploy, used by each of these methods, is to express all knowledge of the computations and the tests

Path Sequence (Reversed)	Right Hand Sides (r)				PC's
	$\underline{X}$	$\underline{Y}$	$\underline{Z}$	$\underline{YD}$	
	X'	Y'	Z'	YD'	$-\ -$

7 $\mathbf{prove}(Z\times(X\uparrow Y)=A\uparrow B\wedge Y\geq 0);$

$$Z'\times(X'\uparrow Y')=A\uparrow B\wedge Y'\geq 0$$

6 $Y\leftarrow YD;$ $(r:\ Y'')$

$$Z'\times(X'\uparrow Y')=A\uparrow B\wedge Y'\geq 0\wedge Y'=YD'$$

5 $X\leftarrow X\times X;$ $(r:\ X'')$

$$Z'\times(X'\uparrow Y')=A\uparrow B\wedge Y'\geq 0\wedge Y'=YD'\wedge\\ X'=X''\times X''$$

4 $\mathbf{assume}(Y=2\times YD);$

$$Y''=2\times YD'\supset(Z'\times(X'\uparrow Y')=A\uparrow B\wedge Y'\geq 0\wedge\\ Y'=YD'\wedge X'=X''\times X'')$$

3 $YD\leftarrow Y\div 2;$ $(r:\ YD'')$

$$(Y''=2\times YD'\supset(Z'\times(X'\uparrow Y')=A\uparrow B\wedge Y'\geq 0\wedge\\ Y'=YD'\wedge X'=X''\times X''))\wedge\\ YD'=Y''\div 2$$

2 $\mathbf{assume}(Y\neq 0);$

$$Y''\neq 0\supset\{(Y''=2\times YD'\supset\\ (Z'\times(X'\uparrow Y')=A\uparrow B\wedge Y'\geq 0\wedge\\ Y'=YD'\wedge X'=X''\times X''))\wedge\\ YD'=Y''\div 2\ \}$$

1 $\mathbf{assume}(Z\times(X\uparrow Y)=A\uparrow B)\wedge Y\geq 0);$

$$(Z'\times(X''\uparrow Y'')=A\uparrow B)\wedge Y''\geq 0)\supset\\ (Y''\neq 0\supset\{(Y''=2\times YD'\supset\\ (Z'\times(X'\uparrow Y')=A\uparrow B\wedge Y'\geq 0\wedge\\ Y'=YD'\wedge X'=X''\times X''))\wedge\\ YD'=Y''\div 2\ \})$$

VC:

$$(Z'\times(X''\uparrow Y'')=A\uparrow B\ \wedge\ Y''\geq 0)\ \supset\ (Y''\neq 0\supset\{(Y''=2\times YD'\supset\\ (Z'\times(X'\uparrow Y')=A\uparrow B\ \wedge\ Y'\geq 0\wedge Y'=YD'\ \wedge\ X'=X''\times X''))\ \wedge\ YD'=Y''\div 2\ \})$$

Figure 5D. VC-generation Using Method D

(assumptions) along a path, exclusively in terms of program variables associated with a single point in the program (either the path begin or path end). Then all of the information is expressed in the same *mathematical* variables and standard mathematical tools can be applied (e.g., theorem proving).

Assignment statements reassociate *values* and *variables*. The compensation for their changes is handled in two different ways by the four methods depending on whether the focus is on the values (Methods A and B) or the variables (Methods C and D). Consider Method B processing over statement 3 ($YD\leftarrow Y\div 2$) as shown in Figure 5B. Predicates P_3 and P_4 are identical except that P_3 contains ($Y\div 2$) wherever P_4 contains YD. The value of YD after the execution of statement 3 was ($Y\div 2$) as evaluated in the environment just before statement 3. Suppose that that common value were α. Then P_3 and P_4 are identical statements about α but P_3 is associated with a point in the program where α can be described as the value of ($Y\div 2$), and P_4 is associated with a point where α is the value of YD. From this unconventional view (focusing on values) P_3 and P_4 are the same constant statement over values, but the assignment statement renames one of those values, α, from ($Y\div 2$) to YD. If P_3 is *true* before statement 3 the renaming yields the same statement *true* in the new notation.

Carried to the extreme, this view of assignment statements gives an unusual conceptual model of program execution. Imagine the program executor (computer) having all possible values from the domain of program variables laid before it. Associated with each value is a (possible empty) list of program variables names and expressions over program variable names. Computations, as specified by assignment statements, are accomplished by updating these lists to correspond with the new associations of program variables to values. Thus the execution of statement 3 in the example removes YD, and any expressions involving it, from all lists. Then YD, and possibly $(Y \div 2)$, are added to the list associated with α. Of course, the executor may have to find some β whose list contains Y in order to discover that $(Y \div 2)$ and α are associated (i.e., $\alpha = \beta \div 2$). In this way, the actual numeric computations would still occur, but indirectly. This discussion, which has been about Method B, applies to Method A as well. Both methods move predicates "through" the statements along the path, adjusting them for variable/value reassociations imposed by assignment statements. Method A does this in a forward pass and Method B does the same thing in reverse.

The introduction of existential quantifiers ($\exists$) in predicates using Method A but not occurring using Method B makes the methods look more dissimilar than they are. However, an analysis of the quantifiers ultimate effect on the VC's generated by Method A, shows that they "go away". The last derived predicate, denoted P_m above, contains one existential quantifier per assignment statement unless they are discarded by a simplification. Note, however, that the VC takes the form $P_m \supset Q$ where Q is the final path-end assertion. The free variables in the VC are the program variables in the context of the end of the path. To prove the correctness of the path the VC must be *true* *for* *all* values of these variables. That is, the notation

$$\vdash P_m \supset Q$$

assumes implicit universal quantification ($\forall$) over all free variables. In the expression $((\exists x\ R(x)) \supset S)$, $\exists x\ R(x)$ is a "negative" term and if x does not occur in S, $((\exists x\ R(x)) \supset S)$ can be rewritten as $\forall x(R(x) \supset S)$. In the case of a VC generated by Method A, all of the existentially quantified variables in P_m do not occur in Q and they become universally quantified when brought to the outermost scope and can be dropped. Of course, this discussion does not apply to quantifiers originally written in the program assertions but only to those invented for use in Method A. The need to have bound variables introduced in Method A but not in Method B derives naturally from the "one-way" destructive nature of assignment statements.

Methods C and D consider program execution in the normal fashion focusing on program variables. At each point along the path each program variable has a value. This association of variables and values is updated by the execution of an assignment statement which revises the value of one variable.

The differences between program variables and mathematical variables can be resolved in another well known and general way by requiring that no program variable ever be associated with more than one value. That is, program variables are "write-once" and each can occur at most once on the left side of an assignment statement. Variables are undefined up to a point in a program execution and thereafter are associated with exactly one value. If the program variables are considered only *after* the program execution, the undefined case can be disregarded and the program variables strictly behave as mathematical variables. Mathematical descriptions of algorithms are often written in this form. For example, the summation of a vector of elements $(a_1, a_2, ..., a_n)$, avoiding use of the summation operator (Σ), can be written using partial sums as:

$$S_0 = 0$$
$$S_i = S_{i-1} + a_i, \quad \text{for } i=1, 2, ..., n,$$

where S_n is the desired sum.

The difficulties found in actually using such a notation for writing programs is that an arbitrary number of variables (variable names) must be used. The programmer is forced to use vectors (arrays) of arbitrary size where a scalar variable would usually do. The problem can be seen in the summation example where the number of S's required is $(n+1)$, when the typical program uses only one. Some analysis is required to see that, in fact, all S's can share the same storage cell. A serious proposal along these lines, attempting to exploit parallel processing, is presented in [4]. Also the functional programming languages such as pure LISP have no reassociation of values and variables except at function invocation, and consequently lend themselves nicely to mathematical analysis.

The approach discussed here and used extensively in Good's thesis [10] is to use the notion for the analysis of programs, even though they, themselves, do not satisfy the write-once property. In the context of this discussion the idea applies quite nicely since only finite-length program paths (path sequences) are being considered. In fact, as the following discussion attempts to show, the four methods for generating VC's can be viewed as specialized methods for implementing the same basic analysis. Each attempts to reduce the number of artificial variables introduced strictly for the sake of the analysis.

For a path sequence, S, a path sequence, S', which does satisfy the write-once property can be constructed by a simple renaming of program variables. This construction is "proof preserving", in that, a proof of correctness for S' is possible if and only if one is possible for the original sequence S. Sequence S' is derived as follows. Let s denote the first statement of S and s' denote the first (next) statement of S'.

a) If s is an **assume** statement, make s'=s. The following statements in S' are defined by repeating the process using (S − s), (S with its first statement removed), in place of S.

b) If s is an assignment statement say:

$$x_i \leftarrow f(x_1, x_2, ..., x_n)$$

then make s'

$$x_i' \leftarrow f(x_1, x_2, ..., x_n)$$

where x_i' is a new variable name not used in the original program nor previously in this process. The following statements in S' are defined by repeating the process using R in place of S, where R is (S − s), with all occurrences of the variable name x_i in all statements replaced by x_i'.

The write-once sequence equivalent to the sequence of Figure 3 is shown in Figure 6.

1	**assume**$(Z \times (X \uparrow Y) = A \uparrow B \wedge Y \geq 0)$;	(same)
2	**assume**$(Y \neq 0)$;	(same)
3	$YD' \leftarrow Y \div 2$;	(new YD')
4	**assume**$(Y = 2 \times YD')$;	(uses YD')
5	$X' \leftarrow X \times X$;	(new X')
6	$Y' \leftarrow YD'$;	(new Y' - uses YD')
7	**prove**$(Z \times (X' \uparrow Y') = A \uparrow B \wedge Y' \geq 0)$;	(uses X', Y' - Z never altered)

Figure 6. Write-Once Path Sequence Corresponding to Figure 3.

The VC for a write-once sequence $S = \{s_1, s_2, ..., s_m\}$ can be generated very simply as:

$$(r_1 \wedge r_2 \wedge ... \wedge r_{m-1}) \supset Q$$

where Q is from s_m which is **prove**(Q), and each r_i $(1 \leq i \leq m-1)$ is derived from s_i by:

a) if s_i is **assume**(P) then r_i is P, and

b) if s_i is an assignment statement, r_i is s_i with the assignment operator ($\leftarrow$) replaced by an equal sign (=).

Using this technique the VC for the path sequence of Figure 6 is:

$$(Z \times (X \uparrow Y) = A \uparrow B \wedge Y \geq 0 \wedge Y \neq 0 \wedge YD' = Y \div 2 \wedge Y = 2 \times YD' \wedge X' = X \times X \wedge Y' = YD') \supset$$
$$(Z \times (X' \uparrow Y') = A \uparrow B \wedge Y' \geq 0)$$

Suppose one copies the right hand side expression of any assignment statement in a write-once path sequence and evaluates it using the values associated with variables at the end of the path. Since the write-once property holds this will produce the same result as the original evaluation done for the execution of the assignment statement. Thus, changing the assignment operators ($\leftarrow$) to equal signs (=) produces definitions of values of program variables known to be valid at the path end. (A variable once assigned a value will never be redefined). A similar argument about the predicate expressions of **assume** statements make them hold at the path-end, if they were assumed to hold at their original position in the sequence. Since all these expressions are known or assumed to hold independently, they can be formed into one large conjunction known to hold at the path-end. The VC represents the question: does the **prove** predicate, Q, follow from this known information.

For comparison, the VC's generated for the example by all the Methods (A,B,C,D and using the write-once sequence of Figure 6 (denoted *)) are shown together in Figure 7A. The comparison is, perhaps, even more easily made if the path assertions are denoted symbolically by P and Q. Change statement 1 (of Figures 3 and 6) to

$$\textbf{assume}(P(X,Y,Z,YD))$$

and change statement 7 to

$$\textbf{prove}(Q(X,Y,Z,YD)).$$

The resulting VC's for all method are then shown in Figure 7B.

Method	VC Generated
A	$\{\exists X'(Z\times(X'\uparrow(2\times YD))) = A\uparrow B \wedge 2\times YD \geq 0 \wedge 2\times YD \neq 0 \wedge YD = (2\times YD)\div 2 \wedge$ $X = X'\times X' \wedge Y = YD)\} \supset \{Z\times(X\uparrow Y) = A\uparrow B \wedge Y\geq 0\}$
B	$(Z\times(X\uparrow Y) = A\uparrow B \wedge Y\geq 0 \wedge Y\neq 0 \wedge Y = 2\times(Y\div 2)) \supset$ $(Z\times(X\uparrow(2\times(Y\div 2)))) = A\uparrow B \wedge Y\div 2 \geq 0)$
C	$(Z'\times(X'\uparrow Y') = A\uparrow B \wedge Y'\geq 0 \wedge Y'\neq 0 \wedge Y' = 2\times(Y'\div 2)) \supset$ $(Z'\times((X'\times X')\uparrow(Y'\div 2))) = A\uparrow B \wedge Y'\div 2 \geq 0)$
D	$(Z'\times(X''\uparrow Y'') = A\uparrow B \wedge Y''\geq 0) \supset (Y''\neq 0 \supset \{(Y'' = 2\times YD' \supset$ $(Z'\times(X'\uparrow Y') = A\uparrow B \wedge Y'\geq 0 \wedge Y' = YD' \wedge X' = X''\times X'')) \wedge YD' = Y''\div 2 \})$
*	$(Z\times(X\uparrow Y) = A\uparrow B \wedge Y\geq 0 \wedge Y\neq 0 \wedge YD' = Y\div 2 \wedge Y = 2\times YD' \wedge X' = X\times X \wedge$ $Y' = YD') \supset (Z\times(X'\uparrow Y') = A\uparrow B \wedge Y'\geq 0)$

Figure 7A. VC's From All Methods

Method	VC Generated
A	$\exists Y'\exists X'\exists YD'(P(X',Y',Z,YD') \wedge Y'\neq 0 \wedge YD = Y'\div 2 \wedge Y' = 2\times YD \wedge$ $X = X'\times X' \wedge Y = YD') \supset Q(X,Y,Z,YD)$
B	$P(X,Y,Z,YD) \supset \{Y\neq 0 \supset (Y = 2\times(Y\div 2) \supset Q(X\times X,Y\div 2,Z,Y\div 2))\}$
C	$(P(X',Y',Z',YD') \wedge Y'\neq 0 \wedge Y' = 2\times(Y'\div 2)) \supset Q(X'\times X',Y'\div 2,Z',Y'\div 2)$
D	$P(X'',Y'',Z',YD'') \supset (Y''\neq 0 \supset \{Y'' = 2\times YD' \supset (Q(X',Y',Z',YD') \wedge$ $Y' = YD' \wedge X' = X''\times X'') \wedge YD' = Y''\div 2 \})$
*	$(P(X,Y,Z,YD) \wedge Y\neq 0 \wedge YD' = Y\div 2 \wedge Y = 2\times YD' \wedge X' = X\times X \wedge Y' = YD') \supset$ $Q(X',Y',Z,YD')$

Figure 7B. VC's From All Methods (Using Symbolic Assertions)

Using Figure 7B as a guide one can convince oneself that Method A and Method *, excluding simplifications, produce the same expressions except that * does not introduce the existential quantifiers (which can be dropped in the VC anyway) and variables are renamed differently. Method A gathers information going forward which involves variables which must be renamed (using $\exists$'s) to avoid conflicts with the same names which remain in the subsequent statements but represent, possibly, new values. Method * renames variables in the program statements in a "forward" way yielding a VC with "opposite" renaming.

Methods B and * also produce results whose difference can be simply explained. In Method *, all assignment statements produce expressions of the form:

$$x = e$$

where x is a variable name and e is some expression. Since these equalities always occur with a global scope in the VC (e.g., they never occur as $(x_1 = e_1 \lor x_2 = e_2)$) they can each be removed by substituting e for all occurrences of x in the VC. The remaining difference in the results come about because of the backward traversal of Method B. Let R be called the "hypothesis" of the VC produced by Method * which has the form $R \supset S$. Method B produces $R \equiv \ldots \land R_2 \land R_1$ in a piecemeal fashion as

$$\ldots (R_2 \supset (R_1 \supset S))\ldots).$$

This difference can be removed by the tautology $((R_1 \land R_2) \supset S) \equiv (R_1 \supset (R_2 \supset S))$.

The equality elimination described, eliminates exactly all of the new variables. Method B can be considered to have the equality elimination "built in" to the processing. It avoids introducing new variable names by being able to use the corresponding expressions appropriately. This feature of Method B accounts for its common use in implemented systems. The basic operation needed is the substitution of an expression for a variable. No mechanism for inventing new variable names is required.

Method C is seen to produce the same results as Method B provided the variables are renamed, and since it processes forward through the program, it produces the hypothesis, R, in the conjunctive form of Method *. Method C shares this cleanliness with Method B but is more clumsy to implement as a computer program. It requires a table of values (or right hand sides) and some table look-up procedure. However, being able to view Method C as symbolic execution, allows experience in building and understanding program executors to be applied, which is of considerable value. The new names generated by Method C are exactly one per program variable once at the beginning of the path. The new names generated in Methods A and * are created once per assignment statement.

SUMMARY

The presentation discusses and compares several methods for generating verification conditions for program correctness proofs. A novice could complain "don't confuse me with alternatives, but show me the best way." The discussion of known methods may not contribute to the knowledge of the experienced program prover, either. An analogy can best explain why such a comparative presentation should be of value. A solid object can be viewed from many angles. The conventional *top*, *side*, and *front* views give a great deal of information about the solid object. Each view, however, is a two dimensional picture devoted exclusively to that view. Only by comparing more than one view can the observer begin to develop an understanding of the true three dimensional object.

The field of programming is a very new one, let alone the sub-field of program proving. Deep thorough understanding of the basic principles is essential to its further development. A comparison of known alternative techniques, as a comparison of different views of a solid, should contribute to a better basic understanding.

ACKNOWLEDGEMENT

Edith Welfel did a patient and careful job of typing this manuscript.

REFERENCES

[1]   Basu, S. K. and Yeh, R. T. Strong verification of Programs. Soft. Eng. and Sys. Lab., Univ. of Texas-Austin, Techn. Report SESLTR-13, 1975.

[2]   Boyer, R. S. and Moore, J. S. Proving theorems about Lisp functions. JACM, vol. 22, no. 1, January 1975, pp. 48-59.

[3]   Burstall, R. M. Program proving as hand simulation with a little induction. Information Processing 74, Proceedings of IFIP Congress 74, J. L. Rosenfeld, ed., North-Holland, 308-312, 1974.

[4]   Chamberlan, Donald D. The single assignment approach to parallel processing. FJCC, Las Vegas, Nov. 1971. pp 263-269.

[5]   Darlington, John. A semantic approach to automatic program improvement, Ph.D. dissertation, Univ. of Edinburgh, 1973.

[6]   Deutsch, L. P. An Interactive Program Verifier. Ph.D. dissertation, Dept. Comp. Sci., Univ. of Calif., Berkeley CA., May 1973. (Also Xerox PARC Report CSL-73-1, Palo Alto, CA.)

[7]   Dijkstra, E. W. Guarded commands, non-determinacy and a calculus for the derivation of programs. CACM, vol. 18, no. 8, August 1975, pp. 453-457.

[8]   Elspas, B. et al. An assessment of techniques for proving program correctness, Comp. Surveys, Vol. 4, No. 2, June 1972, pp. 97-147.

[9]   Floyd, R. W. Assigning meanings to programs, Proc. Symp. Appl. Math., Amer. Math. Soc., vol. 19, pp. 19-32, 1967.

[10]   Good, D. I. Towards a man-machine system for proving program correctness. Ph.D dissertation, Univ. of Wisc., 1970.

[11]   Hoare, C. A. R. An axiomatic basis for computer programming. CACM, vol. 12. no. 10, Oct. 1969, pp. 576-583.

[12]   King, J. C. Proving programs to be correct, IEEE Trans. on Comp., Vol. C-20, No. 11, November 1971, pp. 1331-1336.

[13]   King, J. C. A Program Verifier. Ph.D. dissertation, Carnegie-Mellon Univ., Pittsburgh, Pa., 1969.

[14]   King, J. C. A new approach to program testing, 1975 Int. Conf. on Reliable Software, April 1975, pp. 228-233. (Also appears in Programming Methodology, Lect. Notes in Comp. Sci., 23, Springer-Verlag, 1974, 278-290.)

[15]   Manna, Z. *Introduction to Mathematical Theory of Computation*, McGraw-Hill Book Company, New York, N. Y., 1974.

[16]   Naur, P. Proof of algorithms by general snapshots. BIT 6, 4, 1966, pp. 310-316.

[17]   Topor, R. W. Interactive Program Verification Using Virtual Programs. Ph.D. dissertation, Dept. of AI, Univ. of Edinburgh, 1975.

[18]   Waldinger, R. J. and Levitt, K. N. Reasoning about programs. Artif. Intell., 5, 3, 1974, pp. 235-316.

ANSCHRIFTEN DER AUTOREN:
AUTHORS' ADDRESSES

Dr. E. Bertsch
A. Müller-v. Brochowski
Universität des Saarlandes
FB Angewandte Mathematik und Informatik
Im Stadtwald
66 Saarbrücken

H.-W. Brügmann
H. Lehr
A. Rudert
Universität Erlangen-Nürnberg
Inst. f. Math. Masch. u. DV (II)
Egerlandstr. 13
8520 Erlangen

J. Ciesinger
Inst. f. Informatik der TU München
Postfach 202420
8000 München 2

Dr. A. Cremers
T.N. Hibbard
University of Southern California
Computer Science Program
University Park
Los Angeles, Cal. 90 007
USA

Prof. Dr. Karel Čulík
Čápkova 31
602 00 Brno
CSSR

Prof. Dr. F.L. DeRemer
University of California, Santa Cruz
Information Sciences
Applied Sciences Building 220
Santa Cruz, Cal. 950 64
USA

H. Ganzinger
Institut für Informatik der TU München
Postfach 202420
8000 München 2

Prof. Dr. G. Goos
Universität Karlsruhe
Inst. f. Informatik II
Zirkel 2
7500 Karlsruhe

Prof. Dr. David Gries
Cornell University
Dpt. of Computer Science
Ithaca, N.Y. 14850
USA

z.Zt.

Mathematisches Institut der TU München
Postfach 202420
8000 München 2

G. Hommel
S. Jänichen
W. Koch
Techn. Universität Berlin
FG Programmiersprachen und Compiler II
Ernst-Reuter-Platz 7
1000 Berlin 12

U. Kastens
Universität Karlsruhe
Institut für Informatik II
Zirkel 2
7500 Karlsruhe

Dr. James C. King
IBM Thomas J. Watson Research Center
P.O.Box 218
Yorktown Heights, N.Y. 10598
USA

Dr. H. Kron
Technische Hochschule Darmstadt
FB Informatik, FG PU
Steubenplatz 12
6100 Darmstadt

W.M. Lippe
Universität Kiel
Institut f. Informatik u. Praktische Mathematik
Ohlshausenstr. 40-60, Haus A1
2300 Kiel 1

A.L. Luft
Universität Erlangen-Nürnberg
Inst. f. Math. Masch. u. DV (III)
Martensstr. 1
8520 Erlangen

Dr. R. Marty
Inst. f. Informatik der Universität Zürich
Kurvenstr. 17
CH-8006 Zürich

W. Polak
Universität Karlsruhe
Institut für Informatik II
Zirkel 2
7500 Karlsruhe

J. Röhrich
Universität Karlsruhe
Inst. f. Informatik II
Zirkel 2
7500 Karlsruhe

Dr.-Ing. P. Rütters
c/o BBC AG
Postfach 351
6800 Mannheim 1

H. Schmeck
Universität Kiel
Inst. f. Informatik u. Praktische Mathematik
Ohlshausenstr. 40-60, Haus S10
2300 Kiel 1

F. Simon
Universität Kiel
Inst. f. Informatik u. Praktische Mathematik
Ohlshausenstr. 40-60, Haus A1
2300 Kiel 1

Prof. Dr. A. v. Staa
Prof. Dr. Carlos José Pareira de Lucena
Departamento de Informática
Pontificia Universidade Católica
do Rio de Janeiro
Rua Marques de Sao Vicente, 209/263
Rio de Janeiro .
Brasilien

H. Steusloff
Fraunhofer Gesellschaft
Inst. f. Informationsverarbeitung in Technik u. Biologie
Sebastian-Kneipp-Str. 12-14
7500 Karlsruhe